2

AN INTRODUCTION TO EDUCATIONAL RESEARCH

ROBERT M. W. TRAVERS

Director, Bureau of Educational Research
University of Utah

AN INTRODUCTION
TO EDUCATIONAL
RESEARCH

Second Edition

The Macmillan Company, New York
Collier-Macmillan Limited, London

Third Printing, 1965

Library of Congress catalog card number: 63–22746

The Macmillan Company, New York
Collier-Macmillan Canada, Ltd., Toronto, Ontario

Printed in the United States of America

PREFACE

Since the first edition of this book was published, some dramatic changes have begun to mark the appearance of educational research. These changes call for the training of a new breed of educational research workers. They demand, too, that teachers and educational administrators have a deeper and closer understanding of the nature of research and the peculiarly difficult task it attempts to undertake. The time is not far off when one can hope for the disappearance of those texts which imply that educational research is a suitable hobby for anyone in education. Of course, teachers and administrators, like persons in other occupations, will have to continue to collect data about their problems and to remain constantly on the alert for cues as to how to improve their practices. This is a part of the job of every professional person. Such educational personnel can gain a grasp of what professional research involves through study of a book such as this one, but the study of any book is not sufficient to train a person as an educational research worker. Most of those who read this book will do so in order to acquire some understanding of research; for a few, it will provide a starting point from which they become professional research workers.

·Notable among the changes in the field of educational research over the last few years is the development of significant research programs by colleges of education, particularly those attached to universities. These programs, sponsored largely by funds from the federal government, have played a major role in the training of a new generation of educational research workers. This new generation is already exerting its influence on the growth of educational inquiry and on the content of research courses in colleges of education. This book has been planned and revised with the thought that this new generation of educational scientists may find it suitable as a text in classes they may teach.

The development of the University Council for Educational Administrators, which emphasizes the promotion of a thoroughly professional program of research, is an encouraging innovation. In addition, departments of educational psychology have demonstrated leadership in developing research on problems of teaching and learning. Furthermore, the wide interest expressed by psychologists in the development of a technology related to education has resulted in extensive research on the development of automated teaching devices. This trend has provided an invigorating influence and has done much to revive research activities within the area of educational psychology.

Much of the change is due to the fact that during the last decade, for the first time in history, research related to education has received substantial financial support. The Cooperative Research Program of the U. S. Office of Education has been the central source of such support and has exercised important leadership. With this support have also come pressures to take shortcuts and to make direct attacks on important broad problems, as that of improving instruction in particular subject-matter areas, such as English, physics, and social studies. Such proposals are seductively attractive for they offer the alluring possibility of producing rapid educational reform. This book takes the more conservative view that educational reform comes slowly and that most educational problems cannot be solved by direct attack. One objective of this book is to give the student an understanding of the importance of indirect approaches to the solution of educational problems and the reasons why such approaches have been successful in the past and are likely to be successful in the future, as they have been in other fields of human endeavor. The alchemist set himself the important problem of turning base metals into gold. His problem was an important one and he took the direct approach to it. The consequence of this direct approach was that he not only failed to solve the problem, but also he held up the development of a science of chemistry for centuries. A similar direct attack on educational problems is likely to prove as futile as the efforts of the alchemist.

Many of the improvements in this new edition are a result of suggestions made by Dr. James W. Becker, who reviewed a rough draft of the revised manuscript. Many ideas which he contributed have been incorporated in the final manuscript. His help is very much appreciated.

ROBERT M. W. TRAVERS

CONTENTS

Chapter 1. Groundwork for Research

ix

Chapter 2. Conducting Research Within a Framework of Theory

Chapter 3. Selecting the Problem

Chapter 4. Some Problems of Conducting Historical Research

Chapter 5. Measurement in Research

Chapter 6. *The Use of Multiple Observations in Measurement*

Chapter 7. *The Validity of Measurement*

Chapter 8. The Nature of Observation and Some Direct Approaches

Chapter 9. Observation: More Complex Procedures and Indirect Approaches

Chapter 10. Survey Methods

Chapter 11. Prediction Studies

Chapter 12. *Studies of Development*

Chapter 13. *Experimentation in Education*

Chapter 14. Problems of Research Design

Chapter 15. Data-Processing and Reporting

Chapter 16. Some Final Considerations

ILLUSTRATIONS

TABLES

AN INTRODUCTION
TO EDUCATIONAL
RESEARCH

CHAPTER 1

GROUNDWORK FOR RESEARCH

INTRODUCTION

The Impact of the Scientist on the Problems of Education

EDUCATIONAL problems did not attract the interest of scientists until very recent times. A few descriptive studies were undertaken in the field of education in the nineteenth century, but not until the twentieth century did educators recognize the impact that research could have on educational progress. Clearly, both educational practice and thought have been influenced by research, but there is not much agreement on the procedures the scientist should adopt if he is to contribute to educational progress.

In the nineteenth century many philosophers attempted to describe in general terms how the scientist went about his work, perhaps in the hope that pointers might be found which could be used to guide men in the pursuit of knowledge. The most notable of the nineteenth century philosophers to pursue this problem was John Stuart Mill. He believed he had succeeded in identifying the essential mental processes which lead to the making of a scientific discovery. Mill wrote with a certain finality about how the scientist proceeds, but his thoughts on the subject are considered today to be important contributions rather than the final word. How the scientist goes about his work is still a matter of controversy, and the working scientist often disagrees strongly with descriptions of his procedures written by philosophers.

B.F. Skinner (1956), famous experimental psychologist, has written of this matter, comparing his personal experience of how discoveries are made with textbook accounts of the procedure. The following quotation well reflects the gap between the person who teaches *about* scientific methodology and the practising scientist:

But it is a mistake to identify scientific practice with the formalized constructions of statistics and scientific method. These disciplines have their place, but it does not coincide with the place of scientific research. They offer *a* method of science but not, as is so often implied, *the* method. As formal disciplines, they arose very late in the history of science, and most of the facts of science have been discovered without their aid. It takes a great deal of skill to fit Faraday with his wires and magnets into the picture which statistics gives us of scientific thinking. And most current scientific practice would be equally refractory, especially in the important initial stages. It is no wonder that the laboratory scientist is puzzled and often dismayed when he discovers how his behavior has been reconstructed in the formal analyses of scientific method. He is likely to protest that this is not at all a fair representation of what he does.

The usual formula for conducting educational research is based on the idea that there is such a procedure as "the" scientific method. This is a notion that has had to be discarded, simply because scientific knowledge is arrived at by a variety of procedures and methods. Scientists vary greatly in this respect. A few prefer to follow the time-honored formula. Some, once they have even a vague idea of what they want to do, like to collect small samples of data and conduct rather rough-and-ready experiments; in this way, further cues are derived which may help to sharpen up a hypothesis. Still others may begin their explorations by reading widely in related fields, without too much concern about what they are looking for or what they may find. Some rely tremendously on personal hunches, while others reject anything that savors of intuition. *Techniques of arriving at knowledge, as they are manifested in the behavior of scientists, are highly personal and individualized. "The" simple scientific formula that all well-behaved scientists use simply does not exist.*

This book emphasizes systematic development of knowledge through research. Since the graduate student of education is at the apprentice level, not at the level of advanced discovery and leadership, the book attempts to help him avoid some of the traps which experienced research workers have learned to avoid. Some of the material presented is based on the fact that much can be learned through study of some of the pitfalls into which mature scientists have, at times, fallen. Even the most experienced research workers make errors, stumble down deadend alleys, make unwarranted generalizations, and mistake artifacts for real effects.

Levels of Research

Research includes many different kinds of activities; some simple, others highly complex. The reader who has had little experience in research may jump to the unwarranted conclusion that basic research and complex research are the same, and that applied research is simple research. This is not necessarily the case. Although much of what is commonly classified as basic research is very complex, many studies conducted within the scope of basic research programs are relatively simple and easily executed; for example, studies which reproduce important experiments to determine whether the results will stand up. In the field of applied research some studies are very complex but some are very simple. Basic and applied research do not differ in the level of complexity involved, but rather are they differentiated by the goals they help to achieve. Basic research is designed to add to an organized body of scientific knowledge and does not necessarily produce results of immediate practical use. Applied research is undertaken to solve an immediate practical problem and the goal of adding to scientific knowledge is secondary. The most complex levels of research involve the discovery of laws that apply to a wide range of phenomena. At the simpler levels are research enterprises which involve no more than the application of a familiar technique to a new situation to see how well it works under the different circumstances. For example, a research worker might apply an aptitude test which had been shown to be effective for predicting the capability of pupils for learning French and German and attempt to find out whether it could be used for predicting success in Slavonic languages. At a much more complex level, another researcher might undertake a program of research designed to discover some of the mechanisms involved in transfer of training. The student of education conducting research may be expected to work at a level somewhere between these two.

While skill in research is an important factor in the choice of the level at which to start, there are other considerations in making this decision—one is the matter of the time involved. Research at complex levels generally involves an ongoing program pursued over many years. The graduate student of education could hardly be expected to commit himself for such a long time. On the other hand, he is also not expected to engage in an inquiry which merely involves little more than the routine collection and tabulation of data.

Educational Research: The Present Scene

The term *research* has come to be applied to such a wide range of activities within the field of education that it has ceased to have a single identifiable meaning. Within some school systems there are research departments that serve only the function of maintaining records of pupil enrollment and attendance and related data pertaining to the operation of the system. There are educational research organizations that devote their energies to the tabulation of data pertaining to such matters as the expenditures of the different states on education or the teacher-selection practices of different communities. Other educational research organizations administer tests, develop norms, prepare distributions of scores, and engage in routine testing programs.

Somewhat different are the activities of a few educational research institutes that conduct studies of variables related to and affecting the efficiency of learning, or studies of problems related to the development of personality. Such activities perform a function that goes far beyond that of data-gathering, because the data are collected for the purpose of deriving scientific generalizations that can be applied to the solution of a wide range of problems. This is the meaning of the term *scientific research* that will be employed throughout this book.

Educational research, as it is conceived here, represents an activity directed toward the development of an organized body of scientific knowledge about the events with which educators are concerned. Of central importance are the behavior patterns of pupils, and particularly those to be learned through the educational process. A scientific body of knowledge about education should enable the educator to determine just what teaching and other learning conditions to provide in order to produce desired aspects of learned behavior among young people who attend school. Presumably, learning conditions will also have to be suited to the aptitudes and other characteristics of the learner. Where the researcher can most advantageously begin to develop such an organized body of knowledge about educational events is still a matter of conjecture. He may decide to begin by studying pupil behavior itself, or by studying conditions that affect the pupil only indirectly, such as economic conditions and school finance. Wherever he does begin, however, the assumption is made that the phenomena studied affect, in the ultimate analysis, the pupils in the schools.

The scientific goal of educational research is to discover laws or generalizations about behavior which can be used to make predictions and control events within educational situations. For example, the early studies of transfer of training undertaken by Thorndike indicated that a curriculum based on the doctrine of formal discipline was unlikely to achieve broad educational goals. Later research on transfer of training, while embracing a more complex and sophisticated theory of transfer than that proposed by Thorndike, has generally supported his conclusions and has had important implications for educational planning. The goal of educational research workers is to produce a body of knowledge consisting of generalizations about behavior which can be used to predict behavior in educational situations and for planning educational procedures and practices. Such a body of knowledge would, of course, include knowledge about the physical environment and its relation to the behavior of pupils and teachers. This conception of educational research does not exclude the study of buildings and classroom structures in relation to the behavior of pupils, teachers, and other participants in the educational process, however it emphasizes the idea that the central focus of educational research must be on the behavior of those engaged in educational transactions. Enough has been said at this point concerning the author's conception of the scientific objectives of educational research, but something remains to be said concerning the scope of its applications.

In order to clarify this point, consider some of the areas of education where a mature science of behavior in educational situations could be applied. It could be applied to the selection and training of teachers, to ensure that their behavior in the classroom was as effective as possible in promoting specific kinds of pupil change. It could be applied to the design of textbooks and other learning aids, to insure effective use. It could be applied to the design of classrooms, not only to provide good physical conditions for personal comfort but to insure that the social organization of the class is optimum. It could be applied to helping the pupil make long-range plans by forecasting what he could and could not accomplish. It could provide the principal with a sound basis for organizing the faculty and could guide him in providing conditions that would permit teachers to develop fully their potential as professional persons. Thus one can continue. There is not a single phase of the educational process that a mature science of behavior in educational situations could not render more effective.

Research and Value Judgments

A few contemporary philosophers have expounded the view that the role of research in education is minor, and that the central problems of education are problems of moral and ethical judgment. Once the major problems have been solved, these men claim, then research can play some small role in the solution of local problems. The following quotation from Mortimer Adler (1939) presents this point of view with some vigor:

> The basic problems of education are normative. This means, positively, that they are problems in moral and political philosophy; and, negatively, that they cannot, they have not and never will be solved by the methods of empirical science, by what is called educational research. . . . Neither the facts nor the generalizations [of science] can by themselves answer questions about what *should* be done in education . . . ultimate questions . . . are all moral. They cannot be answered by science. . . . [Ideals are not] relative and subjective, culturally determined or matters of individual opinion. . . . The major problems of education—whether in relation to the individual or to the state . . . have already been solved, for their solution does not depend on scientific research. Scientific research is relevant only in a minor connection, namely, the application of universal principles to local and contemporary circumstances. . . . [1]

To the author of this book, this quotation presents a one-sided point of view. He prefers to believe that advances in thinking about the moral and ethical problems of education must surely go hand in hand with the acquisition of scientific knowledge about the behavior of persons in educational environments. What is the use of establishing lofty goals for education if human beings are incapable of achieving them? What point is there in establish-

---

[1] From "Liberalism and Liberal Education," by Mortimer J. Adler, *Educational Record*, XX (1939), pp. 422–23. Reprinted by permission.

ing standards of conduct that should be the mark of the educated person unless it is known just what are the heights that the human being can expect to achieve in this respect? It is clearly possible to propose solutions to what Adler believes to be the major problems of education, and then to find that they apply only to an imaginary universe. The philosopher and the scientist must surely work closely together on educational problems.

There is no doubt in the author's mind that the usefulness of educational research would be greatly enhanced if the researcher were more often sensitive to the central ethical and moral problems of education. There is little worth in developing research on problems unrelated to these central issues. This does not mean, of course, that the researcher should try a head-on attack, for such a direct approach is often out of the question because of the unavailability of techniques. He can, however, work at points along the fringe of these problems where available techniques seem to apply, or he can seek to develop new techniques appropriate to particular aspects of the problem. At all times he should remain aware of the nature of the central problem, even though he is working on the fringe.

Relation of Educational Research to Research in the Social Sciences

A science of behavior in educational situations of course should draw heavily on what has been learned in related fields. Psychology forms an important part of the background for educational research, but the other behavioral sciences also provide pertinent material. What has been learned about economic behavior is essential knowledge for those who would study the influence of economic factors on pupil behavior, teacher behavior, teacher selection, peripheral matters such as guidance services, and other phases of the educational process. Educational research represents more than the mere application of the methods and theories of the related social sciences to educational problems. If it is ever to develop beyond the stage of an information-gathering activity, research in education must develop its own body of concepts, theories, and principles uniquely adapted to the ordering and prediction of events within the educational sphere.

The need for a framework to guide research is apparent when it is understood that theories of behavior have been developed largely in special contexts. Theory of personality is derived largely from a clinical context. Learning theory has evolved largely in the animal behavior laboratory. Psychometric theory has its background in industrial psychology. In each of these instances, a body of theory has been evolved that is uniquely adapted to the solution of problems in the area in which it developed. A misfortune of educational psychology is that those who have attempted to develop a science of behavior in classrooms have more often borrowed ill-adapted theories from other fields than they have developed theories useful in the study of educational phenomena. One might doubt, for example, that a theory derived from the psychiatric study of seriously disturbed patients would be particularly useful in the study of day-to-day classroom events. The success that psychologists have achieved in developing theories in other applied areas suggests that the same success could be achieved in the development of theories of educational behavior.

There is much to be said for the view that most sciences have been started by the discovery of principles applying to a quite limited range of events, rather than universally applicable principles. For example, scientists had established the general nature of the laws of the motion of falling bodies and the laws of the motion of the planets around the sun long before Newton demonstrated that both of these phenomena could be understood in terms of more general principles. Newton would probably not have arrived at his laws had not his predecessors provided him with a wealth of discoveries of limited significance. Einstein integrated theories pertaining to motion, electromagnetic phenomena, and astronomical phenomena within a larger, more refined, and more comprehensive system. The point of this discussion is that comprehensive theory is characteristic of a very mature science. In the early stages of the development of a science, the most profitable procedure seems to be to develop a set of theories each of which applies to a rather limited field. Attempts to develop comprehensive theories in the early phases of the growth of a science have been, in the past, notorious failures.

Until recent times, psychologists were concerned with the development of comprehensive theories of human behavior. The theoretical developments of Freud, derived from limited clinical situations, illustrate well the comprehensive type of theory that was characteristic of psychology in the late nineteenth and early twentieth centuries. Freud's theory attempted to account for all forms of behavior. It included within its scope a theory of development, a theory of social as well as individual behavior, a theory of forgetting, a theory of creative behavior, and so forth. The weakness of psychoanalytic theory seems to have been in its comprehensiveness, for only in limited areas has it provided a useful basis for predicting and controlling behavior—specifically, the behavior of clinical patients.

The same observation, generally speaking, is true of the other major systems of psychology that developed in the second and third decades of the present century. They have been, so to speak, universal systems designed to encompass all behavior; but experience in the application of such theories shows that their ambitiousness does not bring with it a corresponding amount of success. Indeed, the success of such broad theories has been so limited that in recent times many psychologists have sought an alternative approach, which involves the development of theories that apply only to limited segments of behavior. For example, theories have been developed that cover such restricted phenomena as rote learning, discrimination learning, and speed of word recognition. Somewhat broader in scope are theories that attempt to organize the field of instrumental learning, or the function of drive in learning. Such theoretical developments of limited scope are widely regarded as the very essence of a modern science of psychology.

This trend in modern psychology has not been generally understood by educators, and misunderstandings have often led to rejection of it as "impractical." Educators are heard to say that modern learning theories cannot be applied to classroom situations, and therefore the teacher must either fall back on some of the earlier psychological theories of learning or rely on common sense. What is not often appreciated is that these modern theories of learning are intended to apply to only the most limited domain, and those who develop them have no intention of applying them to educational problems. Indeed, any attempted application of this type would be regarded as unjustifiable generalization. Nevertheless, these theories can provide concepts that may be used in the building of a theory of learning concerned primarily with the problems of classroom learning. The author suggests that much too little effort has been made to extract from current theories of learning those ideas which may have possible significance for education and to use these extracted ideas as the foundation for new educational theories. Such new theories of classroom learning would be limited in their applications and might not be particularly useful for describing the learning and re-education that the clinician tries to produce in his patients. Thus, while educational research workers should watch the contributions made by scientists in related fields, they should also attempt to formulate theories that are specially adapted to the understanding of educational problems.

The need expressed here for a body of theories designed as a basis for educational research is not novel, if one is to judge from the history of educational thought. The most influential theory of learning of the nineteenth century, insofar as education is concerned, was that propounded by Herbart—that human learning proceeded by adding concepts to an "apperceptive mass" of concepts already acquired. This theory formed a basis for research and practice, and, although admittedly it was inadequately stated according to modern standards, its limited scope and educational context made it more useful than many modern theories. The later theory of learning developed by John Dewey also represents, not a comprehensive learning theory, but a theory of learning in school situations, and as such it has formed a basis for vast numbers of educational studies. Nevertheless, the Dewey formulation of learning in classroom situations should be considered a very rudimentary type of theory.

Just as the laws of falling bodies and of the motions of the planets ultimately were integrated into a more comprehensive theory, so may laws of learning used for predicting learning in classroom situations ultimately be integrated with laws of learning derived in laboratory and other situations. In that way, more comprehensive theories of learning will slowly evolve.

SOME DEVICES USED BY SCIENTISTS
TO FACILITATE THINKING

Scientists studying problems of behavior have had to learn to watch their thinking processes carefully to insure that they retain some degree of precision. Perhaps one of the most important lessons the beginner in educational research can learn is to be constantly on his guard for fuzzy thinking which can spoil a study before it even begins. For this reason, a good point at which to start the training of the educational research worker is to consider some of the devices—the theories, constructs, and models—which the scientist uses to organize his thinking about natural phenomena.

Facts and Discoveries

Scientific research results in much more than the accumulation of items of information. The scientist cannot get along without information, but mere accumulation of facts does not constitute scientific research. This often has not been properly understood by educators. Indeed, some agencies devoted to so-called research give their entire energies to the accumulation of information, and often such information is of doubtful value because it has been collected through questionnaires and other techniques of limited value. The product of the scientist is not a table of "facts" but a generalization. The generalizations that the scientist develops are usually called laws. These generalizations or laws must be such that they can be used to predict events. A generalization that applies only to past events is not a particularly useful one, although many of the generalizations derived from history are of this type. Generalization that can be used only for accounting for events in the past provide what are called *postdictive* systems; the generalizations developed by the scientist must be *predictive*.

The generalizations and laws of science are always based on considerable quantities of information, and sometimes this information is derived from daily experience. Newton's law of universal gravitation is a generalization derived from a great deal of daily experience as well as from the specialized experience of the astronomer and the previous work of Johannes Kepler. The laws of thermodynamics also do much to bring order into innumerable daily experiences. Some generalizations are based only on the kind of data that the scientist collects. The discoveries of the great mathematician and astronomer Johannes Kepler would have been unthinkable if he had not acquired the voluminous data his predecessor, Tycho Brahe, collected over a period of several decades.

Nevertheless, it is not enough for the researcher to have voluminous facts if he is to discover laws. Many students have arrived at graduate schools of education with files of data collected in their school systems and have found that those vast quantities of facts could not be used to form the basis of a doctoral dissertation. Somehow, the data never suggest a problem that they can be used to solve. Masses of data should not represent the starting places of research. The data for a major research should be collected only after the problem to be investigated has been well defined. Hypotheses that form the basis for a major research are not derived from masses of unorganized facts but from the available body of organized knowledge.

Theories and Laws

Theory has a place in educational research as in all other types of research. The place of theory is not usually adequately recognized or identified. Too often theory is mentioned in terms of a gulf between theory and practice, and frequently with some ridicule concerning the theory side of this gulf. A distinction is made between the practical people who deal with facts (and who are alleged to "get things done") and the researcher who deals with theories. Such distinctions and discriminations serve only to produce confusion, because they are based on misunderstandings concerning the function and nature of theories.

Those who misunderstand do not recognize that all actions of a practical nature in educational situations are based to some extent on a theory of behavior. The teacher who attempts to enrich the curriculum with field trips and demonstrations is basing actions on a theory that learning is most efficient if the experiences provided for learning occur in a variety of different milieus. The principal who institutes a series of staff conferences in order to install a new experimental curriculum is basing his action on a theory of social behavior insofar as his approach to the faculty is concerned, and a theory of learning insofar as the new experimental curriculum is concerned. The actions of practical people who operate educational programs nearly always are based on some kind of theory of behavior. In this respect they differ from the researcher only in that the researcher must state explicitly the nature of the theory underlying his work, while the practical educator does not have to do this.

Campbell (1952), who has written at some length on this phenomenon, points out that the practical man always seems to be willing to discuss his theories, which he has in abundance, but which differ from those of the scientist in both the way they are derived and the way they are used. The practical man's theories are formulations of what he has observed, but his observations always tend to refer to whatever events he *wanted* to see. A principal we know advocated teaching reading in kindergarten. He perhaps had arrived at this point of view by observing just one or two teachers who were particularly effective in teaching reading to a young group of very bright children. From that point on, he probably responded like most persons who have formulated or initiated a theory—he remembered only those subsequent instances that fitted his theory and forgot or disregarded the instances that did not.

One does not have to wander far in educational circles to find theories pertaining to every type and aspect of learning. There are advocates of socialized learning, individual problem-solving learning, rote learning, meaningful learning, learning by doing, and the rest. Many of these theories go back to such notable thinkers as Aristotle and Thomas Aquinas; some are local in origin. Most, however, are based only on the type of observation that the scientist considers as merely a beginning for his activity while the lay person looks upon them as a sound basis for theorizing. The scientist takes up at the point where the layman rests his deliberation; but, as Coladarci (1954) has so neatly pointed out, "to relate research efforts, continuously, to theoretical considerations is not a disservice to 'practical' interests—they are mutually inclusive categories."

There are, nevertheless, certain real difficulties in bridging the gap between the theories of the "practical" educator and those of the researcher. The theories of the former are couched in the language of the layman and are relatively easily communicated. Those of the researcher are stated in a technical language derived from the behavioral sciences and often are of a type that few scientists and far fewer laymen understand. Thus the practical educator, because he does not understand them, may often feel that the theories of the researcher have little application to actual educational problems. The ultimate interpretation of these theories into terms that the educator understands presents difficulties that have not yet been solved.

More often than not, educational policies and practices are based very largely on such popular theories. What is commonly referred to as educational theory is much more appropriately described as folklore than as science. The transition of theory from a folklore status to a scientific status is what the researcher in education aims to achieve.

Since the context of the discussion has been education, a contrast has been made between the theories of the practical educator and those of the scientist. A similar contrast could have been made between practical men in business, industry, and government and the scientific students in those fields.

The layman and the scientist also use theories in a different manner. The layman usually fails to recognize that a theory is only a tentative statement of a possible law, and he is likely to treat theories as if they were laws. All too often, the professional acts like a layman. If he is a principal and believes that elderly teachers are more effective than young teachers, he is likely to use this credo as a basis for action and to favor elderly teachers in appointing new members to his faculty. He operates as if his theory were an established fact. The researcher does not do this when he is engaged in a study. In the pursuit of research, a theory is a beginning point, used to generate hypotheses that are later tested by experiment and inquiry.

A theory as developed by a scientist is, like the theory of the layman, a set of generalizations believed to have some value in predicting important events. But the scientist and the layman differ in the way in which they derive their theories—the theory of the scientist is derived from well established knowledge and is formulated in as precise terms as he can find; that of the layman is rooted in casual observation. A theory may be formulated in a set of carefully worded statements or, if the state of knowledge is far enough advanced, in a set of mathematical equations. From the theory which he has formulated the scientist derives *hypotheses*, which are simply statements of some of the consequences that can be expected of the theory if it is true. He can then investigate these hypotheses in order to determine whether the theory he has formulated stands up when it is used for making predictions.

A researcher, for example, has a theory that if a young child is given freedom he tends to develop greater motivation to achieve and to succeed than if he is raised in an environment that places many restrictions upon him. He cannot test the theory as a whole in a single experiment or in a single study, but he does examine specific aspects of it. One hypothesis might be that children whose parents greatly restrict their freedom to visit places outside of the home tend to obtain lower school grades than children of comparable ability (as measured by an intelligence test) who enjoy greater freedom of movement. This is a specific, testable hypothesis generated by the general theory on which it is based. Nevertheless, data collected in any particular experiment that substantiated the theory would only be what one might call circumstantial evidence. Evidence collected from various sources would be necessary before one could make any real statement concerning the use of the theory. The hypothesis might be supported in the study of some sample populations but not others, because several factors combine to explain behavior on routine tasks. In the behavioral sciences, the findings presented by various studies of hypotheses related to a single theory usually provide a picture with much greater ambiguity than do studies related to a physical theory.

When studies consistently support a particular theory, their results are customarily stated in the form of a set of generalizations or principles, which in turn form the basis of predictions. In the behavioral sciences, the generalizations and principles that thus far have been derived have only limited value in the making of predictions, and one must suppose that they have been based on rather poor theories and quite inferior evidence.

The experienced research worker who conducts a series of related studies, based on a common theory and designed to extend knowledge in a common field, is said to be conducting a programmatic type of research. Nearly all good research today is of that type. This presents a difficulty to the graduate student of education who conducts a single study that is likely to be both his first and his last. Consequently, a graduate student should seek to develop a study that is part of a continuing program with which he has become familiar through his reading or through personal contacts in the institution in which he is at work. Except in the rare instances, he should avoid investigating some isolated problem which has deep personal appeal and which he desires to investigate for that reason alone.

Constructs and Theories

In the behavioral sciences, it is common practice for the scientist to develop theories that postulate underlying mechanisms to account for behavior as it is observed. In a sense, these ideas concerning underlying mechanisms may be considered to be products of the scientist's imagination, but they help him immensely in thinking about the phenomena that he is studying. These imaginary mechanisms are known as *constructs*. Sometimes they are referred to as *hypothetical constructs*, to indicate that they are not considered to be real objects or events. Most theories of behavior involve many constructs.

It is almost impossible to discuss behavior in terms of modern psychological theory without introducing constructs, and even much ordinary speech involves their use. Unfortunately, in common speech there is a tendency to reify hypothetical constructs; that is to say, we tend to refer to them as if they were real and observable entities. An important part of the research worker's training is to learn to discriminate between hypothetical constructs and observable events, a distinction the scientist strictly observes. We may speak of a person as having a "liberal" attitude, although we cannot observe his attitude directly; all we can ever observe is the result of this attitude as it is manifested in behavior. The attitude itself is a hypothetical construct introduced by the observer to "explain" consistency in behavior as it is seen. Abilities such as verbal ability, mechanical ability, and numerical ability are hypothetical constructs. The abilities themselves cannot be observed, for only behavior that *results from* these abilities is observable.

Hypothetical constructs may be taken from many sources. First, there are those derived from neurology. Although relatively little is known about the functioning of the nervous system, something is known about the location of specific tracts and nuclei and about the transmission of impulses along these tracts. With this limited knowledge, it is possible to postulate the existence of certain mechanisms to account for behavior as it is observed. For example, the student who has read elementary textbooks on psychology usually is familiar with the diagrams of the supposed nerve mechanism that underlies the conditioned reflex. Now in actual fact, no person has ever directly observed such a mechanism. It is postulated on the basis of general knowledge of the nervous system. It is, in fact, a hypothetical construct introduced to account for behavior. A further example of neurological constructs is seen in the type of associationist psychology with which the name of E.L. Thorndike is connected. In this sort of theory, it has been common to think of the development of connections between stimuli and response as representing changes in the synapses, the areas of tissue that separate one nerve cell from another.

A second source of hypothetical construct is the scientist's own field of consciousness, or his *phenomenal field,* as it is called. Many constructs are derived from this source. Most of the constructs of the older systems of psychology were derived from personal experience, but many modern psychologists doubt the usefulness of this procedure.

Nevertheless, the phenomenological theories have a strong group of supporters who work mainly in the clinical field. Carl Rogers, for instance, has exercised leadership within this group for many years, and a number of his students have written extensively concerning this type of construct and the theories that result from its use. Despite the extensive literature they have produced, there is a striking absence of extensive experimentation based upon phenomenological formulations of human behavior, for experimentalists have usually favored other types of theories.

A third source of constructs is physics. The research worker may take the position that the inner, unobservable mechanisms underlying the behavior of the pupil in the classroom can be described in terms of *forces, fields of force, movements,* and similar terms derived from physics. Gestalt psychologists used such terms extensively in discussing behavior and considered that they presented useful and convenient ways of describing the roots of behavior internal to the organism. The late Kurt Lewin also made extensive use of such ideas derived from the physical sciences and would draw diagrams showing the operation of psychological forces analogous to the physical forces of attraction and repulsion exerted by electrically charged particles. These and other analogies from physics are considered to be merely convenient ways of representing underlying phenomena which cannot be directly observed. The system of constructs which they involve are introduced as convenient crutches for thinking about behavior. Constructs are discarded as soon as they are found to be of little value or as soon as they are replaced by constructs of greater utility for research.

Definitive advice cannot be given at this time concerning the relative utility of the three main sources of constructs discussed. The author is under the impression that constructs derived from neurological and physical analogies are preferred by many contemporary theory-builders. They seem greatly to distrust the type of theory that derives its constructs from the content of conscious personal experience. But the fact that a construct is derived from a particular area does not guarantee its utility. Each construct should satisfy at least one important condition, which must now be discussed.

In the development of constructs, the essential condition, as Hull (1943) has pointed out, is the avoidance of circularity of argument. This common defect in theory construction may be clarified by means of an example. In the study of problem-solving behavior, the custom in the past has been to "explain" such behavior in terms of a construct called intelligence. This procedure involves circular argument, for specific problem-solving behaviors are used as a basis for postulating an underlying ability referred to as intelligence, and then this underlying ability is used to explain the problem-solving behavior on the basis of which it was originally derived. In such a situation, the invention of a construct serves no useful purpose.

On the other hand, consider the case of a scientist working on a different problem. This scientist was concerned with the responses of subjects to a certain projective test, which he believed to be a measure of achievement motivation. In order to test this hypothesis, he was able to show that high scores on the test were related to the existence of childhood conditions judged to produce achievement motivation. The reader should note that in this latter case the construct of *achievement motivation* can be usefully introduced because it is related both to the conditions that produce it and the means through which it is measured. This construct involves no circularity of argument because it is firmly rooted both in the conditions through which it is produced and in the consequences observed in behavior. Such a construct is commonly referred to as one that is "tied down at both ends."

Philosophers such as Northrup (1948) have pointed out that in the early stages of a science the concepts introduced are developed on an intuitive basis—that is, that they are derived from personal experience. In later stages, concepts are derived by postulation—that is, they refer to hidden events that are inferred only rather indirectly from observed events. For example, the early stages of physics were characterized by concepts, such as that of force, that were derived from the direct and personal experience of tensions in muscles occurring when the body exerts a force on an object. In the later stages of physics we find concepts, such as that of the neutron, that are postulated on the basis of other events to which they are only remotely related.

Nearly all research on problems of behavior in educational situations is based on the more primitive of these two ways of deriving concepts. This is unfortunate, because the history of psychology shows clearly that research based on intuitive concepts derived from conscious experience is quite unproductive. The great advances of psychology have come when psychologists have postulated mechanisms and variables other than those which they could observe directly. Freud, for example, postulated a whole series of unconscious mechanisms that had no counterpart in conscious experience. All modern work on motivation is necessarily based on hypothetical constructs because individuals have no direct awareness of their own motives and indeed, according to clinicians, commonly misinterpret them. It is hard to find a field in which the study of behavior has advanced on an intuitive basis without the need for postulating hypothetical constructs.

Models

The student cannot long pursue graduate studies without encountering the term *model*, a term which is used very freely and in many different meanings. The treatment of models in this chapter follows closely that of Chapanis (1961).

A model is an analogy, a way of representing a particular phenomenon. Models are widely used by teachers for helping pupils understand phenomena. One of the models most commonly found in the classroom is the globe which should not be construed as being merely a miniature of the earth. Although the shape of the globe represents the earth in miniature form, other features of the earth are not represented realistically; for example, the color of a country on the globe has nothing to do with the color of the actual terrain of that country. The surface of the earth is generally represented as smooth, but if mountains are represented they have to be grossly exaggerated in size otherwise they would not be visible to the student. The lines of latitude and longitude are drawn on the globe, but of course they are imaginary lines on the planet. The globe is merely a convenient way of representing the earth. It is not designed to be a realistic miniature in all respects, but despite this lack of realism its value as a teaching device has been recognized by generations of teachers. Other examples of models are found in the administrative offices of the school system. The table of organization found in the superintendent's office is a model of the administrative machinery of the school's system. The architect's plans for a new school building provide yet another example of a model.

Models are analogies. Chapanis (1961) states the matter in this way: "Scientific or engineering models are representations, or likenesses, of certain aspects of complex events, structures, or systems, made by using symbols or objects which in some way resemble the thing being modeled." No clear-cut line can be drawn between models and constructs. Some scientists have adopted the custom of limiting the use of the term *model* to concrete representations of objects or phenomena while *constructs* are left to refer to more abstract representations of unobservable aspects of phenomena, but no widely accepted distinction has been adopted. The reader might as well recognize that in reviewing research literature he will come across what are called models which have been developed for the purpose of representing behavior with its underlying mechanisms, but that other research workers using the same framework of ideas refer to them as "constructs."

Chapanis, in following through on his definition, classifies models as *replica models* and *symbolic models*. A replica model looks like the object or phenomenon that is represented. A globe is roughly a replica model of the earth, although it does incorporate many symbolic features—the little circles representing cities, for instance. Symbolic models, on the other hand, use abstract symbols to represent either parts of an object or the relationship among phenomena. A symbolic model of perception and communication provided by Broadbent, shown in Figure I, is an example of a symbolic model. This model is able to represent some of the events that have been observed in experimental studies of perception. It has also been used to suggest a number of experiments which have actually been undertaken. A table of organization which has little boxes representing job positions and lines connecting the boxes representing lines of authority is another common example of a symbolic model.

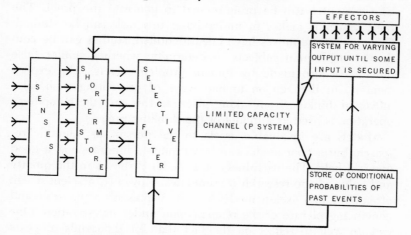

FIGURE I. *Symbolic model of the processing of information received by the human organism.* (From Broadbent, 1958.)

Although a distinction has been made between constructs and models, the scientist may start with a highly abstract set of constructs and then build a model to clarify aspects of them. Niels Bohr's highly mathematical conception of the atom has been presented to generations of students in the form of a simple mechanical model in which an atom is represented as a miniature solar system with the nucleus at the center and electrons spinning around the nucleus at varying distances from it. The scientist passes from constructs to models and back again as it is convenient for the development of his thinking.

The widespread use of models in scientific work derives largely from their value in suggesting experiments and studies and their long history as a means of achieving important knowledge. They have an additional value: sometimes it is possible to experiment first with the model itself and then, with the knowledge obtained, turn to experimenting with the real phenomena. An example of this is found in the study of thinking processes in which computers have been made to simulate the thinking processes involved in, say, the derivation of a proof of a theorem of Euclid. The computer can be programmed to generate the proof. The false moves it makes in undertaking this task can be studied. Once such false moves have been identified, studies can be conducted on human subjects to determine whether similar false moves are also made by human problem-solvers. The experimenter can then go on to find ways of preventing such false moves in thinking from taking place. In this case the computer's operation is used as a model of the thinking process.

Models are invaluable assets to the pursuit of scientific research, but a poor model can be as much a hindrance as a good one is a help. The usefulness of a model is shown in the quality and value of the research it stimulates. However, a scientist can often cling to a useless model because it presents a plausible and convincing picture of the phenomenon under investigation. One can do well to reflect on the fact that for thousands of years men used as a model of the earth a flat disc, a model which confused thinking for generation after generation. Another example of a faulty model was the idea held by the medieval chemist that the phenomenon of burning involved the giving up of a substance called *phlogiston*. The firm hold which this model had on the thinking of chemists not only prevented them from embracing alternative conceptions of combustion but also resulted in a state of stagnation of the field of chemistry for more than a century.

A Conception of the Role of Theory in Research

Up to this point, the nature of theory has been considered only in the broadest terms. When the common man prefaces a statement with the remark "I have a theory that . . . ," he is saying that he believes he knows some law that will be useful to him. He may not be very sure that the law is a sound one, but he is inclined to believe that it will apply in the specific instance. Of course, he has not arrived at the law by any procedure that is acceptable to the scientist, hence the scientist would question whether he really had arrived at a law. In contrast, when the scientist states that he knows a law that will serve the purpose of making a particular prediction or some other purpose, one can be sure that the law has been verified by determining that it is capable of making the predictions that it is alleged that it can make. All laws have their limitations; and since these limits are rarely, if ever, precisely known, there is often question as to whether a law can be relied upon as a basis for a particular prediction. The theories that are used in educational research are usually represented by a series of generalizations about some aspect of education. These generalizations are based on information and are often substantiated by research, but they do not yet have the certainty, usefulness, or status of laws.

An example from a field outside of education may perhaps clarify this point more easily than one from education itself. From the chemical theory that burning represents a compounding of a substance with oxygen, it can be deduced that the products of burning must weigh more than the object that is ignited. Thus, in one of the classical experiments of chemistry, it was demonstrated that mercuric oxide resulting from the burning of mercury weighs more than the mercury from which it was derived. This and similar evidence was collected to support the oxidation theory. Later, as chemistry grew to be a quantitative science, it became possible to predict from a more general theory just what would be the amount of oxygen that would combine with a particular substance.

In its early stage of development, the theory that burning is oxidation involved, like any other theory, one or more basic postulates from which deductions were made; or, to say the same thing but in different words, from which hypotheses were derived. In the simple chemical theory just considered there is a basic postulate from which deductions are made, and which is as follows:

Postulate: Burning is the combination of a substance with oxygen.

Deduction: The product of burning mercury will weigh more than the mercury that is burned.

Later, of course, examples were found of burning that did not involve the combination of a substance with oxygen, and the postulate had to be revised to include such instances. The theory that later evolved pertained to the heat changes produced when all types of chemical elements and compounds were combined.

An example from education may now be cited. The author recently read a doctoral dissertation that was concerned with a problem related to the manifestation of aggressive behavior in children in classrooms. The theory on which the research was based depended on the following three generalizations:

1. Aggressive behavior on the part of the teacher results in aggressive behavior on the part of the pupil.
2. Restriction of movement in the classroom increases the amount of pupil aggression manifested.
3. Aggressive behavior on the part of the pupils tends to be manifested by the stronger toward the weaker.

These three generalizations about aggression in classrooms constitute a primitive theory. Although they are based upon some research, they could not be called laws; much additional research and verification would be needed before they could acquire that status. *Such statements are commonly referred to as postulates, which distinguishes them from laws. Postulates may be considered to be the forerunners of laws.* As more and more evidence concerning the validity of postulates is accumulated through research, they are modified where necessary. When found to be acceptable, they may finally be called laws.

The validity of postulates is examined by testing deductions from them. From the three postulates that have just been given, we may deduce that children in classes with aggressive teachers should show more aggressive behavior in the home than those in classes with nonaggressive teachers. This deduction might also be called a hypothesis. If the hypothesis were tested in research, it might either confirm the validity of the theory or result in a modification of the postulates on which the theory was based.

In general, then, a theory is not a useful one unless deductions can be made from it. These deductions are specific consequences of the postulate or postulates to be tested. If the deductions are ambiguous, they cannot be used to test the validity of the theory; and unfortunately many theories of behavior provide deductions that are highly ambiguous. For example, a theory often stated in articles in the early period of psychoanalysis implied that the psychological development of some individuals remained arrested at a so-called anal stage. Deductions from this postulate were that such individuals would show in later years either excessive fastidiousness about cleanliness or a preoccupation with activities in which dirty materials were handled. Now this theory has almost everything wrong with it. First, it is not really possible to reduce it to a meaningful system of postulates. To do this, it would be necessary to specify the conditions that produce the condition known as anal fixation, so that we could write a postulate of the type, "X produces anal fixation." Then it would be necessary to write one or more postulates stating the general nature of the conditions that anal fixations do or do not produce. Finally, we would have to make deductions of the type, "When X is found in the background of the individual, we may later expect to find the symptom Y [some specific consequence of an anal fixation] occurring more frequently than when X is absent." Obviously, it is simply not possible to test the validity of a theory when it is deduced that either a symptom or its reverse may occur in adult life as a result of a childhood event.

Throughout this discussion, the assumption has been made that the postulates or laws stated in the presentation of a theory are thoroughly understood by all. This is rarely the case, hence it is almost always necessary to present a set of definitions of the terms that are used as a part of any theory. Sometimes variables mentioned in the postulates are defined in terms of the way in which they are measured. For example, a postulate of one theory includes the word *anxiety*. In this theory, anxiety is measured and defined by means of the Taylor Manifest Anxiety Scale. The use of operations yielding an index or a measure is a common way of defining the variables involved in an educational theory.

Summary

1. There is no single well-tried formula that can be used for arriving at knowledge. Despite the attempts of philosophers to formulate simple procedures that will result in the production of scientific knowledge, such procedures do not exist at this time. Scientists differ greatly in the ways in which they arrive at scientific knowledge.

2. Educational research is considered in this volume as that activity which is directed toward the development of a science of behavior in educational situations. Thus it represents a branch of the behavioral sciences that has special implications for all phases of educational planning and that would help the teacher to know what conditions to establish in the classroom in order to achieve particular results.

3. Educational research provides knowledge concerning educational objectives that *can* be achieved and indicates efficient ways of achieving them, but does not determine the ethical and moral values that education should foster.

4. While educational research may, and should, draw upon knowledge acquired in related sciences, it may nevertheless have its own unique characteristics.

5. A scientific body of knowledge acquired through educational research would not consist solely of a body of fact but would provide generalizations and laws that could be applied to the solution of a range of problems.

6. Theories are not just "ivory-tower" phenomena, but are developments of the greatest practical importance. A good theory also marks the point of departure from which a successful exploration of educational phenomena are made.

7. In the behavioral sciences, of which educational science is one, the research worker may build his constructs from a number of different sources of materials. He may build them in terms of his knowledge of the anatomy and physiology of the human being. He may build them out of elements in the content of his own conscious experience. A third alternative is that he may borrow ideas from the physical sciences. Which type of material is used as a basis for theory-building is largely a matter of personal preference.

8. Scientific theories can be considered, under ideal circumstances, to consist of a series of laws related to one another. Most theories in education that are to be used as a basis of research cannot be considered to consist of sets of laws, but rather of sets of postulates that have much less validity than laws. In any case, a theory must include definitions of terms. Deductions from a set of postulates become the means of testing the adequacy of a theory. Such deductions are commonly referred to as hypotheses.

9. Scientific research involves the use of models, which are analogies. Models are used for many purposes, including teaching and administration. Models are used by scientists as devices for helping them think. A useful model may suggest many hypotheses worth testing.

CHAPTER 2

CONDUCTING RESEARCH WITHIN
A FRAMEWORK OF THEORY

IN CHAPTER 1 the point was made that, although scientists show great variability in their methods, there are certain devices which they commonly use in formulating their ideas. Those specifically mentioned were theories, constructs, and models, each of which can play a role in the formulation and advancement of knowledge. This does not mean that every scientist is concerned with the development of theories, the invention of constructs, or the building of models. Some scientists, for example, have very little interest in theories of behavior, devoting their lives to the building of mechanical models which will simulate the behavior of living organisms; others make their principal contributions in theory development.

Most research has some connection with theory, at least insofar as the latter attempts to formulate what has been learned from previous research and to generalize from it. Even the scientist who is least concerned with the development of theory is influenced by theory in this respect. As he reviews the state of knowledge in his field, he cannot help noting the directions in which it points. When he takes his bearings in this way he is formulating theory, though at a primitive level. The position taken here is that educational research would benefit if research workers were to state clearly the theoretical position from which their work begins.

Current Educational Theory as a Basis for Research

Theories in their most rudimentary form are often no more than ways of looking at data; the behavioral sciences were at one time plagued by this type of theorizing. Perhaps one should take a less critical attitude toward such rudimentary theorizing and realize that it was the path that had to be trod before more useful and adequate theories could be developed. From Charcot and Freud up to modern times, clinicians have developed theories that were nothing more than ways of viewing the clinical process, for there was no satisfactory way in which the expected results of the theories could possibly be tested. For example, there is no possible way of testing the Freudian theory that nothing is ever forgotten, for it is quite impossible to conceive of an experiment in which it might be demonstrated conclusively that some event had actually been forgotten.

Any theory that has merit for scientific purposes should be such that one can conceive of evidence that might be inconsistent with it. All scientific theories that have played a major role in the advance of knowledge have been of this type. The rudimentary type of theory we have considered here can be classed only as a kind of crutch to thought.

Theories may be stated with varying degrees of precision. Most educational theory is stated in an informal manner and in the language of everyday speech. One section of Dewey's theory of problem-solving (1910), for example, implies that learning to identify accurately the problem to be solved is an essential aspect of learning to solve problems. This statement of a small segment of Dewey's problem-solving theory could be said to be an informal statement of one aspect of an educational theory, attempts to state in a very general way what is believed to happen in one phase of the problem-solving process.

Such theories have often provided useful guides for action in the classroom, but they have had relatively little influence in providing guide lines for research. The writer is not aware of any study of consequence that has emerged from Dewey's theory of problem-solving. Theories need to be stated in somewhat more precise terms to be of value to the scientist, and while it may not be necessary or even possible to state educational theories in completely formal terms for satisfactory research to result, a greater degree of precision than that ordinarily found seems desirable.

The student's concept of some of the characteristics of a theory needed as a basis for teaching and research may be developed by examining a theory of some historical interest. Consider, for example, the theory of education propounded by Dr. Montessori, which several decades ago aroused a great deal of interest. This theory takes as its primary postulate the statement that freedom of movement within the classroom is an essential condition for effective learning and, as a second postulate, that certain objects have intrinsic value in stimulating the interest of young children. The latter objects, the "apparatus" of the Montessori system, would be discovered by trial and observation. These postulates represent theory in a very rudimentary form. The deductions that can be made from them are only of the most direct type and involve no more than statements concerning the validity of the postulates themselves. Thus, one may "deduce" from the first that children in a free-movement situation should learn more than children in a movement-restricted situation. A test of the validity of this "deduction" provides evidence of the validity of the postulate. There seems to be no way in which it is possible to make deductions from more than one postulate in a manner that links together the various elements in the theory. There is also only a limited rationale on which the postulates are based. They do not stand on a firm foundation of carefully collected data, but, rather, they are based on general observation.

Educational theories which bear a close resemblance to that

developed by Montessori have gained considerable popularity in recent years, even though there is only the most limited evidence of their worth. Enthusiasm for application must be replaced by enthusiasm for research before education can be expected to be built on a solid foundation.

The Montessori theory of education has merit as a theory, in that it stresses the manipulation of concrete conditions and therefore is closely tied to observable events. This simplifies the task of the teacher, who can manipulate the events and their related conditions. A similar desirable feature is not shared by most educational theories. They tend to be preoccupied with the personal experience of the pupil and the manipulation of events within his inner life. Such theories assume that by the provision of verbal materials and various visual and other cues it is possible to generate personal experiences described as "feelings of security," "understanding," and "thinking." Such theories rarely refer to variables that can be measured through some form of objective and recordable performance. The end products are hidden.

One of the handicaps presented by educational theories is that they are also often influenced by sentiment, rather than by a desire to manipulate conditions so as to make education as efficient as possible in the achievement of certain goals. This is reflected in the stress placed on the feelings of the teacher toward the pupil and similar traditional variables of personal experience. Theories based on sentiment often stress how the teacher should feel, as in primitive theories that emphasize that the teacher should love the pupils. Such theories tend to become somewhat mystical when they are probed to the point of answering the question concerning how the teacher's love of the pupil is functionally related to the learning process. Merely to state that it provides a favorable climate in which learning can flourish, just as certain regions have a climate in which grapefruit can flourish, does not provide a satisfactory answer to the question.

The sentimental type of educational theory is particularly perplexing to the student of the behavioral sciences because it is based on postulates that are inconsistent with a large body of data concerning both human and animal behavior. Despite this fact, it has been a widely held type of attempt to state a theory concerning the conditions necessary for effective education and was originally popularized in the writings of Jean Jacques Rousseau. It is a type of theory that is wholly useless to the scientist and of doubtful value to the educator. Statements of the theory never indicate to the teacher just what are the positive conditions that must be manipulated if the teacher is to achieve a particular objective in education. From the scientist's point of view, the theory does not generate a testable hypothesis.

The wide gulf that exists between scientific theories of behavior and educational theories does not have to exist. Ultimately, such theorizing may attain a certain unity. A theory that is clearly stated and provides a useful basis for action in the classroom also should provide a sound basis for research. The gulf that exists between educational theory and behavioral theory simply does not have to persist.

The Statement of a Theory as the Starting Point of a Research

From what has been said, one would infer that theories vary greatly in their complexity. Some contain a single idea, others incorporate many. The single-idea theory, based on a single postulate, commonly has been used as a basis of master's theses. For example, one student started with the postulate, "The rate at which pupils learn to recognize words is a function of their ability to discriminate differences in shape." The student was careful to define what he meant by the ability to recognize words and the ability to discriminate differences in shape. He then proceeded to determine whether this was the case for a given group of words that a certain class of pupils was learning to recognize.

What would have been the advantage of having stated a more complex theory for the purpose of the research? It would have served the purpose of stating as clearly and as concisely as possible the state of knowledge in the area in which the student proposed to work. That is really the function of a theory that has been stated comprehensively. It gathers together the various ideas in the field—once that has been done, it is possible to see more clearly what must be done and where are the major gaps in present knowledge. There is no absolute need to bring together the ideas in a field in order to do research, but since the research worker usually has made a careful review of the literature in the field, he might as well do this. If he does not organize the theory of his area of interest in this way, he is always in danger of basing his research on a single postulate that includes an idea or concept that really does not tie in with other already acquired knowledge.

Bergmann (1957) has very neatly stated this point. He asserts:

A concept is significant if and only if it occurs, together with others, in statements of lawfulness which we have reason to believe are true. . . .

Assume that somebody proposes a new concept, call it the C-coefficient. A person's C-coefficient is, by definition, the number obtained by multiplying his white blood count by his weight in ounces and dividing the product by the number of hairs on his legs. Clearly, it is not difficult to ascertain a person's C-coefficient. Equally clearly, the concept is not significant. Why, one may ask, are we so certain of this? After all, there could be laws in which it occurs. In principle this is so. Yet we are certain that there are none. To understand the reasons we have for this certainty, assume that the proponent of our new concept is a crank who expects to use it for the prediction of cancer, that is, he hopes to find a law that makes the incidence of cancer a function of the C-coefficient ("C" from "cancer"). Again, why do we call him a crank? The point is that we know a great deal about cancer, and that neither the C-coefficient itself nor the law our friend expects to find "fits" with existing laws and theories about cancer.[1]

What Bergmann is saying is that one should use as a basis for research only those concepts that are linked to other concepts.

[1] From *The Philosophy of Science*, by Gustav Bergmann, Copyright © 1957, The University of Wisconsin Press. Reprinted with permission of the copyright owners, the Regents of the University of Wisconsin.

The isolated idea, however brilliant it may seem to the person who has generated it, has no real place in science, for the scientist attempts to build *relationships* among ideas. He builds upon the ideas of the past, though sometimes he may radically reorganize these ideas and see them in a new light. The related ideas that constitute a theory are the postulates of the theory. At this point we should begin to consider some examples of theories from the educational field, deriving our main example from the area of reading, where a very large amount of knowledge has been acquired.

An article describing a method of teaching reading in the very early stages of learning the skill provides an illustration of theory-construction and deductions from postulates. This article, widely considered to be one of the better pieces in the field, is based on a fairly definite theory of reading, although the theory is not very well stated. The nature of the theory may be represented by defining some of the key terms that were used by the author and then setting out the three major postulates that appear to form the core of the theory. Definitions of the key terms and the three postulates formulated by the present writer are set out in Table 1.

The next step is to determine whether the theory can be used as a basis for finding problems for research. In other words, what deductions that serve as hypotheses in a research program may be made from the theory? The writer then thought through some of the logical consequences of the theory and listed them as deductions. One can be sure that some of these deductions have already been tested, but probably at least one has not. Many other deductions also could have been listed.

To those who have been raised on Newtonian mechanics, this attempt to state an educational theory may appear pathetically inadequate. In the theory presented, the deductions *more* or *less* follow from the postulates, but they lack the tight logic of mathematical deductions. The theory lacks precision in the sense in which precision is found in the theory of physics. Yet it can hardly be denied that a theory stated in the fairly terse and organized form suggested in this chapter may be much superior for scientific purposes to a theory presented in a long and wandering article in which the definitions, postulates, and deductions, are all mixed together. Undoubtedly much could be done to improve the statement of the theory presented in the illustration, and the writer's attempt at theory-building probably does not do justice to the article from which it was derived.

TABLE 1. A Theory of the Early Stages of Learning Reading

Definitions

1. *Reading* is defined as a controlled form of talking in which the words that are said are controlled by the nature of the written symbols presented.
2. *A correct reading response* is defined as the act of saying the agreed-upon interpretation of the written symbol presented.
3. *Accuracy of response* to a word is defined as the percentage of attempts to say the word that is correct.
4. *The perception of learning to read as a goal* is evidenced by such behavior as the pupil asking the teacher for reading activities, participating voluntarily in reading activities, choosing reading activities rather than others.

Postulates

1. When reading is learned by means of the sequence: written word presentation, vocal response by the teacher, vocal response by the pupil, the frequency of occurrence of this sequence is related to the accuracy of response of the pupil. (This method of learning to read is commonly referred to as the "look-and-say method" and will be so referred to here.)
2. The effectiveness of the look-and-say method in generating correct reading responses in the pupil is related to the ability of the pupil to discriminate form and shape. Pupils must have a minimum of the latter ability if the method is to produce learning. Additional increments of the ability beyond the minimum result in increased rates of learning.
3. The effectiveness of the look-and-say method in producing cor-

rect reading responses is related to the extent to which the pupil perceives the learning of reading as a desirable goal and is motivated to achieve that goal.

Deductions

1. Measures of motivation to read will be correlated with accuracy of response in the early stages of reading in the case of those pupils who perceive reading as a desirable goal.

2. Failure to discriminate two words is a function of the similarity of the shape of the two words.

3. The look-and-say method produces greater accuracy of response when it is supplemented by procedures that emphasize discrimination of the form of one word and the form of another than it does when such methods are not used.

Since any theory is likely to be a product of intensive study of the scientific knowledge available in an area, it is apt to appear to the person who has not undertaken such studies to be intensely technical and perhaps even incomprehensible. For this reason, some fairly simple examples from areas known to most readers are presented in the main body of the text. A few readers, however, may like to inspect a more sophisticated example of theory construction, even if it does involve a great deal of technical vocabulary. Therefore, an example of a theory which involves somewhat greater sophistication is included in an appendix. Drawn from Ammons (1954), it obviously is the product of careful study and thought, and it provides a fairly complete example of a theory stated in terms of postulates, and one in which the vocabulary has been very carefully defined.

Level of Comprehensiveness of a Theory

Theories vary considerably in the extent to which they cover all of the factors that affect the events being studied. To explain this point, a fairly familiar example may be taken from the field of physics. Consider the problem of predicting the trajectory of a projectile fired from a gun. By simple deductions from Newtonian physics, it is possible to appoximate this prediction if the muzzle velocity of the projectile and the value of G, the gravitational constant, are known. A more comprehensive theory would take into account the resistance of the atmosphere, the barometric pressure, and the direction and velocity of the wind. The more comprehensive the theory, the more precisely is it possible to predict what it is desired to predict, but this is true only insofar as it is feasible to measure the variables that the theory includes.

In the development of a science of educational behavior, we can also build theories of varying degrees of comprehensiveness. We could, for example, build a theory of child behavior in the classroom that took into account a tremendous range of variables, including immediately prior circumstances as well as circumstances farther in the background of the child. Such a theory would have a high degree of comprehensiveness, but it would obviously not be completely comprehensive because it would not include many important variables that had not yet been recognized. Nevertheless, our theory would probably have little utility. It would involve too much that could not be measured at this time and too much that scientists will not, with any likelihood, be able to measure at any time in the foreseeable future. The main defect of such a theory is that it is *not* firmly rooted in current knowledge. A theory that is so rooted is likely to be relatively simple.

A simple theory that deals with relatively few major variables, all of which can be measured, can be a much more productive enterprise than one that deals with a larger number of variables, most of which cannot be measured. It is important in this respect, as in others, to prevent oneself from becoming mentally suffocated under a mass of detail. Relatively simple and incomplete theories have had a history of usefulness in the behavioral sciences and an unexpected degree of success in terms of what was anticipated fifty years ago. A good example of this is the theory that educational achievement is merely a function of a few variables such as the verbal factor, the numerical factor, the deductive reasoning factor, and so forth. Such a theory fails to take into account the facts that achievement is also a function of motivation and that the presence or absence of numerous external conditions affect learning; for example, the way in which the teacher interacts with the pupil. Despite these limitations, this simple type of theory has been the basis of a vast amount of productive research and has formed a basis for much that takes place within the general area of guidance. It has also become the foundation for the entire system of assigning men to training programs within the armed services. Its success has been nothing short of astounding.

Unfortunately, predictions made in terms of this simple type of theory have only moderate accuracy and leave approximately 50 per cent of the variability (variance) of the predicted variable unaccounted for in terms of the prediction variables. In this connection it is of considerable interest to observe that students of the behavioral sciences are not the only scientists who effectively use theories that have only, so to speak, 50 per cent efficiency. Many industrial manufacturing processes in the field of complex chemicals are based on traditional concepts of organic chemistry. On the basis of such chemical theory one would expect a given amount of component chemicals to yield 100 per cent of the chemical product that it is desired to manufacture. In practice, the manufacturing may in fact produce only 50 per cent of the expected yield. For reasons unknown at the present time, side reactions generate a great number of subsidiary products, some of which are usable and some unusable. The theory is a valuable one in spite of its limitations, and it is certainly widely used as guide in the development of industrial products.

The researcher wants to extend theories already existing so that they become more comprehensive, but not to a point where they involve many variables that cannot be measured at this time. Modest extensions may be extremely valuable, and these do not have to be grandiose to represent a substantial development over the previous state of the technique.

Formalizing a Theory

The reader undoubtedly has heard discussions of the need to formalize theories. The concept of a "formal theory" has been used with a great diversity of connotations, and often these two words are uttered as if they had some special magic power. The implication is that all one has to do is state a theory in "formal terms" and great scientific achievements will result. But what is meant by a "formal theory"? The author has a preference for the meaning used by Bergmann (1957), who regards the formal statement of a theory as one in which all of the words have been translated into abstract symbols such as are used by mathematicians. A theory stated in the form of a series of mathematical equations is a formalized theory. The science of behavior in educational situations is not advanced to the point where a formal theory of this type is feasible. Perhaps we may ultimately aspire to the statement of educational theory in such terms. At the present time it is not known whether this is even possible.

Causal and Functional Relationships

It is stressed at various points in this volume that the educational research specialist should seek to establish organized systems of relationships among events and among variables. Such relationships can be stated without introducing the notion that some events cause other events. For example, from the data collected in the past concerning the motions of the planets in the solar system, positions of the planets at some future time can be predicted. The lawfulness of planetary behavior is neither increased nor decreased by introducing the notion that the state of the planetary system at one point in time is a consequence of prior conditions. The concept of cause is irrelevant to the statement of the laws of the planetary system and is unnecessary for making predictions from the laws. The reader may here jump to the conclusion that the concept of cause has no role to play in the development of a science, but this conclusion is not justified. While the concept of cause may not enter into the statement of the laws that are the final products of the work of the scientist, it does nevertheless play an important role in his thinking and may help him in the discovery of laws. Even scientists in advanced fields of knowledge admit to *thinking* in terms of cause and effect. For example, biographical accounts of Einstein's early thinking illustrate this point vividly. A personal concept of the nature of the universe seems necessarily to involve some concept of the causation of events, and this way of thinking plays an integral part in the process of scientific discovery. A brief discussion of the origin of the concept of cause may make this point clear.

Personal experience leads one to believe that all events are the products or results of other events, which are referred to as their causes. The product of these causes is referred to as the effect. The origin of the belief in the existence of causal relationships is found in personal experience, in that each of us performs at least certain acts for the purpose of producing certain effects. In addition, we have the experience of other events producing certain effects on us. This has led ultimately to a concept of a universe in which every thing or event has a cause and in which there is thus a continuity and order among events. Certain major scientific concepts are deeply rooted in this concept of causation—for example, the principle of the conservation of energy, which states that energy can neither be created nor destroyed. A similar principle, deeply rooted in the conception of causation, is the principle stated by Pasteur that only life gives rise to life.

While it is desirable to avoid the projections of one's personal experiences onto the universe at large, there still seems to be merit in retaining a conservative conception of cause in thinking about natural phenomena. Indeed, it is almost impossible to conduct such thinking without the concept of causal relationships. This conception retains the idea that in order for a particular event to be produced it is necessary for certain conditions to exist; the necessary conditions are referred to collectively as a cause.

Much of what has been learned by scientists, such as the educational psychologist's concept of maturation, would be difficult to think about at this time without the concept of causation.

Some scientists prefer to state that they are seeking to establish systems of *functional* relationships rather than causal relationships. This must now be explained. Consider, for example, a simple and well-known law, such as Ohm's law, which can be stated in the following form:

$$\text{Potential difference} = \text{current} \times \text{resistance.}$$

This may be interpreted in popular language as follows: When a current passes through a wire, the drop in voltage along the wire is proportional to the product of the resistance of the conductor times the current. Now one cannot say that the potential difference is caused by the resistance to the current, for the causal relationships are complex. Nevertheless, the relationship expressed by Ohm's law represents interrelationships among phenomena, which, if fully described, could be represented by a set of causal relationships. These relationships could be described in terms of the electron theory of the structure of matter. A description of the system of causal relationships on which the law is based would be complicated, and much more elaborate than the law itself. For this reason, some scientists may prefer to say that Ohm's law represents a functional relationship among variables. Hence the reader will see that the term *functional relationship* refers to a situation in which is described a relationship that is not directly causal but is based on a complex system of interactions.

Most relationships in the behavioral sciences are not expressed in a form like that of Ohm's law or similar simple relationships. However, a few such simple relationships have been postulated —for example, that postulated by Hull (1943) in the form R = HD. When translated, this equation reads: response evocation is equal to the product of habit strength and drive. Insofar as this simple equation expresses a true relationship, it does not represent a simple causal relationship but the result of a great complexity of relationships.

There is perhaps a certain safety in using the term *functional relationship* rather than the term *causal relationship*. When we demonstrate that rewarding a child for performing certain acts increases the probability that the child will perform those acts in the future, we may say that we have established a functional relationship. In doing this, we avoid stating that there is a direct causal relationship between the reward and the heightened tendency to perform the rewarded behavior. Nevertheless, the implication is that the relationships are more than just coincidental, but are a necessary part of the phenomena studied. We can be almost certain that the relationship between the reward and the changed response probability is an extremely complex one, not one that is well described in terms of a simple and straightforward causal relationship. Some philosophers would even go so far as to say that almost any relationship that appears on the surface to be a simple causal relationship is, in fact, a matter of great complexity. For this reason, throughout this book we propose to use the term *functional relationship* rather than the term *causal relationship*. Of course, we will not quarrel with those who prefer to use the term *causal relationship* from time to time.

Knowledge Can be Acquired at All Levels of Precision

There has been a tendency in psychology as it has developed within the American culture to emphasize the need for expressing theories in terms of variables that can be measured. For the most part this emphasis has been a healthy one, for it has led psychology away from the field of philosophy in which it had its beginnings and developed it as one of the biological and social sciences. In this matter, however, one can carry the emphasis on measurement too far. There are those who would prefer to quantify the trivial rather than to study the significant with qualitative methods that fall far short of the precision to which modern sciences aspire. It is perhaps worth reflecting on the fact that most of the generalizations of science began as qualitative statements and later developed more fully in a quantitative form. For example, one hundred years elapsed between Newton's postulation of a universal gravitational constant and Cavendish's successful attempt to measure this important constant. The basic principles of thermodynamics were first stated in a qualitative form. Harvey's discovery of the circulation of the blood, together with the other qualitative discoveries of the great school of medicine at Padua, laid the foundation for what became ultimately the quantitative science of physiology. The important discoveries that represent the very cornerstones of a quantitative science are almost invariably of a qualitative nature.

The author is not advising the graduate student of education to plan qualitative studies for his master's thesis. Major qualitative contributions in research are made by the few, rather than by the many who make substantial but not brilliant contributions. It is almost essential that the graduate student build his research on the qualitative contributions and generalizations of others. He should appreciate the great importance of these qualitative generalizations and realize that the quantitative studies that follow build on the foundation which they have laid. Our present emphasis on quantification should not prevent us from perceiving its merits in their true light.

Types of Laws

The scientist is able to make predictions when it has become possible to state a generalization, or law as it is commonly called. Laws may be either highly limited or broad in the range of events that they include. In this connection, the reader should note that two broad classes of laws have commonly been considered in the behavioral sciences, and these must now be considered.

The traditional goal of a science of behavior has been the discovery of laws that apply to all individuals; that is to say, laws that have wide applicability. Some psychologists have suggested that such laws may not be the only type of law that can be used in the development of a science of behavior. Indeed, some have even suggested that such laws may have only the most limited value. An alternative proposition, particularly highly favored by those who work in the clinical field, is that there are laws that pertain to the behavior of one individual but do not apply to the behavior of other individuals. Thus it is claimed that the sequences and orderlinesses of behavior manifested by one person may be entirely different from those manifested by another under similar circumstances. The orderlinesses of individual behavior that are unique to that individual are referred to as *ideographic* laws, a term that distinguishes them from *nomothetic* laws applying to all individuals. The clinician seeks to establish the laws of behavior of his patient so that he can predict how the patient will react to various possible modes of treatment and so that he can identify those aspects of the environment of the patient that should be changed in order to facilitate therapy. Nevertheless, the clinician also usually assumes that the unique aspects of a patient's behavior were generated through the operation of laws that apply to all individuals. He may assume, for example, that certain basic laws of learning may cause one individual to learn one set of habits and motives while the same laws may result in other habits and other motives in another person.

Allport was the first to raise this problem, in his book entitled *Personality* (1937). He suggested that different people were characterized by different traits, and that a major problem of the psychologist was to determine just what traits were operating in particular individuals. He recognized the difficulty of this problem, and could suggest no satisfactory method of determining which traits were operating or how they could be measured.

One of his students, McKinnon (1938), demonstrated the reasonableness of this conception of personality in a study wherein he showed that, in handling a series of test situations, some individuals were consistently honest, others consistently dishonest, and still others showed great variability of performance. The behavior of the last group could not be considered to reflect an underlying trait of honesty, but the behavior of those who were consistent could. However, the elaborateness of the technique needed to make a simple determination of the presence or absence of a single trait suggests that it is not feasible to determine by the McKinnon type of technique the presence or absence of a whole set of traits. Allport had suggested that individuals might be grouped into types. Each type would consist of those whose laws of behavior were closely related. Thus it would be necessary to develop a technique for sorting individuals into types. But Allport pointed out that this solution was not a very satisfactory one, since it dealt only with approximations and necessarily introduced large errors in the prediction of behavior.

Interest in this whole problem was revived through the publication of Stephenson's work on Q-methodology (1953). In this book a new approach to this problem is offered, and considerable material is also brought together from some of the older approaches. One of the techniques that he has invented is the structured behavior sample, which offers some hope of identifying which ones of a set of traits are useful in characterizing an individual. He also proposes to apply factor analysis to the problem of categorizing individuals in groups of persons whose behavior can be understood in terms of particular patterns of traits.

These ideas of Stephenson should be considered at this time to be only explorations that may lead to the development of techniques that can solve practical problems. The techniques proposed are, at present, of use only for research purposes; they do not yet seem to be developed to the point where they can be used in the applied field.

A Program of Research As a Long-Term Development

The discussion up to this point has been directed toward helping the graduate student of education develop a concept of the nature of research processes in education. The student may well wonder why large projects with which he is familiar often seem to end in relative failure. Such projects often have substantial financial backing; their failure is not due to lack of funds, and the probable reasons for this are worth examining at this point.

In recent years, foundations have provided large sums of money for research on specific problems. An assumption on which such grants are based is that it is possible to formulate and plan at one time an extended program of research which can be undertaken more or less as planned. In the experience of the author, such projects in the field of education usually have been tragically ineffective. The money has been spent, and almost nothing remains as evidence of accomplishment. The author can recall one program with which he was associated as a graduate student that dragged on for some years after he left it. It contributed nothing to substantive knowledge, and the staff slowly drifted away as funds ran out. Whatever it accomplished was relegated to the graveyard of forgotten and inconsequential events of educational history. The fact that memories of such projects carry with them all the pain and anxiety of failure makes them all the more easily forgotten, so the lessons of failure are not learned. The author has pondered this situation for long, and he believes that a substantial case can be made for the existence of certain conditions that make it virtually impossible to develop at one time an extended program of research under the existing conditions. Let us consider these conditions.

First, it has been stressed here that a unified program of research should be based on a common system of constructs and a unifying theory. Such conceptual systems cannot be developed in short order; they require an extended period of development. They may be derived in some initial and crude form from the literature describing previous research. The adaptation of the conceptual system so derived to the field under investigation, however, requires much experience with the field, and such experience comes only through close contact with the planning and execution of research. It is not enough merely to read about research, but the concentrated thought that should accompany the undertaking of research appears to be an essential ingredient of good theory-building. Thus, actual participation in research is a necessary prerequisite for the adequate formulation of plans.

Second, a program of research develops out of a series of often loosely connected investigations, each of which is designed to explore one of several possible directions along which the program might develop. Such explorations are likely to be a necessary precursor of systematic and programmatic research. If approaches based on particular theories have been developed and appear to be profitable, then the way is clear for the development of a program of research.

Third, educational research has been taught to the graduate student of education as if it could be undertaken by the application of a simple formula. *This idea of research-by-formula has been the nemesis of many major projects. It neglects the creative aspect of research, which is essential for genuine discovery and which is the heart of every significant research enterprise.* Research by formula becomes less and less adequate as the size of the program increases. The approach may be adequate for the small local investigation, but not for a large and continuing program.

Fourth, there is a matter the author believes has not received adequate recognition: maturity of judgment in deciding what is and what is not investigable. There certainly seem to be vast differences between individuals in their ability to identify problems that, at the present time, can be investigated. Some researchers are extraordinarily "good guessers" in this respect, while others just do not seem able to perform this function. Undoubtedly, it is an ability that is highly dependent on experience. One is not likely to be a "good guesser" unless he has had wide experience in the undertaking and planning of research. Without such experience, the evaluation of prospective research projects is a virtual impossibility. The execution of successful independent research requires a lifetime of preparation. At the present time, education lacks a sizable group of high-level personnel who have made research a lifetime pursuit. Only through such individuals can large programs develop successfully.

Fifth, related to some of the previous points and yet in addition to them is the tendency for a researcher granted a large sum of money to overestimate what can be done with it. A sum such as $250,000 may seem immense to the poorly paid college professor, but the fact is that research is an expensive activity to undertake, and even the carefully planned use of a sum such as this may result in what seem to be relatively small corresponding gains in knowledge.

The large educational projects observed by the author that have ended without yielding useful knowledge have in all cases failed to develop according to the pattern that has been outlined. Rather have they been planned as grandiose ventures that have attempted to solve problems of central importance in the field of education through some comprehensive design laid down at the outset. Most of us have become much wiser in this respect over the last two decades—and perhaps much more modest in what we can aspire to discover in return for financial support for research.

Early Theory-Oriented Educational Research

The reader should not be left with the impression that educational research began by investigators collecting a vast amount of empirical information, followed by a period when theory became an ever increasing influence—much as the data-gathering period in astronomy was followed by Kepler's organization of the vast quantity of facts within a single and unifying theory. In education, such has not been the case, for much early research was greatly influenced by what was then current behavioral theory even if it were not based upon it. Herbartian theory is easily seen in the work of Joseph M. Rice in his pioneer research on teaching. Rice, it will be remembered, had spent a period of time in Germany, where he became acquainted with new developments in pedagogical theory. This experience fired him to conduct his investigation on spelling and the relationship of achievement in spelling to certain teaching conditions, such as the amount of time devoted to drill. In addition, it must also be brought to the attention of the reader that Edward L. Thorndike's arrival at Teachers College, Columbia University, near the turn of the century, marked an era of educational research dominated by the type of associationist theory that formed the basis of Thorndikean psychology. There was hardly an area of psychological educational research to which Thorndikean theory of learning was not applied. The learning of arithmetic, reading, and writing was scrutinized in terms of this theory, and thereby a great quantity of knowledge was acquired about these processes.

Research of a so-called fact-finding nature, which is typical of much that is done today, represents a phase that finds its roots in the 1920's, with the growth of research departments within the big-city school systems and within the educational departments of the various states. Such research was intended to solve the various problems that were constantly arising and that needed to be solved in order to be able to map out effective educational policies. It is one of the misfortunes of our times that the policies of such research departments were often set by men in high position who had little understanding of what research workers could or could not accomplish. Such individuals were largely unaware of the research worker's purpose, as it is stated in this volume, but rather did they regard him as an inventor of gadgets and knick-knacks and an unearther of odd facts. With this type of "research" policy in mind, research offices were staffed with workers interested in devoting their lives to the collection, tabulation, and interpretation of facts. Under this influence, educational research became a massive fact-finding enterprise. It is hardly surprising that the resulting large-scale projects have failed to produce generalizations that have added to our knowledge of the laws of behavior in educational situations. Indeed, the provincialism that underlies this domain of research is designed to produce local answers to local questions.

SOME SPECIAL RESEARCH PROBLEMS

Institutional Research

It is of interest to consider at this time the function of what has been termed institutional educational research and its value in developing a scientific body of knowledge. Research of this type has a history that goes back more than a quarter of a century. The discussion here refers to the small educational research units that have been established in many large universities for the purpose of solving their own educational problems. A pioneer in this endeavor has been the University of Minnesota, which since the early 1930's has attempted to gain knowledge about its own educational problems through a small department developed for this purpose. Such departments have usually been staffed by both professional research workers and graduate student assistants. Typical topics for the reports that have been produced are such matters as the knowledge of the student at various stages in his career, his problems after he leaves college and the relation of these problems to the education received, the development of methods for establishing an equitable salary scale, the utilization of space within the school plant, the development of procedures for promoting faculty, and the reasons for failure to graduate. This sampling of topics is given because it reflects the element of administrative expediency that determines whether one study or another is undertaken by the unit. It also illustrates the close relationship that must exist between the institutional research unit and the administration of the university. To facilitate this cooperation, it is of advantage for the unit to be attached to the general administration of the university rather than to one of the teaching units.

In appraising what can be accomplished by such units, let us start by considering their merits. First, they represent a rational approach, not an arbitrary one, to the solving of major and pressing educational problems. They emphasize in a most healthy way the need both for the collection of facts and for reflection concerning these facts in the solution of educational problems, in contrast to the method of opinion and argument that is the common way of solving such problems. To many a member of a liberal arts faculty, the methods of a research unit represent entirely novel approaches to the solution of educational problems. The new approach offered by the research unit provides stimulation for thought and sometimes even makes for a realization on the part of the faculty that traditional methods of solving educational problems should be discarded. Once the latter has been accomplished, the faculty should attempt to define its problems in terms that are investigable. Much of the characteristic vagueness of liberal arts thinking about educational problems should be dispelled. The educational research unit should provide an adventure in thinking for the faculty.

Of course, not all such units have served this worthy purpose. The head of the unit must have not only the research skills necessary for executing the studies that are initiated but also a certain political acumen. Judgments have to be made concerning what ideas will and will not be acceptable to the faculty. The researcher who attempts to cast doubts on the most cherished educational ideas of the faculty is likely to be soon seeking another position, but there are some professional researchers who have been extremely successful in providing a stimulus to the thinking of a faculty.

Such is the positive side of the picture, which presents a strong case for the development of such research units. In terms of the function they fulfill, institutional research units have justified their purpose. But what is their role in contributing to a body of knowledge to which other scientists contribute? The answer the author gives to this is that only rarely have such studies made a contribution to scientific knowledge. The reasons are several, and they do not reflect in any way on the competence of the work that has been done by institutional research units. The author believes that genuine scientific work can be undertaken while working on practical problems, but scientific contributions are likely to be made where the research is programmatic and where a particular type of problem is persistently attacked in an integrated series of studies. In institutional research, administrative pressures are likely to be such that as soon as one study is completed, another study in an entirely different area must be started. By this process institutional research solves numerous separate and isolated problems, some of which probe a subject to the point where a real contribution to knowledge can be made. To the administration, the results are often immensely useful, but to science, there is unlikely to be any permanent contribution.

The author's opinion is that units undertaking institutional research should attempt both the answering of problems posed by the administration and the building of a body of knowledge about some problem of central and scientific importance. For this to be done, it is necessary to free some of the labor available for concentrated programmatic research and to protect this aspect of the work from pressures to handle local problems. If this is done, it is believed that slowly there can be built up a substantial program of research related to an important educational problem, and it is likely that this body of knowledge may be of greater use to the institution than are the answers provided to day-to-day questions. Once a program has been initiated, it should be possible to implement the resources of the research unit with funds obtained from foundations that sponsor basic research. That "basic" research on educational problems can be undertaken along with "applied" problems is a position institutional research units should take if they are to grow and flourish.

Relationship of Research to Practical Problems: Action Research

Scientific research in education, like research in any other field of endeavor, is not necessarily directed toward the solution of some immediate and pressing practical problem. Many such problems can be solved only after a large body of knowledge has been accumulated, at which point they become researchable. We have emphasized here that the long-term program of research is the one that ultimately provides educators with the power to predict and control events. The educator has felt impatient with the research worker who takes this position, and his impatience is shared by practical men in other fields who desire to introduce improvements but who are not willing to wait for research to tell them what to do. During World War II this issue became a serious one, and some of our European allies tried out schemes of employing scientists to recommend and institute innovations without recourse to full-scale research. The scientists were required to formulate plans in terms of the best knowledge available, and after the plans were placed in action some attempt was made to obtain evidence concerning their worth. They were not expected to undertake complete and thorough inquiries concerning the value of their innovations. The procedure was designed to expedite change and development and was probably an influential one. It was the father of what is now termed *operations research*.

Operations research was developed as a highly sophisticated approach to problem-solving and involved the most advanced scientific techniques. Unfortunately, a parallel movement in education aimed at making head-on attacks on educational problems, known as *action research,* shared little of the same sophistication. The advocates of action research took the position that the main participants in educational research should be those directly involved in the educational process, notably teachers and school administrators. Thus, it was suggested that teachers in schools should attempt to solve their own educational problems by establishing action research programs. Such participation of teachers was believed to insure that whatever changes were demonstrated to be desirable would be adopted without resistance. The approach is in marked contrast to that of operations research, which is undertaken by highly trained scientists. Just how teachers, wholly lacking training in research, were to conduct investigations of complex problems of education was never made clear. Even relatively simple educational problems resist the efforts of highly trained research workers to find solutions.

A perusal of the literature indicates to the author that much of what is advocated as action research is nothing more than good management. Any modern book on management will suggest that when problems arise an attempt should be made to draw up a list of alternative solutions, then to collect data to determine which one of these proposed solutions is best. This is good management practice but, in education, it goes by the name of *action research.* It is contrasted with scientific research in that it does not, except by chance, build up a body of organized scientific knowledge. It may be highly effective in solving local problems.

It may also serve the very important function of stimulating thought as well as change. It may produce useful knowledge. While there is much controversy in modern educational literature concerning the value of this approach to educational problems, the practices of action research are so obviously consistent with good management practices that they are here to stay even though they may be given a different name a few years from now. Despite all these merits, the author cannot see that action research and scientific research, as conceived here, have much in common.

Summary

1. Most educational theories do not form an adequate basis for research. They tend to be vague, and do not specify what conditions produce what. Many fail to identify the variables that may be involved and hence give no cues as to what should be measured.

2. Theories developed for the purpose of providing a basis for a program of educational research probably should refer to limited phenomena. This means that they should be fairly simple. Complicated theories may have their place when the science of behavior in educational situations is at a more advanced level than it is today and when the variables can be measured or evaluated in a meaningful way.

3. Attempts to state theories related to limited aspects of education are primarily ways of organizing one's knowledge so that what is known can be clearly seen and so that gaps and deficiencies can be noted.

4. The author believes that the educational research worker should attempt to establish functional relationships, not merely statistical relationships, among events.

5. The research worker in education should attempt to add to the body of knowledge that already exists in the field. He should not seek to contribute isolated items of information that may be interesting in themselves but that do not contribute to an organized body of knowledge.

6. The present need for educational research to be based on

explicitly stated theories represents, to some extent, a need to return to an earlier period when theory-oriented research was the rule. The impressive contributions of such persons as Thorndike early in the century are convincing evidence of what theory-oriented research may be expected to achieve.

7. Knowledge can be acquired at all levels of precision. In the early stages of inquiry, knowledge about phenomena is likely to be very inaccurate and general, but it may be of immense importance for later developments.

8. Educational research conducted within an institution for solving local problems usually contributes little to the development of a body of knowledge of broad significance to education as a whole. The pressure to solve one local problem after another prevents the development of a broad program consisting of a series of related studies. Institutional research does not have to be of this character.

9. Research, as it is discussed here, has little relationship to what is referred to as action research. There seems little hope that action research will build a body of knowledge which can serve as a basis for educational planning. While a problem-solving approach should be taken towards most aspects of educational planning, there is hardly a need to dignify this approach with the title of action research.

Some Problems for the Student

1. Study John Dewey's theory of problem-solving in his book, *How We Think* (1910). On what kind of information is this theory based? What kind of deductions can be made from the theory to test its validity? Why is the theory not very useful as a basis for research?

2. What kinds of deductions that could be used to test its validity can be made from the Montessori theory?

3. Examine a textbook that describes procedures for teaching children to spell. Draw up a set of postulates that describe the general theory on which the procedures are based. A similar exercise can be performed in other curriculum areas.

CHAPTER 3

SELECTING THE PROBLEM

THE CONTENT OF EDUCATIONAL RESEARCH: AREAS FROM WHICH A PROBLEM MAY BE SELECTED

THE selection of a problem suitable for a study or dissertation requires the student to take stock of himself and to identify the area of educational research in which his knowledge, talents, and abilities will permit him to make the most successful contribution. Too often this is not done—the student jumps ahead with enthusiasm to tackle a problem which intrigues him but which he is hardly prepared to study. Ideally, the student should have had good training and have already undertaken intensive reading in the area in which he plans to undertake research.

Before considering the task involved in the selection of the problem, a brief review will be presented of the different areas in which educational research has often been undertaken. Certain of these areas are discussed in greater detail in subsequent chapters for the purpose of illustrating some of the technical problems which the research worker may face.

The Broad Areas of Educational Inquiry

Educational research as it is known today is a relatively new branch of knowledge. Little more than half a century has elapsed since Joseph Mayer Rice planned his researches on the teaching of spelling and other skills, and hoped through his studies to bring reforms to education. While research has not yet become the tool for educational reform which Rice conceived it to be, it has some substantial changes to its credit. The reforms brought about by research have not matched expectations because the best part of a half-century has been taken to find out a little about how to conduct research in education, what can and what cannot be accomplished with the crude tools at the disposal of the researcher. The relatively little that has been accomplished has been the product of great effort. Nevertheless, educational research is now beginning to pass beyond the adolescent stage of ambitious but unrealistic dreams and to conceive of its role in more mature terms.

Although accomplishments have been much less than early developers hoped, research has had substantial effects on education. In the lower elementary grades, we find today readers that have been carefully designed so that each new word is presented a sufficient number of times to give the child opportunity to learn it adequately. Such readers have been developed on the basis of learning studies. The measurement of the pupil's reaction to reading is determined by means of tests that are the products of extensive research. So, through the grades, the influence of educational research is evident in the techniques that are used. However, research still provides only meager advice concerning the way in which the teacher should manage the classroom situation in order to maximize learning or to produce specific results. Our study of the methodology of educational research begins with a brief overview of the kinds of problems that are dealt with by those engaged in this field.

Educational Research Related to Development

At the very core of a science related to educational phenomena is research related to the development of the pupil. Here lie the problems of central importance to education and, in contrast, all other problems are peripheral. The emphasis placed on this area of research is seen in the fact that the *Review of Educational Research* devotes an entire issue to the topic once every three years. The 1961 issue covered over 850 references to research on development. In addition, a very large volume edited by Mussen (1960) is devoted to problems of child development. To state the over-all purposes of such research is not easy because they are so varied. The best one can do is to make a broad statement to the effect that such research attempts to identify all the factors that influence human development and to describe the course of development under different conditions.

Early studies of development, undertaken in the first third of this century, emphasized the internal factors which controlled development. Such studies were particularly concerned with the description of the pattern of development and in identifying the sequence with which particular behaviors emerged. Such studies had only limited implications for educational planning, for they had little to do with the environmental conditions which influence development. Since education attempts to influence development through control of certain aspects of the environment, knowledge of internal factors which cannot be controlled has only meager value for educational planning. Recently research has moved to the study of external factors which influence development, with results that have greater significance for educational practice.

Studies of external conditions in relation to development may involve the study of changes over a short period of but a few months, or long-term changes over periods which may last many years. Short-term studies are generally concerned with those conditions in the environment which can be expected to exert fairly immediate influences on behavior. The effect of education on child development has been the central theme for such studies. Long-term studies of development over periods of years have more often been concerned with those environmental conditions which may be expected to have a slow but cumulative effect. The various influences which home, neighborhood, peer relationships, and church affiliations may exert fall into this general category.

Interest in the study of development at particular age levels has varied from time to time. During the Thirties, concomitant with the emphasis then found on expanding adult education facilities, many studies were made of development during the years of maturity and the problems which adults encountered in learning new skills. More recently, interest has been shown in the study of development during the preschool years, for evidence has been accumulating that much closer attention must be paid to providing effective learning conditions during these early years.

Explorations of the usefulness of various theories of learning for designing conditions which produce effective learning in schools have also formed the core of many significant researches. While much of learning theory emerges from laboratory research, studies need to be conducted under conditions which are more similar to those existing in classrooms. Such studies need not be undertaken in actual classrooms but may involve groups of children in classroom-like situations.

Curriculum Research

The term *curriculum research* covers a multitude of very diverse activities. This is partly because the concept denoted by the word *curriculum* has had an evolving and expanding meaning and curriculum research has shown a corresponding evolution and expansion. A century ago, the concept of a curriculum was that of a body of subject matter to which the pupil was exposed. Today the concept is different, although the old-time meaning has not entirely vanished.

In Carter V. Good's *Dictionary of Education,* second edition, published in 1959, the following three distinct meanings of the word *curriculum* are noted:

1. A systematic group of courses or sequence of subjects required for graduation or certification in a major field of study, for example, social studies, physical education curriculum.

2. A general over-all plan of the content or specific materials of instruction that the school should offer the student by way of qualifying him for graduation or certification or for entrance into a professional or a vocational field.

3. A body of prescribed educative experiences under school supervision, designed to provide an individual with the best possible training and experience to fit him for the society of which he is a part and to qualify him for a trade or profession.

The first and third of these definitions involve the notion of a body of content; the second introduces the idea that an *over-all plan* is also an essential feature of a curriculum.

Further light is thrown on the development of the concept of a curriculum in the *Review of Educational Research,*[1] prepared on the occasion of the twenty-fifth anniversary of the founding of the *Review.* This particular issue traces the development of curriculum research, pointing up some of the changes that have taken place in the educator's concept of a curriculum. It is implied, in this review, that the tendency in the past was to think of the curriculum as consisting of all the *experiences* that a pupil had during schooling. The emphasis, according to this outlook was on the experience aspect, hence the curriculum was considered important insofar as it represented an element in the pupil's conscious experience. This was, in fact, a very narrow conception of the curriculum, for surely there are important factors in the pupil's environment that have powerful influences on his behavior but of which he is never aware. Any useful conception of the environmental influences that play a role in the development of the child must not be limited to those to which he consciously responds. For this reason, the emerging concept of the curriculum held by research workers and others is that it consists of all the

[1] Vol. XXVI, No. 3, 1956.

planned conditions and events to which the pupil is exposed for the purpose of promoting learning, plus the framework of theory that gives these conditions and events a certain coherence. Recognition that a framework of theory is needed to give meaning to the happenings in the school is an important step forward. Virgil Herrick and other modern writers on this subject stress that a curriculum can have no real meaning unless it is part of a theory of education.

The introduction of the idea that a theory is a central and essential aspect of a curriculum has been an important step in the development of curriculum research. If one looks back over the research accomplished in the area, he will be impressed with the fact that the chief weakness is a lack of theoretical foundation. There was a tendency to study the effect of one set of materials in comparison with the effect of another set of materials. Analyses were made of the contents of textbooks. One procedure was compared with another. Sometimes a clearly stated curriculum theory was presented, but most often it was absent. The current emphasis on the need for stating clearly curriculum theory should do much to remedy this defect in curriculum research. Indeed, the effect of this trend in thinking is already noticeable.

Techniques for the study of curriculum problems exist to some extent; these must be wedded to a body of theory. For example, there are already many methods for measuring many important characteristics of textbooks. Readability is one of the best explored of these characteristics. Much needs to be done to improve readability formulae, but those at present available are valuable research tools. There is a need for techniques that will measure the complexity of written materials. An excellent beginning has been made in the development of techniques of content analysis, and enough has been accomplished to inspire research workers to apply these techniques to the study of curriculum problems. Much less well developed are techniques for measuring the important characteristics of the other curricular materials to which the pupil is exposed, such as excursions, visual aids, and workbooks. In recent years considerable interest has been shown in studying the value of radio and TV for educational purposes.

Extensive research in this area has resulted in the development of many techniques that can be used as the tools for further studies.

A particularly difficult area of curriculum research is that involving the actions of the teacher and the relationship of his personality traits to his classroom behavior. This is an area largely lacking in theoretical constructs, although considerable work, designed more to explore than to test hypotheses, has been initiated on an empirical basis. In the older studies attempts were made to determine the relationship between the measured or rated personality traits of the teacher and "teaching effectiveness" as measured by ratings. Since it is becoming more and more apparent that there are difficulties in measuring teacher effectiveness, recent efforts have been devoted to discovering relationships between the personality of teachers as measured in various ways and characteristics of teacher behavior as they appear in the classroom.

Numerous other curriculum problems have formed the basis of various inquiries. Studies of pupil needs in relation to curriculum design are legion, and so, too, are studies designed to discover the extent to which various skills can be learned at particular levels of maturation. Historical and sociological studies also constitute an important part of curriculum research, as do studies of the social and political forces that influence the curriculum.

Research Related to Sociological and Economic Conditions Affecting Education

Many of the conditions external to the classroom that affect education are investigated by educational research workers interested in studying the sociological conditions that ultimately influence the educational process. Political pressures that influence the educational philosophy of a school system in one direction or another, the financial aspects of the system, and the sociological conditions that result in increased or decreased support for education may be studied. But answers to the questions, "What philosophy of education is implied in the curriculum of the school?" "What kinds of individuals constitute school boards?" "What barriers exist to the raising of funds in communities of certain specified types?" supply information that can be applied only indirectly to improvement in the effectiveness of learning in schools. Many such studies attempt to answer questions of local significance only, and the results cannot be applied to other communities. Such studies result in the production of what may be termed low-level laws.

Although the central topic of educational research is the development of a science of behavior in educational situations, peripheral studies pertaining to sociological and anthropological problems also are of considerable importance. Studies of the latter type and those pertaining to behavior in the classroom can be considered to be on different levels of description. Just as classroom behavior may be described at various levels, from those that involve the movement of the constituent elements or muscle twitches of the body to descriptions of the over-all behavior of the individual, so, too, can one conduct studies either at the level of individual behavior or at a level where the unit studied is a group. Sociological and economic studies of educational problems are concerned more with group than individual phenomena. To some extent, historical studies are of this type. Studies of school finance are of this character, and at the same time they present many of the difficulties inherent in sociological approaches to educational problems.

Sociologists, economists, and anthropologists use quantitative methods in their respective areas in a way rather different from that of the psychologist. Only rarely can the former group of scientists set up experiments that provide simplifications of the conditions that actually exist. Without experimentation, the scientist is faced with a vast multiplicity of phenomena, which do not always lend themselves to arrangement in a metric scale. Nevertheless, present-day sociologists and economists, and to a lesser degree anthropologists, are developing quantitative approaches to the study of human behavior that could be adapted to the ends of educational research.

Even if one turns to such a relatively well-structured field as school finance, where one would expect to find that phenomena were well quantified since much of it appears to deal with quantities, it is quite clear that researchers have struggled long to develop useful variables. The reader may well be referred, at this point, to a work by Mort and others (1961) which illustrates the problems of obtaining useful measures that can be used by research workers. A particularly informative example is presented by their chapter on educational need, which discusses attempts to develop measures of the educational requirements of communities. These measures must be such that they are comparable in some way from community to community. At first sight one might be tempted to take the pupil as the unit of need, but it soon becomes evident that this is not a satisfactory procedure. If the pupils are widely scattered, schools tend to be small and the unit cost greater than when schools are large. Scattered pupils also increase the cost of transportation to the school, and then the pupil unit has to be adjusted for such factors if it is to represent a unit of educational service to be provided. These complexities have resulted in the development of an extensive technical literature, which has attempted to derive a useful measure of educational need that could be used in subsequent research. Studies of the economics of education often provide useful data for the solution of immediate problems, but rarely do they provide generalizations useful for the solution of a great range of problems. The generalizations that can be derived are qualitative and usually lack any property that might be described as precision. The late Paul Mort, who thought through this matter at great length, pointed out that these generalizations are not scientific laws but categories under which may be classified a "multitude of rule-of-thumb canons" widely accepted as the major lessons that have been learned through studies in this area. One of these is the equalization principle, which states that financial disbursements are such that poorer districts are helped more than wealthy districts. Another is the reward-for-effort principle, which posits that funds are disbursed in ways that encourage other bodies also to release funds for education. An example of the operation of the latter principle is the case in which states provide educational funds for local communities on condition that the local communities expand their educational expenditures by a certain amount.

Professor Mort was perhaps too modest in the description of these and other principles. They represent low-order generalizations that are essentially scientific in nature. When one considers the limited degree to which this area of educational research has developed quantitative methods, it is gratifying to note the order that such principles have apparently introduced.

An area of educational research dependent upon sociology is demography, the study of population changes. Its importance to education is substantial from many points of view. First, if the supply of teachers is to be related to need, then it is necessary to predict several years in advance the number of classes of a given size that will have to be staffed. These long-term predictions are required for adequate educational planning because it may take four or five years to train a teacher, and perhaps another two years to recruit him. In addition, some experience on the job under qualified supervisors also seems to be most desirable. Thus, if there is to be an increased number of teachers available in 1980, it will be necessary to start an active recruiting campaign possibly as early as 1970.

In demographic studies, there are no great difficulties in estimating pupil enrollment five or six years ahead since the future pupils already have been born by the time the estimate is made. Death rates and immigration and emigration rates can be estimated with considerable accuracy. On the other hand, real difficulties are encountered when estimates are to be made ten or more years in advance, for the birth rate may show sudden changes in response to a great complexity of causes. Hardly more than a beginning has been made in establishing scientific laws of population change. Just as the prediction of pupil enrollment is an area fraught with difficulties, so, too, does the problem of estimating future teacher supply present numerous unsolved problems that may challenge the student of education.

Demographic studies have only the most limited value, largely because school authorities cannot recruit enough teachers at the present time and little control can be exercised over the flow into and out of the profession. The latter movements are controlled far more by prevailing economic conditions than by any action that those in charge of teacher education take. There is, perhaps, only one aspect of this branch of the sociology of teaching that has any practical consequences. Through the information derived, it may be possible to persuade students in training to enter those phases of teaching in which there is the greatest need for new teachers and to avoid the few areas where there may be an oversupply.

Mention must be made of a rapidly developing area of research on educational administration. Social psychology, specifically work in the area known as group dynamics, has provided both the theoretical framework and the techniques needed for a research approach to problems of educational administration. Much of the impetus behind this movement has come from the academic staffs of departments of school administration in colleges of education. Through their efforts was formed the University Council for Educational Administration with headquarters at Ohio State University. The Council is now actively engaged in sponsoring and stimulating research. In addition, research programs of a substantial nature have been developed in a number of universities associated with the Council. The most notable of these centers is the Midwest Center for the Study of Educational Administration at The University of Chicago.

Educational Engineering Research

In industry there has developed a branch of knowledge, referred to as *human engineering*, which serves the purpose of adapting machines to their human operators. This problem has already been touched on in the discussion of developmental studies. If a body of knowledge exists about the requirements, abilities, and physiological properties of the human operator, machines can be designed that are well within his capacity. The design of equipment to conform to anatomical, physiological, and psychological requirements is an important aspect of industrial design, and is now backed by a substantial body of knowledge. In education, there are certain types of related research that must be considered at this point.

First, a type of developmental study that has recently found prominence in the literature attempts to determine the pattern of physical development for the purpose of providing a basis for the design of school equipment such as tables, chairs, and desks. This might be termed the human-engineering approach to educational problems. The application of this approach is difficult in the educational field when it is realized that, despite wide variation in the physical characteristics of any age group, all pupils have to be accommodated in the school. In contrast, the human engineer may often design his equipment so that it can be operated by only 60 per cent of potential users.

Another problem that is raised by studies of growth in relation to equipment design is that there are not only large differences between pupils of the same age, but that these are related to differences in sex, in locality, and in other factors. Equipment therefore must be chosen for particular groups of pupils, not for particular age groups. A study designed to provide a sound basis for the development of such equipment is one by Tuddenham and Snyder (1954). Such studies involve difficulties, which are considered in the section devoted to developmental studies.

Second, there is the problem of the design of educational equipment that is more closely related to the learning process itself. The field of education has been notoriously deficient in the development of mechanical devices—the printing press still represents the chief point of impact of technology and industrial development on the educational process. During the first half of this century, there were few who saw the need for greater mechanization of the classroom. Indeed, during that period the only champion of the cause was Sidney Pressey of Ohio State University. He proclaimed that the industrial revolution must come to education and developed a number of mechanical teaching devices. But the lone voice of Pressey did not arouse public interest; neither did it stimulate professional research.

During the last two decades certain influences have generated an interest in the mechanization of the classroom. Among them is the fact that learning research has come to involve complex instrumentation which has some potential for being applied to the management of classroom learning. Psychologists have come to realize that in the study of learning phenomena with animals the use of proper equipment is an essential condition for effective learning. With the use of such equipment psychologists have been able to produce learning in animals which could not have been produced otherwise. With these advanced techniques for producing learning, one can easily give public demonstrations of animals learning rapidly complex skills before the eyes of large audiences. Such public demonstrations of learning of skills— skills which could not have been taught to animals twenty years ago—have dramatically demonstrated the advantages that can accrue from the proper use of mechanical devices in the learning situation. Inspired by the very evident worth of such equipment for facilitating animal learning, psychologists have sought to develop equipment which could be used for the facilitation of human learning.

Although the pioneer of the development of teaching machines in the pre-World War II era was Sidney Pressey, postwar developments emerged in the laboratory of B.F. Skinner at Harvard. This laboratory, devoted to the study of learning, was probably the best equipped in the world with respect to instruments and mechanical devices. Skinner himself had been impressed by the fact that the training of animals, particularly rats and pigeons, could be enormously facilitated by the use of proper equipment. He argued that similar gains could be made in human learning through the design and installation of suitable devices, and he set himself the task of developing equipment to illustrate his point. He was aware of Sidney Pressey's earlier developments but believed they had been limited by the fact that learning theory in the prewar era had not advanced to the point of providing a sound basis for teaching-machine design. It was Skinner's opinion, during the early Fifties, that the science of learning had at last reached the point where it could provide an adequate basis for the management of classroom learning. Figures II and III show a student using one of Skinner's early teaching machines.

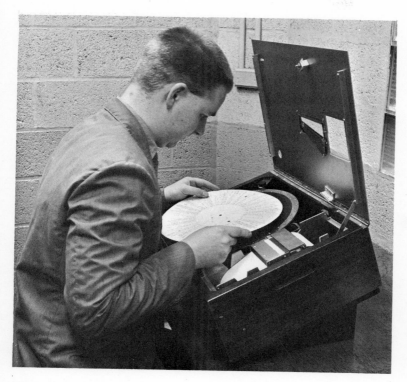

FIGURE II. *Preparing to use a learning machine. A student inserts a disc bearing questions into a teaching machine developed by Professor B.F. Skinner of Harvard University.* (Photo by courtesy of Professor Skinner.)

The development of teaching machines, or auto instructional devices as they have come to be called, presents many theoretical and technical problems. Unfortunately, the tendency has been for commercial manufacturing enterprises to dash ahead with the production of devices of unknown worth and to promote sales on the basis of wild claims. Although research has not so far produced any dramatic evidence to demonstrate that the devices available provide any great superiority over the more traditional

FIGURE III. *Learning by means of a machine. A student uses new teaching machine designed by Professor B.F. Skinner of Harvard University. Student reads question in left window, writes answer in right window.* (Photo by courtesy of Professor Skinner.)

methods of instruction, it is much too early to pronounce any final verdict. In making judgments one is in a position similar to that of a person in the nineteenth century who had just seen his first automobile blow up in a cloud of steam and who concluded that the contraption had no future. The history of technology suggests that a long history of development is needed before a device can be expected to improve upon current practices.

A few currently important research problems related to the development of auto-instructional devices will be mentioned here to indicate to the reader the scope of such research. First, it should be noted that in nearly all such devices the learner is presented with a problem to solve in what is called a "frame." The frame may also supply some information relevant to the solution of the problem. Skinner has generally favored feeding information in small quantities and in taking the learner along the road of knowledge a very small step at a time. When this is done the learner makes few errors in solving the problems provided. Skinner believes this to be a desirable learning condition. On the other hand, there are those who consider that substantial quantities of information should be provided in each frame. When the latter plan is followed, the chances of the learner making errors in the solving of problems is greater because he has more new material to draw upon and the step from the last problem is relatively large. Thus the design of such machines raises problems: How much information should be provided per frame? To what extent should the learner make errors, perhaps to profit from them? How much redundancy is necessary for the efficient presentation of information? There are also problems to be explored concerning the merits of mechanical devices for auto-instruction versus the merits of other techniques. The programmed textbook is an attempt to incorporate in book form the desirable features of the mechanical teaching machine. Whether the programmed textbook accomplishes this end remains to be demonstrated. There are still many issues to be investigated concerning the best plan for designing a programmed textbook. Little knowledge is available concerning the relative merits of these new types of books in contrast with the textbook-workbook combination much used in classorooms. In terms of the meager knowledge available at this time, the problem of how to program learning seems to be a much more significant one than that of how to mechanize it.

An Overview of the Content of Educational Research

When the range of phenomena that the educational researcher may study is contemplated, it is realized that he should approach his task with considerable humility, recognizing that only a few of the foundation stones of an organized science can be laid within his lifetime. The hopes of those who first started research work in this field some fifty years ago have not yet been realized, and will not be realized for a long time to come. Research did not provide a rapid revolution in which knowledge of the soundness of educational procedures was to replace prejudice and tradition, for only after research workers began their inquiries did they realize the immensity of the task before them. The areas of educational research may be likened to areas on a map that have been roughly circumscribed to indicate gross differences in terrain. Some penetration has perhaps been made within the borders of these areas, but most of them remain unexplored. Explorers of the future will provide broad knowledge of these general areas, and then must come the developers who will exploit the resources that each domain has to offer. The boundaries that have been set up are artificial, for each one of the areas of educational research fuses into the others. The criterion of relevance for study is purely a matter of whether an area has impact, direct or indirect, on the development of the child.

THE SELECTION OF THE PROBLEM AND THE PLANNING OF THE RESEARCH

The foregoing broad overview of the content of educational research has been given as an introduction to the matter of selecting a problem. The student is likely by this time to be overwhelmed by the vastness of the unexplored territory which the educational research worker may begin to study. Our next step must be to narrow down the problem and to consider how a research problem is evaluated.

Allowing Time for Planning

The planning of research is commonly thought of by the novice as an initial stage that is quickly passed, to be followed by the more elaborate and prolonged stage of collecting data. Many of the weaknesses in current educational research are attributable to this fundamentally unsound viewpoint. The fact is that the major effort in the undertaking of research should be devoted to the planning stage, which may include not only a careful formulation of the problem, as outlined in the second chapter, but also some preliminary data-collecting activities. Once a research has been well planned and the techniques have been given a preliminary trial to make sure that they are feasible methods of attacking the problem at hand, the actual execution of the research is a simple and mechanical matter, which requires more patience than brilliance. Weeks may go into planning an experiment that may be completed in a single day. The hard part of all research is the planning stage, which is the thinking stage.

Conant (1946) has pointed out that there is no simple formula to help the researcher in the most crucial stage of the development of research, which is the stage of developing hypotheses. The would-be researcher must recognize that much brilliant work owes its brilliance to the significance of the hypothesis that is tested. Some researches, of course, are brilliant because of the unusual and ingenious way in which the hypothesis was tested. The unfortunate fact is that most research conducted in education is nothing short of drab in both conception and development. If this chapter can do anything to reduce even a little the drabness in research in education, it will have done much.

There can be no doubt that individual researchers differ greatly in their sensitivity to problems. Guilford, in his studies of creative talent, has found that such an ability appears to be quite independent of other aspects of talent. This is in keeping with the experience of research administrators, who know that some researchers seem quite unable to locate and identify problems even though they may do a workmanlike job in solving problems assigned to them. Experience is an important factor. Intensive reading is essential for identifying important problems in an area. The student thoroughly familiar with the technical literature of his field of interest cannot fail to become conscious of the problems which other research workers consider to be important. Attendance at and participation in research seminars may help to sharpen the student's ability to discriminate between researchable and nonresearchable problems. Seminars may also bring the student into contact with researchers who are highly sensitive to the existence of researchable problems, and this experience may help him in developing his ability. While it is possible in this chapter to offer the student some help in identifying problems, little is likely to be achieved in the direction of making the student more sensitive to those that are researchable.

The student of educational phenomena should embark on research with full respect for the complexity of the phenomena with which he is faced. In this regard, much educational research lacks the humility that is essential if matters of importance are to be discovered. The author can recall instances where persons who should have known better have approached educational problems as if they were of the complexity of a party game. On one occasion, a professor in charge of an educational research project remarked to him, "This year we are going to settle the problem of measuring teacher personality so that next year we can move on to other matters." From our present perspective, it is quite clear that a hundred years from now scientists will still be attempting to measure some aspects of teacher personality. The student may reflect that even in an area where problems seem so simple, relatively speaking, as in rote learning, investigation soon reveals that the phenomena studied are of enormous complexity. How much more complex must be the phenomena that take place in the classroom, or even those occurring in miniature educational situations set up for research purposes. Herein lies the central difficulty in identifying researchable problems.

Much of the deceptive simplicity of educational phenomena stems from the fact that considerable progress has been made in predicting success and failure in different types of curricula. The fact that persons with little research experience have been able to develop tests for accomplishing just this adds to the deception. Such straightforward relationships are fortuitous, not typical, circumstances. The discovery of clear relationships beyond this point is a much more difficult matter. Sometimes even years of research on a single problem may yield but small returns.

The Acceptability of a Research Project in Relation to the Social Milieu in Which It Is Undertaken

When he embarks on any research, the student of education should recognize that, while he may wish to pursue his own whims and fancies, he is not entirely free to do so, for the acceptability of his product to others may determine whether he does or does not obtain a degree. Most scientists work under a similar restriction. The industrial scientist needs to recognize the goals of the concern for which he works, and at least to some small extent he must modify his own goals to make them compatible. In government service, it is necessary to realize that only certain types of research projects can survive over the years, and if a scientist embarks on a long-range program he should also have other short-term programs that will yield more immediate results of practical value.

This problem is an old one. Leonardo da Vinci found it necessary to spend much of his time devising instruments of war so that his patron would permit him to engage in scientific research. The system of patronage of the last century always required the scientist to modify at least a part of his pursuits to conform to the desires of his sponsors.

There is, of course, much evil in the fact that in most situations the scientist must take cognizance of outside forces that can influence the acceptance or rejection of his work. It might even be argued that many notable discoveries have been made in flagrant opposition to current ideas. The work Galileo pursued in the face of social opposition is familiar to every reader. While the older scientist who is well established can perhaps afford to be insensitive to the social milieu within which his work takes place, the younger scientist finds need of this sensitivity, if only to reach the point where he can afford to present highly novel ideas that oppose current concepts. Here the author is not endorsing the idea that the graduate student should pursue a line of thought thoroughly acceptable to his elders. He is only pointing out that the faculty of a school of education represents what might be called a subculture, and that, like other subcultures, it will accept some ideas much more easily than others. A graduate student would do well to select a school where his ideas and those of the faculty display some degree of harmony. Related to this is a matter that must be considered now.

It is a mistake for the researcher to orient his work in relation to some social issue about which he has deep personal convictions. While such convictions may stem from the most desirable and highly esteemed values, there are reasons why they form an unsound basis for research. In the first place, they usually lead the graduate student to attempt a problem that is way beyond his capabilities, and often beyond the scope of available techniques to solve. The common trait of overambitiousness seen in so many doctoral studies is most often an outgrowth of the individual's own personal values, and that he seeks evidence that will support some private belief. Much wiser would such an individual be if he developed a research project as an outgrowth of another's systematically developed program.

A further difficulty also stems from the researcher's personal involvement in issues that pertain to his research. This is the difficulty of maintaining an objective attitude in the analysis and interpretation of data. Darwin noted that he found a tendency in himself to forget those facts that were not in accord with his theory. Even more prone to forget such disagreeable facts is the person who has the deepest beliefs about the value to be attached to a particular viewpoint.

Finding Problems

It is difficult to supply definitive ideas concerning how the student should obtain ideas for his research. Part of the trouble arises from the fact that we know little, as yet, about the usefulness of various techniques for this purpose, and the scientist who is asked to say how he finds his ideas is usually quite unable to give a definitive answer. Certain procedures that the student may possibly find useful can be suggested, but these have not been validated.

One method of deriving research ideas is to read articles published in the current literature and to consider how the techniques and ideas discussed therein might be applied to the solution of other problems. The adaptation of techniques to the solution of new problems is a profitable and worthwhile enterprise in which many scientists engage. Indeed, many such enterprises may be judged to have high originality.

A second approach is to identify in the literature studies that would have had merit except for some central defect that makes it impossible to draw conclusions from the findings. This is not to be looked down upon as an activity, for it often yields results of great importance.

A third procedure is to refer to the discussion section of technical papers (usually it is the final paragraph), wherein the author presents reflections concerning the significance of the results and what type of investigation should be undertaken as a follow-up. Such suggestions appear in considerable numbers in the concluding sections of technical reports. Many, of course, present only ideas rather than practical suggestions, and many are beyond the realms of usability at the present. Nevertheless, fruitful ideas may still be found in quantity.

All of these procedures involve a review of the literature. Since the latter is not the simple matter that it may seem to be, some comment on this activity must now be made. Locating published material requires well-developed techniques for using a library, and this book assumes that the student has those skills. If he does not, he is referred to an excellent book by Alexander and Burke (1958) designed specifically to provide that type of training. It is limited to the mechanical aspects of using a library; it does not concern itself with the more subtle subject of how information derived from a library should be used. A person may locate all relevant references but fail to derive from them relevant information.

The identification of the research literature pertaining to a field may begin in any of several different places. The *Education Index* is one good place to start, but the student should avoid accumulating a massive bibliography before reading a few important articles of recent vintage. The *Encyclopedia of Educational Research* should be consulted for major references. Some of the articles in it provide outstanding overviews of particular areas of inquiry.

Unfortunately, a tradition has grown up that a "review of the literature" is a low-level task, which can be undertaken by the student who is not very advanced. Many, of course, would disagree with this view, as is evident in the fact that the chapters in each *Review of Educational Research* are usually written by the senior members of the profession. In a similar spirit, the *Annual Review of Psychology* is, for the most part, written by persons who have had considerable experience in the fields they cover. A first-class review of the literature requires the maturity of viewpoint that comes from years of study and research. The student of education who has had a brief experience in graduate school cannot be expected to have the intellectual maturity to prepare a thoroughgoing review of research in an area of education in which he is interested, but the experience of making the review can be a worthwhile one, and with a few precautions much can be done to give it a professional and polished appearance.

Advice commonly given in making a review is to start by preparing a fairly complete list of references, but this is poor counsel, and any person who has engaged extensively in such work will know it. The first thing that a would-be reviewer must do is familiarize himself with the issues and problems of the field. Until he has done this, he cannot possibly know what are and what are not relevant contributions.

Familiarization with the issues and problems of a field can be accomplished by reading articles that treat of this matter. In most areas, such articles exist, but these should not be confused with the type of article that is noninterpretative. For example, most chapters in the *Review of Educational Research* are noninterpretative, mere listings of studies that have been made in the previous three-year period.

Critical review-type articles serve the purpose of indicating to the student what are the central issues to be taken into account in his own reading and review of the literature. He would also do well to discuss his early impressions of the literature with some professional person thoroughly familiar with the area. He will then be ready to begin work on his own review.

Through his preliminary reading, the student will have located some of the major references. These should be consulted next. At this stage a good plan is to enter the title of each reference at the top of a five-by-eight-inch card and to use the remainder of the card for summarizing the article with particular reference to the light it throws on major issues. A small section at the bottom of the card may be reserved for critical comments and further hypotheses suggested by the author of the study.

Additional references will be found in each article reviewed, and thus most of the significant sources will be obtained. At this point, the reader may ask why it has not been suggested that he prepare a comprehensive list of references from a source such as the *Education Index*, which lists every article and publication that has any relevance at all to educational problems. The answer is that in such a source the classification of references is necessarily very crude and often depends more on the title of the article than on its content. Such comprehensive lists of publications may supply a rough check on what is available, but they cannot provide a basis for a critical review. However, such lists do permit a superficial independent check of the completeness of the references obtained from published articles.

In the development of his review of the chosen field, the student will have opportunity to discover a problem that he can use as a basis for his research. Once such a problem has been found, the review can be written in terms of the relevance of the various studies to it. Until such a problem is found, it may be well to postpone the final integration of the material into a single review, which will usually constitute the first chapter of the thesis or dissertation.

The reader should pause at this point and link the considerations of this chapter with the earlier discussion of the need for conducting research within a framework of theory. *The review of the literature, if it is conducted in the way described here, should provide an overview of the current framework of theory in the area in which it is proposed to undertake an investigation. The student may be expected to abstract from his review of the literature a theory in terms of which he plans to work. A minimum requirement should be that he draw up a statement covering the essential features of the theory, but preferably he should be more ambitious and draft the theory as a set of postulates. He should then show how his hypotheses represent a series of deductions from these postulates. This he will find to be a worthwhile exercise in clear thinking.*

SOME POINTS ON THE EVALUATION OF RESEARCH STUDIES

In previous sections it has been emphasized that the person who embarks on a research should be thoroughly familiar with previous work in the area and should attempt to organize this knowledge into a theory that can form the basis for future work. It is perfectly obvious that all that has been written and published in an area cannot be given equal weight in such a review. Indeed, much of the available material may be disregarded when the final summary is made. Up to this point no advice has been given

concerning the evaluation of published studies as a basis for retaining or discarding material.

In a sense, this entire book is concerned with the evaluation of
research, for any attempt to teach the student something about
methodologies, if it is successful, must help him to judge between
adequate and inadequate research. A summary of much of this
book would be a list of procedures that some scientists have found
useful for advancing knowledge, plus a list of common errors
that are likely to render studies useless or to reduce their value
greatly. The chapter summaries collectively do this in a fairly
concentrated form. However, the author feels that there is merit
in presenting at this stage a brief section on the topic of evaluating research studies. If the student is developing a research project at the same time he is taking a course on research methodology, he will need to perform these evaluative functions long
before he has studied problems of research development and
design. Nevertheless, a mature ability to evaluate research will
require much more extended study than has been undertaken up
to this point.

Evaluating the Problem

There are several ways in which it is possible to evaluate the
problem that forms the focus of a research, and most of these
have already been stated in one way or another. First, in reviewing a research study and evaluating its worth, the reader may
well ask, "Is the problem clearly stated?" If the problem is not
clearly stated, it is quite evident that the research cannot make
any significant contribution to knowledge. The statement of the
problem should be found in the early paragraphs of the research
report and should be preceded by only those materials that are
necessary for a full understanding of the problem.

Second, it may be asked, "Is the relation of the problem to previous work in the area clearly stated?" This is a point on which
it is a little more difficult to evaluate a study than is at first evi-

dent. Sometimes an expert reading an article may see very clearly the relationship between the problem and previous work, while a novice in the field may not. This is in part due to the fact that many technical journals frown on long introductions to articles, although such introductions are really necessary for the novice to see clearly how the research is related to previous work. Such journals cut down on introductory materials merely as a space-saving device. It is unfortunate that this is necessary, since as a result such articles can be fully understood only by those who have already read extensively in the field.

Third, the reader must ask himself, "Is the problem broad enough to provide a study of real significance?" Many researches that are conducted in the educational field pertain to local problems, and their results have no significance whatsoever for other areas. The narrowness of a problem is a particular problem in experimental studies where the results apply only under conditions of a highly specific type.

Perhaps one further question may be asked in the process of evaluating the problem—"Does the solution to this problem pave the way for the development of further knowledge?" A problem should not lead up a deadend street; rather it should be an avenue that opens up new territory. A research designed to solve some local problem within a school system is unlikely to meet this criterion. Such a study will probably, although not necessarily, be given little weight in a review of the literature, and much less weight than one that attempts to solve a problem of rather broad significance.

Evaluating the Procedure

The first point to note in evaluating the procedure adopted in a study being appraised is that the description of it should be sufficiently precise to enable another person to reproduce the study. If essential aspects of the procedure are not described, it is not possible to verify the results by undertaking a similar study. If the procedure is not adequately described, it is also not possible to evaluate its merits, since the aspects omitted from the description may have been quite inadequate even though the remainder may have been adequate. Of course complete description is rarely if ever possible, as will be pointed out later in this volume.

While the procedure is often well described, it is common to find that the nature of the population to whom the procedure was applied is not even mentioned. This is an important omission, for if a study were undertaken using as subjects state patrolmen, it would hardly be reasonable to apply the results to, say, elderly spinster teachers.

Then the reader must ask himself, "Are the procedures adopted in the study clearly related to the solution of the problem?" Much more is to be said about this point in later chapters. For the present, we wish only to warn the student that many published researches never amount to anything simply because the procedures adopted could not accomplish what they were supposed to accomplish. A common error in research is to use a psychological test without being sure that the test is valid for the purpose for which it is being used. If the procedures and techniques are not suitable for solving the problem at hand, it is evident that the study can be of little value. Sometimes a research worker recognizes the fact that the use of certain procedures involves certain assumptions, and if he is wise he states those assumptions. He may make the assumption, for example, that a measure of spelling skill derived from a published objective test of the skill provides a true indication of the pupil's habitual skill in spelling as it is manifested in his schoolwork. The research worker, or the reader of the account of the research, may be able to point to other studies that supply evidence in support of or contrary to this assumption. This evidence may, in turn, be used as an aid in the full evaluation of the study.

The Design of the Study and the Adequacy of the Analysis

Any research that is reviewed must be appraised partly in terms of the extent to which it was adequately designed. Problems of design are considered at some length in later chapters, but a brief discussion of them is in order here. Design has two aspects. First, there is the matter of whether it permits the collection of the evidence necessary to solve the problem. Second, there is the matter of whether it is efficient—that is to say, whether it permits the collection of the maximum amount of information with the least amount of effort. The evaluation of designs is quite a technical matter, and there are no simple and straightforward methods for it that can be given in a few paragraphs. At this stage the student should look only for gross flaws. It is surprising how many such flaws occur in published studies.

The Evaluation of the Results and Conclusions

No study is of any real value unless the results are clearly stated in a form that permits one to know precisely what was found. If one cannot determine just what was found, or if there is ambiguity concerning it, the worth of the study must be questioned. Sometimes one does not know just what was found because some of the data appear to have been omitted. The author recalls a study in which a series of tests was administered to five hundred subjects, but the results were reported for only about four hundred. What happened to the other one hundred subjects? Were the data for them lost? Were they cases that provided data inconsistent with what the researcher was trying to demonstrate? One can only hope that was not the case; for all the information given, it might have been. Many ambiguities in the presentation of results are due to the fact that the research worker does not indicate exactly what happened to the data that he collected.

If the results are clearly presented, the reviewer should proceed to examine the conclusions to determine whether they follow from the results. Then he should determine whether the conclusions are consistent with those of other studies in the same general area. If they are inconsistent, he should see whether the researcher has a reasonable explanation for the inconsistency.

Some Additional Criteria for Evaluating
Published Research

There are certain other criteria that the student may wish to use in evaluating research. Place of publication is certainly an important cue. If a research study has been published in a well-established technical journal with a high reputation for the quality of its contributions, it is probable that it has been reviewed by competent experts in the area and has been found to be a study of quality. Of course, the experts are sometimes wrong. Articles published in obscure sources and in journals that require the author to pay all publication costs are often poorly selected. It is hardly surprising that the sources of free publication are able to select the best contributions.

Authorship is a somewhat controversial basis for evaluating research publications. Books and articles in technical fields are usually evaluated for possible publication without the name of the author being indicated on the manuscript. The novice in research, and perhaps the mature research worker too, may well feel that the work of the renowned expert can be expected to be outstanding. This is not always so.

The Effect of Selective Publication on
Reported Results

In reviewing the literature, the reviewer should be aware of the factor of selective publication. The writer believes that this phenomenon is well illustrated by the studies on the merits of progressive education that appeared during the years 1920–40. Those that appeared in the literature during this period were designed mainly for the purpose of comparing the relative merits of what was termed *progressive education* and what was termed *traditional education*. The general procedure was to measure the achievement of two matched groups that had been exposed to one or the other of these two types of curricula. Some years ago the author reviewed this literature and noted that the small studies almost always favored the progressive curriculum while the larger studies were much less favorable. The best explanation for this seems to be that strong feelings are involved in this area, and most of those who undertake studies in it are motivated by the desire to demonstrate that progressive education is superior to the traditional approach. On this account, one suspects that, when a small study is undertaken and produces results that are unfavorable to the cause of progressive education, the tendency is simply not to publish the study. In contrast, when a small study produces favorable results that confirm the research worker's opinion, considerable effort may be made to find a publisher. However, when a large and extensive study is involved, the research worker is likely to have invested so much time and effort that he cannot afford not to publish, even when the results run counter to his previous opinions.

The reader can see that selective publication is likely to result in the data providing a biased idea of the extent to which a particular point of view can be supported by evidence. A reviewer of technical literature should keep this possibility in mind.

DESIRABLE CHARACTERISTICS OF THE PROBLEM

The problem that is eventually isolated may be stated in terms of a question for which the proposed research is designed to obtain an answer. Sometimes the question to be answered is referred to as a hypothesis. Sometimes in this book it has been called a deduction from a postulate. Certain criteria may be suggested for judging the merits of hypotheses, and these need to be discussed further at this point. It will be assumed in this discussion that the hypothesis is firmly rooted in a framework of theory, hence this particular criterion will not be discussed here at further length.

Hypotheses selected for research should be testable. One of the commonest sources of difficulty for the graduate student who embarks on a dissertation is the selection of a hypothesis that is not really testable. The same difficulty is also apparent in the researches of some of the more mature members of the educational profession. For example, one educator selected for his research the hypothesis that secondary schoolteachers did not know enough algebra to teach their pupils competently. This is not really a scientific problem; nonetheless it was one of some interest. He proceeded to test this untestable hypothesis by administering an algebra examination he had devised to a group of secondary-schoolteachers. Since the questions in his test gave the appearance of having been devised to confuse, it is hardly surprising that most of the teachers achieved a very low score. His conclusion was that the teachers did not know enough algebra to teach with competency, which was just a reiteration of the opinion he had held in the first place. The data really provided no genuine information to endorse or reject the conclusion. He wanted to prove a point, and he had done so by devising a test that measured the essential knowledge of the teacher, according to his own judgment (and few might agree with him). What was needed in order to make his hypothesis a testable one was a prior study establishing what mathematical knowledge was, and what was not, essential or desirable in an algebra teacher.

This point should be emphasized because some of the most interesting and important hypotheses are quite untestable at this time. It is important to learn this lesson, because a common way of attempting to select problems for a program of educational research is to start by listing the problems that are in most urgent need of attack from the practical standpoint. The author has been associated with several projects set up in this way and has invariably protested the use of this procedure, but the result has always been the same. The research program has bogged down in a swamp of untestable hypotheses. While the researcher may begin his thinking with some focal point in education where answers are urgently needed to important questions, he should start by struggling to find a contact point between available organized knowledge and the problem with which he is confronted. If such a contact point does not exist, the researcher must assume that he is attempting to operate in an area that, because of its isolation from organized knowledge, is likely to yield untestable hypotheses.

Hypotheses should state relationships between variables. A well-developed hypothesis that meets satisfactory standards should state an expected relationship between variables. Unless hypotheses can be stated in this form, they have not reached the point where they are appropriate as a basis for research. A hypothesis such as "Children who attend Sunday school show greater moral growth than children who do not" is not testable, because the term *greater moral growth* does not refer to a variable that is measurable at the present time, or likely to be measured in the near future. On the other hand, a hypothesis such as "Teachers who manifest aggression in the classroom have pupils who also manifest aggression" refers to a variable, aggression, that can be measured through such procedures as counting the number of specific types of aggressive incidents that occur. However, the reader should recognize the fact that it is often necessary to use quite indirect means of measurement. This is true of all sciences. The physicist measures the amount of various elements in the sun by studying the spectrum of its light. The psychologist may attempt to measure emotional disturbance through the response of the individual to an ink blot. Although hypotheses should state relationships between variables, it does not mean that these variables have to be measured by any direct method, although any indirect measurement should be based on a clearcut rationale.

Hypotheses should be limited in scope. A common error of the graduate student of education in planning research is to develop hypotheses of global significance. It is perhaps natural for the beginning research worker to be overambitious in his initial efforts, partly because of his earnestness and partly because it takes maturity of viewpoint to realize how little can be accomplished in a lifetime. The more mature research worker is likely to choose hypotheses narrower in scope and therefore more testable. The student should seek hypotheses that are relatively simple to test yet highly significant. He should try to bring order into a very limited corner of the universe—but it should be an important corner.

Hypotheses should be consistent with most known facts. Any hypothesis formulated as a basis for research must be consistent with a substantial body of established fact. It is too much to expect that it be consistent with *all* established facts because in so many areas the facts themselves appear to be inconsistent with one another. For example, in the area of vision, it is known that single nerve fibers cannot carry more than one type of impulse; yet there do not seem to be a sufficient number of nerve cells in the retina to make up three distinct mechanisms for the three primary colors. No theory of vision has been able to resolve all of the apparently inconsistent facts, and almost any hypothesis formulated is likely to be consistent with some of the facts and inconsistent with others.

Hypotheses should be stated as far as possible in simple terms. This is desirable in part to permit the meaning to become clear to others, but it is also desirable since, in order for a hypothesis to be testable, it must be stated in relatively simple terms. The simplicity of the statement has nothing to do with its significance. Some of the most important hypotheses ever tested have been such as could be explained to an average child in junior high school. It is the simple truths tentatively formulated as hypotheses that form the fundamental cornerstones of science. For example, Pasteur's hypothesis that life would not be spontaneously generated from organic matter if all living matter were first destroyed is an easily understood concept, yet it is one that deals with an idea of fundamental importance. Newton's hypothesis that a body continues in uniform motion until acted upon by a force is a simple one, yet it became a cornerstone of physics.

Hypotheses should be simple from another point of view. They should avoid the use of vague constructs, however popular these may happen to be in current educational thought. It is quite useless to formulate a hypothesis such as, "The adjustment of the

pupil to the classroom situation will depend upon the total classroom situation." Such a hypothesis includes several vague concepts, one of which is *the total classroom situation*. To say that
an event depends upon everything else that is happening fails to
do what the scientist has to do, namely isolate a few aspects of his
environment that have special relevance as factors in the production of the phenomenon in which he is interested. The specifica-
tion of these characteristics must be undertaken in the formulation of a clear and simple and important hypothesis.

*The hypothesis selected should be amenable to testing within
a reasonable time.* The student of education is too often exces-
sively ambitious when he first seeks to undertake research. This
is usually a result of the fact that he is in close contact with the
pressing problems of education. He is frustrated by being per-
petually confronted with problems that must be solved before
major advances can be made, and to overcome his feeling of personal frustration he sets himself the goal of solving one of the
major problems. Yet the fact is that nearly all such problems cannot be solved for a long time to come. They are mainly problems
of immense difficulty, which cannot be profitably studied because
the essential techniques for attacking them are not available.
This is well illustrated by the numerous graduate students of
education who suggest each year that they develop a doctoral
dissertation in the field of teacher effectiveness. The common
proposal is that a study be made of personality traits as related
to teacher effectiveness. Such studies assume that measures of
relevant teacher traits are available—and of course they are not.
These studies also assume that the effectiveness of the teacher in
achieving various kinds of significant objectives is known, and
that the growth of the pupils with respect to these objectives can
be measured. It is almost certainly true that most of such achievements cannot be measured at the present time and that no means
will be found to measure them for a long time to come. Most
studies of teacher effectiveness that the graduate student is likely
to consider are impractical because the techniques for carrying
them out simply are not available and cannot be developed
rapidly.

The student should be warned against doing what is commonly done when the would-be researcher finds that techniques are not available for the study of a particular problem—that is, using what are often hopelessly inadequate techniques. For example, many who have wished to study personality characteristics of teachers related to their effectiveness have ultimately settled for studies involving the correlation of ratings of teacher effectiveness with ratings of personality characteristics. Such activity can be described only as pseudo research. It bears a relation to well-conducted research in that it involves the statement of a hypothesis and the collection of data, but the data have only a superficial relationship to the testing of the hypothesis. The serious research worker would find it hard to accept the belief that actual teacher effectiveness in achieving a particular objective is related, except to a slight extent, to ratings of effectiveness produced by an observer, for the judgments of an observer are likely to be very erroneous. Similar doubts may be expressed about the validity of ratings of the teacher's personality characteristics. What such research produces is correlations between one obscure variable and another, and in this obscurity little light can be discerned. If, on the other hand, it were possible to measure the true amount of learning produced by each of several teachers working with comparable classes, it would be of the greatest interest to determine the relationship between the personality characteristics of the teachers and the amount of learning produced. In this case the data would be meaningful and would not represent the type of worthless substitute for meaningful data so commonly introduced into educational research. Educational literature is full of examples of studies in which a student's enthusiasm for a problem has blinded him to the weaknesses of the techniques through which he has tried to study it.

Sometimes, in order to test a given hypothesis, it is necessary to test a hypothesis related to it by some rather remote channel of reasoning. An example from the physical sciences illustrates this point more clearly than examples from education. In order to test a hypothesis concerning the nature of the chemical and physical processes that result in the release of the sun's energy, it is necessary to make a spectral analysis of the light coming from the sun. From this analysis, it is possible to make inferences concerning the conditions that resulted in the production of the light.

SOME ADDITIONAL CONSIDERATIONS IN SELECTING A PROBLEM

Some Practical Matters Related to Research

Before the final selection of a problem is undertaken, the student should ask himself a number of quite practical questions which only he can answer. The first of these is whether he is well equipped in terms of his background to carry out the research. A student in school administration may be fascinated with the idea of exploring faculty-principal relationships, or some phase of these phenomena. However, if he has never undertaken work in social psychology he will rapidly find himself out of his depth. The would-be research worker must ask himself whether he has sufficient mastery of the area to undertake an attempt to advance knowledge. The advancement of knowledge can be undertaken only by those who have already covered all of the territory up to the frontier of knowledge.

A second question, somewhat mundane but important nonetheless, is whether the study falls within the budget the student can afford. For this reason, a careful estimate must be made of the cost of apparatus, tests and other printed devices, and other equipment called for by the study. In addition, the cost of computational work must be considered. A later chapter discusses this cost. Sometimes a study cannot be undertaken because adequate space is not available. In recent years the matter of space has become an acute problem, for enlarged enrollments have stretched university facilities to the limit.

A third very practical consideration is whether the necessary cooperation can be obtained from those who must participate in research as subjects. Many studies require the cooperation of schools, and although they will generally cooperate with faculty on major research projects, school districts are becoming increasingly unwilling to work with graduate students on research projects.

Indirect Versus Direct Approaches

A common error in educational research results from the researcher attempting a too direct attack on his problem. For example, generations of educational researchers have attempted to appraise the level of motivation of students and others by asking persons directly to indicate how well motivated they are, or by asking observers to indicate how well motivated these persons appear to be. Such approaches are well known to be quite futile, for the work that Freud initiated, which has now been pursued for nearly a century, has shown quite clearly that motivation is a matter of which the individual is largely unaware and that he has the greatest difficulty in explaining. The same clinical studies indicate that direct observation of behavior as it occurs on a day-to-day basis reveals little concerning motivation. Motivation is, as it is commonly said, a hidden variable that cannot be observed directly and cannot be assessed directly. It is the indirect approaches to motivation, such as those of the clinician or those that began with the work of H.A. Murray and his associates in the 1930's, that have yielded the little knowledge we now have concerning it.

Indirect approaches to problems are typical of all branches of science. The realization that the laws of falling bodies could be studied best by studying not free-falling bodies but such artificial situations as objects moving down inclined planes, opened an entirely new era in physical experimentation. The study of human genetics has been made possible through studies of the microscopic structure of plant cells. The development of radioactive materials has made it possible to investigate human metabolic processes that have defied any direct approach. Much scientific knowledge has to be acquired by indirect methods. Even the practical problem of measuring the diameter of the earth does not lend itself to the direct approach, which would involve the stretching of a measuring tape around its circumference. All knowledge about the atom and its supposed structure is acquired by extremely indirect methods, where the measurements made are connected only remotely with atomic phenomena and where the conclusions involve a long chain of supposed events.

The directness of approach of many who work in educational research is not too different from the approach of the physical scientist of the Middle Ages who wished to solve the problem of converting lead to gold by simple and direct means. Part of the reason for this is that our ingenuity has not led us yet to useful indirect methods of attack on more important questions that are likely to arise, and thus we tend to keep hammering away with direct approaches, which mostly have no value at all. However, we can take a few steps in the right direction. Even an opinion survey at times can avoid to advantage a direct question concerning a problem. For example, a person may be unwilling to admit what he pays his servant, but he may be quite willing to state, without embarrassment, what he believes to be the prevailing wage in the community for that kind of work.

Sometimes the indirect approach to problems involves the conduct of a study in a laboratory situation rather than in a real-life setting. Many problems of reading have been attacked successfully in this way, and subsequent classroom studies have validated the results. There are advantages in a direct approach whenever it is likely to yield results, but the student who finds that only an indirect avenue is open to him should not feel discouraged. He should remember that some of the most important discoveries of science were made by a similar means.

Research in administration is an area in which a direct approach is often not feasible but in which indirect attacks on the problem may be highly productive. The author can recall the suggestion of a student interested in the question of how information was passed around in a large board of education building. The suggestion was the simple one of keeping a record of who called who on the telephone within the building. There was no intention of keeping a record of what was said, for the purpose was only to draw up a diagram rather like a sociogram that would indicate the channels through which information passed during the course of daily business. Of course, there has also been much laboratory work conducted on the effect of various administrative practices on the morale of groups, and these studies are being slowly extended into the field of real administration. The choice of level of reality of a study, its directness or indirectness, is determined by a multiplicity of factors, including the amount that is already known about the phenomena.

The Data Language

The behavioral sciences, as they have developed in recent years, have shown a tendency to develop their own language and to discuss events in terms quite different from those used in everyday speech. Those engaged in research have become increasingly aware of the importance of selecting a suitable language with which to describe and discuss the events in which they are interested. The problem to be investigated and the specific hypothesis to be tested must be stated in a language that is appropriate. The language selected is referred to as the *data language*. Since the data language of a study is used, in the first place, in the statement of the hypothesis to be tested, some problems related to the selection of a data language must be discussed at this time.

The language of daily usage is not only often inappropriate for scientific usage, it may be misleading. In the early developments of many branches of scientific knowledge scientists have been actually led astray by common language. The great French chemist Antoine Lavoisier was one of the first to point out this fact. He noted that the names given to most chemical substances in his day were quite misleading. The chemists of his time talked about such substances as *oil of tartar, butter of arsenic, flowers of zinc,* and so forth. To think of these substances as oil, or butter, or flowers, hindered rather than helped the chemist for the substances did not have the properties of oil, or butter, or flowers.

The break which Lavoisier made with popular language and the introduction of a more appropriate language for describing or discussing chemical phenomena and chemical substances was an essential step for the founding of a science of chemistry.

The phenomena of education can be discussed in many different ways using many different vocabularies. Consider the case of the researcher studying some aspect of the behavior of the teacher. Much of the data of any such study must be derived in some way from the movements of the teacher in the classroom or from disturbances that he produces in his physical surroundings, as when his vocal cords cause vibrations in the atmosphere. Now an educational researcher who described all of the movements of a teacher and all of the physical disturbances produced by his behavior in the physical environment during a one-hour period would not have a description of events that would be in the slightest respect meaningful to another research worker. A graph showing the decibel level of noise produced by the teacher's larynx would not convey to most of those who inspected it just what had happened in this respect in the classroom. A language that described teacher behavior in terms of the physical properties of movement, direction, force, pitch, and the like, would at the present time be an entirely inappropriate data language for any researcher who wished to study the classroom behavior of teachers. Now it is quite conceivable that a time may come when such a data language may be appropriate and meaningful to other researchers, but until that time comes it must be considered as inappropriate.

The development of a suitable data language for any program of research in the behavioral sciences must take cognizance of two facts. First, it must be based on the recognition that all behavioral events that occur during a data-gathering procedure cannot be recorded as part of the data, for much more occurs than can ever be recorded. Second, what is recorded constitutes only certain aspects of behavior, and terms must be employed that are generally recognized as referring to the particular aspects of behavior that are abstracted. Third, the terms used must refer to objectively identifiable events; that is to say, events that independent observers can identify. Thus, in describing the behavior of the teacher, the researcher may record the number of instances in which the teacher threatens the children with keeping them after school, gives them additional homework, discusses behavior problems with the parents, and similar specific matters. Such a category of teacher behavior will be meaningful to other researchers who read about it, and one hopes that the researcher will plan his work in such a way that this category of behavior can be postulated to be highly relevant to the phenomenon that will be the object of the research.

A data language should not contain unnecessary references to unobservables. For example, a researcher recorded the statement, "The teacher felt frustrated because he was unable to maintain order." This statement referred to the teacher's feeling of frustration, which could not be observed but only inferred from observables. The kind of inference that is implied in the researcher's statement should never be included in the data language; the data language should refer to the events on which the inference is based.

The data language used by a specific researcher in the behavioral sciences will depend to a considerable extent on the nature of his academic training and background. In the illustration used two paragraphs above, the data language was derived from the language of common speech. The key word was *threat*, and this word was used in one of its common meanings, but the researcher is in no way bound to this type of language. Often categories of behavior that will be understood well only by scientists will be used. For example, one researcher found it convenient to classify teacher behavior as learning-oriented or threat-oriented. These terms refer to behavior that is hypothesized to contribute to the organized learning of the classroom and behavior that serves the purpose of defending the teacher's ego against some external threat. The latter is exemplified by a teacher whose principal tended to judge teachers in terms of the orderliness of the pupils in the classroom. For this reason, this teacher spent almost the entire time exercising control over every movement of the pupils. Now the terms *learning-oriented* and *threat-*

oriented in this context are familiar to the person with thorough training in psychology, but are quite meaningless to most other people.

In selecting a data language, the scientist sometimes makes up new words or defines common words in new ways. Occasionally this is necessary, but such a procedure should be reduced to a minimum for several reasons. One is that it requires each reader to learn a new vocabulary before he can study the results of research. Few readers of the research will be inclined to do this, and still fewer will be willing to master the language to the point where it can be easily manipulated. Another problem arises from the fact that if familiar words are used in unfamiliar ways, the groundwork is laid for a long history of misunderstandings. Indeed whole areas of knowledge have been confused by this practice. A good example of this difficulty is presented by modern learning theory, where the term *reflex* has different meanings in the language of different theorists.

The data language usually refers to only a limited range of phenomena. The researcher should try to specify the range of phenomena to which his data language applies. This is important because often readers will assume that the researcher is referring to a much wider range of phenomena than was the intention. For example, a researcher may have defined the phrase *aggressive behavior* in terms of certain aspects of the behavior of the pupil in the classroom. A reader in going over the report may easily forget the way in which *aggressive behavior* was defined and assume that the term and the conclusions that refer to it apply not only to behavior in the classroom but also to behavior in other situations.

The data language may also refer to characteristics of the physical environment that are hypothesized to effect behavior in some way. These characteristics have been referred to in this book as stimulus variables, and they may include such varied features as intensity of lighting, number of books in the school library, number of pupils in the class, and the area of classroom space per pupil. The data language for discussing such variables is derived from the language of everyday speech and presents no special problem. However, there are many important characteristics of the school that cannot be so easily described. For example, what is commonly referred to as *degree of permissiveness* is a characteristic of the school that is difficult to define in terms most persons would understand, and thus it becomes extremely important to tie this term down to observable events that can be recognized.

At a primitive level of scientific development, the data language usually consists of qualitative and descriptive terms. These terms become progressively more remotely related to the language of everyday usage as the science develops. At a more mature level, the terms of the language begin to refer to variables rather than to qualitative phenomena. In the ultimate stage of development, the language is in terms of mathematical symbols that refer only to measurable variables.

The Advantages of Breadth and Narrowness in Defining Problems

There are disadvantages in the definition of a problem in narrow terms, particularly in the early stages of exploration. Narrowness hampers the possibilities of an imaginative approach. This can be appreciated by presenting a concrete problem from a field other than education. The example here is one developed by John Arnold, who, in his classes on creative engineering, stresses the importance of defining problems at first in broad terms. He points out that in one of his classes some students embarked on the engineering problems of designing an improved automatic toaster. By stating the problem in this way, the possible ideas that could be incorporated in a plan of action were restricted. If the problem had been defined as that of *developing new methods of providing the consumer with toasted bread,* a wide range of new ideas would have become available for exploration. For example, one can conceive of the possibility of providing the consumer with ready-packaged toast. Industrial methods of large-scale toast-making could then be considered.

There was also the possibility that some commercial substitute for toast might be developed. So long as the problem was that of *developing a better toaster,* these latter possibilities could not receive consideration. Now there is no question that ultimately a problem has to be narrowed before it can be worked upon, but this should not happen until opportunity has been provided to explore the problem on a wide base with the full play of imagination.

There are similar disadvantages attached to the early narrow definition of problems in the field of education. Thus, in the search for a problem to work on in the field of mathematics, the researcher might well start by asking himself the question, "In what ways is it possible to improve the teaching of number operations?" rather than the question, "In what ways is it possible to improve the teaching of long division?" When the student begins to think in terms of the broad problem, he is free to identify some crucial aspect of the teaching of arithmetic, the improvement of which would result in the improvement of the teaching of arithmetic in general. On the other hand, if the student thinks only in terms of teaching long division, the outcome of the resulting research is likely to be applicable only to the teaching of long division. The student should direct his thinking in such a way that the ultimate product of the research envisaged is a principle that has at least the possibility of being widely applicable.

It should be pointed out here that we are referring in this section to the early stages of developing research. As thinking progresses, it is necessary to consider more and more specific aspects of the problem.

Preliminary Explorations of the Problem

The selection of a problem for study is not usually undertaken in a single step, for it is commonly necessary to run a preliminary study before the decision is finally made. The need for such a preliminary study does not arise when the problem requires the conduct of a research closely similar to one that has already been done, for it is then known that the research can be undertaken. However, when the field of inquiry is relatively new and does not have available a set of well-developed techniques, a brief feasibility study must almost always be run. Such brief trial runs demonstrate whether it is practical to undertake the research, whether the professional techniques are sufficiently sensitive to measure differences that it is desired to measure, and whether one can obtain the necessary cooperation of others involved in the study. Negative results in any one of these directions may be sufficient to cause the researcher to change his problem.

A preliminary trial or pilot study also provides some indications of the availability of subjects, if human subjects are used, or of other needed materials. Certain studies may require specific population characteristics, and it is necessary to determine whether populations having these characteristics actually exist. For example, one study required a comparison of the performance of children who did not like their teachers with that of children who did, and each one of these categories of children had to be divided into a bright group and a dull group. A preliminary study was needed to determine whether enough children existed who would admit not liking their teachers to make the study possible.

Preliminary trial runs involve not only the selection of a problem, but also the selection of some kind of design for the study. In practice the design of the trial run may be much simpler and less sophisticated than the design that is finally adopted. The trial run may provide much information that is needed for the final design.

Developing a Research Plan

A stage arrives in the development of every research at which it becomes desirable for the worker to arrange his ideas in order and write them down in the form of an experimental plan. A few experienced and sophisticated research workers may never actually write out such a plan, just as most experienced writers do not start by making an outline, but most research workers need a formal plan just as most writers need to make an outline. The student of education who is embarking on his first research enterprise will certainly need to develop and outline a research plan that will serve a number of different purposes.

First, the research plan helps him to organize his ideas in a form whereby it will be possible for him to look for flaws and inadequacies. Many research studies appear to offer excellent promise until the details are laid out in black and white. Only then do the difficulties of executing the study become apparent.

Second, the research plan provides an inventory of what must be done and what materials have to be collected as a preliminary step to undertaking the study.

Third, the research plan is a document that can be given to others for comment and criticism. Without such a plan it is difficult for the critic to provide a comprehensive review of the proposed study. Word-of-mouth methods of communicating the proposed study are more time-consuming and less efficient than that provided by a written plan.

A research plan should cover at least the items discussed in the paragraphs that follow. Only a brief discussion is presented here, since many of the points are treated at greater length in the chapters that follow.

1. *The problem.* The plan should include a clear statement of the question or questions that the research is designed to answer. These are the hypotheses. The plan should also provide a concise account of the background of the problem and the theory on which it is based. The questions must be clearly and precisely stated. The statement of the problem must be complete, and it must be presented in a form that makes absolutely clear just what information must be obtained in order to solve the problem.

2. *The method to be used in solving the problem.* This section of the plan provides an over-all description of the approach that offers an avenue to the solution of the problem. Sometimes it is necessary to adopt methods that make special assumptions, and these should be explicitly stated in this section of the plan. For example, if the method involves the measurement of attitudes

by means of verbal attitude scales, then it may be necessary to assume that verbal expressions of attitude are related to other expressions of attitude. In the latter case it might not be desirable to continue with the research unless evidence can be marshaled showing that the assumption was justified. Usually it is necessary to introduce assumptions about methods simply because direct attacks on the problem are not possible, and the indirect nature of the approach that must be taken introduces the need for assumptions.

3. *Procedures and techniques.* While the previous section describes the over-all approach to the problem, this part of the plan is concerned with the details of the techniques to be adopted. If interview methods are to be used, an account of the nature of the contemplated interview procedures should be given here, also whether the interview is to be structured and in what way, and the characteristics that the interviewer should possess for the purposes of the study. If tests are to be given, the conditions under which they are to be administered should be specified, as well as the nature of the instruments that are to be used. This section is an appropriate place for describing apparatus to be used or to be built. If public records are to be consulted as sources of data, the fact should be recorded here. The details of the procedures and techniques would not be complete without an account of the sample that is to be included in the study. A statement should be included indicating how the sample will be drawn, the universe from which it is to be drawn, and its size.

4. *The population of events to be studied.* The population of events to be studied will depend upon the population to which the results of the study are to be generalized. If the results are to be generalized to all seventh-grade pupils in a certain school system, the research plan should state this fact. Since it probably will not be possible to include all seventh-grade pupils in the study, but only a sample, the research plan should state how the sample is to be identified. The method of identifying the sample should be such that generalization from the sample to the original population is feasible. If textbooks are the subject of the research, the population of textbooks to which the results are to be general-

ized must be specified as must the method of identifying the sample of textbooks to be studied.

5. *Methods to be used in processing data.* A research plan should indicate the statistical and other methods that are to be used for processing data. Such methods should not be left until the data have been collected. Many students have completed considerable work on a study, only to find that statistical techniques did not exist for answering the questions that were asked. This part of the plan should be reviewed by a person expert in the field of statistics, since such a specialist can often suggest changes that result in substantial savings of time and effort.

Summary

1. Educational research was initiated little more than half a century ago and set iself the ambitious task of producing a rapid revolution in educational practices. Time has shown that research in an area develops only slowly, and that decades may pass before suitable research methodologies are developed.

2. Since the central focus of educational research is the development of the pupil, and particularly insofar as this is produced by the practices of the school, it is hardly surprising that developmental studies constitute a major area of educational research.

3. Developmental studies have shown an evolution in the theoretical position from which they have been undertaken. Earlier studies were often dominated by the standpoint of the maturationist, who sees development as largely the product of inner forces. Current research, in contrast, emphasizes the role of learning in the development process, and studies have become more and more concerned with the acqusition of new behavior as it is brought about by the school. The wealth of theoretical viewpoints from which the research worker may draw his ideas insures that research in the area can be thoroughly theory oriented.

4. Since those who work in the field of curriculum emphasize the need for curriculum *theory* as an essential element of curricu-

lum development, the stage is well set for programmatic curriculum research that is firmly rooted in clearly stated theories. This is a relatively recent development, for curriculum research of the past has tended to be a fact-finding enterprise. Many techniques are now available that permit research on important curriculum problems, the application of which has hardly yet been explored.

5. The influence of sociological and economic conditions on education is an important field of inquiry. There are, of course, real difficulties in developing generalizations that have any wide applicability in this area of investigation, but some that have been made are extremely important in their practical consequences.

6. The design and engineering of equipment for schools is a relatively new field of educational research and development. Current attempts to develop devices that provide effective learning situations represent a most important innovation. Such devices can play an important role in the acquisition of a wide range of thinking skills.

7. The planning stage of research is the critical stage and should not be hurried. Often it is the most time-consuming stage.

8. The student should be aware of the great complexity of the phenomena that are studied in educational research. Even the simplest of these are extraordinarily complex.

9. There are dangers in the student seeking to investigate some problem related to a social issue about which he has deep feelings. The difficulties of maintaining an objective view of the results under such conditions present serious problems.

10. One method of identifying a researchable problem is to become fully absorbed in the technical literature of the area of interest. Another is to identify previous studies that should be repeated with refinements.

11. A review of the literature is an important part of the activities that prepare the student to undertake research. He may well start this by studying articles by the outstanding scientists in the field. The review of the literature should provide the student with the framework of theory required for research.

12. The hypothesis selected for study should be testable and should be stated in terms of variables that can actually be measured. The hypothesis should also be limited in scope and consistent with known facts, and should represent a deduction from a theory that the student can identify.

13. Most problems that are researchable at all must be attacked by indirect means. Most of the questionnaire studies that abound in education are misguided efforts to obtain information by direct means.

14. The problem must be stated in a language that is appropriate; that is to say, a suitable data language must be selected. The data language in terms of which a technical problem is stated is usually considerably different from the language of ordinary communication.

15. The fact that the student is able to identify a problem does not mean that he is ready to jump ahead and carry through the collection of data. Some preliminary studies are usually necessary in order to determine whether the proposed study is or is not feasible. Preliminary studies often indicate that a problem needs to be restated or modified before it can be considered researchable.

16. A research plan that outlines the essential features of the proposed research should be prepared. An important function of this plan is to provide an outline of the inquiry that others may review and criticize.

Some Problems for the Student

1. Students who have already identified research problems should present them to the class for criticism. Much can be learned by such a critical review. It is suggested that the problems be presented in the form of the research plan that has been outlined in this chapter. The student should be prepared to defend the theoretical position to which the proposed research relates.

2. Students who have not yet identified research problems should review the technical literature in the general areas in which it is proposed to work. The central theoretical concepts of the selected areas should be identified, and problems should then be outlined for criticism by others.

CHAPTER 4

SOME PROBLEMS OF

CONDUCTING HISTORICAL

RESEARCH

Historical Research and Case History Research

RESEARCH conducted by historians has differed from research conducted by the majority of scientists in so many fundamental ways that a chapter on the subject almost seems out of place in this volume. Nevertheless, its inclusion is justified on three grounds. First, many theses written by students in schools of education are historical in character. Second, a review of research literature is in itself an historical study, for the reviewer is attempting to reconstruct what was done and what happened in the past. Third, the last few decades have seen a rapprochement between historical research and research in such areas as anthropology, sociology, and psychology. The Social Science Research Council has made persistent efforts to bring together scholars in history, anthropology, sociology, and related disciplines so that each can profit from the knowledge of technique and method acquired by the others.

An example of this rapprochement is found in a Social Science Research Council Report by Gottschalk *et al.* (1945) in which the knowledge of a historian, a sociologist, and an anthropologist is pooled to provide a more complete understanding of the use of the personal document in research. In this report each outlines the problem of using personal documents as data upon which to base research. Psychologists have also conducted inquiries on the fringe of historical research. For example, the writings of Allport (1942) on the use of personal documents in research has had some impact on students of historical method.

Historical research is concerned with man's past, and while it has as its aim the reconstruction of the past, such a reconstruction can never be fully achieved. The problem of the historian is similar to that of psychologists working with case history material who seek to reconstruct from such material the nature of the person to whom it pertains. The information is always fragmentary and the reconstruction provides a sketch rather than a finished portrait. Different students of a case history may arrive at different reconstructions from the same evidence, but the student of personal case histories sometimes has an advantage over the historian in that he may go out and study his case further and validate through the collection of additional evidence the reconstruction he has built. The clinical psychologist typically does this. From the evidence he collects about a case, he attempts to reconstruct the person. Then he validates his reconstruction by further observing the person. For example, he may infer from the patient's performance on a projective test that the patient would be well adapted to doing work involving attention to detail but poorly adapted to work requiring broad over-all planning. The psychologist could then collect information on the patient's past and present success in work situations and continue to collect data in the future which might validate the inference he had made. The historian cannot look to the future to validate his reconstructions of the past.

Reconstruction of the past, which is called history, is based on inferences made from documents. The term *document* is used here in a broader sense than it is used in daily living. A document is an impression left by a human being on a physical object. The impression may be made with ink on a piece of paper, with a sculptor's chisel on a piece of stone, with the artist's brush on canvas, with the potter's hand on soft clay, and in any other way in which a human may leave a trace of his activity. This conception of a document is derived from the writings of Gottschalk (1945), who makes no distinction between written impressions and other impressions. In any case, the latter distinction is not easily made, for primitive written communications may be pictorial, and every object on which the human hand has left an impression tells a story.

Documents are derived from sources. A particular observer is an example of a source; he may be the source of many documents. A newspaper is another example of a source. However, the word *source* also has another meaning in that a document is commonly referred to as a source of information.

That sound inferences about a culture can be made from objects is so obvious that the point hardly needs to be pressed further. If a visitor from another planet were able to procure some of the common objects used by modern civilization but died on the return trip home, the objects themselves would permit the inhabitants of the other planet to go far towards reconstructing a picture of our civilization. Take, for example, a good quality kitchen knife. The fact that it contained high-grade steel would indicate that the civilization from which it was derived had an advanced technology in the processing of metals and had probably made substantial scientific discoveries. The name of the manufacturer on the knife would indicate a knowledge of writing and the widespread use of writing and printing in daily life. The plastic handle would provide further cues concerning the scientific and technical development of the culture. Additional inferences from other objects in the collection would not only provide some verification of the inferences made from the knife, but would also add to the reconstruction.

The reconstruction of the past is undertaken in terms of a set of written symbols. The assumption is that the words of history which constitute the symbols bear a well-defined relationship to past events, much as an equation of a physicist bears a relation to the processes occurring in an experiment. One important difference is that the physicist can always reproduce the process in order to check whether his formula actually corresponds to real events. The historian has much greater difficulty in doing this. In an earlier chapter the use of models in the development of science was discussed. In a sense, history is a model of certain events of the past.

The thinking habits of most people are such that they have difficulty in thinking of written history as merely an attempt to build a verbal model of past events. One can understand why this is so. To read a chapter by a great historian of high literary talent is to have a vivid experience of living in the past with a feeling for the reality of the past much as one has a sense of the reality of the present. The compelling reality of the image of history imparted to us is an illusion conjured up through the literary and research skills of the historian. The reality of history is illusory, for one cannot know the past in the way in which one can know the present. One cannot know it in the way in which it was known to those that lived it. Written history is only an attempt to provide, through the use of words and symbols, some representation of what are inferred to be events which actually took place. How close the relationship between the written symbols and the actual events is always a matter for conjecture. Language itself, with its many limitations, probably has only limited capacity for representing the events as they actually happened. Perhaps here again there is a parallel with physics. Newton's equations of motion are useful for describing the motions of bodies under conditions such as occur under certain unusual circumstances. They have limited capacity for describing motions occurring in cars and airplanes, as these devices perform in daily experience. The language of physics, as expressed in the equations of the physicist, has only limited capacity for representing the complex events of the real world as it impinges on living individuals. The language of everyday speech probably has even less capability of representing the events of history. Its apparent capability of doing this is a dangerous illusion.

The problems of selecting, examining and making inferences from documents are the problems of historical method. They present essentially the same difficulties that are encountered in making inferences from psychological tests and other materials, but they have the added difficulty that there is often no direct way of validating the inference. When one considers that trained psychologists have been relatively unsuccessful in making predictions about individuals even from very extensive case histories, one may well wonder whether the historian is likely to be more successful in reconstructing history from the documents available.

The Choice of a Subject

Every historical study begins with the choice of a subject. This may seem to be an easy decision to make, but the fact is that it is not and there is considerable controversy among historians concerning the criteria to use in the selection of a topic. Gottschalk (1951) suggests that four questions should be asked in identifying a topic:

1. Where do the events take place?
2. Who are the persons involved?
3. When do the events occur?
4. What kinds of human activity are involved?

Other prescriptions exist for defining historical topics. One of these is to define the topic in terms of some important idea or set of beliefs. One school of historians has taken the position that history is the history of important ideas and if it is not this, then it lacks significance.

The scope of a topic may be varied by varying the scope of any one of the four categories; the geographical area involved may be increased or decreased; more or fewer persons may be included in the topic; the time span involved may be increased or decreased, and the human activity category may be broadened or narrowed.

In a sense, historical studies can only begin with a very rough determination of what is to be the topic involved. Since in the beginning stage the research worker does not yet know the scope which his topic may acquire after all of the facts have been assembled, he can only indicate in a rough way the scope of the projected research. As he studies the sources available to him, he may find that the proposed topic involves so many and complex events that he must limit its scope. He may also find that the area is an impoverished one and that a broadening of the scope of the study is desirable.

Selection of Sources

Historical studies usually begin with a delimitation of the general category of events that is to be reconstructed. The next step is the establishment of sources from which inferences can be made concerning the nature of the events. A common classification of sources is into *primary* and *secondary*. A primary source is one which has had some direct physical relationship to the events that are being reconstructed. A person who observes directly an event would be classified as a primary source, and so, too, would a photograph or sound recording of the event. A reproduction of such a photograph would also be considered as a primary source. The writings of a person whose life is being reconstructed as a history would be considered a primary source even if he wrote about himself in the third person, as certain writers have done. Secondary sources are those that do not bear a direct physical relationship to the event that is the subject of study. They are related to the event through some intermediate process. Thus, if the historian is interested in the life of a character who we will designate X, he may have to use documents produced by Z who never knew X personally. Z may have derived his information about X through an interview with Y, a close personal friend of X. In such a case both Y and Z introduce distortions, hence Z as a secondary source is necessarily a poorer source of information than Y. If the chain involved in the transmittal of information is lengthened from X—Y—Z to a chain of four elements, the adequacy of the information is again decreased. Psychologists have conducted experiments on the transmittal of information by this kind of human chain and have found that substantial distortions may occur in very short chains, even to the extent that the information transmitted loses all its original characteristics.

Many sources include both primary and secondary elements which the person conducting historical research, or research involving the use of personal documents, may have to sort out. Many biographies have been written by close personal friends of the principal character involved. The biography will be a mixture of information derived by direct observation and material obtained by the writer from other sources. Often there is no way of determining which parts of a source are primary and which are secondary, although this may be a vital issue in determining the inferences to be made from the material.

Criteria of the Validity of Inferences and Reconstructions

The scientist uses many different criteria to determine the validity of the ideas which he develops. One criterion is what may be called an *internal* criterion—whether the idea fits with other ideas derived from different sources. The wave theory of light derived from a study of lens phenomena and interference phenomena does not fit with the quantum theory of light derived from such phenomena as the photoelectric effect. Both conceptions of light must be inadequate—they are incompatible with one another, although each is compatible with the evidence on which it is based. Inferences made from different sources about the same historical event must be compatible and fit together if they are to be considered valid. This type of validation procedure used by the historian closely resembles that used by the scientist. But the scientist has another method of validating his inferences; namely, by making predictions on the basis of the inferences and determining whether such predictions are correct. The historian is not able to use the latter approach to validate his inferences.

A difficulty which the historian faces when he attempts to validate his inferences is that this process always involves a considerable degree of personal judgment and subjectivity. The scientist attempts to overcome this difficulty by using measuring devices and laboratory procedures which eliminate, as much as possible, the factor of judgment. For example, by inference from other data Einstein developed an equation relating mass to energy. This inference could be validated by finding situations in which there was a conversion of mass to energy and *measuring* the amount of energy produced by a given loss of mass. There is very little guesswork involved in this kind of validation. There is much greater difficulty in validating the inference that a Supreme Court justice held a particular personal view with respect to a particular issue although to hold such a view was in conflict with a decision which he had endorsed. Indirect information may *indicate* that his personal views were in conflict with the position, but how much evidence does one have to have, in this case, to substantiate the hypothesis? The answer is strictly a matter of opinion, a matter which makes the task of the historian a particularly difficult one.

While agreement among sources and the criterion of internal consistency is commonly used, it cannot always be justifiably applied. The psychologist is, in this respect, in a much better position than the historian, for very rarely in psychological work can the criterion of internal consistency not be applied. In contrast, the historian often encounters instances in which much evidence appears on the surface to point in one direction, but the inference is wrong. Consider, for example, the documents left in Germany after the end of the Nazi regime. Document upon document takes the position that the difficulties of Germany were manufactured by the Jews. Clearly, the position is nonsense and although the documents show consistency, the criterion of consistency cannot be applied.

The Evaluation of Written Documents

Before a written document can be used as a basis for making inferences, its worth for the purpose must be evaluated. This is generally done from two distinct points of view. First, an appraisal must be made of the authenticity of the source. Second, if the authorship can be established, the characteristics of the author must be weighed in order to determine whether the document he produced can be considered a sound source of information. Each of these presents problems in evaluation which must be considered separately.

The evaluation of authenticity. Sometimes a problem of authenticity will arise in the research that students of education are likely to undertake, although less often than in other kinds of historical research. For example, if a student were to make an analysis of the content of speeches made by superintendents during a given period of time in order to study the educational policies of the period, he would be faced with the problem of determining how many of the superintendents used ghostwriters. The same problem arises in the case of correspondence, for it is very common for an official letter to be composed by a person other than the signer. "Autobiographies" are also commonly written by ghostwriters and throughout history there have been persons who earned their livings by such writing. The educational researcher with an interest in the history of education is unlikely to come across forgeries or documents to which the names of famous persons have been appended for prestige purposes.

The historian is plagued by the fact that the details of many documents are incorrect and, unless checked, may give rise to incorrect inferences. Barzun (1957) gives an interesting example of how an incorrect date on a letter might lead to incorrect inferences. He cites the case of a letter written by Berlioz to his publisher about the preparation of an index for a book. According to the letter, it was written from Paris on Thursday, June 23. No year was indicated. Establishing the date of the letter presents an interesting problem. Barzun points out that other sources indicate that Berlioz lived in Paris from July 1849 until April 1856 and hence a reference to the calendar should indicate in which one of these years June 23 fell on a Thursday. The calendar indicates that the year would have been 1853, but Barzun then goes to point out that the year could not have been 1853 for at that time

Berlioz did not have any manuscript in the final stages of completion. The year must have been 1852 and the day Wednesday rather than Thursday, June 23. The evidence indicates that Berlioz made an error in noting the day of the week.

The evaluation of the writer as a transmitter of information. The authors of documents may represent excellent sources of information or worthless sources. A number of characteristics are commonly considered in making evaluations of writers.

1. Was the writer a trained or untrained observer of the particular event? If a biologist recorded that he observed the Loch Ness monster, greater credibility would be given the report than if a person not trained in biological observation had reported it. Related to this is the matter of the expertness of the observer. The biologist in this case is not only a trained observer but also an expert on animal life. More credence is given to the observations of experts than those of amateurs.

2. What was the relationship of the observer to the event? The closer the writer was to the event recorded, the greater the value of the source. Persons who arrive *after* an event has taken place or who were some distance from it are not in a position to provide reports to which great significance can be attached. An accident report of a principal who arrived on the scene after the incident occurred is likely to be worth less than that of a teacher who saw it happen.

3. To what extent was the writer under pressure to distort? There are many cases in which educational documents must be considered as almost certainly representing a distorted picture of what happened. A school board that meets behind closed doors and then releases for publication a report of the deliberations is likely to produce a distorted statement of what occurred. The statement is likely to be designed to please the public and the personnel of the school system. Again, in a public session of a school board a newspaper reporter is likely to give greater stress to those aspects of the proceedings which might be of political interest to his particular newspaper.

4. What was the intent of the writer of the document? This is related to the previous item, but covers a greater range of cir-

cumstances. Documents may be written for many different purposes: to inform, to remind the writer (as in the case of a personal memorandum), to command (as in the case of a directive), to produce a particular effect on a particular reader or on a group of readers, or sometimes even to unburden the mind of the writer (as is sometimes the case with personal correspondence). The intent of the writer of the document, if it can be determined, should have a powerful influence on the evaluation of a document as historical evidence.

5. To what extent was the writer expert at recording the particular events? The well-trained newspaper reporter is much more likely to provide an accurate report than the casual tourist who happened to observe the same event. Untrained observers in schools may report entirely erroneous impressions. Many critics of the public schools have not been inside one since they left school and base their criticism on anecdotes brought back by their own children. Such children would be considered to lack expertness in recording events that occurred.

6. Were the habits of the author of the document such that they might interfere with the accurate recording of events? This is an interesting problem. A good writer is not necessarily a good reporter. The writer with literary talent may be unable to control the temptation to embellish. The opportunity to display a clever turn of phrase or an apt analogy may interfere with precise reporting. The talented writer is also often imaginative and creative and experiences difficulty in discriminating between what actually happened and what he imagines happened.

7. Was the author of the document of such a nature that he might omit important materials or distort others in order to avoid being sued for libel? Every writer will yield to some extent to this, but the bold will still report more than the timid and with less distortion. While this point is an important one, advice cannot be offered which will help the historian distinguish the bold writer from the timid one.

Cause and Effect Relationships

Just as the behavioral scientist generally avoids referring to Event A as being caused by Event B, so too is the historian very cautious in his use of the concept of cause. No historian would want to discuss the *cause* of war or the *cause* of depressions. Both are highly complex events with complex relationships to other events. Only the physicist dealing with very simple isolated laboratory phenomena can use the word *cause* without running into difficulties. A physicist can appropriately say that a given force causes a given acceleration in a given mass. He can make such statements because he is dealing with an isolated phenomenon. The historian is never in such an enviable position.

The historical research worker must accept the fact that he is not dealing with clear-cut cases of cause and effect and must avoid such notions in his writing. It is very easy to make such a statement as "John Dewey's experiences with the experimental school which he founded in Chicago caused him to recast his views on education." Such a statement is quite inaccurate since, although Dewey's experiences in connection with the Chicago school were extremely important to him in the development of his ideas, they were only one set of circumstances among many others from which his later conception of education finally emerged. The historian generally deals with chains of related events, but he cannot say that one event in the chain was caused by the previous event in the chain. A student might undertake an historical study of the changing role of the school faculty in establishing educational policies during the last twenty-five years. In undertaking such a project, the research worker would realize that many conditions and circumstances have been responsible for the changing role of the school faculty in this respect, but he cannot identify clear-cut cause-and-effect relationships. The change that has taken place is a result of many factors and the influence of a particular factor cannot be accurately assessed.

In addition, there are events and conditions that have had some influence but which have not been identified. For a discussion of this problem, the reader is referred to Barzun (1957).

The Synthesis of Information

If the preparation of a history were merely the digging out of facts, the task would be a simple one. But we have already seen that the study of documents often raises puzzling problems of what is fact, and that judgment is always involved in determining the extent to which the inferences made have a high probability of being correct. These processes present difficulties enough, but even more difficult is the step involved in using the facts and inferences to build an organized account of the events which the history is to cover. This process of putting together a history after the basic research on sources is completed is referred to as the *process of synthesis*. How this should be done is a matter of controversy.

One cannot clearly separate the search for documents and their examination and study from their synthesis into a coherent work. The synthesis of historical material is closely related to the whole problem of making inferences from historical data. Consider, for example, a history which is focused on the life of a central character. If it included only the objective facts—what the person had been observed to do or had left some record of having done—it would be a dull and lifeless history, lacking any unifying ideas. In order to avoid producing such a cold, lifeless, and objective history, the writer may infer from the data that the person was motivated throughout life by certain powerful and enduring motives. What would be a life of Thomas Jefferson if one could not see in it dedication to the achievement of certain values? What would be a life of Galileo if one could not see in it his devotion to the pursuit of truth and his imperviousness to the social pressures of the times? The historian generally infers from his data that there are underlying characteristics which give unity to the personality which he is studying. But, as every psychologist knows, there are substantial hazards involved in making such inferences, and two persons studying the same historical character may not infer the same underlying motives or other basic characteristics.

Since psychologists cannot agree upon a list of fundamental motives or underlying personality traits, the historian must choose a system which he prefers for the description of behavior. Typically, he chooses a popular conception of personality organization rather than a technical one. One is unlikely to find a biography of Napoleon written in terms of how he was *conditioned* to manifest power-seeking behavior; neither is one likely to find one written in terms of psychoanalytic concepts. True, a few historians have attempted to describe their human subjects in terms of psychoanalytic concepts, but these are notable exceptions and are regarded as bold experiments rather than as orthodox treatments. Perhaps the two major reasons why interpretations of behavior undertaken by historians follow popular conceptions of personality structure are that historians are most familiar with this conception of personality and that history is written for a consumer and the popular conception of history is the only one that the consumer is likely to understand. Synthesis of conceptions of historical characters in terms of popular conceptions of behavior will continue to be made.

The point being emphasized here is that the historical reconstruction of human behavior can be undertaken in many different ways, unless it is the reconstruction of an empty frame. Historians aim to reconstruct real persons with motives, values, fears, inner conflicts, struggles with their consciences, hates, loves, and the wealth of internal processes which make man more than a mere empty frame. This procedure involves many assumptions about human nature which research may ultimately show to be unsound.

While the historian is limited in his interpretation of historical characters by his own conceptions of psychology and behavior, he is also limited by the inevitable fact that he must interpret the past in the light of contemporary thought. He may attempt to build a verbal model of the past, but the model is always a product of contemporary thought. A history written today reflects events of today as well as events of the past. The mind of man can mirror the past, but the image may be distorted by the very shape of the surface. Our picture of the schoolrooms of the Middle Ages is colored by what we know about our schools to-day.

Even at a much simpler level of synthesis than the one which has just been considered there are difficulties involved in putting together what are ordinarily considered to be the facts of history. Consider, for example, two items about the French revolutionary Georges Jacques Danton: (1) Danton said, "I always act in accordance with the eternal laws of Justice," and (2) Danton was a man of violent and extreme views. The two items differ in their derivation, one being reproduced from a document while the other has been inferred from many separate documents. Now consider the problem of putting these two "facts" together. One might write any one of the following statements:

While Danton was a man of extreme and violent views, he said, "I always act in accordance with the eternal laws of Justice."

Danton said, "I always act in accordance with the eternal laws of Justice" but he was a man of violent and extreme views.

Although Danton said, "I always act in accordance with the eternal laws of Justice," he was a man of violent and extreme views.

Even though Danton was a man of violent and extreme views, he said, "I always act in accordance with the eternal laws of Justice."

Words such as *while, although,* and *but* can introduce meanings which may take the history beyond the realm of reasonable inference.

Quantitative Methods in Historical Studies

Many attempts have been made to apply the quantitative methods of the scientist to the solution of historical problems. So far the impact of these methods has not been extensive and much research in history, like much research in anthropology, must remain on a qualitative level. Most of the quantitative methods which have been developed are applications of content analysis.

Some of the earliest efforts to apply quantitative methods involve the use of word counts. Writers typically use particular words at their own frequency rates. A word which has a high usage rate by one writer may have a low usage rate by another. The usage rates of different words may be studied to throw light upon the authenticity of the source of a document. Word usage rates may also be used as a basis for inferring inner emotional states, such as anxiety.

A second and related type of analysis has been developed by McClelland (1961) in an attempt to throw light on the motives operating in individuals in different cultures at particular times in history. McClelland argues that, if the writing appearing in a culture reflects strivings after excellence and provides what he terms "achievement need imagery," the culture may be considered as one with high achievement need. If such an inference can be made, it opens the way to the study of the social conditions which lead to high achievement need in the population. It also opens the way to the study of history in terms of a modern psychological theory of personality. The approach is a novel one and still too new for any appraisal to be made of its ultimate value for the interpretation of the past.

During World War II elaborate and careful attempts were made to make analyses of the public speeches made by Nazi officials for the purpose of identifying possible underlying conflicts within the Nazi party. In addition, some attempt was also made to use such content analyses for the purpose of inferring probable next moves on the part of the enemy.

This brief discussion of the introduction of quantitative methods into historical research may stimulate some readers to explore the possibility of applying such methods to the analysis of educational documents. For example, what motives have been stressed in elementary school readers over the last century? How have these motives changed, and how are the changes related to cultural change during this period? These are but a few of the problems that might be worth investigation.

History as the Study of Nomothetic or Ideographic Phenomena

In Chapter 3 the distinction is made between nomothetic laws, which apply to all persons, and ideographic laws, which reflect the individual's unique history and which, hence, do not apply to others who have had different life histories. Allport (1961) has stressed this distinction in his writings and a parallel distinction is made by historians. Just as some psychologists emphasize the unique characteristics of each individual person, so too do some historians stress the uniqueness of each historical sequence of events.

The issue is as unsettled in the study of history as it is in the study of psychology. In both disciplines there are those who emphasize the nomothetic qualities of their subject matter and those that emphasize the ideographic. Toynbee, for example, has taken a nomothetic approach to history and has attempted to show that within a group of twenty distinct cultures common trends are found, much as there are, to some degree, common trends in the psychological development of all children, even though each child has unique characteristics which distinguish him from other children. Certain historians emphasize the unique development of each and every culture.

The issue is one mainly of theoretical interest and has relevance to the issue of the extent to which the historian can predict the future turn of events, or may be able to do so one day. Contemporary historians, good scholars that they are, make few claims that historical trends are so well established that the future of a civilization can be predicted. Hopes of being able to make such predictions go far beyond expectations reasonable at this time, but there is another important relation which historical research has to future events.

While historians may not be able to predict the future of a civilization, the study of history does affect the future by influencing the decisions of those who participate in government.

Such persons as Roosevelt and Churchill have had a deep and scholarly interest in history, and their knowledge must influence their decisions. At least, some of the grossest follies of mankind may not be repeated, although perhaps this is setting our hopes too high. In the same spirit, those responsible for the establishment of educational policy are influenced by their knowledge of the history of education. The amateur reformers in the field of education would probably drop most of their plans for the remodeling of public education if they had a better understanding of the failures of the past.

The Planning of Historical Studies

This chapter has been concerned with the difficulties encountered by historical research workers and with some of the means used for overcoming these difficulties. It has not been concerned with the details of planning historical studies. That some plan is necessary before historical research is begun is generally accepted, but there is diversity of opinion concerning the extent to which such a plan should be detailed. Certainly, the planning which can be done in the undertaking of a scientific study cannot generally be undertaken in typical historical research. Nevertheless, some planning is both necessary and desirable and might well follow the points listed below.

1. The problem. This involves the choice of a subject for study which can be stated in the way already indicated. The problem may be further elaborated by the statement of specific hypotheses concerning the subject for research. Some historical research workers are very insistent that hypotheses should be stated with the maximum precision possible so that they can later be tested by other research workers, perhaps using different sources. As in the scientific area, the more that is already known about a subject, the more possible it is to formulate specific hypotheses. In the early stages of the exploration of an area, the research worker may have only vague ideas of what to look for.

2. The sources. Some exploration of possible sources is usually made before the subject of historical research is definitely selected. The plan should specify the sources to explore and places where new sources might be discovered. Some evaluation should be made of the value of available sources and whether they can be expected to provide a sound foundation for the historical reconstruction planned. There is little point in undertaking a study if the sources of information are very limited and of doubtful authenticity.

3. *The psychological, sociological, economic, and other concepts to be used as a basis for making inferences.* This part of the plan involves stating some of the assumptions which will underlie the inferences to be made from the documents to be studied. If this section of the plan is properly completed, the historian will know what he is doing. A life of Froebel based on assumptions about personality derived from psychoanalysis is going to be very different from a life of Froebel based on the same documents but interpreted through commonly held conceptions of behavior. The assumptions involved in the preparation of a history should be clearly stated though the historian himself may never be fully aware of what all the assumptions are.

4. *The evidence needed to support or reject the hypotheses.* In scientific studies this problem does not arise beyond the fact that levels of confidence have to be set for accepting or rejecting hypotheses. In historical studies there are difficulties in establishing the amount of evidence needed to reject or confirm a hypothesis. By making such judgments in advance of the study, the research worker can prevent himself from rationalizing that a hypothesis is confirmed even though the evidence to support it is slight. Now this process of indicating the evidence required to support or reject a hypothesis can only be done to a limited extent because the historian can know only in very general terms the nature of the evidence which a search of sources may reveal.

Summary

1. The methods of historical research and those of the scientist have certain common characteristics and attempts have been made to bring together historians and social scientists to find unity among their methods.

2. Historical research attempts to provide a verbal reconstruction of man's past. Written history attempts to provide a verbal model of the past much as an equation of a physicist is a model of physical phenomena.

3. History is reconstructed from a study of documents, defined as objects on which man has left an impression. Inferences are made from these documents. Historical method deals with the problems of selecting, examining and making inferences from documents.

4. Historical research begins with the choice of a subject which may be narrowed or broadened in scope as the inquiry is pursued.

5. Sources of historical information are generally categorized as *primary* or *secondary*, according to their proximity to the event about which they are considered to be sources of information.

6. The historian is limited in the procedures he can use in validating inferences made from documents. He is unable to use the scientist's criterion of making and checking predictions of future events on the basis of the inference. To some extent he may be able to validate an inference by checking with other sources and documents. However, he must use caution in the application of this method because consistency alone is not a sufficient condition for the validity of an inference.

7. Written documents must be carefully evaluated before inferences are made from them. The historian must evaluate the authenticity of a document. He must also evaluate the standing of the writer as a transmitter of information, the extent to which the writer was trained to observe the phenomenon he describes, the relationship of the writer to the event, the extent to which there were pressures on him which might have led to distortion,

his intent, his expertness, his habits, and the legal system of the culture within which the document was produced, as well as other factors.

8. The concept of cause should be used with caution in the writing of history. The historian typically deals with chains of related events in which causal relationships are generally complex and not clearly identifiable.

9. The end stage of historical research is a synthesis of the information and inferences which have been thus derived. A synthesis of history, like the process of making historical inferences, generally makes assumptions about human nature within a framework of psychological theory. The choice of a theory of behavior is crucial to the writing of a history and should be explicitly stated.

10. Quantitative methods are slowly influencing historical studies. The main influence in this respect are the methods derived from content analysis.

11. Controversy exists whether history should be considered the study of nomothetic or ideographic phenomena.

CHAPTER 5

MEASUREMENT IN RESEARCH

Measurement and Science

IT IS difficult to conceive of a scientific approach to problems that does not involve the use of measurement. When measurement is involved, it is usual to say that *quantitative* methods are being used, as contrasted with *qualitative* methods, which do not involve the use of measurements. Quite obviously, much of importance can be learned by the use of qualitative methods, but the organized body of knowledge that is called a science seems to require measurement techniques for its development. The histories of most areas of knowledge show that in the early stages of development knowledge is acquired by qualitative methods, without resort to measurement. Such knowledge is usually lacking in precision and often hopelessly vague, but the kernel of truth that it contains opens the way to the development of progressively more precise knowledge.

Sometimes these early qualitative observations are of immense importance. For example, the observations of Freud formed the basis for the development of much of clinical psychology, although many years had to elapse before the development of measuring techniques and experimental methods permitted the systematic testing of aspects of his theories. Qualitative observations seem to be essential for the development of any branch of science, at least in its early stages, but it is ultimately careful work involving measurement that builds a science of real value. At a rudimentary level, even qualitative concepts can show some organization, as did Freud's; but the ultimate test of the validity of such concepts is whether or not they facilitate prediction. Tests of the accuracy and validity of prediction almost inevitably involve measurement.

The statement that measurement is central to the development of a science is justified more by history than by logic. Each field that has become a science has shown a dreary period of slow advance prior to the introduction of methods of measurement.

Perhaps it would be well to pause here and reflect briefly on the role that measurement has played in science. Consider, for example, the well-known studies of Gregor Mendel. He started out with the observation, familiar to most farmers, that crosses of different types of the same plant produce a new generation in which the characteristics of the parent plants may be distributed in various ways. Mendel was able to count the frequency with which each of the characteristics appeared in the offspring, and on the basis of these counts he was able to lay the foundation for a science of genetics. It is quite inconceivable that a mechanism underlying the inheritance of attributes would ever have been discovered without the use of such measurements. The crucial fact was one that involved quantity; namely, that approximately 75 per cent of the offspring of a cross between dwarf peas and tall peas were tall.

Numerous other examples could be given of the dramatic role played by measurement in the founding of other areas of science. A science of mechanics came into being when Galileo was first able to introduce a simple way of measuring the rate at which bodies fell. Much of the work that Newton had begun came to a standstill for nearly one hundred years until that great experimentalist Cavendish was able to measure the gravitational constant. Lavoisier's careful measurement of the weight of the products of combustion demonstrated that the phenomenon of burning involved a combination of a substance with a component of the air, and this in turn revolutionized chemistry. Later, the measurement of atomic weights supplied the basis for laws of the combination of the elements. Almost every major advance in science has been closely allied to the development of new methods of measuring or handling quantities.

Much the same seems to have been true in the behavioral sciences, of which research in education constitutes a part. Binet's attempts to measure intellectual power advanced immensely the possibilities of making predictions of behavior in ways that the earlier qualitative methods had been unable to do. When J. Maynard Rice first developed methods of measuring certain outcomes of the educational process, he made it possible to compare systematically one classroom procedure with another. E.L. Thorndike made it possible to exercise control over certain aspects of the curriculum by providing measures of the relative difficulty of various words, which in turn made it possible at a later stage to measure the difficulty of reading materials. Further development of evaluation techniques has made it possible to conduct research in education that simply would not have been possible fifty years ago. Even though the measurement techniques that have been introduced in education are crude, they have permitted a great expansion in our knowledge of the educational process.

Measurement involves the assignment of numbers to events according to some rule. The scale used at the post office for weighing packages assigns to a package a number that indicates its weight. The scale has been built to assign numbers to packages according to a rule prescribed by the National Bureau of Standards. A much simpler type of measurement is illustrated by the assignment of numbers to baseball players in order to label them. In the technical meaning of the term, the latter also involves measurement because it involves the assignment of numbers to objects or events according to a rule. Measurement, as the term is used in their book, is hence rather broadly defined.

Levels of Description

It used to be said, not so many years ago, that only insofar as the observer was describing specific acts was he describing behavior with any precision. Actually this is not true, for behavior can be described in a whole range of terms, from those that refer to the minutest detail to those that refer to gross total units of action. This concept is better understood by illustration. It is possible to describe behavior in terms of large units, such as, "The teacher showed the class how to carry out long division by working several simple examples on the blackboard." It is also possible to describe the same situation in terms of smaller units of behavior, such as, "The teacher (1) entered the class, (2) said, 'Good morning, children. Today we are going to learn long division,' and (3) explained the general idea of long division and why it was useful to learn it, . . ." Still further details could be given by describing the movements of each part of the teacher's body in space and in time, and by providing a record of the sound vibrations produced by her larynx. Such a detailed level of description of behavior probably could not be used because of the vast quantity of data it provides and the immense difficulty involved in handling such massive quantities of facts. On the other hand, the broad descriptions provided by observation of the gross over-all type provide too little data for the purposes of most research. All levels of description refer to behavior, and both stimuli and responses can be described in terms of a great range of complexity. What the scientist has to do is choose the level of description that will ultimately permit him to make useful predictions. This may be said in a different way, which is explained elsewhere; namely, that the scientist must choose a data language suited to his purpose.

In this connection it is common to distinguish between "molar" and "molecular" approaches to research in education. This distinction comes from the field of chemistry, where the term *molar* refers to a rather large mass of material in contrast to *molecular*, which refers to a small particle. When research in the behavioral sciences is said to be undertaken at a molar level, it means that it is concerned with gross aspects of behavior rather than with minute details. Research can involve the minute aspects of behavior, but this is not generally considered to be profitable. Hence, most educational research is molar.[1]

The choice of the proper level of description is important in all aspects of educational research. If one is concerned with school plant and facilities, it is probable that he will not be concerned with the size of the brick used, but the classroom may be a convenient unit with which to deal. Then, again, all of the buildings in a school system would probably compose much too large a unit with which to be concerned. Much the same is true of behavior. A unit of behavior must be selected that is neither too large nor too small for the particular purposes that the researcher has in mind.

If a study is being conducted in which pupils are required to read as quickly as possible words which are flashed on a screen, it is likely that the experiments will be concerned only with

[1] When Hull originally considered his molar theory of behavior, he was inclined to think that all of the response dimensions, such as speed of response, forcefulness of response, and others, would all be related and indeed positively correlated dimensions. Empirical research has shown that this is not the case. It seems far more correct to assume that measures of two response dimensions will be correlated only when they are learned (reinforced) together. The Hull theory of the interrelationship of response dimensions, which has become known as the micromolar theory, avoided the need of measuring any other than the gross consequences of behavior. Considerable question has been raised in recent years concerning the soundness of the assumptions on which it is based, and some have advocated a micromolar approach that admits the necessity of the study of behavior in greater detail and that recognizes each aspect of a gross response as a separate response in itself, to be studied in its own right. This leads into a field in which relatively little is known. Little advice can be given the student concerning the degree to which he should plan his studies on a macromolar or a micromolar level. Nevertheless it may be pointed out that, as research proceeds to a more detailed level of behavior, there is increasing difficulty in measuring the characteristics that it is desired to measure, and more and more complex laboratory instruments are needed. There are strictly experimental advantages in the study of molar behavior rather than molecular, and these exist quite apart from any theoretical advantages. From the point of view of the educator, it is molar behavior rather than molecular behavior that is of interest.

whether the words are or are not correctly read, and not with all the variations that may occur in how the word is said. The response involved in saying a particular word is an involved constellation of events, and the word may be said softly or loudly almost immediately on presentation of the stimulus word or after considerable delay; it may be spoken clearly or slurred; it may be said in a monotone voice or it may be said with fluctuations in pitch; and so forth. In addition, the reading of the word on the screen may involve a variety of processes. Sometimes the word may be recognized immediately, and sometimes its pronunciation is elucidated by means of the application of phonetic principles. In the molar approach we are not concerned with the myriad variations that may be related to the making of a particular response. It is evident that when this is done, a certain amount of information is lost.

CLASSES OF VARIABLES IN EDUCATIONAL RESEARCH

In order to test hypotheses in ways that determine whether they should be rejected or accepted, it is almost always necessary to use concepts that permit measurement. It has been found convenient to classify variables on three rather distinct bases, with which the reader should be familiar.

First, it is common to classify variables into the categories of dependent and independent variables. In experimental studies the condition that is varied is referred to as the *independent variable*. If the amount of time devoted to drill in spelling is varied in a study, then this is the *independent variable*. If the effect of drill is measured by means of a spelling test, then the score on the spelling test is referred to as the *dependent variable*. These terms have second meanings, commonly used by statisticians: the variable that is being predicted is called the *dependent variable*, while the variable from which predictions are made is called the *independent variable*.

Second, one may classify variables in terms of the phenomena to which they relate. Thus it is common to distinguish between variables related to the stimuli that impinge on the individual and those that are related to his responses.

Third, one may classify and consider variables from the point of view of their mathematical properties. While a very large literature has been written on this last type of classification, it will be touched on only briefly in this chapter because up to the present it has had only limited consequences for research methodology.

Each one of these three classifications of variables must now be considered.

DEPENDENT AND INDEPENDENT VARIABLES

Consideration must first be given the primary meaning of the distinction between these two classes of variables, which derives from experimental psychology. The experimenter, whether in education or elsewhere, varies certain conditions in order to determine how variations in these conditions produce certain consequences. In most educational experiments, the experimenter varies some condition in the environment of the child, such as some aspect of the teacher's behavior. He then seeks to determine how this affects achievement as measured by a test or some other device. The variation in the teacher's behavior is the independent variable, while the achievement score constitutes the dependent variable.

The second and broader meaning of these terms seems to have been derived from statistics rather than from any other source. In most scientific research, events are considered to occur in a time continuum, and certain events precede and are considered to be necessary antecedents of other events. The researcher usually measures certain characteristics of a situation as it exists at a particular time and tries to relate his findings in this respect to measures of previously existing conditions. It has become customary to refer to the variable to be predicted as the dependent variable, since it is viewed as being dependent on previously existing conditions.

The type of event that it is sought to predict is occasionally an all-or-none affair, such as whether a person will or will not graduate from high school, will or will not commit a crime. More often it is desired to predict some aspect of behavior that can be given a position on a continuum—as, for example, what grade a pupil will achieve in a particular course, or the liking a student will express for specific curricular materials, or the change in the absentee rate when a new building is provided. In such cases, and in most cases in educational research, the research worker desires to predict the value that a variable will assume under given conditions.

The variables that educational research is ultimately concerned with predicting are response variables, characteristics of the way in which the person responds to his environment. This may not be apparent to many educational researchers, so further comment is necessary. Much curriculum research, for example, appears to have as its main goal the development of a curriculum. The curriculum developed exists only because the researcher believes it will have a better effect on the child's behavior than other existing curricula. In a similar way, research on problems of school plant are justified only because it is believed that the type of plant provided affects the behavior of pupils. Much research is based on the assumption that certain educational events affect behavior, and ultimately such assumptions must be tested even though this cannot be done at the present time.

The variables that are used for making predictions are commonly referred to as the independent variables of research. It is not the nature of the variables that makes them dependent or independent but the way in which they are used. Indeed, it frequently happens that the dependent variables in one study become the independent variables of another study.

In a study of predicting reading skill resulting from training in a foreign language, a measure of skill at the end of the period of training would probably be the dependent variable. The independent variables would be chosen according to the nature of the inquiry. They might include various aspects of the way in which teaching could be varied and aptitude tests given prior to training. The independent variables might also include earlier conditions related to the ability to learn the particular language, such as exposure to related languages in childhood. They might also refer to such matters as the rewards, incentives, or reinforcements provided by the learning situation, or to any other condition related to the learning process.

The dependent variables of educational research, which ultimately are response variables, may refer to the frequency with which certain types of behavior occur or to qualities of behavior in particular situations. Often they represent verbal behavior, which, in a civilized society, is one of the more important aspects of behavior. The ways in which response variables are derived from the vast number of events that constitute the flow of behavior are discussed elsewhere in this book. It is sufficient to say at this point that many unsolved problems are involved.

The ultimate purpose of a science is to permit both the prediction and the control of events. Some sciences must be content with only the prediction of events, as is the case of astronomy, where control appears to present insuperable difficulties. The educational researcher is relatively fortunate in this respect, because not only can he expect to be able to predict events—such as who will succeed in college—but also he can aspire to exercise control over events—as when he seeks to develop a curriculum that will achieve a particular goal with maximum efficiency. At the present time, it is probable that the educational researcher knows much more about predicting events than he does about controlling the educational process to achieve particular ends. Prediction alone fulfills an extremely important function in education, and the capacity provided by research to do this has had a very important influence on educational practice. If it is possible to predict who will succeed in medical school and who will not, it may then be possible to prevent many from experiencing the frustrations of failure. If it is possible to predict who will become delinquent unless remedial action is taken, there is a possibility of making a radical change in certain aspects of our culture. If one could predict which students of education will become highly neurotic, if not psychotic, teachers, a major problem of educational administration would be solved.

While prediction performs an extremely important function in education, an even greater contribution could be made by educational research if it could tell the educator how to arrange conditions in order to produce specific results. Some progress has been achieved in this direction. A little is known about the types of classroom conditions that are effective for particular purposes. Some knowledge is available about the effects of particular types of classroom organization. But knowledge concerning the control of educational conditions is still fragmentary because it is hard to acquire. The reader will note, in subsequent chapters, that it is generally much easier to conduct studies that lead to prediction than to conduct those that lead to control.

The conditions which produce effective learning in one pupil will not necessarily produce effective learning in another. When it is said that the function of the educational research worker is to discover the conditions related to effective learning, it is assumed that these will be such that they can be modified as required by individual differences. The fact that children come to the classroom from different backgrounds and with different abilities results in their responding to the learning situation in different ways. Our knowledge of conditions related to effective learning should make us flexible in prescribing for particular pupils; it does not imply any rigidity of educational practice. In addition, teachers vary in the conditions they themselves are capable of producing. For example, some who may be otherwise capable are unable to generate a warm, friendly atmosphere. Such teachers will probably have to use somewhat different teaching techniques from those of teachers who have sympathetic dispositions. All such differences among persons, whether pupils, teachers, or others, must be included among the variables with which educational research is concerned.

STIMULUS, RESPONSE, AND INTERVENING VARIABLES

Stimulus Variables

An important classification of variables that has had great influence on the language of current theories of behavior is that of stimulus variables, response variables, and intervening variables. Twenty years ago this classification could have been glossed over in a few lines and summarily dismissed, but its current importance is such that it cannot be treated so briefly today. Over the years it has become necessary to specify with increasing precision what is meant by these classes, and although full agreement has not been reached, it is important that tentative definitions be given here.

The first class of variables that we must consider here is the stimulus variable. The term *stimulus*, or the corresponding quantitative term *stimulus variable*, we now recognize does not define a clear-cut class of phenomena, as it was once thought to do. The best analysis that the author has yet come across concerning the varied senses of the term is supplied by Verplanck (in Estes *et al.* 1954), who distinguishes four usages.

Usage I. In this usage, the term refers to a part of the environment or to a change in the environment. In this meaning, a stimulus is considered to be a stimulus even though it has no observable effect on the organism. Since most psychologists are interested mainly in those aspects of the environment that affect behavior, this meaning of the term includes a wider range of phenomena than is usually needed.

Usage II. This is the usage most commonly found in textbooks of physiology and in most general textbooks on psychology. It refers to any form of energy that produces a response in the receptors. What constitutes a response is often a moot question, for it is also common for psychologists to refer to subthreshold stimuli, which individually may not produce a response but which collectively do. Thus a light of low intensity may not produce a retinal response when it is of one millisecond's duration, but five similar successive one-millisecond flashes may do so. The distinction between forms of energy that produce a response and forms that do not is far from being as clear cut as it is presented to be in elementary texts.

Usage III. This is the usage implicit in most educational research. In this sense, which is also accepted by B.F. Skinner in studies of animal learning, a stimulus is not considered as such until the subject manifests an observable behavioral response to it. Thus a black square on a white background is not regarded as a stimulus in many rat studies until the animal has learned to respond to it in some way, as by moving a lever or pushing the square back so as to gain access to a food box. In a similar way, one would not usually refer to a chart on a wall as a stimulus if the children never showed any evidence of responding to it. A stimulus variable in this sense of the term would be described as *response-inferred.* This is an undesirable property in many ways, since the stimulus is inferred to be a stimulus through a rather remote chain of events. Many psychologists believe that a rigorous science of behavior would not include such remotely inferred classes of events.

Usage IV. In this usage, the stimulus is identified as in Class II with a physical event, but the event may occur within the organism. Sensations arising within the muscles would be identified with stimuli in this category. In the latter case, the physical event is not as easily identified as it would be were it Class II; it is only inferred to exist from behavior. Until the event which functions as a stimulus is actually identified, it must be considered hypothetical—that is to say, an unobservable event postulated to account for observed behavior.

In listing these different ways in which the term *stimulus* is used, Verplanck states that it is most unfortunate that a single word should be used to refer to all of these phenomena. It should be noted that only in the case of the first two of these usages does the term refer to a class of environmental variables that the experimenter can vary. The researcher should be aware of this fact, and when he himself refers to a stimulus or a stimulus variable, he should know which one of the various usages he has in mind. He should not perpetuate the confusion that has existed in the use of the term *stimulus*.

The definition that we prefer to accept at this time is the first one given by Verplanck, except that in educational research we are concerned with only those environmental conditions that may be *hypothesized* to effect behavior.

Examples of Stimulus Variables in Educational Research

Any measurable aspect of the pupil's environment that in some way may be expected to affect his behavior is considered here to be a stimulus variable. These aspects include not only the characteristics of the buildings, textbooks, visual aids, and other features of the physical environment, but also the behavior of teachers, counselors, parents, principals, and others with whom the person seeking education comes into contact. So far, relatively little effort has been devoted to the isolation and measurement of stimulus variables related to the educational environment, but a few may be mentioned by way of illustration. A first example is presented by measures of reading difficulty such as those provided by the Lorge index or the Flesch index. These measure an important property of printed verbal material.

A second example is found in measures of the amount of behavior in various categories emitted by the teacher. For example, Wallen *et al.* (1961) systematically recorded samples of verbal behavior emitted by teachers during the pursuit of their classroom duties. These statements were later classified in order to obtain measures of various aspects of the teaching performance. One of the categories used in the classification scheme was *controlling behavior*. The measure of controlling behavior was the number of controlling statements made by the teacher in the sample of verbal behavior studied. Such a measure represents one characteristic of the environment of the child exposed to the particular teacher.

Relatively little is known about the relevance of physical aspects of the surroundings of the child, and most relevant stimulus dimensions that have been defined refer to the behavior of persons with whom he comes into contact. It is hardly surprising that this is so, since the major influences in a person's life result from contacts with other persons rather than from contact with physical events as such. This may be due to a very great extent to the fact that educators have not yet learned how to arrange physical conditions to maximum advantage. Recent studies in the teaching of foreign languages have shown that much is to be gained by isolating students in booths where they are instructed by tape recorders. In this learning situation, not only is the student isolated from distracting stimuli, but also it is possible for him to repeat parts of the lesson on the tape recorder as many times as he wishes. While research in the past has emphasized the importance of the role of the teacher and the resulting interpersonal relations, educational research may become more and more preoccupied with the physical conditions related to learning.

Many studies of classroom learning are concerned with a whole range of stimulus variables represented by conditions other than teacher behavior. Of particular interest at the present time are so-called visual and auditory aids, which are extensively used although there is little evidence to justify their use.

The growth of the use of visual and auditory aids unfortunately has been influenced by factors other than those derived from rational planning. Since visual aids are an easily observable but probably superficial aspect of the classroom environment, there is always a temptation for the teacher to cover the walls of the room with charts and other devices, for these may be the basis on which parents, school board members, and even supervisors may judge the merit of the teacher's performance. While this basis for judging a classroom is seen frequently enough in civilian schools, it is probably the most common way of judging teaching effectiveness in military establishments, where the in-

spection system is such that major emphasis is placed on superficial detail. This emphasis on the importance of what can be
easily observed has stimulated not only the worst features of the
current use of visual aids but also some of the best features.

Research on the use of visual and auditory aids has had a long
history. Slide projectors came in for their quota of educational
research forty or more years ago. In the early Thirties substantial research was undertaken on the use of the film as a teaching
device. Some of this research was undertaken by well-known
scientists, among them L.L. Thurstone of the University of Chicago who conducted extensive studies of the use of the moving
picture for the changing of attitudes. The use of sound pictures
by the armed services for training purposes also stimulated substantial research within the military establishment.

Additional impetus was given to research on the new educational media provided by an advanced technology by the arrival
of Sputnik and the resulting frantic efforts to improve our educational system. Soon after the Russian satellite made its spectacular
orbit of the earth, Congress appropriated funds to make it possible for the U.S. Office of Education to undertake research on
new media through which education might be expanded and en-
riched. Despite the extensive efforts that have been devoted to
the exploration of movies, film strips, television, tape recorders,
kinescopes, and so forth, the knowledge so far achieved concerning the value of these items of equipment for improving
and extending education has been rather meager, but perhaps
too much may have been expected in the first place. Some of
the reasons for the small return in knowledge for extensive effort
may be considered briefly.

First, there is the fact that visual and auditory aids to learning
have not generally been introduced as a part of a systematic
learning program. The use of such equipment is often justified
by some vague hope that it may liven up the learning situation.
This fact immediately brings into focus a major difficulty encountered in research in this area. For example, during World
War II, a series of films was developed entitled *Why We Fight*.
Considerable efforts were made by psychologists to evaluate

these films as devices for producing attitude change, but it was soon found that the films had not been made with clear purposes in mind, and that, as a result, they seemed to contribute to the development of a whole series of rather independent attitudes.

Second, it is suspected that most visual aids do not present a sufficiently extended experience to produce either measurable changes or changes of any great permanence. The author's opinion is that unless a whole program of visual aids is directed towards a specific goal, little is likely to be achieved and no measurable changes in level of achievement will occur.

Third, most visual aids are not related to the learning process in a theoretically sound way. Often they are only knick-knacks designed to enliven the classroom in some manner, as if such enlivenment would necessarily have any effect on the course of learning. The same mistaken notion is that an irrelevant joke somehow makes the circumstances of learning more congenial. A joke in the classroom is often just a substitute for effective teacher behavior. In the case of many visual aids, one suspects that the student remembers the gimmick but not the point the gimmick is designed to illustrate. One may remember a cute gadget while forgetting the meaning it was supposed to convey. This is a matter that could well be investigated.

Fourth, a related difficulty in the planned use of various devices is that only limited knowledge is available concerning the advantages of feeding information through several sensory channels rather than through one. Some research indicates that there are advantages in utilizing one sensory channel at a time. There is also some information that the attempted transmission of information through more than one sensory channel may produce a jam in knowledge intake. Certainly the human organism can very easily become disorganized when excessive information simultaneously pours in through several sensory channels. These are matters requiring experimentation and study so that learning situations can be developed which will provide the maximum of information input with the minimum of overloading and disorganization.

Fifth, some of the indirect effects of some of the stimuli in the learning situation need to be studied. One of these is the possibility that they may sometimes increase the effectiveness of learning, not by providing information in a more effective way, but by raising the level of arousal or excitement of the learner.

Visual and auditory aids have been considered as manipulable aspects of the pupil's environment. In this sense, the total curriculum may be considered an extended program of this type, since the visual and auditory senses are the main channels through which curricular materials have an impact on behavior. In view of what has been said, the best possibility of obtaining differences in pupil behavior as a result of differences in educational treatment would be when two matched groups of students are exposed to fundamentally different curricula. However, there are difficulties in this approach, which need brief consideration.

First, there is the difficulty of locating curricula that differ in any fundamental and permeating respects. Social pressures are such that most curricula contain a common core of material required by society if not by school boards. Few bodies that control education permit much deviation from the social norm in the design of curricula.

Second, it is often difficult to determine just how curricula do differ. We must not be fooled by names and assume that, just because they differ in name (as do the so-called traditional and progressive curricula), they differ in significant stimulus characteristics as far as the pupil is concerned. The results of much research on curricula in the past have had little validity because the differences in curricula have been differences only in name. What are needed are measures of various properties of the curricula. This is feasible in many cases; for example, when measurements are made of the amount of time spent in various activities such as lectures by the teacher, class recitations, group activity, individual study, and so forth. The main difficulty in obtaining such measures is that of observing classrooms without altering the process that is observed. One suspects that, if obervation is sufficiently prolonged and is extended over a period of more than a week, the teacher and class will become accustomed to the presence of an observer and will show a typical pattern of behavior.

The difficulty of quantifying differences between curricula stems partly from the fact that quantification must depend partly, if not largely, on judgment. Detailed analysis of recordings of what happens in the classroom is not a feasible venture because of the vast amount of material that it entails. Although it is possible to obtain rough quantitative estimates of the time spent by the teacher in lecturing, in conducting recitations, and the like, it is not easy to qualify by present methods the time spent by the teacher in imparting information, in asking questions, and in correcting pupil's products; hence these must usually be estimated by the observer and the results of the estimations recorded on a rating sheet.

In summary, while a science of education requires that measures of important characteristics of the environment believed to have relevance to the educational process should be available, there are as yet few aspects that can be measured satisfactorily. At least a part of this difficulty stems from the fact that most other branches of the behavioral sciences have devoted little of their effort toward the measurement of environmental conditions related to behavior.

Response Variables

The ultimate purposes of education are defined in terms of desirable ways of responding to life situations. It is clearly not enough for the educator just to believe that he has produced certain internal changes in those who have passed through his educational program. It is generally conceded that the success of any educational program lies in its effect on behavior in those situations that the program has been designed to help the pupil face. If a program has among its objectives that of developing a critical attitude toward political propaganda, it is a failure unless in later years the person who has passed through that program shows through his behavior a critical attitude toward political propaganda. It is always through responses that the success or failure of an educational program can be established.

The common approach to the measurement of the way in which a person responds to his environment is best understood if we turn to some of the classroom responses that are commonly accepted as evidence of achievement. A useful illustration is provided by the teaching of reading, in which it is common in the early stages to build up a recognition of fifty to one hundred everyday words. The pupil becomes able to recognize these words although he has no knowledge of phonetics, and this recognition enables him, with a little help, to read simple books designed around them. The pupil's recognition ability for these words can be measured in terms of the number he recognizes and speaks correctly. His learning in this respect is measured in terms of the frequency with which he makes a correct response in a standardized situation. Frequency of response is one of the commonest types of response variables that the educator is likely to encounter. Many personality variables are measured in terms of frequency of occurrence of a particular response. Frequency of occurrence of a particular class of behavior is used as a major method of measuring response characteristics. Not only may we measure the progress of learning in the case of a rat that is acquiring the skill of running a maze by determining the frequency of occurrence of errors (wrong turnings), but similar techniques may be applied to charting the course of learning of the pupil. Aspects of the pupil's personality development may be measured by counting the number of antisocial acts shown toward other pupils, or the number of acts of hostility shown toward the teacher. Frequency of occurrence of many kinds of maladjustment is often used by counselors as an important item of information to be used in helping the pupil.

While frequency of response is a very common measure used both by the practicing teacher and the research worker, there are other response characteristics that are also commonly recorded. Latency of response or speed of response is often measured for the appraisal of certain skills. For example, the level of skill achieved in typing and shorthand is commonly measured by determining the speed with which the pupil can perform the skill. This amounts to measuring the speed of response to either the words on the page from which typed copy is being prepared or the spoken words which are being taken down in shorthand. In some cases the vigor of response may be measured as in the case of a speech teacher who watches her pupils give speeches ín almost inaudible timid tones at the beginning of the year but six months later hears them holding forth in a vigorous and dynamic manner. The athletics coach also attempts to develop vigor of response, among other characteristics.

Sometimes the response variable involved in educational research is a scale value assigned to a response. Frequency measures of particular events, such as the frequency of saying "No!" or the frequency of physical aggression, are easily understood. More difficult to understand are measures derived from scaled systems of events. The scale value of a particular event is a more complex concept. It may be illustrated by studies of racial attitudes, in which persons are required to respond to some situation involving a member of another racial group. The response may vary from positive and friendly to negative and hostile. The response may be assigned by one of a number of procedures to a position on a numerical scale that varies between the extremes. Another example of a scaled response is the response to a vocabulary test as measured by the total score. Such a test presents a series of words of graded difficulty, and the person taking it may be expected to define correctly all of the words up to a certain point but none beyond that point. The point where passing an item changes to failing an item can represent the number answered correctly and also the position on the scale that represents the maximum level of difficulty of the words that are successfully defined. Here again various methods may be used for assigning scale values. However, it should be noted that the vocabulary test described here represents an idealized situation that is unlikely to be duplicated in actual practice. What happens in a well-constructed vocabulary test is that, although there is not a completely sharp break between the point of passing and the point of failing all items, there is a limited zone within which this break occurs in a rather irregular fashion. Scaling is approximate rather than precise in such a situation. Behavior theory development, insofar as it has been attempted on a rigorous basis, has been concerned with response-frequency measures or their correlative response-probability measures.

In research in education there are many frequency-of-response variables of great significance. In the early stages of reading, the frequency with which particular words are recognized represents an important class of variables. Frequency of errors in written compositions in English or in foreign languages is one of the commonest variables measured by teachers in those areas. They are not concerned with the level of seriousness of these errors, but with the number of times they occur within a given range of opportunity. Computational errors are also of this type. The arithmetical operation 9×9 is performed perhaps one hundred times by a child, and on 95 per cent of the occasions he performs the operation correctly, but from time to time, even though the response is highly overlearned, an error occurs. One might say that the probability of a correct response in such a case is 0.95. In other children the correct response probability is perhaps 0.75 or 0.42. There are differences at any given time in the response probability for groups with exposure to equal amounts of training. In practice, we are likely to be interested in predicting a sum of such response probabilities, as when we administer a test of one hundred simple computational problems from the multiplication tables and count the number of errors that are made. In measuring computational skill, this procedure is more likely to be adopted than is the procedure involved in preparing a set of problems of graded difficulty—which, in this case, would be problems graded in terms of complexity.

In the case of response variables, great difficulties are also encountered in establishing scales in which the units can be considered to be equal in any way. Attempts have been made to scale responses in various ways so that the resulting scale can be considered to consist of equal units, but objections can be raised to all of these systems. Many psychologists would accept the viewpoint expressed by Alfred Binet that, in the measurement of responses, all one can do is to rank individuals and that true scaling is rarely if ever possible in this domain. This problem will be discussed at greater length later in this chapter.

Intervening Variables

A few psychologists have taken the view that a science of behavior can be built simply by studying the relationship of stimulus variables to response variables. Such psychologists assume that response variables are direct functions of stimulus variables. If this were the case, education would simply be a matter of arranging and scheduling stimuli so that the desired responses would be elicited. On this basis, a theory that accounted for behavior in the early stages of learning to read might perhaps consist of two postulates, worded as follows:

Postulate I: The probability that a correct response will be made in recognizing a word is directly related to the number of times the correct response has already been made.

Postulate II: The probability that a correct response will be made on a specific occasion in recognizing a word is inversely proportional to the time elapsing between practicing the response and measuring the probability of its occurrence.

This miniature theory, which covers the early stages of learning in which facility is acquired in the recognition of common words, is really a practice-makes-perfect type of theory. It states in a straight-forward manner that the ability to recognize words is simply a function of practice. Every schoolteacher in the first and second grade can testify to the inadequacy of such a theory and can show why it is wrong. Pupil after pupil in the first grade shows no improvement at all in recognizing words, even though extensive practice is given. The simple deduction from the theory that the child who has to build up a recognition vocabulary simply needs more practice to remedy the deficiency is a deduction that is just not in accordance with the facts.[2] Some pupils in the first grade are not capable of reading, hence a theory of reading that has at least minimum adequacy must include the concept of capability, an internal condition that is not directly observable and that accounts for individual differences in the responses of children to equal amounts of word-recognition practice.

Even in the simplest cases, it is not possible to describe events merely in terms of the relationship between stimulating conditions and responses. Consider, for example, the case of the eyelid reflex produced by a slight puff of air on the cornea. If the puff is very light, the response may or may not occur, depending on the condition of the individual. Responsiveness varies according to internal conditions such as fatigue, attentiveness, the degree to which certain chemicals are present, and so forth. In the case of more complex behavior, the intervening conditions cannot be identified with any known chemical condition or identifiable neural structure. The intervening conditions that must be postulated therefore are said to be hypothetical. Whatever varies when these intervening conditions are varied is referred to as an *intervening variable*.[3]

Intervening variables have been described as hidden variables. In more technical terms, they can be said to have transcendental

[2] If the theory were to be used for any other purpose than to illustrate a few points in the immediate discussion, it would be necessary to define the terms used in some detail. Terms such as *response probability* and *practicing a response* would need careful definition if the theory were to be used as a basis of research. The theory is used here only to illustrate the absurdity of one that uses only response variables and stimulus variables.

[3] The terms *intervening variable* and *hypothetical construct* (or *construct*) are used by many writers almost interchangeably. At one time an attempt was made by Meehl and MacCorquodale (1948) to draw a clear distinction between these two concepts, but objections were raised to the distinction they proposed. The suggested distinction was that a *hypothetical construct* involved ideas over and above those included in an *intervening variable*. Much of what is referred to as a hypothetical construct in current psychological theory represents mechanisms that are postulated to mediate between stimulus and response. These mechanisms are not observable and should really be considered as imaginary mechanisms. The utility of such devices for guiding the thoughts of the scientist will depend on the extent to which they lead to variables that have predictive value.

properties, in that they represent conditions that transcend experience and cannot be observed directly. Aptitude for reading or reading readiness is not a property that can be observed with any directness in a child. All that can be observed are the results of this variable as they are manifested in the task of learning to read.

The reader should be warned against the introduction of intervening variables by circular argument. The fact that children differ in the rates at which they learn to read is not a sufficient basis for inferring a variable referred to as reading aptitude. It helps little to postulate the existence of an intervening variable and then to use this variable to explain the differences on the basis of which it was postulated. Such circularity serves little purpose. On the other hand, if it can be shown that equal conditions of learning still result in individual differences in reading skill, the investigator is on rather firmer ground in postulating such a variable. Indeed, some variable must be postulated to account for the lack of relationship between the stimulus variable and the response variable. The theory would be on still firmer ground if it could be established that a variable measured by a certain specific test (other than a reading test) could be used as if it were a measure of this aptitude. If, for example, a measure of physiological maturity were to account for individual differences in reading skill after exposure to equal training conditions, it might be said that this variable operated as the intervening variable that must be introduced to account for reading behavior.

Intervening variables may refer to a wide range of conditions. Sometimes they may have a clear relationship to tissue functions, as when a condition of hunger is produced by food deprivations over a period of hours. Studies of changes in behavior in pupils at various stages of food deprivation have been conducted which have shown that behavior changes as food deprivation is increased. The condition of deprivation may be considered to be a measure of an intervening variable in such experiments. An experimenter might, for convenience, refer to the condition of food deprivation as a condition of hunger, but by doing this he is likely to confuse the issue. While children deprived of food for a period of four hours might refer to themselves as "hungry," it is quite possible that the vague inner state of discomfort of which they were aware might be of only minor importance in modifying behavior in comparison with the effects of deprivation of which they were not aware. For this reason, the wise experimenter would do well to refer to this variable as "deprivation" rather than "hunger." He would also do well to measure deprivation by the number of hours without food rather than by any subjective estimation of hunger.

By the example given, it is not suggested that research on food deprivation in children is likely to be particularly profitable. It is merely a convenient example of an intervening variable that illustrates many of the problems of defining such variables.

A major class of intervening variables is the so-called aptitude variables. These are presumed to measure conditions that facilitate learning, and there is substantial evidence that many of them measure facilitations produced by previous learning. It is possible that some measure rather permanent conditions in the nervous system, which have been influenced only to a small degree by learning. Relatively little is known at this time about the generation of these variables, but the fact that they can be measured and that these measures have predictive value have given them a position of the greatest importance in educational research. One of the rather surprising facts about this class of variables is that relatively few aptitudes that have definite predictive value in learning situations have been discovered.

Motives also represent intervening variables, and they also represent variables that are commonly but erroneously postulated on the basis of direct observation of behavior. Strictly speaking, motives are unobservable. If two persons perform the same task but at different rates, there is no value in stating that the one is better motivated than the other, for by this is meant only that the one worked more rapidly than the other. A beginning has been made in the measurement of motives by independent techniques, and also a beginning has been made in a useful classification of human motives. At one time it was thought that interests might constitute powerful measures of human motivation, but these promises have not been fulfilled. Many variables that we have considered here as stimulus variables may be treated as intervening variables. For example, we have treated variations in training as stimulus variables in this chapter. We could have viewed them as external conditions that generate internal conditions, which in turn operate as intervening variables in an actual reading situation. When the child is tested for his ability to recognize words, the printed words are the stimuli, what he says when they are presented constitutes the responses, and internal conditions—some generated by previous training and others by complex conditions including heredity —represent the factors that produce intervening variables. The latter is just a different way of viewing the situation, and it may be just as satisfactory a way as that discussed.

CLASSIFICATION OF VARIABLES IN TERMS OF THEIR MATHEMATICAL PROPERTIES

Students of psychometrics have emphasized the importance of the mathematical properties of psychological measuring devices, because these properties determine the operations that can and cannot be performed legitimately with measures derived from them. The classification given by S.S. Stevens (1946) will be outlined here. Modifications of this system by Coombs (1953) add the concept of a partially ordered scale, which will be mentioned.

At the least powerful level of measurement is the *nominal scale,* which is simply a system of assigning number symbols to events in order to label them. The usual example of this is the assignment of numbers to baseball players in order to identify them. If these players were arranged in order of the numbers on their shirts, the order would have no meaning. Thus the numbers cannot be considered to be associated with an ordered scale, for their order is of no consequence. In educational research, it is quite common to identify events by numbers. All hostile gestures of the teacher may be recorded by placing a check mark against the number 11, while words of praise administered by the teacher are indicated by checks against the number 15. The numbers are just convenient labels for the particular class of events. In these scales, the numbers refer to events that cannot meaningfully be placed in some order.

The lowest level of the *ordered scale* that is commonly used or discussed is the ordinal scale.[4] The *ordinal scale* places events in order, but there is no attempt to make the intervals of the scale equal in terms of some rule. *Rank orders* represent ordinal scales and are the commonest used in educational research.

Stevens distinguishes two types of scales in which the intervals can be said to be equal in some way. These are *interval scales* and *ratio scales*.[5]

In the case of the interval scale, the intervals are adjusted in terms of some rule that has been established as a basis for making the units equal. The units are equal only insofar as one accepts the assumptions on which the rule is based. For example, in psychophysics it is common to accept as a unit the smallest difference that can be perceived. This unit is referred to as the *differential threshold*. Interval scales may have an arbitrary zero, but it is not possible to determine for them what may be called an absolute zero.

Ratio scales do have an absolute zero of measurement. The term *absolute zero* is not as precise as it was once believed to be. We can conceive of an absolute zero of length, and similarly we can conceive of an absolute zero of velocity. One object would have an absolute zero of velocity with respect to another when the distance between the two objects remained constant. Nevertheless, an absolute zero of temperature is theoretically unobtainable, and it remains a concept existing only in the

---

[4] Coombs introduces an intermediate category, *partially ordered scales*, in order to cover certain psychometric measuring devices that fall between nominal scales and ordered scales.

[5] Coombs also distinguishes *ordered metric scales*, which might be considered as a class between ordinal scales and interval scales.

scientist's mind. One could also change the present system used to number calendar years so that the zero on the scale would not approximate the birth of Jesus but would approximate the beginning of the universe (based perhaps on an expanding monoblock theory). Many assumptions would have to be made in establishing such a system for numbering years, and such assumptions would be more tenuous than those involved in the establishment of a zero of temperature. By means of even less acceptable assumptions, it would be possible to establish a scale of intelligence that would have an absolute zero *if the assumptions were accepted,* but there would be many who would balk at the assumptions. Indeed, so many would reject them that the enterprise would not be considered worth while. It is of interest to note that E.L. Thorndike suggested at one time the establishment of a scale of intelligence that would have something approximating an absolute zero.

This discussion serves to point out that an absolute zero, for the most part, is a concept rather than a reality. Whether an absolute zero on a scale that claims to have one is accepted as such depends on the general acceptability of this concept to those who might use it. The actual existence of such a zero is not always demonstrable, nor is it necessarily some directly observable condition.

While measurement involves the assignment of numbers to events, when these numbers can be considered to represent a scale, then it is clear that the events have some order. Thus the scientist who selects events that have these properties has thereby succeeded in perceiving some order in the general domain that he is studying. Measurement may thus in itself be an ordering process, and it is this kind of ordering that in the past has been particularly effective in enabling man to exercise some control over his environment.

At the highest levels of measurement, it is also possible to perform certain arithmetical operations with the measures, such as addition, subtraction, multiplication, and division. However, it is obvious that, in the case of scales that have no absolute zero, one measure cannot be multiplied by two in order to obtain a measure indicating a quantity twice as great.

One cannot justify performing any arithmetical operations with most of the scales of measurement used by the psychologist. One cannot assume that a mental age of eight years on the Binet type of scale represents a level of intelligence twice as great as that represented by a mental age of four years. It is also unreasonable to say that a standard score of 60 on a standardized achievement test represents twice as much knowledge as a standard score of 30. It is just not possible to make such direct arithmetical comparisons between scores on most tests that are available today.

Some Problems of Scaling

Certain aspects of scaling that have not ordinarily been considered in the past have appreciable consequence for educational research. Attention was first drawn to this matter by Lloyd G. Humphreys (1956) in an address to the annual testing conference sponsored by the Educational Testing Service. He pointed out that Cattell many years previously had noted that scales could be divided into two categories, *normative* and *ipsative*.[6]

Normative scales are represented by intelligence tests and tests of achievement, and generally by tests in which a scale consists of a distinct set of items where the total score represents some function of the number of correct and incorrect answers. Scores on normative scales are usually interpreted with respect to the performance of persons collectively described as a norm group. On a set of normative scales such as are represented by an achievement test battery, a person may have all high scores or all low scores, and we are interested in considering each score separately and independently of all other scores.

In contrast, *ipsative scales* are illustrated by those derived from the *Study of Values*. This instrument attempts to provide measures of the extent to which each of six values influences a person's life. These six value systems are the economic, the religious, the social, the scientific, the political, and the aesthetic. The test is

[6] C.H. Coombs had drawn a similar distinction between relative and irrelative measurement.

set up so that the person taking it must express a number of preferences for one or the other of these values. Where he is asked to make a choice between a decision based on religious values and a choice based on economic values, he must choose one or the other; he cannot choose both. The result is that if he tends to choose religious values, scores on the other values tend to be depressed. The scores are derived in such a way that the average scores on all scales are the same for all persons. A person scoring high on some scales must necessarily be low on others. The scores can thus be used for ranking the values for a single person. They compare the strength of one value with another *within that person.* They do not permit comparisons of one individual with another. This fact has certain important consequences when these scores are correlated with other variables that it may be desired to predict—this is a particularly significant point to notice when tests of interest are used in an attempt to predict performance in some activity. Since many tests of interest employ ipsative scales, it is as well to remember that in predicting performance with such tests we are correlating ipsative scales with normative scales, such as class grades, or with other measures of achievement.

When ipsative scales are used, they should be used for predicting ipsative characteristics. A test designed to provide ipsative measures of interest in school subjects should be used for predicting an ipsative criterion, such as the rank order of the success achieved by pupils in these subjects. The rankings on the interest scales and the rankings on the achievement scales would be compared for each person included in the study. It is possible that the interest rankings might predict the achievement rankings for some persons and not for others.

Another aspect of scaling that has particular importance for educational research is the difference between altitude and breadth. The distinction is important in building achievement tests, and it can be explained fairly easily in terms of the problem of building an achievement test in American history to be given to college freshmen. Such a test might call for information concerning the major facts of American history from the days of the early settlers up to modern times. It would not call for any of the more obscure facts of history but would measure the breadth of a person's knowledge of the important facts.

A different test in American history could also be made covering the same period. The latter could be divided into sections, such as the Colonial Period, the Revolutionary Period, and so on. Within each of these periods, questions could vary from those that call for commonly known facts to those that pertain to relatively obscure events. A person answering the questions within any one of these sections would tend to answer questions up to a certain point, failing items beyond that point. Such a test would measure something different from breadth of information; what it measures might perhaps be termed "altitude."

Oddly enough, those who construct tests do not seem to be too concerned over whether they are measuring breadth or altitude. Usually no mention is made of this in test manuals, and it is necessary to examine the test in order to determine whether the emphasis is on the one or on the other. As a result, relatively little is known about the relationship of breadth scores to altitude scores.

Does the Research Worker Predict Behavior?

An ambiguity commonly occurs in referring to behavioral measurement. Current usage is to say that we measure behavior. What in actual fact we do measure is *some property of behavior*. When the researcher states that he is measuring the behavior of the teacher in the classroom, he is really measuring only certain properties of behavior. To state that the behavior of the teacher is being measured carries with it the implication that the measurement supplies a complete description of behavior. In actual fact, the researcher is likely to measure, and that only rather roughly, certain limited aspects of behavior. From the measures themselves, it is possible to reconstruct to only a very limited degree what happened at the time the measurement was made. We are never likely to be able to perform the literal function of predicting teacher behavior in the classroom. Nevertheless, this should not discourage us, for what is important is to predict, not teacher behavior as a whole, but those aspects of it that have some crucial effect on pupil behavior.

Even if it were possible to predict accurately every aspect of teacher behavior, there would be no particular purpose in doing so. Much of what can be observed represents a great range and variety of events that have little bearing on what is accomplished. A teacher who is restless and moves around the classroom may be displaying merely the consequences of a long period of sedentary work. The activity may function only as a means of restoring the circulation in the muscles of the legs. It is clearly a phase of behavior that there appears to be no particular use in predicting. The same is true of pupil behavior. We are not concerned with predicting the numerous isolated actions that the pupil may perform after he leaves school, for most of these are specific responses to incidental situations and have only immediate consequences. On the other hand, we are very much concerned with the prediction of trends in behavior and characteristics of behavior that appear in a wide range of situations.

An analogy that has been commonly used in discussing this problem is that of transmitting information over a circuit. In any circuit, a fraction of the energy transmitted is relevant to the transmission of the information; the remainder represents unorganized and irrelevant energies introduced into the circuit by unknown and uncontrolled sources. The latter unwanted source of energy is commonly referred to as "noise." In a good circuit, the energy changes are mainly signal energy changes and the noise energy is reduced to a minimum. In the analogy under discussion, the signal energy is compared with the aspect of behavior that it is desired to measure, while the noise represents the stream of minor behavioral events that have no consequence insofar as the building of a science of behavior is concerned. As a matter of fact, this has been used as a basis for a general theory of behavior developed by Miller and his associates (1955). Their theory is much more comprehensive and, as it is said, global than any type of theory that the author would recommend as a basis for research, but it is of interest to note the possibilities that communication theory has as an analogy to behavior. Also, it may be mentioned that workers in fairly specific research areas have used the communication theory analogy and have built miniature theoretical systems on this basis.

Summary

1. The development of most sciences has usually been accompanied by the introduction of quantitative methods.

2. The scientist must decide the extent to which he is to study details or gross events. He chooses a level of detail that is convenient and appropriate. In educational research it is molar behavior that is likely to be examined.

3. It has become customary to refer to the variable that is predicted as the *dependent variable* and the variable that is manipulated or used for making predictions as the *independent variable*.

4. Variables that are predicted in educational research are usually responses to the environment—either the frequency with which certain responses occur or the characteristics of the responses.

5. A stimulus is defined, for the purposes of this volume, as a condition existing in the environment, which is hypothesized to produce a response in an individual. Educational research restricts its interest to those environmental conditions that are hypothesized to affect behavior. Studies in the field of curriculum are studies of environmental conditions and their relationship to the learning process. Studies of visual aids are studies of the manipulation of stimulus conditions.

6. Studies of visual aids present certain difficulties that are likely to interfere with positive findings. The main difficulty in such studies is that they are concerned with very limited aspects of the learning process.

7. Differences produced in learning by differences in curricula are more likely to produce positive findings than are studies of the effect of specific learning devices. However, curriculum stud-

ies are difficult to undertake, and differences between curricula are difficult to measure.

8. The central difficulty in the conduct of curriculum studies, apart from administrative difficulties, is the measurement of differences between curricula. Curricula may differ in rather complex ways, and their characteristics cannot usually be measured in a simple manner.

9. The child's and the adult's responses to his environment are commonly measured in terms of the frequency with which a particular response is made. This is generally the simplest type of measurement procedure.

10. A more sophisticated procedure for measuring responses is the use of an ordered scale. Achievement is commonly measured by tests that approximate such scales.

11. Intervening variables represent characteristics of the person that influence behavior. Most of these characteristics cannot be observed directly and hence have been referred to as *hidden variables*. Such variables are used to predict individual differences in performance to learning situations, and they include intellectual aptitudes as well as motivational characteristics.

12. Scales may also be classified in terms of their mathematical properties. These properties determine the extent to which various operations such as subtraction and addition can be performed meaningfully, with scores derived from them.

13. Normative scales are used for comparing the performance of one person with that of another. Ipsative scales compare a person's performance in one area with his performance in another area. Normative scales should be used for predicting normative characteristics. It is not meaningful to predict normative characteristics with ipsative scales.

Some Problems for the Student

1. A psychiatrist developed a test that, he claimed, could be used for identifying certain types of mental abnormality. A research worker, interested in the problem, administered the test

to groups of persons who were characterized by these abnormalities and in whom these abnormalities had been properly diagnosed, and also to a "normal" control group. He interpreted the test results according to the rules provided by the psychiatrist but found no relationship between the results and the presence or absence of particular abnormalities. However, when the test results were given to the psychiatrist alone and without further information, he was able to make a very accurate prediction of which patient suffered from which abnormality. What hypotheses can you suggest to account for this situation?

2. List some of the characteristics of textbooks that result in the facilitation of learning. How might these characteristics be measured? Can they be measured without devoting an excessive amount of labor to the task? How could the reliability of these measured characteristics be estimated?

3. A teacher suspected that many of the academic difficulties encountered by the children in her class could be attributed to the unfavorable home conditions under which homework was accomplished. In order to study this problem, she administered a questionnaire to the children, asking about the extent to which there were distractions such as television and radio going on while they were doing their homework. A score derived from this questionnaire was then correlated with school grades. What is wrong with this procedure for studying the problem?

CHAPTER 6

THE USE OF MULTIPLE

OBSERVATIONS IN

MEASUREMENT

The Single Observation

Most inferences that can be made as a result of educational research are based on multiple observations. From observing a child respond to but a single problem assigned by the teacher, no responsible person is likely to make inferences concerning the child's educational achievement level or his scholastic aptitude. The single observation provides insufficient information for making either one of these inferences. Multiple observations can be used for making fairly accurate inferences about a child's achievement. Achievement tests are such means of providing multiple observations about a child's achievement, and the scores derived from these multiple observations have been demonstrated to measure certain achievements satisfactorily.

In other phases of educational research a similar state of affairs is found; the single observation has only the most limited value. If it is wished to obtain a socioeconomic index for comparing the background of children, it is unlikely that reliance could be placed on a single observation such as whether or not a child's home is equipped with a telephone. While the presence or absence of a telephone is undoubtedly related to general socioeconomic conditions, it is only one of many possible criteria. What would probably be done would be to prepare a checklist of a number of items, each one of which is hypothesized to be related to socioeconomic conditions. The list might include items such as the presence or absence in the home of a telephone, a bathroom, an encyclopedia, a refrigerator, a separate bedroom for the child, and so forth. What would be done would be to add up the scores on each of these items by counting the checks according to a key. The total information provided by all of the items might be of use, while the individual items considered separately might be almost useless. The smallness of the amount of information encapsulated in each single item makes the use of many items necessary.

The reader should not conclude that there are no areas of science in which single observations are of great importance. Medical science is replete with examples of instances in which a single test provides almost certain knowledge about the presence or absence of a particular disease. Chemical analysis depends upon the making of a sequence of observations, each one of which is quite unambiguous in its interpretation. In physics, too, a single observation, such as is made in the determination of the density of a body, may provide highly valuable information that can be used to predict the behavior of the body in a multitude of situations. The contrast with educational research is marked.

The Combination of Observations

Once it is recognized that observations must be combined in order to provide information that has any utility, two problems immediately arise. First, there is the problem of *what* observations are to be combined. Second, there is the matter of *how* they are to be combined. Most of the knowledge available about these two problems has been derived from studies of verbal responses to verbal problems such as appear in tests. Such knowledge, however, does have applicability to the wider range of materials used in educational research.

Consider the problem of estimating the size of a child's vocabulary or the relative size of the vocabularies of different children. One way of doing this might be to ask the child to define a series of words selected at random from a standard dictionary. If in this way we were to ask the child the meaning of ten words, and the child were to define five accurately, we might infer that the child could define 50 per cent of the words in the dictionary. However, a random sample of ten words would provide only the most limited amount of information about the child's total vocabulary. Chance may have resulted in the selection of common words, or perhaps very rare words, or words that the pupil happened to know. If any of these things were to happen, our estimate of the pupil's vocabulary would be far wrong. In order to avoid this eventuality, several courses of action might be taken. One of these would be to use a larger sample of words, the purpose of which would be to increase the precision with which it was possible to estimate the total vocabulary. The problem is the familiar statistical one of estimating the characteristics of a universe from the characteristics of a sample.

There is also a second way in which multiple observations may be used, which may be described by returning to the problem of measuring vocabulary. If we were to draw a sample of one hundred words from the dictionary by taking the last word on each right-hand page, or every twentieth right-hand page, it is probable that our list would contain many common words with which almost everybody was familiar. These words would waste time in administering the list and provide little information. Another procedure might be to select ten words that 90 per cent of the children to be tested would know, ten words that only 80 per cent of the children would know, ten words that 70 per cent would know, and so forth. This would form a rudimentary type of scale, which would be used to determine how difficult a level of vocabulary the individual can define. When such a scale is used, the purpose of measurement is no longer that of estimating the responses of the individual to the universe of possible items, although this can be estimated indirectly. It may be possible to infer that a person who scores 70 correct on the scale can define in a similar way 90 per cent of the words in a given dictionary. However, the main purposes of such a scale are to compare one child with another so that deficiencies in vocabulary may be remedied, and to predict expected achievement in related fields.

Dimensionality and the Clustering of Observations

There are unsatisfactory features in the procedures discussed for the measurement of vocabulary which stem from the fact that knowledge of vocabulary cannot be considered to be a unitary trait. Consider, for example, the case of the student confronted with a vocabulary test consisting of equal numbers of scientific and nonscientific words. Such a test might contain fifty test items in each of these two areas. Now it has been fairly clearly established that knowledge of scientific words is not very closely related to knowledge of general vocabulary, and thus the test measures two rather distinct abilities. If the student taking the test obtained a score of sixty items right, it would be impossible to determine from the score alone whether the student had answered most of the scientific items right, or most of the nonscientific items right, or a considerable number of both types of items correctly. Two persons might obtain equally high scores, one by obtaining a high score on the scientific items, and one by knowing the nonscientific items. The score alone would not indicate whether the person was strong in the one area or in the other. This is because the test does not consist of a homogeneous group of items all of which are measuring the same ability. If a measuring instrument is to have maximum utility, it should be designed so that it measures only one variable.

If a collection of items has such a mixed nature, then the score derived from it has only limited meaning. What is needed for meaningful measurement is a group of observations or items that belong together in some significant way and that can be used collectively as a measuring instrument. Such a group of items is sometimes referred to as a *homogeneous scale,* but one has to be careful about the use of the word *homogeneous.* Some writers who talk about a homogeneous group of items mean only that the items all *appear* to be measuring the same kind of variable, as would be the case with a test of scientific vocabulary or a check list for measuring the socioeconomic status of the home. Others use the word to refer to a group of items that all belong together because it can be shown statistically that they all measure the same variable. What one really needs for meaningful measurement is a group of items or observations that not only belong together in some meaningful way but that also can be demonstrated by statistical means to measure a common property.

The problems of using multiple observations involve the case in which it is possible to build up a measure to a point of usefulness by including additional observations. It was also pointed out that the observations added must be homogeneous with those already available if the variable is to be truly meaningful. More commonly the research worker is faced with the problem of having at his disposal numerous observations that must be grouped together into separate and distinct scales in order to provide meaningful measures. It is this problem of grouping that must now be considered.

Combining Observations in Meaningful Ways

The scientist who approaches educational problems is commonly faced with an abundance of observations and must find some way of grouping them so that they provide useful information. In the conduct of many types of school surveys, such as are undertaken by school and college accrediting associations, the accrediting agency may accumulate large numbers of items of information about educational institutions. Such information is not easily handled as a mass, and in some way the observations must be combined into groups if they are to be easily interpreted.

If the home backgrounds of children are being studied, the social worker or research worker may collect hundreds of items of information about each child. Such data may include items indicative of socioeconomic level—home ownership, car ownership, size of home, value of home, and the number and type of appliances in the home. In addition, data might be obtained on a range of phenomena such as the number of brothers and sisters, the health of the parents, the sibling rivalries manifested by the children, the education of the parents, the number and type of books in the home, the preferences of the parents for the children, the father's occupation, the age of the parents, the number of neighborhood friends of the child, the religious affiliation, and the like. If, say, three hundred items of information were collected about each of two hundred children, the resulting collection of sixty thousand items is not usable for most scientific purposes until it is organized in some way. Some of the ways of doing this must now be given brief consideration.

The a priori method. It is probable that the research worker who planned to obtain a large quantity of information about the background of the pupils had some theory about the characteristics of the background that were relevant for his purpose, which might have been that of predicting the level of academic achievement of the pupils. He might have started out by postulating a number of different kinds of conditions in the background that might be related to achievement. One of these conditions might be the economic status of the home, another might be the degree to which tensions and frictions were absent from the home, another the cultural status of the home as indicated by the number of books or the presence or absence of a piano, and so forth. The list of items of information to be collected might well have been drawn up after a set of broad categories had first been established. After the data had been collected, the items would be grouped into these broad categories and a score derived for each. Thus, one score would indicate the relative socioeconomic status of the home, another the degree of psychological tension in the home, and another its cultural status. Thus, the three hundred items might be made to yield a dozen or fewer scores and the data would be reduced to manageable proportions. Advantages of the method are that it produces a set of measurements closely related to the theory on which the study was originally based and that the measures are quite likely to have considerable reliability.

While this method is attractive, it has its limitations, particularly in studies in which not too much is known about how the items of information should be grouped together. The latter is true of such an area as school characteristics, in which a checklist might be used to describe a school by summarizing what are believed to be certain important facts about it. On the other hand, there are areas in which much is known about how items of information should be grouped. If the items referred to the biographical history of adults, it might be useful to group them in terms of the extent to which they reflected mechanical interests, scientific interests, clerical interests, and so forth.

The a priori method of grouping items of information rarely produces measuring devices that have particularly desirable properties as measuring devices. Too often the scales thus produced are too highly correlated with one another, which means that they measure characteristics that overlap. Considerable further work often has to be performed with these scales to refine them to the point where they are actually useful. A discussion of these additional steps is beyond the scope of this book.

Methods of grouping that depend upon the interrelationships of the items. The student is familiar with the concept that two tests are said to measure the same variable when they are highly correlated, and that they measure different variables when they are uncorrelated. The same concept may be applied to items of information of all kinds. On the basis of this concept, it is possible to sort a pool of items into groups on the basis of whether the items are or are not correlated. Each group of items would then include all those items that were highly interrelated from a statistical point of view. Also, the items in one group would have little correlation with those in other groups—at least this would be so under ideal conditions. The actual procedure for doing this and the technical concepts involved are considerably more complex than is indicated here. Those who wish to explore the matter further are referred to an article on a special technique for doing this, called the *homogeneous keying technique,* which was developed by Loevinger, Gleser, and DuBois (1953).

Procedures for grouping items of information according to their interrelationships can be applied quite mechanically. Indeed, some of these can be undertaken almost completely by electronic computers. This is an advantage in terms of the speed with which the work can be performed, but the results are often difficult to interpret. Items that do not appear to belong together in any way are often grouped together. It is not that there are no good reasons why the items should be grouped in this way, but the reasons are not at all apparent. The reasons for the grouping often lie in the accidental way in which events happen together in our culture and in perhaps remote historical causes. For example, in one study of biographical material, it was found that three items grouped themselves together. These were (1) a knowledge of Latin, (2) a conservative political attitude, and (3) the ownership of a small business by the parent of the person being studied. It happened that in the city in which the study was undertaken, adherents to the Catholic faith were likely to share these three characteristics. This resulted in these three items being grouped together in a large number of biographical items tabulated by one of the statistical methods mentioned here; but without a knowledge of the community from which the data were derived, the grouping would be meaningless.

A second approach to the sorting out of items of information in terms of their relationships depends upon a whole series of techniques that have collectively become known as *factor analysis.* These techniques have evolved mainly for the purpose of attempting to identify the abilities that can be considered to underlie most of the aptitude tests that have been developed. Thus it can be shown that most of the numerous aptitude tests at present available can be considered to measure relatively few variables. One can classify tests in terms of the extent to which they measure each of a small number of reference variables, such as verbal ability, numerical ability, arithmetic reasoning, and so forth. By this means tests may be grouped together in terms of the *factor* that they measure. When large batteries of tests are used, say twenty or more, the procedure for conducting the factor analysis becomes arithmetically very laborious, if it is to be conducted by hand, though electronic computers have enormously facilitated the procedures involved. There are also difficulties introduced by the fact that the procedures usually permit of more than one interpretation concerning the variables that are to be considered to underlie the battery of tests.

These same types of procedure can be applied to the grouping of test items or other items of information. One cannot point to examples where this procedure has used such items of information with striking success, but it is a procedure that is widely suggested in the literature. A major difficulty in its application stems from the fact that the arithmetic becomes extremely elaborate if the technique is applied to any large pool of items. Other difficulties arise in choosing, from the many possible sets of underlying variables that might be considered, the one that is most useful for the purpose at hand. At the present time the methodology of factor analysis has not demonstrated itself to be well suited to the sorting of items of information of the type considered, though it may have excellent uses in dealing with test variables.

The grouping of items of information in terms of the variables it is desired to predict. In a later chapter on problems of prediction, it will be pointed out that items of information are often assembled in order to make predictions. There are, for example, many studies in which information about the home and cultural background of children has been collected in order to predict and anticipate difficulties in school. Let us consider such an example in order to illustrate the method of grouping items of information.

Let us suppose that items of information about home and cultural background were collected for the purpose of predicting (1) reading disability, (2) social difficulties in school, (3) absenteeism, and (4) degree of success in an academic curriculum. The research worker collected 150 items of information about the background of each child entering a junior high school in a large city. The school served a residential area of varied economic circumstances. The data collection was continued until a record was obtained of the backgrounds of each of 400 pupils. These pupils were followed through the school. A reading disability group was slowly and carefully identified. Reports that enabled the research worker to identify a socially maladjusted group were obtained from teachers and added to by counselors. Records of absenteeism were available, and so were records of grades. Once the research worker had obtained all this information, he selected from the pool of background information items a group that predicted reading disability. When a total score was derived from this group of information items, the score was found to predict reading disability with considerable success in subsequent samples. A similar procedure was adopted for predicting each one of the remaining three variables that the study had been designed to predict.

While the procedure that has been just described does have a certain logic in it, there are procedures considerably more complicated that could be used to provide more accurate and efficient predictions. These other methods take into account not only the relationship of the items to the variable to be predicted, but also the extent to which the items provide overlapping information. This involves rather complicated statistical procedures which really require the use of computers if they are to be efficiently undertaken.

This method of using multiple items of information has been used successfully for combining items for all kinds of purposes. It has been used for predicting performance in various types of training programs, for predicting success in certain occupations such as that of salesman, for predicting delinquency, and so forth. In most studies that have used items of background information, the resulting predictions have been extremely limited in accuracy. Of course, this does not mean that the method might not provide highly accurate predictions when used to combine other types of information.

The disadvantage of the method lies in the possibility that the measures it produces, as in the example discussed, often are closely related to one another. One may suspect that three of the four scales produced may have all been measures of the extent to which the atmosphere of the home was favorable to intellectual development. The fourth scale, related to social adjustment, may have measured a different characteristic.

Some Cautions Regarding the Fractionation of Pools of Items

The procedures that have been discussed in this chapter are analogous to mechanical procedures for the fractionation of crude oil. The crude oil is fed in at one end of the fractionating plant, and a whole range of petroleum products, some useful and some not, comes out at the other. Procedures for grouping and selecting test items are of this character. They can be applied and used without much knowledge of the why and the wherefore, and their application can be considered in most cases as a step in the direction of developing tools for research, but it can hardly be considered research.

This point is made because the author has frequently been faced by the graduate student who has come to him with the proposal that his doctoral dissertation consist of the application of a certain technique to a pool of items that the student proposes to build. This is not an activity that should be encouraged in the graduate student. It represents a laborious and time-consuming routine. It does not encourage the type of activity often considered to lie at the very core of a program of doctoral studies—namely, the thinking through of an important problem to the point where ways are found of arriving at a solution. Research of any consequence requires more than the mere application of a mechanical routine. If it could be undertaken by the latter means alone, it could be produced in a factory by a relatively uneducated labor force.

Much of what is undertaken in the name of research, and

which is the wholesale application of a technique to some universe of items, fails to note that the mere identification of a variable is no guarantee that it is going to be of any use. As a matter of fact, new measuring instruments in the behavioral sciences can be developed very easily. The great difficulty is to discover and develop variables that have predictive value. This usually requires prolonged endeavor and what has been termed scientific insight. It does not result from any mechanical procedure, but rather from the development of a sound theory and the testing of deductions from this theory.

It thus behooves the scientist to begin all work on the development of measuring instruments with a theory concerning how the variables he is attempting to measure relate to the specific aspects of behavior that he is studying. If this is done, it will be necessary to test the instruments in order to determine whether the measures they provide permit the making of the predictions that were anticipated. If they do not, one should discard not only the instruments but also the theory on which they were based. Measures that have merit in terms of their internal properties do not help in building a sound theory and do not contribute to knowledge if they show no signs of operating in the way expected.

Finally, it must be reiterated that the information provided by a single observation related to education is extremely limited, and even a group of relatively homogeneous items cannot be expected to provide more than a hint about other types of events. This may be looked upon in another way in the case where the observations refer to behavior. If a group of test items occupies five minutes of time, this must be recognized as an extraordinarily limited sample of a person's behavior. What a person does in a five-minute period is only the most limited basis for generalizing about what the same person will do during other five-minute periods. At the same time it should be recognized, of course, that a test situation is not *any* sample of behavior, but should be a sample of behavior that has been demonstrated to have particular significance for predicting how the person will behave in certain other situations. Nevertheless, there is a definite limit to the amount of information that can be obtained about behavior in a given period of time.

Finally, a word of caution must be said concerning the development of tests that cover a very narrow range of phenomena. Such tests, because they cover a very limited range of phenomena, can be used to predict only a very limited range of phenomena.

There is something of a paradox here. The more specific the variable measured the greater its chances of being independent of other variables, but the less its chances of being a measure that has wide utility as a predictive device. It may be remembered at this time that the measures that have had the most widespread use in predicting behavior are those that tend to be rather generally correlated with a wide range of tests. For example, verbal-factor tests have the most general utility for predicting trainability, and yet these tests show considerable correlations with other tests. It is likely that the fact that they correlate with other tests is, in itself, symptomatic of the capacity to predict.

The items considered must cover a range of activity in order that the resulting measuring instrument may apply to a range of activities. If one postulates that liking for mechanical activities and objects clusters, it would be undesirable to limit the range of mechanical objects and activities included in a test to those involved in the repair and maintenance of automobile engines. Such narrowness of range is unlikely to be of use for most purposes for which the instrument is to be used. The most striking failure of this kind in the development of instruments emerges when the same question is repeated several times within the same test. One test that attempts to measure needs is of this character. What such a procedure does in this case is to build up reliability for each measure of need, since when approximately the same question is repeated, it is going to be answered in approximately the same way. However, what this does is to measure a highly specific characteristic, which may have little generality in other situations in which it may be expected to appear. On the other hand, it is this specificity that will ensure that the various measures of need are independent of one another.

The result is that the instrument appears to provide a series of measures of need that have both high reliability and high independence of one another. This is generally considered to be a most desirable state of affairs, but it is not so when it is achieved by measuring responses to extremely restricted situations. Exactly the same would be true in dealing with other kinds of observations. If a checklist were made to be used for obtaining a measure of the adequacy of a school plant, it would be undesirable for most of the items to refer to the size and adequacy of the library. There would be agreement that a score to be derived from the checklist would be useful only if it provided a comprehensive coverage of the school facility.

SOME SPECIAL PROBLEMS OF UTILIZING MEASUREMENTS

Measures in Which the Responses Are a Function of Time

The measures that have been discussed to this point are those customarily administered in such a way that increases in the time available for responding would not appreciably change the score. This is inevitably the case in most tests of information, knowledge, thinking skill, attitude, interest.

Test instruments that involve speed of response do not involve the problems of item selection that have been discussed in the previous sections of this chapter. The reason is that speeded instruments are almost invariably such that the score is the number of units completed in a given time, and it is important that each unit be equivalent to every other unit. A common type of speeded test is the clerical aptitude type, which requires the individual to compare two lists of closely similar names and to mark those where corresponding pairs of names do not match.

Each pair of names corresponds to a unit of work, and the test should be so designed that all pairs are equivalent as units of work. In order to approximate equivalence, the person making the test will need to have some theory concerning the factors in these stimuli that are related to behavior. He may, for example, believe that long names are more difficult to compare than are short names; hence, in order to make all units of work equivalent in terms of this factor, he will make all names equal in length.

It may be pointed out here that when time is used to control a test score, the method commonly used is that of controlling the time on the total test. Customarily, all examinees start and finish at the same time. Under this procedure, a person who works at the maximum speed of which he is capable and completes ten items obtains the same score as the person with facility for the task who works along in a way that is leisurely for him and also completes ten items. A superior way of controlling the speed factor in such tests would be to expose each item separately for a given interval of time. At the end of that time, the next item would be exposed, and so forth. In this way, the examinee would be paced all through the test. The time per item might stay constant under these conditions or might be reduced as the test proceeded.

Pattern Analysis as a Method of Combining Observations

The discussion of the problem of combining observations that has been presented up to this point has disregarded a problem that clinical psychologists have frequently stressed. It is that the pattern of responses to particular situations may provide more information than a simple summation of those responses. Problems of pattern analysis will be first discussed here with reference to the problem of combining and utilizing scores for different tests, since such problems are already familiar to the teacher.

Rorschach test administrators have commonly stressed that it is the interrelationship among the various scores on the instrument that provides information of real significance, and that the absolute values of the scores mean little. The author knows of no cases that have clearly demonstrated that the patterns of scores on the Rorschach, rather than the scores themselves, are of real significance. There are, however, cases with other types of measures where substantial evidence has been collected to show that patterns of scores may be extremely important as predictors. In some of French's studies (1956), effectiveness in particular situations has been predicted well in terms of the relative strength of affiliation and achievement motives. In such studies, situations have been presented that produce a conflict between affiliation and achievement motives, and the action that results is a product of primarily only one of these motives. As one might expect, it is the stronger of the two motives that ultimately becomes the major determinant of behavior in these situations. In such a situation, three patterns of motivation are possible. Either achievement motivation is the stronger of the two, or affiliation motivation is the stronger, or they are both equal in strength. If a third motive were involved and each motive were considered to assume three levels (high, middle, and low), twenty-seven possible patterns of motivation may occur.

It can be readily seen that if as many as 6 motives are involved, the number of possible patterns becomes large, and if data are to be collected with as many as 100 cases showing each pattern, then very large numbers of cases are to be collected—a minimum of 62,900. In practice, far more than this minimum would have to be collected, since there would certainly be far more cases in some categories than in others. Perhaps 1,000,000 or more cases might have to be collected before there were at least 100 in each category. The cumbersomeness of the data to be collected makes profile analysis unsatisfactory where many possible patterns exist. For this reason, some restrictions must be placed on the process.

One method of reducing the number of patterns is to use only a high-low dichotomy instead of a high-middle-low division. Another is to group together patterns that can be considered similar on some rational basis. While this latter approach is attractive, there are difficulties involved in developing a rationale that can be used for the grouping of patterns. The author is inclined to believe that comprehensive studies of patterns in which every pattern is studied in relation to a criterion are unlikely to provide useful results. It is too much of a hit-or-miss procedure. However, studies of the patterning of a few variables for which there is strong reason for believing that differences in pattern are associated with differences in performance may well prove to have value. Here again the author is attempting to stress the need for well-defined hypotheses or problems before data are collected or analyzed. Massive pattern analyses conducted in the hope of finding a vague "something" run counter to this concept of research.

The problem of pattern analysis becomes important in the scoring of specific tests when it is desired to produce a score that will predict a particular criterion with maximum accuracy. Meehl (1950) was the first to see the real significance of this problem when he pointed out that two dichotomously scored items could each correlate zero with a dichotomous criterion, and yet from the pattern of responses to the two items it might be possible to predict the criterion with perfect accuracy. This phenomenon is illustrated in Table 2. It is clear in this table that two patterns Yes-No and No-Yes predict passing, and two patterns Yes-Yes and No-No predict failure. It is also shown that each one of the items considered separately has no value at all in predicting the criterion. It can be shown that what is happening under such circumstances is simply that a curvilinear function is being used for making the prediction, instead of the linear function that fails to predict.

The Meehl phenomenon is a special case of the proposition that scoring a test in terms of patterns provides the best possible prediction of a particular criterion. Scoring in terms of number right may provide as good a prediction in some cases, but it cannot provide a better prediction than when all possible patterns are used in making the prediction.

TABLE 2. Patterns of Responses to Two Items in Relation to a Criterion

	Response on Item I	Response on Item II	Number in Each Pattern	Pass or Fail
Pattern I	Yes	No	25	Pass
II	No	Yes	25	Pass
III	No	No	25	Fail
IV	Yes	Yes	25	Fail

Relation of Each Item to the Criterion

ITEM I	Pass	Fail		ITEM II	Pass	Fail
Yes	25	25		Yes	25	25
No	25	25		No	25	25

Ordinary scoring methods in which all persons obtaining the same score (say the number right) are placed in the same category—even though they answer different combinations of items—present a case in which many patterns are classified and grouped together. The conventional method of scoring is likely to be less efficient than would be a scoring system which kept all patterns separate.

In the case of certain types of scales, known as Guttman scales, only a limited number of patterns are possible. Consider, for example the following five-item scale:

1. $4 + 6 =$
2. $3\frac{1}{4} \div 2\frac{1}{2} =$
3. If $2x + 4 = 0$, then $x =$
4. If $x^2 - x - 12 = 0$, then $x =$
5. If $y = 3x^4 + 2x^2 + 4$, then $dy/dx =$

In the case of this five-item scale, the person able to answer the last item would almost certainly have been able to answer the preceding four items. The person who answered the first two items but was unable to answer the third would almost certainly fail on the last two. The scale is so graded in difficulty that a person is able to answer items up to a certain point but will fail all items beyond that point. In the case of such a five-item scale, only six possible patterns of response are possible, and these would be as follows:

	Item I	Item II	Item III	Item IV	Item V
Pattern I	Wrong	Wrong	Wrong	Wrong	Wrong
II	Right	Wrong	Wrong	Wrong	Wrong
III	Right	Right	Wrong	Wrong	Wrong
IV	Right	Right	Right	Wrong	Wrong
V	Right	Right	Right	Right	Wrong
VI	Right	Right	Right	Right	Right

In such a case there are only six possible patterns. The score can vary from 0 to 5, and from the score alone it will be possible to determine the pattern of responses that produced that score. If the test did not form such an ordered scale, other patterns of responses would be possible. If no semblance of an ordered scale were present, there would be thirty-two possible patterns of scoring categories. Only a very few achievement tests and attitude scales form ordered scales of this type. Most types of measuring instruments are so remote from being ordered scales that numerous patterns of responses are possible. A method of considerable interest for scoring these various patterns has been suggested by Lubin (1957), who has done much to clarify concepts in this field.

The way in which Lubin proposes to score patterns can be shown to be the most efficient of all possible methods of using the information that the test or other device can make available. In order to explain how this is done, let us consider a relatively simple example. Suppose that a measure were available of the satisfaction that teachers derived from their work, and it was desired to relate this measure to a five-item personality test that had been administered at an earlier date. In actual practice, one would not think of utilizing such a short test, because so few items would contain relatively little information, but a five-item test is convenient for the present explanation of Lubin's method of scoring, which is named *configural scoring*. The average score on the job-satisfaction scale for all those who have the same pattern of responses on the personality scale is the score for that pattern. Thus for each one of the thirty-two possible patterns a score on the job-satisfaction scale will be assigned and this will be the configural score. It can be shown that the configural score is the score that will best predict the job-satisfaction scale from the personality scale. No other method of scoring can provide a better prediction, though, of course, it is quite possible that the personality scale may be a poor predictor of job satisfaction in the teaching profession.

In the case of a 5–item scale, there are 2^5 possible patterns of response if there are only two ways of answering each item. In the case of a 10–item device there would be 2^{10} possible patterns, which is 1,024. In the case of a 15–item device there are 32,768 possible patterns. This points up the real difficulty in using this type of pattern analysis: there are likely to be just too many patterns to be manageable if there are more than a few items to be considered.

Just how much is to be gained by pattern analysis in the use of multiple observations? No answer can be given to this question at the present time, since experience with such methods is still limited. It is quite possible that if studies are conducted where there is real reason to believe that patterning has important effects, real gains may be found in the use of this type of method.

Reliability of Measurement

Many of the operations discussed in this chapter that involve the combining of observations are undertaken for building up those characteristics of instruments that in the history of measurement have been referred to collectively as *reliability*. Problems of reliability refer mainly to a special class of inferences from scores. In the history of psychological measurement, a reliable measure has been considered one that would remain stable if the measure were again applied under similar conditions. This statement implies that differences in scores on the measure from one person to another are not merely the product of a great number of uncontrolled events, but that they represent some relatively stable and continuing condition that differentiates persons one from another. For example, absenteeism in any school on February 8 of any year may show great differences from school to school, but these differences are a product of a multiplicity of causes. In one community a high absentee rate is due to a local epidemic of measles, in another it is a result of a blizzard, and so forth. We may expect little relationship between absenteeism on February 8 and absenteeism on March 8 of the same year. Absenteeism on a particular day may be said to lack sufficient reliability to make it a useful measure for any conceivable purpose. A measure that is to have value must be determined by conditions that have some permanence and continuity, and it is this that in turn gives the measure stability.

A central weakness in the whole concept of reliability stems from the difficulty of defining what is meant by *similarity of conditions*. It is quite obvious that if measurements were repeated under truly *identical* conditions, the results would inevitably be identical. Measurements vary because conditions vary. The expression *measurement under similar conditions* cannot refer to *measurement under identical conditions,* but just how far conditions can depart from identity and still be considered similar is entirely a matter of personal judgment.

Reliability is thus a somewhat fuzzy concept. At least a part of the fuzziness is a result of the fact that the term refers to a series of concepts that are confused with one another. Thus the American Psychological Association (1954) has wisely suggested that any manual that accompanies a test and provides estimates of reliability should indicate the method by which it was computed. Different estimates of reliability pertain to different inferences.

In a split-half type of reliability, scores derived from half of the items are correlated with scores derived from the remaining half. If the items are considered to be random samples of a universe of items, and if they are divided into two sections at random, then the reliability coefficient is an attempt to answer the question, "To what extent is it possible to make inferences from a score on one random sample of these items concerning scores on another random sample?" However, if the two groups of items are so matched that for each type of item in the one group there is a corresponding item in the other group, then the inference pertains to the extent to which a score from one sample of items covering certain specific areas can be used to infer scores on other similarly structured samples.

In the case of the coefficient of reliability based upon two successive administrations of the same test, the purpose is to estimate the extent to which it is possible to infer scores at other points in time from a test score obtained at a particular time. It is a rather different inference from that made from a split-half or a parallel-form procedure for estimating reliability.

The estimation of reliability by means of the Kuder Richardson type of formula, which has already been mentioned, refers again to a different type of phenomenon. Cronbach (1951), who has made a careful study of this approach, refers to the coefficient derived from this procedure as *alpha* rather than by the more lengthy name that it has acquired from its originators. Cronbach has also shown that it refers to an internal property of a test, which is a product of the statistical relationship among the items. This property is known as *homogeneity,* and refers to the extent to which all the items on a test can be considered to contribute to the measurement of a single common variable. This is stating the matter in the simplest possible terms. A precise definition of homogeneity requires the extensive use of mathematical terms. The coefficient *alpha* is for this reason now most commonly referred to as a measure of homogeneity rather than as a measure of reliability.

Measuring instruments of the type used in the social sciences can provide only measures that approximate homogeneity. Much of the variance of each item can be attributed to sources other than that which it is desired to measure. However, this may not be as harmful to the total score as one might at first assume. The reason for this is that the unwanted aspects of the variance are derived from a large number of unrelated sources and therefore, so to speak, tend to cancel out one another in a total score.

Summary

1. In educational research it is usually true that a single observation provides only a very limited amount of information. In order to overcome this limitation, it is usually necessary to combine together several observations.

2. Items of information must be grouped together in some way so that they form a meaningful measuring instrument. Under ideal conditions the items should all belong together in terms of some theory, but they should also all belong together in a statistical sense, and in this sense should all measure a common variable.

3. Items of information may be combined together on the basis of judgment either because they appear to belong together or because there is some theoretical basis for grouping them together. This method of grouping together items of information is referred to as the a priori method.

4. A series of methods of using multiple observations have been developed in which the grouping depends upon the statistical relationships among the items. Two general classes of techniques for this purpose have been developed:

a. The homogeneous keying technique represents a method that has been evolved specifically for the purpose of sorting a large number of items of information into groups each of which forms a measuring instrument.

b. A second approach is that of factor analysis, which evolved more as a procedure for the grouping of tests than a procedure for the grouping of items.

5. Observations may be grouped also in terms of the extent to which they predict some other variable.

6. Caution should be exercised in combining items of information. The procedure should be so planned that the resulting variables are meaningful in terms of current educational theory. In any case, the amount of information that one may expect to

obtain from even a group of items that form a measuring scale is limited. The more specific the variable that is being measured, the more it is likely to be independent of other variables and the more it is likely to predict only a narrow range of behavior.

7. Pattern analysis represents a special group of techniques for using multiple observations. While clinical psychologists have long believed that the pattern of scores on a battery of tests might be of greater significance than the actual values of the scores themselves, it is only recently that a theory of pattern analysis has been developed. Pattern analysis can also be applied to the scoring of items, and it can be shown that configural scoring is the most efficient method of utilizing all of the information provided by a set of observations.

8. Pattern analysis techniques are still being explored. Those that are available tend to be extremely cumbersome to use. As yet, it cannot be stated how much is to be gained by pattern analysis techniques as contrasted with simpler and more traditional techniques.

9. The development of methods for using multiple observations rather than single observations has been intimately related historically to the problem of improving the reliability of measurement. As understanding in this area has developed, the concept of reliability has been found to be more and more unsatisfactory, and those who have been engaged in the development of measuring devices have been urged to specify just what technique they have utilized in the estimation of reliability. The concept of homogeneity seems to be a more satisfactory one than the concept of reliability.

CHAPTER 7

THE VALIDITY OF

MEASUREMENT

TECHNICAL problems related to the use of measurement are the concern of all scientists in the behavioral areas. Research workers in sociology, psychology, anthropology, economics, and education all encounter difficulties in their research produced by the fact that the measurements they make do not have the properties they would wish them to have. The fact that psychology, in its early stages of development, was able to attract to its ranks men from other sciences who had a major interest in problems of measurement made psychology a focal point of interest in such problems. In the nineteenth century Francis Galton, who had a background in genetics, and Alfred Binet, who had a background in medicine, began to explore problems of measurement in the behavioral sciences. Edward L. Thorndike followed in their footsteps at the turn of the century. In this century, L.L. Thurstone, a mathematician who at one time was assistant to Thomas Edison, moved into psychology and became the leading theoretician in the field. Although the work of these men and others was in the field of psychology, its implications have influenced every branch of knowledge which has to do with human behavior. For these historical reasons the chapter which follows draws most of its material from the field of psychology and the activities of organizations of psychologists. If history had been a little different the material might have had to be drawn from sociology, or anthropology, or education.

A focal point of discussion, whenever problems of measurement are considered in education, is the concept of *validity*. Unfortunately, this concept has drifted into the behavioral sciences by an adaptation of the word *validity* as it is used in common speech. Had it been introduced by some careful thinker at an appropriate point in the history of the development of the behavioral sciences to denote some well-defined concept, the difficulties that have occurred over the past forty years in clarifying its meaning might not have arisen, but such was not the case.

The present state of thought concerning the problem of validity is probably best understood by reviewing the history of the concept. The struggle for clarification that psychologists have lived through during the past forty years has resulted in much insight and understanding, and the historical review is presented here in order to bring some of this to the student.

Early Attempts to Standardize Measurement of Behavior

The American Psychological Association has had a long-standing interest in the standardization and use of psychological tests. As early as 1895, the Association appointed a committee on mental and physical tests and reported its recommendations at the annual meeting held in Boston in 1896. A more ambitious venture was started in 1906 when the Association established a committee on the subject of measurements. The main purpose of this committee seems to have been the collection of descriptions of tests in use, in order to make them available to other investigators. It was felt that if the results of different experiments were to be comparable, it was necessary for investigators to use at least similar instruments of measurement. The object of this entire procedure was to facilitate the development of generalizations concerning the relationship of test variables to other variables. The implication in much of the report of this committee was that the tests defined the variables that were measured, but the term *validity* was not used. Nothing seems to have been lost by its absence, for the tests discussed in the report were discussed within the framework of a surprisingly well-developed rationale derived largely from the associationistic and Wundtian tradition. Not all modern test batteries have such a rich background of theory as was the case with this battery proposed for general use. However, the excellent work of this committee was ahead of its time, for it is hard to find a single reference to its work in the technical literature of the period.

Psychologists contemporary with this committee continued to develop large numbers of measuring instruments. One of the most prolific of these was Edward L. Thorndike, who in his *Theory of Mental and Social Measurement* (1904) put forward the view that psychological measures represent facts about an individual, and that the problem of the psychologist is to arrange conditions of measurement so that the measures are accurate representations of the facts. In this connection Thorndike uses the example of a person reacting to a stimulus. From this behavior, the psychologist may abstract the quality of speed of reaction, and the problem of measurement is to devise an instrument through which a number that will represent the reaction time can be assigned the individual's reaction. Refinements of the measuring procedure merely reduce various errors that contaminate it. It should be noted that there is a real difference between the argument that measures are an attempt to describe accurately certain physical events, such as reaction time, and that measures are an attempt to represent some underlying and forever unobservable psychological reality. Arguments about "what tests really measure," which for twenty years were considered to be the central problem in determining whether tests were or were not valid, arose at a later date. In Thorndike's subsequent work this problem is raised, and his *Measurement of Intelligence* (1927) opens with the statement that psychological measuring instruments still have three fundamental defects, which are: (1) "Just what they measure is not known"; (2) "How far it is proper to add, subtract, multiply and divide, and compute ratios with the measures obtained is not known"; and (3) "What the measures signify concerning intellect is not known." The first of these three implies that there is an underlying reality, measured by tests, that can be known, and so too does the third. However, in the works of Thorndike up to and including his 1927 volume *Measurement of Intelligence,* the term *validity* is used only with respect to the validity of judgments of the difficulty of tasks. This is true also of his *Educational Psychology* (1913).

The first use of the word *validity* in a technical article, as far as the present writer can determine, is in an article by Freeman in 1914. In this article, Freeman states that "this report deals only with questions regarding the technique and validity of test methods." This statement implies that the term *validity* was then used in discussions of testing problems, even though it was not commonly used in the literature of the day. However, Freeman does not use the term again in the remainder of his article. Just a few years later, the discussion of the concept of validity became involved in discussions of what tests really measure, and a valid measure was defined as one that measured the variable it was supposed to measure.

Discussions of what tests really measure and whether they do or do not measure what they are supposed to measure waxed in the early 1920's, largely as a result of the widespread application of intelligence tests. Discussions of the subject appeared not only in technical journals but also in popular magazines. The disillusionment concerning the value of these tests, which inevitably followed an era of excessive and premature enthusiasm, is well represented by a series of articles on the subject by Walter Lippmann, which appeared in the *New Republic* in the early part of 1923. Most of what he had to say would conform to modern thinking on the subject. The articles probably had some desirable effect of inhibiting those who made immoderate claims concerning test usage, or who claimed that tests measured innate faculties. A more constructive article followed in the June 6, 1923, issue, by Edwin G. Boring. It presented the view that today would be identified with the operational point of view, namely that "intelligence as a measurable capacity must at the start be defined as the capacity to do well on an intelligence test." The implication is that it is not reasonable to ask the question, "What do tests really measure?" Measures derived from tests represent certain characteristics of behavior that have been selected because according to some theory, they have a special value for prediction. Tests measure whatever they measure. They are valuable if they are capable of making the predictions they are expected to make according to the theory on the basis of which they have been developed. Only empirical verification can show whether the predictions hypothesized can be made. The discussion of what tests really measure should have been settled then and there, but it has continued intermittently over the years.

In the late 1920's and in the two decades that followed, the profitless discussion of what tests really measured was gradually displaced by a concern for the problem of what inferences could be made from test scores. But the psychologists both in education and in industry did not state the problem in this way, for their interests were strictly practical.

This new trend was a result of the growth of applied psychology, and the interest of applied psychologists was largely in the matter of what tests predicted. In this context, psychologists began to refer to correlations between test scores and variables that it was desired to predict as *validity coefficients*. The acceptance of this concept of validity was more a matter of convenience than a product of profound reflection. While nobody cared very much any more what a test measured, it became a matter of paramount importance to determine whether a test was or was not capable of being used for the making of predictions. This aspect of the matter has been the central focus of attention when the meaning of the term *validity* has been discussed during the last twenty years.

Since evidence of validity for a test became more and more a guaranty of a good market, test manuals in the 1930's and 1940's showed an increasingly free use of the term, and *evidence for validity* became progressively more and more remote from evidence that useful predictions could be made with the device. A situation rapidly developed where the many new meanings of *validity* had to be defined.

In the late 1940's, voices began to question the clarity and precision of the then current concept of validity. Mosier (1947) wrote a penetrating article pointing out that the term *validity* was used with reference to four somewhat distinct concepts: (1) validity by assumption, where the items of a test appear to bear a logical relationship to the phenomena to be predicted; (2) validity by definition, where a test is used to define a particular variable, as would occur if knowledge of mathematics were defined in terms of a score on a particular mathematics test; (3) face validity, which occurs when a test, in addition to having statistical validity, also appears to have relevance; and (4) validity by hypothesis, which occurs when the mass of previous evidence supports the contention that a test has relevance for predicting a particular criterion.

Mosier's article heralded a series of attempts to clarify concepts in this area. The most ambitious of these attempts must now be considered.

The American Psychological Association's Second Attempt to Order Concepts in the Measurement Domain

As a consequence of the failure to reach any kind of agreement among professional persons concerning the meaning of validity, each test publisher felt free to interpret it in his own way, and often in a way that was at variance with the views of a large fraction of the profession. Other concepts in the measurement field also lacked clarity but perhaps were not obscure to the same degree.

The proliferation of instruments that filled the markets during the postwar era, the varying standards adopted by test publishers, and often the lack of standards, prompted the American Psychological Association in 1949 to take some action in setting up standards that test publishers might follow. The committee, which became known as the Committee on Test Standards, spent the first few years of their effort on the preparation of a report, which has particular relevance here because of its novel contribution to the development of the concept of validity. It is understood that the committee was in favor of discarding the word *validity* but decided to retain it because its usage had become so deeply ingrained in the field of applied psychology. The thought seems to have been that the concept could be discarded and replaced at a later date. In the interim, it was decided to define various aspects of validity and to name them separately. These various meanings need now to be considered.

Predictive validity. This is validity in the customary sense in which it has been used in applied psychology and in aptitude measurement in education. It is validity as represented by statements such as, "The Jones Reasoning Test administered in high school correlates 0.4 with average grades over the first two years in liberal arts colleges having enrollments greater than one thousand students." Such statements represent empirical relationships that supposedly can be used to evaluate the worth of a test for a particular purpose. In the statement that was just quoted, the data—which, let us assume, are unimpeachable—permit us to make statements concerning the value of the instrument in the particular situation in which they were collected. They do not provide knowledge concerning how the test will work in other situations. If inferences are to be made concerning the predictive validity of the test in other situations, it is necessary to make assumptions concerning the relationship between the situations in which the data were collected and new situations in which it is desired to make a prediction. Usually very little knowledge is available concerning this relationship. Indeed, in spite of guesses to the contrary, an investigator might be quite surprised to find that the Jones Reasoning Test did not provide as satisfactory predictions within teachers' colleges as within liberal arts colleges. *Predictive validity really does not provide a basis for using an instrument except in the situation in which it was validated.*

Concurrent validity represents a concept very similar to that of predictive validity. The difference is a relatively minor one. In the case of predictive validity, the variable used in prediction is measured at some time previous to the measurement of the variables that are predicted, as would be the case in predicting college grades from aptitude tests administered in high school. On the other hand, in the case of concurrent validity, performance on a test is compared with a measure derived from some concurrent performance, as when a test given in high school is used to predict high school performance. The fact that a test has concurrent validity does not necessarily mean that it has predictive validity. For example, it is quite conceivable that a test might discriminate in a certain plant between those who had and those who had not been promoted, but it is quite possible that the same test given persons when they were first hired might have no success at all in predicting which of them would be promoted later. The test might involve only information acquired after the person was hired.

Real and important questions can be raised concerning the merit of separating concurrent and predictive validity. When predictions are made over any time interval different from that used in the original validation of the test, assumptions must be made concerning the justifiability of the predictions under the new conditions. Sometimes the assumptions are reasonable, sometimes they are not.

Content validity is the extent to which the situations included by the test are representative of the group of situations that the test is supposed to sample. It is common in the case of achievement tests to compare the content of the test with the content of the curriculum and to arrive at some judgment concerning the relationship of the two. The product of such an operation is a rough-and-ready judgment, and no satisfactory methods have been devised for quantifying this relationship. The central difficulty involved is that of measuring the characteristics of situations so that a sound basis exists for comparing the properties of the test situation with the properties of the situations that they supposedly represent.

The difficulty of measuring content validity reflects a current inadequacy in perhaps all theory in the behavioral sciences. Until it is possible to measure the characteristics of situations to which persons respond, there is little hope of obtaining in psychology generalizations that have really broad significance. If the laws of behavior in situations having characteristics X, Y, and Z are known, one may be justified in making predictions about behavior in other situations having the same characteristics X, Y, and Z—but only if it is genuinely possible to identify these characteristics.

Construct validity is the final category proposed by the committee of the American Psychological Association. Construct validity is demonstrated by showing that measures derived from the instrument can be used for making inferences consistent with the theory on which the test is based. Thus a projective test of achievement motivation is found to provide scores that are correlated with output of work on a task so simple that output must be considered to be mainly a function of motivation. If this were found to be the case, one could reasonably infer that evidence had been elicited to support the contention that the measure could be identified with achievement need. Usually it would require more than the single piece of evidence of the type studied to justify the inference about the characteristics of the variable measured. What is needed is evidence from remotely differing spheres, all of which substantiates the belief that the instrument predicts in those situations in which prediction is expected. The nature of science is such, of course, that one cannot expect all of the evidence to point in the same direction. One can expect some inconsistencies, and it is the function of further work to discover reasons for these inconsistencies and to revise the theory under review so that it becomes consistent with all available evidence.

Sometimes the evidence that is dealt with in the determination of construct validity is derived by correlating scores from the instrument under consideration with scores derived from similar tests, or tests that are related according to some theory. It seems to the author that such evidence is necessarily weak and limited in value. Mere relationships among measuring devices are limited sources of information. What are needed are relationships between measures derived from devices and important variables that one wants to predict.

It should be noted that other writers had discriminated the concept of construct validity from the broad and hazy general concept of validity. Mosier's "validity by hypothesis" (1947) is essentially the same. Gulliksen's term, *intrinsic validity*, also carries with it much of the same meaning. As a matter of fact, as far back as 1936 Bowers (1936) clearly defined the concept of construct validity and pointed out that it was the only real basis for generalization.

An Attempt to Restate the Problem

The present attempt to restate the problem in terms of the general matter of scientific measurement stems from the observation that the behavioral sciences are the only sciences that seem to need the concept of validity. Furthermore, in the field of behavior it is only within the limited domain of testing that the word *validity* is used. Experimentalists, theory-builders, and clinicians do not seem to feel any need for the concept in their respective domains. Works are written on the basis of experiments, and theories of psychology are drawn up without reference to the term. Why do those in the testing field need this concept that researchers in other fields of psychology and in other fields of science find superfluous?

The problem of validity seems to deal with the problem that

in other fields of science is known as that of generalization and inference. When the psychologist asks the question, "Is this test valid for this purpose?" he is asking the question, "From the response of the individuals to this test, what statement can be made concerning the response of these individuals to this other situation that by custom is called the criterion situation?" The question concerns what inferences can be made from test scores.

The concept of validity, as it is commonly discussed, refers to the problem of inference and generalization. Discussion usually involves a test score R_t from which it is believed that some response in a criterion situation R_c is to be predicted. Validity is the extent to which it is possible to base statements about R_c on R_t. Sometimes it refers to the extent to which it is possible to make generalizations from R_t to R_{c1}, R_{c2}, R_{c3}, or a whole class of criterion situations.

Since the usual evidence that justifies such generalization and inference is a correlation coefficient, the value of this evidence must be given some consideration at this point.

Correlation and Inference

The fact that the Jones Reasoning Test has been demonstrated to correlate with the grades of students in, say, an elementary electronics course is extremely limited information, which permits little or no generalization. The fact that the correlation between test scores and grades was found to be 0.4 $(N = 200)$ on a single class cannot be taken as a sound basis for making the generalization that the relationship will be maintained in future classes. The correlation may have been generated by some incidental condition, which may rarely or never reoccur. The author can recall one case in which a correlation between an aptitude test and a set of grades was generated by the fact that the instructors reviewed the aptitude scores of their students just before they assigned grades. In other words, the mere fact that a correlation has been found between an aptitude test and a criterion variable is very inadequate evidence that any generalization can be made concerning the probability that the same relationship will be found on future occasions; or, in terms of the traditional language of psychology, a single correlation coefficient, even if it is of substantial magnitude, is poor evidence of validity. Predictive validity and concurrent validity are really quite trivial concepts, because the correlation coefficients on which they are based are insufficient for establishing a generalization that can be used.

If a correlation coefficient does not permit useful generalization concerning the value of a test, what does constitute such evidence? *The primary evidence on which useful generalizations can be based is the fact that the relationships among the variables are to be expected on the basis of a more general theory of prediction that has been shown to have value in the making of predictions.* For example, consider the problem of constructing a test for reducing the percentage of failures among those admitted to law school. Suppose that an experimental battery for solving this problem included a test consisting of the well-known cube-turning items [1] and a verbal reasoning test that involved a considerable knowledge of vocabulary. Suppose it were found that the reliability of each one of these two tests was 0.95 for an entering class of 230 law students, and that the space test and verbal reasoning test correlated 0.5 and 0.3 respectively with the average grades of this group while in law school. For convenience, let us assume that there were no dropouts. In addition, let us assume that the data show that the cube-turning test is likely to provide as satisfactory a prediction of average grades as an optimum combination of scores from the two tests.

In such a situation, the choice of the empiricist would be clear. He would use scores on the cube-turning test for the selection of the next entering class, for had not this test been established as the *more* valid of the two? In addition, he would reflect that a statistical test of significance had demonstrated to his satisfaction

[1] Cube-turning items usually illustrate a sample cube with a different design on each visible surface. A number of other cubes are illustrated, and the subject must select from among these the one that is the same as the sample cube but turned into a different position.

that the difference in the "validity" of the two tests should not be considered as a mere product of sampling.

However, serious questions may be raised as to whether the choice of the empiricist is a sound one. In criticizing his choice, the scientist would point out that previous studies had shown with monotonous consistency that the type of verbal test used in this study was a more satisfactory predictor of grades in courses involving the extensive manipulation of verbal symbols, and that a space-manipulation test had been shown to be notoriously inadequate for this purpose. The fact is that the data collected in this situation are so inconsistent with data previously collected, and with generalizations based on them, that no acceptable generalization is possible concerning the extent to which these tests are likely to be generally useful for selecting law students for future classes in the same law school or in other law schools.

Most persons familiar with the generalizations that can be made concerning the value of various types of tests for the selection of students would probably agree that the verbal test would be more likely to have selective value for law students than the space test. The verbal test can be considered to have "validity" for the selection of law school students, not just because of the single empirical finding of $r = 0.3$ for this particular case, but because this finding is consistent with an organized body of knowledge. No generalization seems reasonable from the so-called validity coefficient of 0.5 for the spatial test, simply because this coefficient is inconsistent with a substantial body of available knowledge and thus, in traditional terminology, cannot be considered valid as a selection instrument in this particular situation.

The moral of this story is that predictive validity and concurrent validity as defined by a single correlation coefficient are simply not an adequate basis for action. However, if coefficients of correlation are consistent with previous findings and with even a crude theory based on these findings, then there begins to be some basis for generalization, and therefore for justifiable action. In a scientific sense, the only real validity is construct validity.

Some sophisticated reader is likely to point out that the problem here discussed stems from the fact that the prediction study that posed the problem was ill designed in the first place. The investigator should have proceeded by including only those variables that provided some rational basis for believing that they should predict the ability to succeed in law school as it is measured by course grades. If a rational approach had been taken in the planning of the investigation, the perceptual test would never have been included in the study and the paradox provided by the so-called coefficients of validity would never have arisen. All this is perfectly true, and it seems to bring out the point that when prediction studies are rationally planned, it is then and only then possible to consider validity coefficients as evidence that the test will continue to have predictive value in similar situations in the future.

A position similar to the one formulated here appeared in a monograph by Loevinger (1957). Loevinger takes the position that a measure has validity insofar as it has predictive value and the predictions are consistent with the general characteristics of the instrument and the theory on which it is based. The characteristics of the measuring instrument itself are carefully analyzed by Loevinger into what she terms a substantive component and a structural component. The substantive component corresponds roughly to the content of the instrument; the structural component refers to the relationship between items. For further study of these concepts, the reader is referred to Loevinger's monograph.

Summary

1. Throughout the last half-century there has been extended controversy over the problem of the meaning of measurement in the educational and behavioral sciences. Discussions of this problem have had considerable confusion added to them through the introduction of the term *validity*, which drifted into the language of the field and then acquired a number of meanings.

2. In order to bring the word *validity* under better control, a committee of the American Psychological Association was set up to study the matter and to provide definitions of different aspects of the concept of validity as it has been used in recent times. The committee attempted to define four aspects of validity, and the recommendations of the committee have had wide acceptance.

3. It is the opinion of the writer that the only real sense in which a measure can have validity is when it has been shown consistently to be capable of making predictions *in accordance with a theory*. This is the central meaning of what the committee of the American Psychological Association called *construct validity*. It is the only concept of validity that is clearly tied to the way in which the scientist works. Since the serious scientific research worker in education will conduct all of his work within a framework of theory, this is the only aspect of validity with which he should be concerned.

CHAPTER 8

THE NATURE OF OBSERVATION

AND SOME DIRECT APPROACHES

DISCUSSION up to this point has been focused on some of the factors involved in the way in which the scientist thinks and on the general characteristics of the tools he uses in his work. This introduction should not distract the reader from the fact that the scientist does not work in a vacuum: that his research is deeply rooted in events in the real world. The educational research worker cannot sit in an ivory tower. He must, at some time in his work, go out and collect data which has relevance for the building of scientific knowledge about educational events. This chapter and the next are especially concerned with the data-collection phase of the educational research enterprise.

What Is an Observation?

The term *observation* is used by the scientist in a somewhat different sense from that in which it is generally used. The data that form the central core of a scientific study and from which the results and conclusions are ultimately derived consist of observations. Indeed, an item of data may be referred to as an observation even if it was derived from a machine that recorded how individuals in a particular situation behaved, and if it involved the scientific observer only indirectly. The subjects of the inquiry may not have been directly observed at all, but the resulting record is referred to as an observation or as a series of observations, even if never recorded by a human observer.

In the behavioral sciences, observations may be made in two distinct areas. They may be made concerning the situations to which individuals are exposed. They may also be made concerning the responses of persons to those situations. Unfortunately, it sometimes happens that observations on stimulus conditions have to be made, or are made, indirectly from response conditions. When the counselor is faced with an account of home conditions as told by a student who has serious emotional problems, he may have to make inferences concerning what is objective observation on the part of the student and what is the product of his own distorted perceptions. This difficulty has increased and strengthened the role of the social worker in psychotherapy, for the social worker, among his other activities, can assume the role of direct observer of the conditions that affect the patient's behavior.

From a research point of view, the nature of conditions to which individuals are exposed must be determined directly. Response-inferred conditions such as the clinical psychologist or the psychiatrist is forced to consider cannot possibly form a basis for research that is at all satisfactory. Conditions existing in the classroom should be established independently of what pupils say about them. Insofar as feasible, they should not be described in terms of what a human observer believes them to be, because the process of interpreting events introduces distortion in an unknown direction and by unknown amounts. If mechanical instrumentation can possibly be used for recording relevant conditions, it should be used—not only because of its objectivity, but also because of the permanence of the records that such instrumentation provides.

The Functions of Mechanical Instrumentation

Instrumentation represents an observation technique that is generally much better adapted to experimentation than to field observation occurring under existing conditions over which the experimenter does not attempt to exert control. Physical instrumentation, as a result of its very nature, must restrict the recording of observation to a quite narrow channel of events. In the field observation situation, it is difficult to arrange matters in such a way that this narrow channel can be picked up, recorded, and quantified without tampering with the situation that it is desired to record.

The first type of instrumentation is likely to serve only the most trivial ends in educational research. While it is possible to measure such factors as the classroom temperature, the illumination on the page of the book or in the classroom as a whole, or the noise level in a particular situation, it is only rarely that some significant relationship is found between such variables and significant aspects of human behavior. Those aspects of the pupil's environment that can be quantified without resorting to instrumentation are likely to represent the most significant aspects of the educational environment. There is no need to resort to instrumentation to determine the number of books in the school library, the number of pupils in the class, the years of training of the teacher, and such items.

Physical instrumentation in research may serve two primary purposes. First, it may simply provide a record of events as they occur. Motion pictures and sound recordings of classroom happenings are of this character. These serve only the purpose of making it possible to reproduce the essential elements of a particular situation again and again, so that the material may be re-evaluated or re-assessed in some way by other raters or other observers. The bulk of the material that this involves is always substantial, and the process is costly. Instrumentation that permits reproducibility should be embarked upon only when there has been the most careful planning and where adequate funds are available for the purchase of materials and the employment of personnel.

The second type of instrumentation serves more than the purpose of recording events as they occur, for the product is not just a record but a quantification and reduction of events to measures that can be used. For example, it may be possible to determine how much movement the teacher makes around the classroom in a given period of time by equipping him with a pedometer. The pedometer will provide a single over-all score, which indicates the number of steps taken during the period of observation. However, it is rare that instruments which permit the recording of particularly relevant behavior can be attached to a teacher or to pupils in a classroom situation. Instrumentation is much more appropriate to a laboratory situation in which special provision is made both for the appearance of particular aspects of behavior and for their measurement.

It may be pointed out at this time that the use of physical instrumentation necessarily places restrictions on what is to be observed. Most physical instrumentation results in the measurement and recording of only a limited aspect of phenomena. This is true regardless of whether the phenomena are derived from the physical or from the behavioral sciences. Usually, those selected are believed to be crucial elements of the phenomenon that is being studied; and since few can be measured, it is essential that these elements be crucial and that they be of theoretical significance.

The student of education may not be fully aware of the complicated measurement function of instruments in research. An example may illustrate this function. A relatively simple electronic device may be constructed to record the noise level in a classroom. This device registers the various physical disturbances of the atmosphere that fall within the range of audible frequencies, combines the energy values of these various disturbances, and indicates on a meter some linear or other function of these energy values. The device may be arranged so that it will give an average reading of the noise over, say, a ten-minute period. The instrument can be adapted to provide a numerical reading related to the particular function of noise that it is desired to record. It can thus automatically summate and eliminate the need for numerous readings, which otherwise would have to be summated by hand.

Apparatus in Educational Research

Many theses and dissertations in the field of education have had to be abandoned because of apparatus problems, and some have been extended years beyond the expected date of completion for the same reason. It is therefore appropriate that a few comments be made here in order to steer the student away from some of the deeper pitfalls in the use of apparatus.

First, it is perhaps worth pointing out that the author has known a number of graduate students who insisted on developing research projects involving apparatus that took years to build. Some of these students failed to reach the point of obtaining a doctoral degree simply because they never completed the apparatus. If the student doubts that he can build the required equipment within the space of a few months, he usually should abandon his dissertation problem and find another. Students differ greatly in their ability to build apparatus, and only the student himself can judge his capacity for building experimental equipment. One suspects that the person who has high competence in this respect is also the individual who can show the greatest ingenuity in developing simple designs. Many apparatus troubles result from a failure to simplify apparatus to the point where it will achieve the desired purpose with a minimum number of working parts.

Second, in the planning of apparatus, it is most desirable to incorporate working units that are already available, such as slide-projectors, camera shutters, chronoscopes, and amplifiers. Much equipment that is available around a college can be adapted for experimental purposes.

Third, it is of the utmost importance that equipment be such that it will be relatively free of malfunctions. Apparatus that breaks down during the course of data collection wastes one of the assets that the experimenter has to conserve most carefully; namely, the time given him by his experimental subjects. Freedom from malfunction is partly a function of complexity and partly a function of good design and the use of appropriate materials. Do not, for example, build apparatus in which moving parts are made of wood. These are always unsatisfactory. If metal parts cannot be made, then try using plastics, which will not shrink and expand with changes in the humidity of the atmosphere, as will wooden parts. Plastics such as Lucite can be easily bent into desired shapes when warm and can be filed and machined when cold. Electrical contacts are always a serious source of malfunction, and for this reason all connections should be soldered. Where switches are required, it is important that good quality products be used, and the experimenter should never use the homemade variety. Particularly useful are modern microswitches and relays, which can be obtained in good quality at a cheap price. Small mercury switches are also cheap and are most satisfactory where small electrical loads are to be carried.

The building of complicated electrical equipment should be limited. It is rarely desirable for the student to work out his own electronic circuits, since those already available are likely to represent the limit of what can be accomplished at the present time. This is particularly true of DC amplifiers, which provide enormous amplification but are also unstable unless they have rather complicated additional balancing circuits.

The reader should perhaps be warned that the cost of having an instrument company build apparatus is usually prohibitive. This statement does not mean that instrument companies charge unreasonable prices, for the actual cost of producing such equipment is high. Not only does it require expensive and elaborate machine tools hence high overhead charges, it also requires relatively well-paid craftsmen and highly paid supervisors. In addition, even the smallest part that is to be custom made must be drawn by a skilled draftsman before the task of making it is assigned to the machinist.

Finally, whenever a piece of apparatus is made for conducting an experiment, it is desirable that the entire experimental procedure, once it is started with a particular subject, be completely automatic and not require the intervention of the experimenter. Although there are exceptions, it is by and large most undesirable for the experimenter to have to stop the apparatus from time to time in order to interject some addition to the directions. Thus, if the experiment is conducted by running a sound-recording tape, it is desirable that the full directions to the subject also be recorded on the same tape.

With respect to the use of standard moving picture or sound-recording equipment, a word of caution may be voiced. While the products of such equipment may enable the observer to review events at his leisure, this review is usually a time-consuming and tedious procedure and is rarely worth the effort that it involves.

One ingenious adaptation of a photographic technique may be mentioned. This technique was first developed by Arthur Lumsdaine and was later further perfected by Nicholas Rose. The purpose of these investigators was to record audience responses to moving pictures by means of infrared photography, which permitted the taking of pictures in a darkened room without the audience being aware of the fact. The series of still shots was then analyzed. Figure IV shows an example of an audience response recorded by this technique.

THE DIRECT OBSERVATION OF PHENOMENA

Up to this point, discussion has not been centered on the direct observation of phenomena but on the instrumental recording and quantification of events. This procedure circumvents the major difficulties encountered in direct observation and the computation of quantitative measures derived from the observations. The limitations of instrumentation are such that the educational re-

FIGURE IV. *Infrared photograph of an audience watching a sequence from the film* Life of Riley. *This photograph is the result of a technique for studying audience behavior and is part of an unpublished doctoral dissertation—"A Psychological Study of Motion Picture Audience Behavior," by Nicholas Rose, Ph.D., now Chief Psychologist, Wadsworth Veterans Administration Hospital, Los Angeles 25, California.* (Photo by courtesy of Dr. Rose.)

searcher is inevitably brought up against the problems of observing directly both behavior and environmental conditions.

Perhaps a word is necessary to indicate what is meant by the word *phenomenon*. In educational research, observations are derived from environmental conditions, from behavior, or from certain static characteristics of the individual, such as his height, his appearance, and so forth. These sources of observations are referred to here collectively as *phenomena*.

Some Observable Characteristics of the Pupil's Environment

The material aspects of the environment which have the greatest immediate impact on the learner are those closely associated with the curriculum, such as textbooks and other items of educational equipment. The analysis and assessment of the properties of these materials, a difficult and complex matter, will be treated in the next chapter. For the present, consideration will be given to those aspects of the educational environment which can be more easily appraised and studied.

While materials related to the curriculum impinge most directly on the pupil, other aspects of his environment may also contribute to or interfere with learning even though their influence is less direct and probably less extensive. Administrators agree that the arrangement of a school building may facilitate some activities but interfere with others. In recent times schools which have wished to introduce team teaching have often been hampered by the fact that traditional school buildings are not well suited to a team-teaching approach. Architects and administrators have worked together on the development of floor layouts which would permit team teaching and provide a situation in which groups of children can be readily divided up into smaller groups for some purposes and reassembled for others. Little is known about how space provisions in schools are related to function. Even some of the more easily appraised characteristics of the environment, such as the amount of playground space per pupil, have not been properly studied in relation to pupil utilization. State recommendations for minimum amounts of playground space per pupil are based on judgment rather than on knowledge. Such questions as the amount of playground space actually used can be investigated by fairly straightforward observational techniques and interesting results obtained. Other relationships of pupil behavior to directly measurable aspects of the environment need to be explored. For example, classroom space per pupil may be expected to have an effect on quality and frequency of pupil-pupil interactions. The type of questioning techniques used by the teacher—whether the questions merely ask for information or require the pupil to make deductions from knowledge already in his possession—may be an important determinant of what is learned.

Research is still lacking on the effect on learning exerted by some of the more easily identified characteristics of the pupil's social environment. While size of class as an environmental characteristic has been extensively studied, there is still a lack of data on the interaction of the sex of the teacher and the sex of the pupil in relation to learning. It may well be that women teachers are more successful in helping girls while men teachers are more successful in helping boys. Teachers' ages and years of experience are also easily assessed characteristics which, one may speculate, have important relationships to what happens in classrooms. Other easily observed characteristics of aspects of the pupil's environment could be enumerated. Research does not have to involve characteristics of the environment which are difficult to measure for it to be significant, although some research workers may be interested in the study of complex characteristics or characteristics that can be measured only indirectly.

Much less easily measured are the economic and cultural circumstances which form the background of the pupil. While family income can generally be estimated, how the family spends the income may be more important than how much income is spent. Measures of income utilization by the family are still very underdeveloped despite their importance to research in sociology and social psychology.

Problems in the Observation of Behavior

Faith in the value of observing behavior would appear to be a cornerstone of teacher education. Some teacher-education programs emphasize the need for sending the teacher in training out into schools to observe at the earliest stages of professional study. Observation as such is considered a useful activity. Some, however, question this procedure, saying that unless a person knows what to observe the activity may be quite pointless and useless, and that the mere activity of looking and seeing serves little purpose unless certain other conditions have been established previously.

Much the same is true of scientific observation. It would be almost universally agreed that observation is an activity of central importance to the scientist, but it is not just a looking-and-seeing activity. This is a fact that is not always properly appreciated by the person who embarks on his first scientific inquiry. The writer can recall an educator who was starting on one of his first researches, which he decided should be in the general area of teacher effectiveness. He decided that the best way of starting research in this area was to undertake an extensive program of classroom observation. After many hours of this activity, he found that it did not seem to be leading anywhere. Since he felt that his technique of observation might be at fault, he invited some of his graduate students to participate with him in these observation sessions. Much to his surprise, this did not seem to improve matters, and the project was abandoned because it did not appear to be producing results.

The error in this approach lies in the assumption that the mere process of looking at phenomena will reveal what is relevant in them for particular purposes. Conan Doyle in his Sherlock Holmes stories provides an illustration of this fallacious type of outlook. Sherlock Holmes' success is attributed in large measure to his "powers of observation," and it is implied that he is naturally able to see more details in what he observes than are the other characters. This concept is derived from a fallacious psychology, which equates the data of sensory experience with what is perceived. Perception is, in contrast, necessarily an interpretive process. In observing a classroom, the sensory data consist of movements of physical objects and vibrations in the atmosphere which are referred to as sounds, but what is perceived is vastly different from this conglomeration of changes in physical energy. What is perceived is an organized, continuing activity, but the concepts and ideas in terms of which the activity is perceived depend upon the experience and training of the observer.

The latter point can be clarified by describing an experience that happened to the author some years ago, when he was invited to participate in classroom observation as a part of a program of research. One of his fellow observers was a clinical psychologist with strong leanings toward the psychoanalytic point of view. The other was an educator with substantial experience in the training of teachers but with only a meager background in current psychological theory. Indeed, the interests of the latter individual were more in the realm of developing specific classroom skills, and were little inclined toward the interpretation of teacher behavior in terms of personality traits and mechanisms that were products of the individual's own background and personal history. These two observers gave entirely different descriptions of what went on in a particular classroom. In his description, the clinical psychologist referred to the extensive oral aggression of the teacher whenever it appeared that the classroom situation was getting out of control. He also pointed out that such oral aggression (raised voice) was also followed by feelings of guilt, which made her inclined to offer the children various minor rewards, consisting mainly of mild praise. The educator, on the other hand, described the teacher's raised voice merely as disorganized behavior resulting from the fact that she had not acquired genuine facility in using the skills needed for the control of a class of children. What the clinician described as behavior reflecting guilt feelings, the educator described as a return to skillful methods of exercising control over a classroom.

The point here is that any useful description of the tremendous complexities of events in the classroom must be made in terms of a system of interpretation, commonly referred to as a frame of reference. It is necessary for the observer to do more than describe the objectively occurring events, for these are mere movements of conglomerations of matter. What is needed is the abstraction of various classes of these events, in terms of what are believed to be certain relevant determinants of behavior or to have certain important consequences. The situation is considerably different from that encountered by physicists in observing the moving needle of a galvanometer. The physicist would be able to stay closely with the task of describing strictly what he observed in terms of a simple motion in space. No complex interpretations need be introduced. The situation to be observed does not involve the vast complexities of a classroom, which, because of the immense number of simultaneously occurring events, can be described only by reducing these events to certain broad but meaningful categories. Writers on research in the behavioral sciences have often compared observation in the physical sciences with that in their own field without stressing this essential difference between the two.

The reader may well ask at this point, "Surely would not the observer be performing an observation process comparable to that performed by a physicist when he enters a classroom and notes the frequency of such well-described events as yawning among pupils?" However, even when such well-defined phenomena are involved, judgment is not entirely eliminated. The observer must decide whether a student who opens his mouth just slightly and then closes it is yawning. Human activity of even the simplest sort shows a wide range of variation. It is for this reason that the student of behavior must be concerned with the reliability of observation, while the physicist does not have this problem except under very rare circumstances. If human behavior were more stereotyped, the psychologist would not be faced with this problem to the same degree.

What has been said does not lead to the conclusion that observation without clearly defining what has to be observed is always a pointless activity; for the fact is that under certain circumstances it may be useful, particularly in the early stages of an inquiry, but only if it is properly carried out. Suppose that an investigator held the theory that hostile acts on the part of the teacher tended to result in hostile acts on the part of the pupil. He might start by sitting down in his office and listing pupil acts and teacher acts that could be considered as hostile, but his own memory might turn out to be a poor source of materials for this purpose. At this point, he might feel that a better source of information would be the classroom itself. On this basis, the investigator might well visit several classrooms for the purpose of obtaining lists of behaviors that might be considered symptomatic of hostility. At the same time, he could obtain some estimate of the frequency of each one of these behaviors. Clearly it would not be useful to include in such a list of behaviors those that occur only very rarely, because the investigation might not include a sample of sufficient size to include a single observation in this category.

General classroom observation of the type discussed in the previous paragraph also serves the purpose of indicating the extent to which hostile behaviors are identifiable. While careful reliability studies must be undertaken later, it is important to obtain at an early stage a rough estimate of the extent to which observers can agree on the presence or absence of particular aspects of behavior. Items that are not easily identified may then be removed from the list at an early stage. Sometimes items of behavior that one may expect to be easily recognized do not appear so when an attempt is made to identify them in a classroom situation.

Once this initial stage has been completed, the investigator will have in his possession knowledge of what can and cannot be done in the way of collecting in the classroom data that are relevant to the solution of his problem. It then becomes important to systematize the observation process. This is usually accomplished by preparing a schedule that is to be used by observers in subsequent phases of the investigation. Such a schedule both serves the function of indicating what is to be observed and provides a means of recording the observations.

The Recording of Observations

In research, special problems not met in daily life are encountered in the recording of direct observations of behavior. Consider, for example, the observations that are made by the teacher in conducting her class. These represent a range and variety of facts that are singled out from the vast medley of happenings in the classroom because they appear to have some special significance to the development of the pupil about whom they are made. These facts are observed and recorded for a great many different purposes. They may provide information to be passed on to the school psychologist, the parents, or the teacher of remedial reading, or to be used later in counseling the child. They may also be used in helping the child learn by giving appropriate assignments or in some other way. Usually, if they are recorded at all they are set down as brief anecdotes relating the salient elements in the incident. Now while such facts are extremely important from the point of view of running the classroom, they do not constitute the kind of data that the scientist seeks to collect. This fact is often not well appreciated by educators, some of whom have been known to arrive at graduate schools with several crates of such materials and the hope of deriving a doctoral dissertation from them. They are usually embarrassed by the answer to their question, "Here are the data, now what do I do with them?" While the reader at this point will know that the definition of the research problem must generally precede the collection of data, it still may not be clear to him how the data collected by the teacher, and the way in which they are collected, differ from those used by the scientist. Therefore, some expansion in this point is needed.

The first point of contrast has already been made; namely, that the teacher collects data for a multiplicity of purposes while the scientist does so for the sole purpose of testing a single central hypothesis.

A second point is that the teacher uses the data as they are collected, while the scientist processes his findings in order that they may be used to answer the questions that have been asked. The scientist cannot use directly the crude data presented by such material as anecdotal records. For the teacher, such records convey the required meaning directly, but for the scientist the meaning is much more indirect. The scientist prefers to handle his data by first reducing them to quantities and then manipulating these quantities through the application of quantitative methods. In many areas of inquiry, particularly in those where research is a relatively new enterprise, the scientist cannot live up to this ideal. Anthropologists, for example, have typically collected rather large quantities of data through note taking procedures and have attempted to discern general principles running through them. However, even in such a field, quantitative methods are slowly having an impact on research procedures. By way of illustration one may point out that linguists, who make careful quantitative analyses of language characteristics, are having an important impact on anthropological research. In the meantime anthropologists have done much to improve their notetaking procedures. Educational research has tended to place emphasis on measurement rather than on the use of descriptions, and the approach discussed here reflects this trend.

Rating as a Method of Reducing Data

Much of the data that are manipulated in educational research must be reduced to quantitative terms by means of a rating procedure. Unless one is dealing with a case in which the rater judges the relative frequency with which an event occurs, the rating procedure involves the evaluation of numerous events, which individually have only small relevance and probably low reliability but which collectively may have value for prediction purposes. If it were possible to design a machine that would identify these events, score them for significance, and then add up the scores to give a total—and if it were possible for the machine to do this consistently—the results would probably be much superior to those produced by the human rater. The scores or ratings produced by human raters are based on a much less consistent performance than that of our imaginary machine. Actually, the method of reducing data by means of a rating procedure is quite complex, because the rating is usually based not on a well-defined series of events but on a rather vague universe of events, often defined only in the most general terms. If the researcher considers the rater as a rather complicated machine for reducing data, it is evident that in order to have proper control over the measures derived by the procedure he must know what goes into the machine as well as the nature of the operation performed by it. The fact that there is very little control over the data that our statistical reduction machine is given to use accounts to a great extent for the unsatisfactory nature of ratings. An additional complexity in the use of ratings arises from the fact that two ratings (on two pupils, two teachers, or two whatever else) may not be based on the same data at all. This is not quite as damaging as it sounds, for we could compare the achievement of two pupils even if they did not take the same form of test, and even though the items that they answered were different.

When two supposedly parallel forms of a test have been equated and it has been demonstrated that scores from the two can be used interchangeably, the researcher feels little hesitation in treating scores from one or the other as if they were alike. The equivalence of data derived from two sets of facts must usually be assumed in the treatment of ratings. A rater is employed to derive whatever significance may be possible from the data, and this he does on the basis of judgment, which in turn is based upon experience. An illustration may help to clarify this point. Suppose that one were to rate the children in a class with respect to their cooperativeness with the teacher. Cooperativeness might be manifested in a number of ways, such as doing assigned work quietly, attending to the teacher when she is speaking, volunteering to help with chores such as cleaning the blackboard, volunteering information in class discussions, helping other children with assignments, restraining aggressiveness when reprimanded, and through an immense range of additional and varied behaviors. The rater has at his disposal a sample of these behaviors, but no two children present the same sample, since each shows cooperation or the lack of it in a form that is compatible with his own personality structure. The rater must somehow evaluate the evidence provided by each pupil and make some judgment concerning what that evidence shows concerning cooperativeness. The task is obviously an extremely difficult and complex one, particularly so since the ground rules for the whole operation have not been precisely defined. It is small wonder that the results of many studies that involve ratings produce only a mass of data to which there is little rhyme or reason and from which no useful scientific knowledge is derived.

If control is to be exercised over the rating process so that the product is meaningful, it is necessary to control both the type and quantity of information to be used by the rater and the processing that this information is to undergo. Let us consider the first of these problems.

It is extremely difficult to define for an observer just what is the universe of events to be observed, and, in fact, this is not usually done except in the vaguest terms. For example, a teacher may be asked to rate pupils for their ability to work with other children in small groups. It is probable that the researcher engaged in this enterprise would supply the teacher with a rating scale in which various positions would be described in such terms as "Works well with group, seems to add to what the group accomplishes, contributes to the smoothness with which the group operates"; and perhaps at the other end of the scale the statement, "Generally seems to be a source of friction and irritation in a group." Now such a series of statements does very little to orient the rater in the matter of what to observe, but rather it assumes that the rater knows the kinds of observations that are necessary and relevant in order to arrive at the kind of judgment that the scale demands. There is no entirely satisfactory way of remedying this situation. An obvious partial solution is to provide a preface to be read as an orientation to the use of the scale. While such a preface may help to orient the rater on the matter of what he is to observe, it can refer to only a limited sample of the universe of behaviors to be observed, since a long list becomes tedious to read and remember. It may also draw attention to certain specific behaviors, and the rater may easily forget that the behaviors listed are supposed to represent only a sample, not the total universe, of behaviors to be observed.

An alternative procedure, which has considerable merit, is to develop a rating scale consisting of many scales, each of which is directed to a fairly specific aspect of the total domain of behavior that is to be observed. If pupils are to be rated on their ability to work in small groups, each pupil might be rated with respect to each one of several aspects of the behavior and perhaps as many as twenty aspects might be listed. When such a procedure has been adopted, it is usually desirable to perform a factor analysis of the ratings to determine whether they can be considered to contribute to a single principal factor. One major advantage of the multiple-rating approach, in addition to the assistance that it gives in defining the domain of behavior to be observed, is that it usually helps to increase the reliability of ratings.

Efforts to Control the Rating Process

Efforts to exercise control over the rating process are familiar, for the common ones are cited in every textbook in educational measurement. The student is undoubtedly familiar with these the usual rules such as the following:

1. Define several points on each scale with as great precision as possible.
2. Restrict each rating scale to a narrow range of behavior that can be well defined.
3. Change the ends of the scale so that the "good" end is not always at the top or always at the bottom of the scale.
4. Avoid words such as *average* in the middle range of the scale. The rater who does not wish to give too much effort to the rating procedure is likely to class too many as "average."

5. In the directions, indicate the need for honest rating, and, wherever possible, state that a low rating will not have any consequence for the person rated, either direct or indirect.
6. Assure the rater that his anonymity will be safeguarded.

But rules such as these, which are useful tips and provide some little help in rating, do not result in the exercise of adequate control over the rating process, at least not the type of control that an experimenter might wish to exercise over the way in which measures are produced. The usual suggestions are not to be disregarded, for they may perhaps convert wholly inadequate procedures into procedures that, although poor, have enough value to make them usable to a limited degree.

The various attempts to improve the traditional type of rating scale have not produced any instruments that represent a startling improvement over those of several decades ago. It is also doubtful whether any of the more novel approaches to rating have been more successful. One of these, which has been a source of considerable controversy, is the forced-choice approach of the type developed by the Adjutant General's Office. The reader is referred to Guilford's *Psychometric Methods* (1954) for a discussion of this technique, which at this time must be considered of a controversial nature. Unfortunately, it is extremely difficult for a reader to disentangle the merits and demerits of this particular technique, because the enthusiasm of some of its users gives impressions that a more critical appraisal do not justify. Such uncritical appraisal makes it difficult for readers of the literature on forced-choice methodology to determine what has and what has not been accomplished. It is hoped that the reader will review articles on this topic with a much more dispassionate eye than is typical of their writers.

Reliability of Ratings

In theory, if our directions concerning what is to be observed are sufficiently exact, if the observer has been precisely informed concerning the operations to be performed, and if the method of recording the final product of these processes has been well defined, it should be possible for two observers to arrive at closely similar if not identical ratings after observing groups of situations in which there are a range of differences. Interobserver reliability provides some evidence of the extent to which all of these factors have been specified in a satisfactory way. It is possible that good interrater agreement may be achieved even though adequate specifications for the entire procedure have not been provided. For example, teachers may agree on rating pupils for social adjustment even though they cannot provide an adequate definition of what is meant by this characteristic. On the other hand, if all specifications have been accurately made and are capably followed by two observers, it is inevitable that the resulting ratings will agree.

If ratings are to be meaningful, it must be possible to communicate the rating process so that different individuals can achieve the same results. If the procedure is not communicable, then it is evident that the particular research is not repeatable because of the lack of communicability of the operations that it involves. For this reason, in all studies that involve ratings it is necessary to demonstrate that there is interrater reliability, for lack of such reliability probably indicates lack of communicability of the procedures that the research involves.

There is also considerable value to be achieved in determining the consistency of rating from occasion to occasion. If there is consistency among raters but not from occasion to occasion, it indicates that the phenomenon studied is not a stable one. If teachers were to be rated for some aspect of aggressive behavior shown toward children in the classroom, it is quite probable that raters would agree well among each other concerning the amount of aggression shown on a certain occasion, but the teacher might show little or no consistency in this trait from one occasion to another. Indeed, the amount shown might depend primarily on such factors as the time of day and the presence or absence of petty out-of-school frustrations.

In most rating studies an effort is made to work with characteristics that have stability over time, but it is quite conceivable

that studies might be run in which changeability of the characteristic rated was sought—as, for example, if the researcher were
investigating changes in the behavior of the new pupil as he
adapts to the school situation. Under such a condition, the researcher would want consistency from rater to rater, but not from
occasion to occasion if the occasions were so spaced as to cover
a period of time over which changes were hypothesized to occur.
Sometimes it may be desired to collect data in such a way that
the effects of certain changes on the phenomena to be observed
will be eliminated. Thus, in the hypothetical study of the aggressive behavior of teachers, it might be desired to eliminate variations that occur during the course of a day, and for this reason
it might be planned to collect ratings only during the first hour
of each day of teaching. By means of an analogous procedure,
variations during the course of the week might also be eliminated.

The Validity of Ratings

Since ratings are so widely used in educational research a word
must be said concerning their validity; that is to say, the extent
to which predictions and other inferences can be made from
them. A research worker who has collected a great quantity of
data involving ratings is likely to have the impression that he has
obtained reliable measures of important variables. Most of us
think of ourselves as good judges of human nature—when our
judgments turn out to be wrong, we are surprised. This same
tendency leads the research worker to overvalue data which he
has collected in the form of ratings.

Let us consider briefly some of the inferences that might be
made from the ratings of teachers on characteristics commonly
considered to be related to the learning process. Lists of such
characteristics, of which there are many, commonly include
traits such as ability to explain, friendliness, vigor, well-organized, and so forth. Let us suppose that an observer spent two

thirty-minute periods with each teacher before making the ratings. The chances are that the ratings of this observer would show some agreement with those of another observer but that the two sets of ratings for any characteristic would not likely be correlated more than about 0.5. This means that there would be some agreement between the observers who might also agree that the characteristics rated should be related to the amount of learning manifested by the children. However, judging from past experiences with ratings, one could say with some certainty that most of the ratings would show no relationship to measures of learning. In very few cases is one justified in making inferences from ratings of human behavior. At the best, relationships with other variables are small.

The Interview as an Observational Technique

Up to this point, our discussion has mainly centered on the problem of observing classroom and group-activity situations. In such cases the observer is almost always external to the situation observed. In the interview, on the other hand, it is usual for the observer to be the interviewer and thus to form a part of the total situation within which observations are made. Attempts have been made to introduce observers who are outside of the interview situation, but this is not a usual technique. When the latter technique is used, the interviewer can play a role in which he has been thoroughly drilled, and can do so unhampered by recording procedures.

Interviews may vary in the extent to which they are structured. The chief advocates of the unstructured interview have been clinical psychologists, who have used extensively the type of interview in which the conversation is left to wander where it will. The argument has been that, since the causes of particular characteristics of behavior vary from person to person, questions that are appropriate for probing in one case are inappropriate in another. The clinician feels a need to vary his tactics as the situation demands. One consequence of this flexibility is that he is not likely to discover laws that apply to a number of individuals, and indeed that is not what he is looking for.

The researcher, on the other hand, is looking for general laws· and has little, if any, interest in the idiosyncrasies that make each patient a unique person. He cannot possibly consider the idea of collecting each item of data under different conditions from every other item. For this reason, when he conducts an interview the data from which are to be used for general scientific purposes he attempts to introduce as much uniformity as possible into the procedure. If the interview is to be highly structured, he asks the same series of questions of each person interviewed and does not vary either the order of the questions or the tone of voice in which they are asked. He establishes a uniform procedure that he applies whenever the respondent becomes discursive and wanders too much from the question asked. He uses the same introductory and concluding remarks.

If a structured interview is used, and if it proceeds with an organized list of standardized questions, it may be found desirable to ask questions that are open-ended or those that restrict the possible responses that the interviewee may make. In the former case, the interviewee is expected to *recall* or generate an answer. In the latter case, it is necessary only for the interviewee to recognize the response of his choice. There is some evidence that recognition, at least in a test situation, produces more information, and more accurate information, than recall. One presumes this is true also of an interview situation, but there is little empirical fact to support this view. When the interviewee is free to give any answer to the questions of the interviewer, there is danger that the interviewer may incorrectly record what is said or the gist of what is said. While the amount of distraction undoubtedly varies from situation to situation, there is at least one study by Payne (1949) in which 25 per cent of statements recorded by the interviewer were found to be wrong when they were compared with a recording of the entire interview. Such errors are much less likely to occur when the interviewee indicates to an interviewer which one of a number of statements printed on a card represents his particular choice of response. However, even in the latter case, the procedure for recording the response is not entirely devoid of error. There are also a few persons who refuse to choose any of the responses provided, preferring to modify one of them before they accept it.

An important aspect of the interview situation is the interviewer himself. For long it was not realized that it is necessary to know something about the characteristics of this individual if the products of the interview are to be evaluated. Those engaged in public-opinion polls have found that interviewers not only tend to select certain types of persons to interview, but the responses of the interviewee are related to the characteristics of the interviewer. Controlling interviewer characteristics is not a matter that can be undertaken easily at the present time. Some characteristics that influence some types of response are known, but others are not. It is also not known to what extent training may result in uniformity of interviewer characteristics.

The novice in research is likely to feel that interviews and methods by which the personal inner life of the individual can be studied offer special promise for yielding knowledge that can be used ultimately for the prediction of behavior. The behavioral sciences started out with this contention, which dominated nineteenth century psychology. The notion has been perpetuated by psychiatrists, who have consistently advocated the use of individual interviews for selecting persons for special assignments. Yet the rather puzzling fact remains that researches involving inquiry into the inner life of the individual have been extremely unsuccessful. The reasons for this remain quite obscure, but it is perhaps of some value to the would-be researcher to consider certain sources of difficulty in the methodology of studying the individual, with the hope that this may help the student to avoid them.

First, in any interview in which one person conducts an inquiry into the inner life of another, the situation is much more complex than can be described in terms of an observer and the observed. The situation is more accurately described as involving an observer and a person responding to an observer. The responses are a result of the behavior of the observer and the characteristics of the observed. It is quite possible that relatively minor changes in the behavior of the observer could produce quite pronounced changes in that of the observed. The latter can be clearly seen in the administration of the Rorschach. Any behavior on the part of the Rorschach administrator that indicates that the situation involves threat to the ego of the examinee results in restrained responses. What the observer notes is as much a product of his own behavior as it is a product of the observed's characteristics.

Second, it follows from what has been said that, unless the observer can manifest the same uniform patterns of behavior toward all those who are observed, he introduces a series of quite irrelevant variables into the situation. It is clear that observers are unable to reproduce uniform patterns of behavior when faced with varied situations. Even among actors who in the same play, night after night, face the same situation, there is considerable variation in performance. Many times greater is the variation in the performances of a person interviewing another. This variation is quite beyond the control that an individual can exercise over his behavior.

Third, interviewing procedures are usually based on the assumption that the person interviewed has insight into the causes of his behavior. Clinical psychologists, through experience now covering several decades, have come to the conclusion that insight into the causes of behavior is something rarely achieved, and that even with the extended help of the clinician, it is acquired by dint of long and hard effort. The assumption that it is possible to discover the causes of behavior by means of a short interview is a conception of psychological research that has long since been abandoned.

Fourth, there are difficulties in quantifying the data provided by the interview. Often the data are such that they do not lend themselves to quantification. Rarely is it possible to quantify by enumeration, as when the scientist counts the number of words that refer to a given content category. The best that can be done is to rate certain characteristics of the interviewee's behavior.

Fifth, in individual methods of appraisal, the psychologist is often looking for the laws of the behavior of the individual. Insofar as these can be discovered, they yield qualitative statements that summarize trends in past behavior, but these trends may not be related to the making of the desired type of prediction. In contrast, objective methods of appraisal are always designed to measure variables that are empirically or rationally related to the variables that psychologists have sought to predict. The material derived from an interview may have only the most remote relevance.

Sixth, a person who is being studied by another may not be willing to give himself away. There is a real difference between the behavior of a person who visits a clinical psychologist in order to seek help and a person who is not motivated in this way to lay bare his innermost thoughts. In the latter case, there is a certain defensiveness about the individual's performance, and an unwillingness to reveal what is in his mind. Indeed, there are some who refuse to answer the simple questions asked by public-opinion pollsters because they say that this would be an infringement of their privacy. The same difficulty arises in the administration of certain types of tests, particularly instruments of the projective type. The patient at the clinic may be expected to give a much richer range of responses on the Rorschach test than the one who is taking the test as a part of some research study.

Finally, what has been said here does not mean that it is not possible to study individual cases over a period of time, for this can be done by many methods that permit the use of objective measuring devices.

In interview situations, unless it is otherwise desired, the greatest caution must be exercised lest the questions themselves convert the situation into a threatening one. In conducting a study of changes in attitudes from age twenty to age fifty, it would be most unwise to ask the fifty-year-old group how they voted *when they were young.* This would imply immediately that the fifty-year-olds were regarded as an aged group, an implication that might be quite unacceptable to them. Often it is possible to reduce the potential threatening effect of questions by implying that the phenomenon is a common one. If one asks a married person how long it was after he was married that he first contemplated separation or divorce, he is more likely to admit that such ideas have entered his mind than if asked whether he had ever contemplated separation or divorce. The first of these questions carries with it the implication that thoughts concerning divorce or separation are common, or even that they occur in the mind of every married person. The second question implies that such thoughts occur only in certain married persons. Sometimes the element of threat can be reduced by a mere change of terms. It is probable that married couples will be much more willing to talk about sources of friction in their marital relationships than they would be to discuss the things about which they quarrel. The latter is likely to arouse feelings of guilt to a much greater extent than the former.

At this point, the reader may well ask, "Why not just pass out a questionnaire? Why go to all the trouble of conducting an interview when both the questions and the responses are standardized?" The answers are, to a considerable extent, matters of opinion, but there is substantial consensus among experts.

First, and this appears to be well established, it seems possible to obtain a much higher percentage of respondents with an interview than when questionnaires are handed out. Interviewers commonly report less than 5 per cent refusals to answer questions, while returns from mailed questionnaires rarely exceed 40 per cent. There is also a tendency for those who answer questionnaires to omit the answers to some questions, through either forgetfulness or a distaste for facing the particular issue. Incompleteness of returns is rarely found when data are collected by interview.

Second, the interviewer is able to answer questions concerning the purpose of the interview, and the interviewee may be put at ease in a way that is not possible with questionnaire techniques. He is thus able to build up a feeling of confidence that makes for both cooperation and truthfulness.

Third, questionnaires present difficulties to persons of limited literacy, and the respondents to a mailed questionnaire study are likely to represent an undue proportion of the more literate public. In addition, persons who read with difficulty may not exercise the care that they should in finding and selecting the right answer, while the interviewer can take care of all such mechanical details.

Fourth, an interviewer can conduct an interview at a proper speed, while questionnaires are often filled in hurriedly. The writer can recall having to fill in a questionnaire late at night in order that it be available for collection the following morning. True, the questionnaire had lain around the house for two weeks, but somehow time had not been found to answer the questions. This kind of problem can be avoided if an interview is used.

On the other side of the picture, it may be said that it is often much more feasible to present in questionnaire form long and extended lists of questions which it would be very tedious and expensive to present orally. Such questionnaires, administered to highly literate groups, may yield large quantities of information that could not easily be obtained by the oral interview.

Recording of Interview Data

Many different methods are available for recording interview data and each has its own advantages and disadvantages. Circumstances must determine which one will be selected for a particular study.

A first point to note is that the interviewee provides a great wealth of information, only a part of which is likely to be noted and recorded. While the verbal behavior of the interviewee is generally a matter of central interest, he also provides information through his facial expression, body movements and gestures, and even through his dress. The research design involving the interview must specify what aspects of the information provided by the interviewee should be recorded and which of the recorded aspects should be coded. The recording of the interview, as the term *record* is used here, involves the procedure of obtaining a reproduction of what happened without summarization or interpretation. A transcription of a shorthand report of an interview taken down word for word approximates such a record as does a tape recording or a sound movie. On the other hand, the notes taken by an interviewer which summarized what happened do not constitute a record in this sense. They represent the combined processes of selecting, summarizing, and interpreting information which is referred to as the *coding process.*

There are substantial advantages to be accrued from the procedure of recording an entire interview and then, later, coding the information that it is desired to code. Such a procedure presents ethical as well as technical problems. With the development of pocket-size tape recorders there is the possibility of making a complete record of the verbal communication. Many if not most psychologists consider it unethical to record interviews without obtaining permission from the interviewee. The federal government has taken the position that the recording of telephone conversations without the knowledge of the conversants is illegal and the same general principle would appear to apply to the recording of verbal communications under other conditions. But one has to recognize that if the interviewee knows his words are to be recorded, this fact will exercise some influence on what is said. The same applies to the making of visual as well as auditory records.

If a record is kept of an interview, it can be analyzed at leisure and in a much more thorough fashion than when responses are coded at the time they are made. The reliability of the coding procedure can also be investigated when a record is available which can be played back to different coders. In this way a comparison can be made of the coding undertaken by one person and the coding undertaken by another.

A major difficulty involved in the use of complete records of an interview is the voluminousness of the material involved. If one hundred interviews are recorded on tape and each interview lasts thirty minutes, the total time recorded is fifty hours. If each tape has to be replayed four times for obtaining and coding the information an additional two hundred hours of listening time are involved. Since such listening is very tedious, the listening procedure may have to be extended over months, if a conscientious job is to be done. For this reason the records of interviews are not widely used in research, and most research workers have preferred to record certain limited observations during the interview, frequently coding them at the same time.

The Situation in Which Observations Are Made

The observational techniques selected for use depend upon the nature of the situation in which observations are made. If the assumption is made—and it is generally considered a reasonable one—that behavior is a function of both the situation and the personal characteristics of the individual, then it follows that it is necessary to arrange situations in such a manner that the behavior to be observed will emerge. This is generally recognized in experimental psychology, but rarely in educational research. Many studies have been conducted in which children have been observed both at work and at play, but in which no attempt at all has been made to control conditions existing at the time when the observations were made. Such a procedure is similar to administering a different test of achievement to each one of a number of children and then comparing the test score of one child with that of another. In the case of tests, comparability of the instruments used is an essential condition for comparing the scores, and this is rarely forgotten. However, where the situation used for measurement is not a test but a free-play or work situation, this necessary condition is often forgotten. Again, when interviews are used as situations in which observations are to be made, rarely is any comparability found among them.

There are certain aspects of all situations used as bases for observational data that have to be controlled if meaningful data are to be collected. First, there is the orientation to the situation as such. Usually this is a verbal orientation, and great care must be exercised in this process. It is not just when social behavior is being observed that this orientation procedure is of crucial importance. Even when a test is to be administered, the orientation procedure is a matter that may be of major importance in determining the score. It is now well known that, in the case of the Rorschach test, the responses depend to a very great extent on the circumstances surrounding the administration. If the orientation is such as to imply that the scores might be used in some way that vitally affects the person's future, it is likely that the performance on the test will be characterized by reticence or reserve. Whether the person knows it or not, he is likely to withhold information and to be much less free in giving responses when there is some threat involved in the situation than when no threat is involved. Much the same is true in any other situation in which persons are observed or tested, and it should be noted that the threat involved may be implied rather than stated. If a person, due to the serious attitude of the experimenter, is made to feel that whatever is being answered represents a characteristic of great importance to success in life, he will behave differently than if he feels that the procedure is just an experiment and of no consequence to him personally. The implications for the person under study must be clearly spelled out.

Second, if stooges are used as a part of the situation to which persons are to be exposed, it is important that they be well trained so that they respond in the same way to all. Those who are to function as a part of an experimental situation must learn not to respond differently to different personalities. Learning in this respect is probably only partial, since most persons are not aware of the extent to which they are responding to others.

Third, it is important to develop safeguards so that information about the situation is not transmitted from those who have been exposed to those who are still to be exposed. Sometimes the mere separation of subjects from others who have been exposed will suffice. Sometimes other precautions are necessary, such as the selection of persons from different classes or from different schools. It may help if subjects are asked not to divulge information, but even when this is done, there is likely to be some leakage of information.

Finally, it is hardly necessary to point out that some of the more obvious factors affecting behavior, such as time of day, should be carefully controlled, or designs that permit the separation of the variance attributable to these factors should be used.

Role-Playing as an Observational Technique

An interesting extension of the interview technique, in which there has been much interest in recent years, is found in role-playing. An example is given in an unpublished study in which it was desired to explore the personalities of prospective teachers by means of this technique. For this purpose a number of situations were developed. In one of these, one of the participants was given a rather detailed account of the behavior of a pupil in a class that the student was theoretically teaching. The student was given fifteen minutes in which to study the material, and was told that at the end of that period she would have to interview the mother of the pupil in order to discuss with her the problems of the child. Another student playing the role of the mother was instructed to take a very defensive attitude toward the child and a hostile attitude toward the teacher, placing the blame for the child's behavior on the way in which the school was managed. The scene was then spontaneously enacted by the two participants.

The reader can see that there are extensive possibilities for personality measurement and assessment in such a situation. The behavior of the persons involved can be rated for various characteristics, and there are also possibilities for using check lists for enumerating the frequency of occurrence of specific aspects of behavior. While the technique is still in the exploratory stages of development, promise is offered by the fact that persons placed in role-playing situations become deeply involved emotionally. Many play their parts as if they were completely identified with the character portrayed. The technique cannot yet be considered as a ready-made usable product, but it is an interesting invention.

Role-playing also has potentialities as a training technique. It offers promise as a direct means of teaching persons to handle rather complex social situations. Here is a fine field for educational research.

The Usefulness of the Observational Techniques Reviewed

When educational psychology began to develop over half a century ago, it was hoped that relatively simple techniques for observing and recording aspects of behavior would yield information of great value to the educator. This hope has not been fulfilled. Simple rating procedures have not proved themselves to be a satisfactory way of assessing relatively enduring personality traits. Nevertheless, researchers will probably continue for many years to conduct studies in which ratings are used, because it is believed that the small amount of information provided is better than no information at all. Also, at the present time there does not appear to be anything in sight that might be considered an improved substitute.

In recent years it has been hoped that a substitute for rating might be found in measures derived by placing persons in standardized situations and measuring aspects of their performance in these situations. This approach, which has commonly been referred to as an assessment procedure, has failed to yield results that can be considered in any way superior to those obtained from traditional procedures. Such procedures are based upon the assumption that personality traits that appear in one situation will appear in other and different situations also. This simply does not seem to be the case. A person who is aggressive in one situation is withdrawn in another. A person who is happy when he is in one place is unhappy in another. A theory on which observation is based must ultimately take into account the variability of behavior from one situation to another.

Summary

1. The scientist uses the term *observation* in a rather different sense from that ordinarily used. The scientist refers to an item of data as an observation.

2. There are two distinct classes of observations that are made in the behavioral sciences. They may pertain to the characteristics of the environment or to the responses of living organisms to that environment.

3. Instruments may be introduced into the observation process for various purposes. They may improve the precision of the resulting observations. They may eliminate the need for human observers over long periods of time. They may summarize observations that would otherwise be bulky and cumbersome to handle.

4. As far as it is feasible, any instruments or devices used as a part of a research should consist of standard parts that are easily maintained and highly reliable in operation.

5. The underdeveloped state of the art of educational research is such that instruments have only the most limited value. Most of the data that such research involves must be collected by other procedures, and direct observation is probably the most widely used of these.

6. Observation is a procedure for classifying and recording events according to some plan or scheme. The latter is commonly referred to as the *frame of reference* of the observer. The observer should approach a situation with a clear idea about what is to be observed and with some rudimentary theory about the significance of his observations.

7. The classroom data collected by the teacher usually differ in many respects from those collected by the scientist. One marked difference is that the teacher uses his data directly, while the scientist uses them only after they have been processed in some way.

8. Rating is a way by which numerous events that are observed are somehow summarized and combined. Control over the rating process requires that control be exercised over both the nature of the information that is used and the way in which it is used. The unsatisfactory nature of most ratings is a reflection of the difficulties involved in introducing such controls.

9. Any rating procedure developed should be such that it can be communicated to others.

10. The interview is a commonly used technique for obtaining

observations concerning individual behavior. It presents a highly complex situation from which it is difficult to obtain data that can be reproduced in other studies.

11. While interviewer characteristics are important variables in the situation, they are difficult to identify and control. It is even difficult to train interviewers to make accurate records of what happens.

12. The interview must be considered as a complex social situation in which the interviewer and the interviewee are making continuous adjustments to the responses of one another.

13. In planning interviews, caution should be observed in making assumptions about the extent to which the interviewee has insight into his behavior.

14. The interview has certain advantages over the questionnaire, such as a higher percentage of respondents, superior cooperation, and a lack of dependence on the ability to read. It does present many problems of recording information.

15. Attempts have been made to place persons in situations that represent reproductions of real-life situations, in order to observe their behavior.

Some Problems for the Student

1. In a certain teacher-training department, the supervisor of each student teacher is required to observe him conduct several hours of classes, then submit a report on what he has noted. What are some of the factors in the supervisor's background that might result in a tendency for the observation of student behavior to be selective? Suggest methods that could be adopted to insure that the observations submitted by different supervisors would be comparable, at least to some extent.

2. Prepare a rating scale or other instrument to be used in the process of assessing the amount of anxiety displayed by persons in a face-to-face counseling interview.

3. When they know they are being observed, children and teachers behave in a manner different than when the observer is

absent. Suggest several ways that might be used to overcome or partially overcome this difficulty.

4. List some personal characteristics that it might be feasible to rate accurately in an interview situation. List some characteristics that probably could not be accurately rated in the same situation.

CHAPTER 9

OBSERVATION: MORE COMPLEX

PROCEDURES AND

INDIRECT APPROACHES

IN THE preceding chapter the reader was presented with a discussion of the problems of observing and recording the characteristics of individual behavior. However, most behavior that will be observed as a part of an educational inquiry is likely to be seen under rather complex social conditions, such as those that occur in a classroom. While most rating schedules have been developed for use in situations where the person who is performing the rating is highly familiar with the person rated, observation in the classroom situation presents an entirely different circumstance. The observer in the classroom has probably never before seen the pupils he is observing, and he will probably never see them again. For this reason alone the type of rating schedule that has been considered is unsuitable as an instrument for recording aspects of behavior seen in most classroom observation situations.

The types of instruments that are now to be considered have been developed mainly for the purpose of helping the observer organize his work when he is faced with a novel social situation, such as a classroom. The schedule is a means of controlling the observer's behavior so that the observations he makes will not be based on his personal whims and will serve the purposes of the research that is being undertaken.

Classroom Observation Schedules—Problems in Their Development

The reader can turn to a textbook on educational measurement in order to acquire information about the development of rating scales, but he will not find information about the development of observation schedules so readily available.

The development of observation schedules to be used in the recording of events in the classroom is a matter that requires considerable technical knowledge. In order to familiarize the reader with some of the problems that this involves, the development of an observation schedule as it occurred in one study is presented here. The study selected is that by Morsh (1955), which is also discussed in other parts of this book. Examples of other observation schedules are then presented.

In his study, Morsh was concerned with determining the relationship between instructor's and student's behavior and the amount students learn. The study was conducted in technical courses given in Air Force schools. In this research, it was decided to study behavior at a level that involved fairly small segments or what would commonly be called specific behavior. Observers were sent to classrooms in order to obtain lists of what seemed to be relevant teacher behaviors that could be postulated to effect the course of student learning, and also student behaviors that could be hypothesized to be symptomatic of efficient and inefficient learning. On the basis of these preliminary observations, a list of 160 behaviors was prepared. But it was soon found that observers who used it as a checklist could neither keep all the items in mind nor observe on such an extended front. This difficulty resulted in the reduction of the checklist to 80 items. While the author does not have data on which to base any criticism of an 80-item device, it does seem to him that even the abbreviated list included too many items for practical purposes. The alternative is perhaps equally unsatisfactory, for it involves either using a few items that may cover only a limited range of behaviors, or using broader regions of behavior that are likely to be rather vaguely defined.

At this stage of the inquiry, certain observational difficulties soon became apparent. The first of these was mechanical. It simply did not seem feasible to provide observers with an instrument lengthier than a single page. Searching through more than one page in order to record an entry was not a feasible task, particularly when, as in any classroom, much was happening and several different but relevant behaviors occurred concurrently. Second, there was little point in the inclusion in a checklist of those items that happened so rarely that they were not likely to be noted by the typical observer in the study. Third, the observer had only limited time in which to record his information, and thus items that required some reflection before the decision to record was made should not have been included unless they provided information essential to the study. (There is, of course, no clear-cut line to be drawn between items that involve judgment and items that do not. Rather it is a matter of degree. In many areas of observation, if judgment items are discarded, little of value remains. A simple and familiar example of this is the typical English theme or composition. Systems of judging such compositions that are limited to objectively observable items, such as spelling, capitalization, agreement of subject and verb, and so on, have been found to measure only the most trivial aspects of teaching in English.) Fourth, it was considered desirable that the lists be usable by an observer who had had only very limited amounts of training. Fifth, it appeared to be important to make the lists short enough to be memorized by the observer. (The author feels that this is an extremely important property of all well-built observation schedules.) Sixth, only those items were to be retained that had some logical relevance to the learning process as it occurred in the classroom. (This is a point stressed all the way through this book, and is merely the application of one aspect of acceptable scientific methodology.)

As a result of these practical considerations, still further reductions were made in the checklists. That for recording observations pertaining to the teacher's nonverbal behavior consisted of a list of 35 items. Another list of 33 items pertained to the instructor's verbal behavior. A third list of 25 items was used for recording observations of student behavior.

Three observers were given preliminary training and were then assigned the task of collecting data in fifteen-minute observation periods in thirty classes. On the basis of these data, the reliability (consistency) of rating was determined for each item in the checklist. Through this computation most of the items were found to have adequate interobserver reliability. Those that did not were almost without exception items that occurred very infrequently. Examples of such items (sad to say) from the instructor's verbal behavior were "praises student, praises class, admits mistake." From the list of nonverbal behavior, infrequent items included such matters as "uses blackboard for key term, checks time, ignores student answer." All of the items except one in the student behavior checklist showed satisfactory interobserver reliability.

Now Morsh was aware of the fact that raters might well agree among one another and in this sense the measure might have reliability, but this would not necessarily mean that the measure would have consistency from occasion to occasion. Indeed, from the evidence presented up to this point, it is quite possible that the incidents that occurred during the particular fifteen-minute periods were not typical.

In order to determine whether the observations during the particular fifteen-minute periods of observation could be used to generalize about behavior in other periods, a further study was made. In this subsequent study, each observer visited a large number of instructors for six fifteen-minute periods. These were combined into three half-hour periods for the purpose of determining reliability of observation from occasion to occasion. As a result of this procedure, it became necessary to eliminate certain additional items from the checklist because they did not show sufficient consistency from occasion to occasion. As a result of this elimination procedure, there remained 13 items on the instructor verbal behavior form, 12 items on the nonverbal behavior form, and 10 items on the student behavior checklist. The lists were then set up for six five-minute periods of observation to provide a total period of thirty minutes of observation on each form. What were some of the items that were retained as reliable after such an elaborate process of elimination? In the case of the student behavior checklist, the following items were retained:

Talks	Ignores instructor
Answers question	Slumps
Asks question	Yawns, stretches
Looks around	Sleeps or dozes
Doodles	

While the extent to which the student manifests such behavior can be considered as evidence of conditions unfavorable to learning, the same cannot be said of the teacher behavior items. The final teacher behavior checklist included an excess of items such as "stands behind desk, stands at board, stands at side, moves, leans on desk, sits at desk." Undoubtedly such items tended to be retained by the procedure because they could be observed reliably. On the other hand, there were also retained some items that it seemed reasonable to suppose were highly related to the teaching process. Examples of these were "ignores student with hand up, smiles, demonstrates at board." The data selected demonstrate the tendency for highly reliable items of behavior that refer to gross bodily positions to be retained, while the more difficult to observe and more subtle aspects of teacher behavior are rejected in any tryout or procedure for the screening of items.

There is much to be learned from this. The principal lesson is that aspects of teacher behavior likely to be related to learning effectiveness may be difficult to rate and will probably have to be rated or assessed through instruments that the investigator has prepared after long and painful effort. This may mean that the researcher will have to experiment with the rating (or checking) of numerous different aspects of behavior until those that can be reliably rated are identified. A satisfactory instrument for use in observing teacher behavior can be prepared only after prolonged effort.

While the previous discussion was presented in order to illustrate the problems of preparing schedules and checklists for recording observations, it would be unfair to the reader not to present some of the consequences of this study. As might be expected, the items in the teacher behavior checklist showed little relationship with the extent to which the students showed gains in achievement (corrected in terms of both their initial knowledge and relative level of ability). The difficulty of recording relevant aspects of teacher behavior are indicated by these results. The only alternative explanation would be that teacher behavior does not provide important variables in the teaching process. The latter just does not seem to be an acceptable hypothesis in terms of what is known about conditions affecting human learning.

In contrast, the behavior of the students as recorded on the checklist was indicative of the extent to which learning was taking place. This is, of course, entirely reasonable. Students who are yawning, dozing, or sleeping cannot be expected to be learning with any degree of effectiveness. Morsh draws the interesting conclusion that if the supervisor visiting the classroom wishes to make an assessment of the amount of subject-matter information that is being acquired by the student, he might do well to observe what the students are doing. Observable student behavior may provide more valid evidence of teacher effectiveness with respect to certain goals than can the information derived from the observation of teacher behavior. When we learn what aspects of teacher behavior to observe in this connection, this statement perhaps may need modification.

The Morsh study has been presented here because it is one of the better-designed efforts at obtaining observational data from a class situation. It illustrates some of the precautions that must be taken and the care that must be exercised. It also reflects the fact that the screening process may eliminate from consideration all but the most trivial of observations. When this happens, the researcher should not be content to pursue his inquiry with the reliable but trivial. He has a choice of making another attempt to observe relevant events or of dropping the investigation.

Many of the difficulties that are presented in the Morsh study stem from the fact that we are only beginning to learn useful techniques for classroom observation. The complexity of the phenomena are such that any quantification procedure involves difficulties in abstracting that segment of behavior to be observed, and further difficulties in the quantification of aspects of that segment. New ways of doing this will be constantly explored during the years to come, and it is the author's belief that methods far superior to any available at the present time will be developed. How far it will be possible to replace human observation and judgment by physical instruments that record and quantify is a matter about which there can be only speculation at present.

The difficulties that Morsh tried to avoid led him directly into other difficulties arising out of the specificity of the phenomena recorded. Others have recognized this difficulty and have attempted to devise methods that circumvent it. All of these are based on the concept that a whole category of different behaviors may be used to measure a dimension of teacher or pupil behavior, much as the items in a test may be used to measure a relatively homogeneous and single dimension. There are, of course, innumerable different ways of doing this, because the classroom presents a vast range of phenomena that can be observed, and these can be classified in a great variety of ways. On this account, most of the techniques that have been proposed restrict observation to a limited phase of behavior. For example, a technique proposed by Withall (1949) confines the domain of observation to statements made by the teacher. This is done on the assumption that most of the important interactions that occur in the classroom are undertaken through the verbal medium, hence a study of verbal interactions will reveal most of the important events occurring there. These statements are sampled according to some plan that provides that they be as representative as possible of the statements made by the teacher in the classroom. Once they have been recorded—and this is done at the time of observation in the classroom—they are available for later classification, which can be undertaken by persons who were not involved in the original recording process. One may then determine the reliability of the classification procedure. The classification of verbal behavior proposed by Withall uses the following categories:

1. "Learner-supportive statements that have the intent of reassuring or commending the pupil.
2. "Acceptant and clarifying statements intended to convey to the pupil the feeling that he was understood and to help him gain insight.
3. "Problem-structuring statements or questions which proffer information or raise questions about the problem in an objective manner, with intent to facilitate learner's problem-solving.
4. "Neutral statements which comprise polite formalities, administrative comments, verbatim repetition of something that has already been said. No intent inferable.
5. "Direct or exhortative statements, with intent to have pupil follow a recommended course of action.
6. "Reproving or deprecating remarks intended to deter pupil from continued indulgence in present "unacceptable" behavior.
7. "Teacher self-supporting remarks intended to sustain or justify the teacher's position or course of action."

These statements are quoted from Withall since his wording is carefully selected.

Withall's technique is of particular importance because it is based on a theory concerning the determinants of certain classes of events in the classroom. He hypothesized that the teacher's behavior is the most important single factor in creating class-room climate and that the teacher's verbal behavior is a representative sample of his total behavior.

Subsequent work has confirmed the view, expressed by Withall and substantiated by his data, that the statements of teachers can be categorized with reliability. At the time of writing, there is little evidence to show that the measures derived from this categorizing process represent conditions important to the learning process, but on the other hand the categories offer promise. They appear to be good candidates for this purpose since they represent conditions that are commonly postulated to be important factors related to learning, and particularly those related to reward and feedback. In this respect, Withall's study is in many ways ahead of that previously discussed, for it deals with broad categories of behavior that, at least in other contexts, have been shown to be related to the learning process.

Some of the advantages of the Withall technique over the more familiar observational and rating techniques that have already been discussed may be pointed out. It permits the summation of scores derived from a great number of behaviors. In this way, it is possible to build up reliable scores from a great variety of classroom events. The work and thought of categorizing behavior, which may occupy so much of the time of an observer in the classroom and may detract from his observations, is undertaken at leisure after the observations are made. The technique also recognizes the overwhelmingly important role played by verbal behavior in structuring events in the classroom, a fact that has been commonly overlooked in most observational techniques.

Some Examples of Observation Schedules

In contrast to Withall's technique, the observational method proposed by Cornell, Lindvall, and Saupe (1953) does not restrict itself to the observation and recording of verbal behavior but covers a much wider range of events. The purpose is broader, though possibly vaguer, and is summarized in the following words: "Our chief concern is with measures or descriptions of 'what students do in school, what teachers do in school,' or in short, just what a school is in terms of the total learning environment it provides the students." Some further restriction is placed on the domain to be observed by the statement that this is to be restricted to events within the classroom situation. It is clear, then, that these workers are concerned with the development of a series of dimensions of the educational environment of the school child, and the hope is that the dimensions will differentiate among school systems. In actual fact, these workers are concerned with more than differentiating school systems. Mere differentiation is not a sound basis for selecting a characteristic for measurement. If the walls of one school consisted of plaster and those of another of plywood, this would not be considered adequate as a basis for selecting this particular characteristic. Any characteristic selected for differentiation must be one that has relevance to the educational process itself. It should be selected not only because it differentiates but also because it is related to some important aspect of the learning process as it takes place in schools. This is implied in the statement that "the most direct impact of the school upon the child is in the classroom." This is a somewhat vague recognition of what we have been saying here. It does not provide a theory of behavior that is a sufficient basis for selecting those differentiating variables that are relevant to the educational process from those that are irrelevant.

The following dimensions for measuring classroom differences are proposed in this system:

1. Differentiation. This dimension defines the extent to which classrooms provide for individual differences of both intellectual and nonintellectual characteristics. While there is no universally accepted method of providing for individual differences, a number of common procedures that may be scored along a common dimension are adopted for this purpose.

2. Social organization. While this is referred to as a dimension, it seems to the author to be a complex consisting of a number of dimensions such as single-group versus multigroup organizations, pupil leadership versus teacher leadership, and group-leader interaction versus no interaction.

3. Initiative. This dimension reflects the extent to which the pupil directs the learning process or is directed by adults. The amount of pupil initiative manifested is a dimension in which schools show striking differences.

4. Content. This again must be considered as a complex rather than a single dimension. It includes observation of such varied phenomena as one textbook versus several textbooks, the extent to which sources other than textbooks are used, and the extent to which the curriculum is organized around areas of pupil interest or around areas designated by the teacher.

5. Variety. This dimension is used to measure the extent to which there is variation in classroom procedure. It can be measured, for example, by the number of different activities that are observed to occur during a given period in the classroom.

6. Competence. This category represents a dimension in which the teacher is appraised for the extent to which he is inactive or to which he shows positive behaviors that can be reasonably assumed to be related to learning. It is not competence in the sense in which a teacher is said to be effective or ineffective in the achievement of certain goals, but rather is it a difference between playing a passive or innocuous role and playing a positive role in the classroom. The word *competence* is not too well chosen.

7. Climate-teacher. This dimension refers to the extent to which the teacher behaves in a way consistent with the development of good human relations. It deals with interpersonal relations and matters of warmth and friendliness.

8. Climate-pupil. This dimension refers to the extent to which the pupils either respond positively to the classroom situation or tend to be restless and inattentive. It does not refer to what is ordinarily referred to as "classroom atmosphere," since this characteristically includes reference to the degree to which there is tension in the situation.

Regardless of the merits of the various dimensions that have been discussed, there are certain difficulties involved in the use of an observational technique of this kind. The person who applies it uses a sheet entitled "Classroom Observation Schedule" for recording his entries. On this he records his observations by five-minute intervals. However, the observations cannot be recorded directly because the schedule calls for a coded record of what is observed. This is accomplished by means of a "classroom observation code digest," a two-page affair that permits the numerical coding of what is observed. Only the number derived from the code is recorded on the observation schedule. In addition, there is a sixteen-page manual that describes in detail how this process is to be accomplished; it includes a great deal of detail, and also special instructions for handling various aspects of the coding and for dealing with exceptional cases.

The entire procedure quite clearly calls for a great deal of practice on the part of the person using it. If data were to be collected in a specified group of classes, the observers to be used would have to be given practice on another group of classes. It is doubtful that a few hours would provide anywhere near the amount of experience needed to obtain real facility with the system or the minimum facility necessary to provide records with good interrater agreement. The defect in the system stems from the tremendous burden of work that it requires the observer to do in the recording of observations. This is done in the interests of providing accurate data in a form that makes them utilizable for subsequent quantitative analysis. Conceivably, broad overall judgments of the type that were commonly made in classroom studies of the late 1930's may yield as much information as those that deal with the more modern type of observation schedule.

An instrument which has been carefully developed and which has considerable breadth and scope is a device developed by Medley and Mitzel (1958) known as the OScAR. The peculiar name is an abbreviation for *Observation Schedule and Record*. The authors of this device claim that it can be used by a relatively untrained observer, which gives it a considerable advantage over the device previously considered.

The essential core of the OScAR is a fairly elaborate schedule on which observations are recorded. The observer begins by starting his stopwatch and entering in the "Activity Section" as many of the activities listed as he observes. This section includes such items as "pupil laughs" and "teacher works with individual pupil." The observer then turns to the "Grouping Section" in which he records the nature and size of the groups observed. In the "Materials Section" he records the equipment and learning aids available. In the "Signs Section" he records evidences indicative of the social climate of the classroom. He then records the elapsed time and resets the stopwatch to zero. The observer then records the subject matter area which received most attention during the period of observation. Finally, the observer starts again and begins to tally statements the teacher makes in five categories: Pupil-supportive, Problem-structuring, Miscellaneous, Directive, Reproving. In addition, he records gestures of the teacher which might indicate affection, approval, hostility, or reproof. The total procedure also involves certain additional operations. The typical procedure found in most studies which involve the OScAR call for at least two separate visits to each classroom.

The data thus collected are finally scored on fourteen scales:

1. Time spent on reading
2. Problem-structuring teacher statements
3. Autonomous administrative groupings
4. Pupil-leadership activities
5. Freedom of movement
6. Manifest teacher hostility
7. Supportive teacher behavior
8. Time spent on social studies
9. Disorderly pupil behavior
10. Verbal activities
11. Traditional pupil activities
12. Teacher's verbal output

13. Audiovisual materials
14. Autonomous social groupings

A factor analysis has demonstrated that the fourteen keys serve mainly to measure three variables which are described as emotional climate, verbal emphasis, and social structure.

Interaction Analysis

Most of the procedures involved in the observing and recording of classroom events which have been considered up to this point have involved single events or classes of events rather than sequences. Yet the fact is that the effects of teaching are highly dependent upon the nature of the sequences that take place. It obviously makes a difference whether what is discussed at one moment is or is not related to what is discussed at the next. In some classrooms teachers can be observed hopping from one topic to another while in others events take place in an orderly sequence. The difference is a significant one in terms of learning taking place. An important outcome of the research of Heil and Washburne (1962) is that the orderly teacher who behaves in a well-organized manner has the most over-all success in producing academic achievement in the classroom.

Events in the classroom also manifest order and sequence with respect to another dimension. Teaching may be regarded as a process involving an interaction between pupil and teacher, and hence of an alternation between observable activity on the part of the teacher and observable activity on the part of the pupil. In one classroom most of the observable activity in this interaction may be on the part of the teacher; in another, most of the observable activity may be in the pupil phase of the sequence. An analysis of the interaction between the teacher and the pupil is obviously an important approach to the study of the learning conditions existing in the classroom.

The last decade has seen intensive efforts to develop devices which can be used to measure the characteristics of the interactions between teacher and pupil. The problem of instrument development has been approached from many different points of view. Hughes (1960) has approached the problem from the point of view of developing a method of appraising teacher effectiveness. She has taken the position that some interactions are effective elements in the learning process while others are not. If the latter assumption is correct, then a record of the teacher-pupil interactions can be used to measure teacher effectiveness with respect to particular goals. Another approach is illustrated by work under the direction of B.O. Smith (1960) in the area of mathematics. Smith has attempted to study interactions in terms of the logical structure, or lack of it, which they manifest. A third approach to the problem is found in the work of Flanders (1962), whose original contribution lies in the way in which the interaction data are analyzed.

Flanders collects data on classroom interactions by using trained observers who classify verbal behavior occurring during each three-second period. The statements are classified into the following categories:

Teacher talk	1. Clarify feeling constructively 2. Praise or encourage 3. Clarify, develop or make use of ideas suggested by students 4. Ask questions 5. Lecture 6. Give directions 7. Criticize
Student talk	8. Student talk in response to the teacher 9. Student talk initiated by the student 10. Silence or confusion

From the record, which consists of a set of numbers entered by the observer at the rate of one every three seconds, one can tabulate the frequency with which each one of the events occurs. But this is not the main purpose of the data-collection process. The data permits a much more subtle analysis of the ongoing classroom processes. This is done by preparing what is referred to as the matrix, which consists of a table with ten vertical columns and ten horizontal rows, as shown in Figure V.

Catagory	1	2	3	4	5	6	7	8	9	10
1. Clarify Feeling Constructively	—	—	—	—	0.4	—	0.1	0.1	—	0.1
2. Praise or Encourage	—	0.9	1.8	0.9	2.5	—	0.1	0.2	0.9	1.0
3. Clarify, Develop or Make Use of Ideas Suggested by Students	—	0.9	27.8	11.0	20.3	1.7	0.5	4.3	9.9	8.5
4. Ask Questions	0.1	0.1	0.2	13.5	4.4	1.0	0.4	36.5	11.5	3.0
5. Lecture	0.6	1.1	1.6	25.5	440.3	5.1	3.2	0.3	14.7	9.7
6. Give Directions	—	0.1	0.1	1.7	5.5	10.4	1.1	1.7	1.6	6.4
7. Criticize	—	0.1	0.1	1.4	3.6	1.0	9.6	0.4	0.4	2.9
8. Student Talk in Response to the Teacher	—	2.3	16.9	9.1	8.7	1.7	0.7	63.0	3.0	2.8
9. Student Talk Initiated by the Student	—	2.6	35.5	3.8	6.9	0.9	0.9	0.4	45.9	4.1
10. Silence or Confusion	0.1	0.3	0.9	3.7	9.6	6.7	2.7	1.3	13.1	37.4
Total	0.7	8.4	84.8	70.7	502.2	28.6	19.5	108.1	101.2	75.8

per 1000 tallies

N= 13,593

FIGURE V. Interaction matrix for content centered social studies teachers, N = 3 adjusted for 1,000 tallies. (Data from Flanders, 1962, p. 116.)

In this matrix the ten columns and the ten rows correspond to the ten categories of observed behavior. The purpose of the matrix is to permit the tallying of the recorded events in pairs. This is done by taking the first pair of events which might have been recorded in Categories 6 and 9. Such a pair of events would be tallied in the cell where Row 6 intersects with Column 9.

Then the next pair of events is tallied. This pair would be the event classified as 9 and the event that followed it. These are tallied in the same way—and so the analysis is continued. Since this may become a very tedious process when thousands of events have to be tallied, the material can be perhaps best handled by a computer.

An examination of the matrix indicates some of the characteristics of the teaching process as observed. For example, in the case of the matrix given as an illustration, any period of lecturing by the teacher is most likely to be followed by more lecturing. In only 8.25 per cent of the cases does a comment by the teacher stimulate the student to make a verbal contribution to the class. In the case of this particular classroom for which the data are provided, a little more than 70 per cent of the time is occupied by teacher verbal activities and only about 21 per cent by pupil verbal activities. Very little verbal activity is initiated by the pupils, and more than half of the pupils' verbal activity is in direct response to the verbal activity of the teacher. The classroom is conducted along traditional lines, the teacher holding forth and the pupils supposedly absorbing knowledge.

The system of classification used by Flanders is a relatively simple one. It has to be, for the data collection proceeds at high speed and the observer must be able to classify verbal behaviors almost instantaneously. A much more complicated system of classifying classroom behavior is provided by Hughes (1960), but when a more complex system is used the observer is not able to classify events on the spur of the moment. In the latter case, the events must be recorded as they occur and classification must be undertaken at a later time. Such a procedure has advantages, but it is much more time consuming. There is no "best" way of classifying events in the classroom, but classification systems differ in the extent to which they lead to profitable research and significant knowledge. At the present time not enough is known to be able to recommend the Hughes approach over the Flanders approach or vice versa. Both represent interesting devices which will probably yield important knowledge.

The Pupils as Classroom Observers

Attempts have been made to enlist pupils in the task of determining the nature of classroom events generally through the use of a questionnaire. The advantage of this technique is that it may throw light on the pupil's perception of the characteristics of classroom activities and such perceptions may be much more important than the perceptions of an adult observer.

The earliest devices used for this purpose were developed by McCall (1937, 1941) at Columbia University Teachers College in cooperation with the professional staff of the Board of Education of the City of New York. These devices were developed for the purpose of determining the extent to which the introduction of a new curriculum had actually changed classroom practices. For this purpose a "School Practices Questionnaire" was developed for use in Grades 1–9. Later, as a result of experience with this questionnaire, a similar device was developed for use at the junior and senior high school levels, titled "Comprehensive Curriculum Tests." Data concerning the value of these devices were limited, and it is difficult to appraise their usefulness.

A more recent device, which attempts to use pupils as observers, has been developed by Cogan and was used as a part of a series of researches (Cogan 1958a, 1959b). The Cogan device carries the innocent title of *Pupil Survey* and covers a great many areas in which the teacher relates to the pupil. The first section of the survey relates to the kind of homework assignments given the pupil by a particular teacher. The second section covers "extra things you may do, not counting assigned homework." The third section contains 80 questions covering a wide range of matters including how often the teacher loses her temper, the orderliness of the class, the extent to which the teacher allows the pupil to exercise choice, and the punctuality of the teacher.

The main scales derived from the items pertaining to teacher behavior are described by Cogan (1958a) as follows:

I. Inclusive
    A. Integrative
    B. Affiliative
    C. Nurturant
II. Preclusive
    A. Dominative
    B. Aggressive
    C. Rejectant
III. Conjunctive
    A. Level of demand made on the pupils
    B. Ability to communicate
    C. Competence in classroom management

The three terms, *inclusive, preclusive,* and *conjunctive,* are each described by the categories that fall under them.

Distortion in Observation

Instrumentation is introduced into scientific inquiry because of the limitations of the human observer. In physics, the rapidity of many phenomena requires instrumentation in order that highly transitory events that could not be observed can be reduced to events that can be observed by the experimenter. In this field, instrumentation not only reduces nonobservable phenomena to observables but also permits the measurement of observables. In the behavioral sciences, instrumentation serves all these ends and also a very important additional purpose. That purpose is to prevent the observer from introducing into his narration events that never occurred.

Real differences exist in the ability of individuals to report observations without bias. McPherson (1954), who studied this problem of the differences between high distorters and low distorters, came to the conclusion that these two groups were distinguished by the following characteristics:

Low Distorters	High Distorters
1. Able to integrate the content with their own ideas and the ideas of others.	1. Parrot the content and gives little evidence of understanding the material they are trying to present.
2. Tend to relate the ideas introduced by group members to the content and to each other. Will clarify errors and misinterpretations made by group members.	2. Tend to avoid questions about content and accept misinterpretations without attempting to correct them.
3. Demonstrate a freedom with material by using it as a basis for introducing relevant ideas that serve to broaden or extend the range of ideas.	3. Escape the material by using it as a springboard for introducing highly personal experiences that do not forward an understanding of the content.
4. Restate comments of others in an attempt to clarify contributions and relate them to the general trend of the discussion.	4. Restate comments from members of the group but show no evidence of an ability to tie member contributions together in meaningful relationships.
5. Maintain a high level of work orientation. Initiate work and join others in the task.	5. Tend to avoid the work task of the group and engage in frequent "flight" behaviors.
6. Show a greater facility for maintaining an objective point of view in situations that are emotionally laden.	6. Are more inclined to be influenced by emotionality in such a way that they cannot view material objectively.
7. Are able to make decisions about alternatives that contain emotional elements.	7. Become indecisive in certain instances where the alternatives contain emotional elements.

Of particular interest in the McPherson study is his attempt to develop methods of identifying the high distorters. His primary attempt to do this involved the development of a reading test in which the subject was exposed to paragraphs of material and was later presented with a series of questions about it. The information provided by the subject in answering these questions was used as a basis for measuring the amount of distortion. Although these results are valuable, it should be pointed out that one may suppose that a person will distort more in making some observations than others. A person will probably distort most in situations in which, for some reason unknown to him, he is motivated to distort.

Unobservables

It has not been found feasible to develop a science of behavior that includes only stimulus variables and response variables pertaining to directly observable events, although traditional education with its emphasis on drill was based to a great extent on the assumption that the amount a child learned was dependent entirely on what was done to him or on what he was forced to do. There was a time when psychologists attempted to develop a science of behavior that required only observables such as stimulus variables and response variables; that is to say, a system in which the laws sought were of the general type $R = f(S)$, where R, the response, is said to be a function of the stimulus. The character of an individual's response is quite obviously not just a function of the stimuli to which he is exposed, because different individuals show different responses to the same stimuli. This fact can be accounted for only by postulating that individuals differ; or, to use other words, by postulating that different conditions exist and intervene between the stimulus and the response. This is a reiteration of what was said earlier. The concepts are reintroduced here in order to show their relevance to problems of observation.

Intervening variables have sometimes been called hidden variables because they cannot be observed directly, but this fact is

easily forgotten in an observation situation. The tendency of observers is to assume that what can be observed—namely, the
stimulating conditions and the responses to them—is a sufficient
basis for explaining behavior. This is clearly not so except in
certain unusual situations that have little relevance for education. Observers commonly make inferences about the operation
of intervening variables from the responses they observe. These
inferences are not justified. For example, if an observer notes
that one child is attending closely to the teacher while another
is not, he is likely to make the inference that the one is highly
motivated while the other is not. This statement either merely
reiterates that the one attended to the teacher while the other
did not, or it invokes the operation of a new variable referred to
as motivation. There is no real basis for inferring the operation
of such a variable, since the difference in behavior might be due
to the fact that the one child was deaf while the other could
hear, or that the nonattentive one did not understand English,
or was dull, or sick. Innumerable other intervening variables can
be introduced, all equally tentative and questionable. Without
further data, there is no basis for choosing one of these variables
rather than another as the correct one. Those variables must be
measured independently of the situation in which they operate
if they are to be used for explanatory purposes.

Some Problems of Using Untrained Observers

There is much talk in the literature about the need for using
trained observers in research, but just how an observer is trained
or what this involves is usually left to the imagination of the
reader. The problem of training observers can perhaps be introduced by discussing a familiar situation—that provided by a
baseball game. The radio commentator observing such a game
describes the nature of each pitch, whether it is fast or slow,
curved or straight, inside, outside, or down the middle, and so
forth. In contrast, the occasional onlooker, the author among
them, finds it quite impossible to make these discriminations, for
all balls look much the same to him and differ only in what happens to them in the subsequent play. The commentator also

notices and remarks on many other events that pass unnoticed by the amateur. He notices movement in the outfield as different batters come up to the plate, and other responses of the players to the changing situation. The commentator has, in fact, learned to do two things that the inexperienced observer has not yet learned. First, he has learned to make discriminations that the inexperienced observer has not learned to make. Second, he has learned to respond to more cues, as when he responds to movements in the outfield that few others even notice.

A professional psychologist is sometimes referred to as a trained observer, but this does not mean that he is trained in all situations. One who has spent his life working with rats may be called a trained observer of those rodents, but he may not necessarily be considered trained for conducting an experiment with children. Observation of a particular situation may require special experience that is not provided in ordinary professional training.

In conducting studies that require extensive observations, it is usually necessary for economic reasons to employ observers who have had little training as psychologists. Often graduate students in their early stages of training are selected for this purpose. Under such conditions, it is desirable to follow a few simple rules in the establishment of observational procedures.

First, the observers should participate in the development of the system to be used for recording observations. They should be in on the procedure from the beginning of its development. If this is not possible, then they should be in on the tryout of the tentative schedule. During this process they can be of help in determining what they can learn to observe and what they cannot. They can also acquire facility in the mechanics of recording their observations, and at the same time help in the development of a convenient recording schedule. Through the use of such tentative schedules, observers can compare their records after a period of observation, and, when there are differences attributable to misunderstandings of particular words, come to some agreement on the definition of the terms to be used.

Second, do not expect the untrained observer to record frequently occurring forms of behavior as well as other aspects. He can be kept so busy recording one or two frequently occurring items that he has no time to note anything else. Also, the untrained observer is able to cope with only a limited repertoire of behavior. With practice, this range can be increased.

Third, the schedule not only should specify the category of behavior to be observed but should give the observer training by pointing out some actual examples of this behavior as it occurs in an observational situation. The categories of behavior must be as specific as possible; one might possibly suggest the rule that the more naïve the observer, the more specific they should be.

Fourth, categories that involve a considerable amount of interpretation should be avoided. Untrained observers may show little agreement with one another concerning what they consider to be aggressive behavior. Trained observers may ultimately agree on this classification as they learn a common system of interpretation.

Fifth, the observers should be informed of the purpose of the experiment except insofar as this may prejudice the outcome of the study. If the groups or persons to be observed have been exposed to two different treatments and if differences between treatments are studied, it is not desirable to inform the observers of this, lest even a slight prejudice may result in a tendency for the observations to come out in one way rather than another.

Finally, one suspects that if there are great cultural differences in the backgrounds of the observer and the observed, the significance of much that happens may pass unnoticed. This cultural factor is one that scientists are only just beginning to understand.

ADDITIONAL OBSERVATIONAL TECHNIQUES

The Critical Incidents Technique

During the past decade, interest has developed in what is called the critical incidents technique, the invention of John C. Flanagan, who has applied it to a great range of situations. It is, in essence, a method of observation, but it also involves the judgment of the observer concerning what should be observed and recorded. The technique is a method of defining the group's concept of what makes a particular member of an occupation more effective than other members. It is a way of defining, for example, what superintendents mean when they say that Teacher X is more effective than Teacher Y. It avoids the difficulties that are produced when a superintendent is asked the question, "What do you consider to be the characteristics of a good teacher?" The answer to such a question always involves vague generalities, such as, "The good teacher is kind," or "The good teacher provides effective incentives." Such descriptions are not a sufficient basis for developing instruments that can be used to measure the extent to which teachers do actually conform to this ideal. The critical incidents technique may be used to describe more adequately what a superintendent has in mind when he states that Teacher X is better than Teacher Y, but this does not in any way mitigate the fact that the technique is still operating in the domain of judgments. In the ultimate analysis, the pronouncements of any person concerning what makes a good teacher must be based on a reasoned judgment that *this* type of pupil learning is better than *that*.

The procedure involved in the critical incidents technique is well illustrated by a study by Jensen (1951) of the critical requirements for teachers. In the Jensen study, a *critical incident* is an observed teacher behavior or aspect of teacher behavior that is *judged* to make the difference between success and failure in teaching. The term *judged* is italicized here to indicate that what is being accomplished is to summarize such judgments in terms of behavior incidents. There is clearly little point in collecting descriptions of the commonplace behavior that is about as typical of those teachers judged to be good as it is of those judged to be poor. The reader must also note that the method is not a scientific device for deciding what constitutes good teaching. It is only a method of describing what some person or group considers to be crucial matters in judging the merits of teaching.

In the Jensen study, the participants were asked first to recall an elementary teacher judged to be ineffective, and then to relate the incident that made the participant decide that the teacher was incompetent. Similar questions were asked concerning the participant's experiences with effective teachers. Jensen also tried a number of variations of this technique, such as asking the participants to recall childhood incidents of effective and ineffective behavior on the part of teachers.

The material derived from such a technique is voluminous and needs to be reduced to manageable proportions. This may be done in various ways. One of these is to attempt to abstract from each incident the salient feature that caused it to reflect effectiveness or ineffectiveness. Thus one category might be "hypercriticality" on the part of the teacher; another, "fairness and impartiality." One can then compare frequencies between classes, or compare groups of teachers with respect to the frequency of occurrence of any particular class of behavior. In addition, one may use the material for constructing scales for rating teachers. The technique could be applied to the definition of a "good" student versus a "poor" student or a "good" parent versus a "poor" parent—to almost any situation in which one group is to be discriminated from another. Nevertheless, this statement concerning the wide applicability of the technique should not be taken to mean that the results are necessarily useful.

The critical incidents technique has enjoyed a period of relatively uncritical popularity, which is quite typical of new techniques in an area where research workers have often a feeling of helplessness because of the complexity of the problems faced. The technique also has an apparent attractiveness and relevance to the solution of many important problems, though it is the opinion of the author that the attractiveness is superficial. It is, therefore, necessary to examine the technique rather more critically.

First, the technique often provides samples of rarely occurring behavior that are not likely to be observed again. The very rarity of the observations minimizes their usefulness.

Second, the infrequency of the events listed in any study of critical incidents makes them extremely difficult to classify. The event that is remembered and later recorded as a critical incident is often remembered because it is unusual. Thus the technique reflects the phenomena of selective recall and often produces what appears to be a list of unique, and therefore unclassifiable, events.

In addition, the technique may reveal substantial lack of agreement among participants. If this occurs, the product is likely to be a conglomeration of events that cannot be shaped through categorization into any recognizable form. Even if there is some agreement, it may not be possible to arrange the behaviors along any kind of continuum, which would be a most desirable feature of the data if they were to be used as the basis for a check list.

Finally, the technique should be recognized by the graduate student of education as an extremely laborious one. It involves the manipulation of large masses of data through techniques that are extremely time-consuming. It should not be considered as one suitable for a doctoral dissertation or a master's thesis. Even if the difficulties involved in the handling of the volume of data are overcome, there would still be considerable doubt that the lengthy and tedious work involved would yield results of consequence. Although the technique has been applied to several types of educational problems, results have not been of any particular note.

Self-Observation and Self-Report

The oldest technique of the psychologist is that of self-observation, and it still occupies a place in modern psychology. Self-observation has undergone a long history of development, and current techniques that might be considered to fall in this category are far removed from those that would have been used a century ago. Much of what is strictly self-observation is also not commonly referred to by that term and is consequently not recognized as such.

Self-observation techniques began in history with crude introspection of the armchair type, whereby through an inspection of one's inner self an effort was made to discover the laws of events in consciousness. This type of self-observation acquired some refinement in the first psychological laboratory founded by Wundt and reached its highest stage of development in the work of Titchener and his pupils. Despite all the work devoted to the development of the introspectionist approach, it is viewed today as having been a profitless venture. Even though the techniques evolved may have done much to eliminate errors in the observation of mental phenomena, the knowledge acquired by these means was meager. Today it would be hard to find a laboratory in which these techniques would be considered for use.

One plausible reason for the failure of classical introspection techniques to yield useful results was that they did not involve measurement. More recently attempts have been made to quantify certain aspects of personal experience, and the results of such efforts seem promising. Certainly it can be said that advances in the behavioral sciences seem to have accompanied the introduction of quantitative methods. With this in mind, a brief review will be made here of quantitative self-observation techniques.

Self-ratings. Graphic rating procedures have been applied extensively to the situation in which the person rates himself. The early studies of this type were based on the concept that the individual is the person who knows himself best, and that self-ratings could be used as a basis for study of the structure of personality. This concept had some value, naïve though it was. R.B. Cattell, who has worked extensively in the area of personality ratings, is of the opinion that self-rating studies help to confirm findings based upon other sources of information. In the last two decades, self-ratings have come to be viewed in a rather different light as indicators, not of a personality as it actually is, but of a person's self-concept. The distinction between a person's self as it appears to others and as it appears to himself has been found a useful one. Psychologists of the Rogerian school have emphasized that a person's concept of himself may have a powerful influence on behavior. Reference is made here to the school of psychology that emphasizes the importance of events in the phenomenal field. According to this viewpoint, the development of a science of psychology involves the discovery of the laws of the sequence and interrelationship of events as they occur in the person's field of consciousness. This field is described as the *phenomenal field,* a term that has been handed down from German philosophy, where it was used to denote the field of consciousness within which all observable phenomena occurred. Phenomena were events and things in the universe as they were observed, and they were contrasted with noumena, which were things and events as they actually existed independent of an observer. According to the phenomenologist, all the determinants of behavior exist in the phenomenal field. Therefore, in order to understand behavior, it is only necessary to study the phenomenal field. Since the psychologist does not have direct access to the phenomenal field of another, he must rely on the statements made by that person about his own phenomenal field. The statements that a person makes about himself are also used by the psychologist who has a behavioristic outlook. He regards such statements as objective facts and ignores any reference they may have to an inner life.

Q-Methodology. Special methods have been adapted from other fields for treating self-rating data and other forms of self-evaluation. One of the most interesting of these, developed by Stephenson, has been described by him in rather obscure terms in a book (1953). The basis of Q-methodology goes back to a procedure which has long been used by psychologists and which involves computing a correlation between two profiles of standard scores for two individuals. If the two profiles are identical, then the correlation between them will be equal to 1.00. If the profiles show opposite trends and are the mirror image of one another, then the correlation between the two will be −1.00. All degrees of relationship may be found between profiles, and the correlations may vary from −1.00 to 1.00. In this way a person's self-ratings may be compared at various times during psychotherapy. If it were found that the early self-ratings of the patient showed a high degree of correlation with his later self-ratings, the conclusion would probably be drawn that little change had taken place in his concept of himself. However, in actual case studies which have been reported, the technique has demonstrated marked changes in the profiles of self-ratings as therapy progresses. The methodology described by Stephenson involves much more than the simple procedure of comparing one set of self-ratings with another by means of a correlation coefficient, though this is the basis of it. Stephenson has attempted to elaborate this procedure by tying it in with elaborate statistical techniques which, he believes, add greatly to the power of the approach. While Q-methodology offers interesting and ingenious approaches to problems which have not yet been studied effectively, the reader should realize that they involve considerable statistical sophistication and often imply hidden assumptions. They are for the experts in the field rather than for the amateur, and even the experts have sometimes found themselves under fire from other experts for using the techniques inappropriately.

Personality inventories as records of self-observation. Another method by which personal experience may be quantified is through personality inventories, which are mainly devices for recording personal experiences. Some of these devices limit such personal experiences to responses of liking and disliking and are referred to as *interest inventories,* while others are restricted to different categories of personal experience. Still other inventories deal with the course of action that a person would most likely pursue when faced with certain kinds of situations.

It is difficult to provide an appraisal of such an extended field of measurement in the short space that can be devoted to it here. The measures derived by such self-observation techniques have not shown the promise that was originally anticipated of them. However, they have not shown themselves to be entirely useless, for situations have been found in which they have provided predictions of limited accuracy, but there has often been difficulty in reproducing these predictions in related situations. Interest inventories have perhaps been the most widely used of these instruments. In comparison with the recent success achieved with some types of projective techniques, the success of the inventories considered here has been meager.

Self-observations have come under criticism from two quite distinct standpoints. First, it must be pointed out that clinical psychologists since the days of Freud have emphasized that a person is an extremely biased observer of his own behavior. Much behavior of great significance escapes his observation, and he is a poor judge of what are its significant aspects. In addition, many of the important determinants of behavior are not considered by the intellectual descendants of Freud to be within the realm that is open to personal and direct observation. Motives, for example, are said to be in the category of unobservables in the person who has not undergone psychoanalysis, although the latter therapeutic technique is said to provide some personal access to this aspect of personality. Second, the person who is observing himself is a biased observer. He wants to present himself to others in the best possible light, and his answers to questions about himself are colored quite inevitably by this tendency. The person observing himself is not untruthful in his report, but he is selective in what he reports and how he reports it. He may at times report in a way that is truthful yet biased.

The Utilization of Biographical Data

Biographical data have always been of immense interest to the educator. Every teacher recognizes that the problems and difficulties of children are, at least in part, the product of previous conditions. Most of us have the implicit belief that if we could know the complete life history of an individual, then we would understand his present behavior. The teacher, the counselor, the social worker, all seek information about the past history of the individual in order to understand his present actions. The research worker interested in such problems may attempt to obtain data about the past in order to determine how present behavior came into being. Since biographical information is one of the more important classes of observations that are made in educational research, some consideration needs to be given here to the data-collection problems that it involves.

In the traditional type of biographical study, biographies are examined on an intuitive basis much as the clinician examines a patient. An example of this type of approach is manifested by Anne Roe in her studies of creative talent. The purpose of the examination of the biographies in this case is to determine whether the group of creative individuals show any common characteristics running through their lives. In the case of Anne Roe's studies the attempt seems to have had some success, and the results of the biographical studies have been confirmed by other sources of evidence. Nevertheless, the success of this method in the case of some studies does not mean that it is always successful. The truth seems to be that the method has many dangers, and unsuccessful applications tend to be overlooked.

A major danger is illustrated by the early biographical studies of neurotic patients. In these it was shown again and again that such individuals often had been exposed to traumatic experiences. The conclusion was erroneously drawn that traumatic incidents in childhood produce neurotic behavior in adult life. This conclusion is not justified, for when the background of well-adjusted individuals is also examined, it is found that this group, too, shows a similar incidence of traumatic events. A related error was made at one time as a result of investigations on the family background of psychotic patients. It was found that such patients had a large number of relatives who were "queer" in some way. It is not reasonable to conclude on this basis that psychoses are inherited, since further investigation shows that so-called normal individuals also have numerous relatives who are commonly described as "queer." The reader will recognize that the way to prevent such erroneous conclusions is to introduce a group of "normals," whose background is also examined. The introduction of a control group is really necessary in order that any conclusions at all may be reached.

The biographical information presented by autobiographies or derived from interviews is difficult to treat in any scientific study because of its diffuse nature and because of the multiplicity and variety of the events that it may cover. These characteristics force on the investigator the intuitive approach that must be taken in examining such material. The intuitive approach involves the interpretation of the material, but an interpretative process invariably introduces error. In order to avoid such errors, inventories have been developed for recording biographical information.

In the typical biographical inventory, a standard series of questions is asked about a person's background. The questions are answered by choosing one of a number of alternatives. Typical questions are the following:

In what type of community did you spend most of your time before entering school?
1. In the country
2. In a town with less than 5000 inhabitants
3. In a town with 5000 to 10,000 inhabitants
4. In a town with 10,000 to 50,000 inhabitants
5. In a town with more than 50,000 inhabitants

Which group of school subjects did you prefer when you were in high school?
1. English, speech
2. Social studies, history, geography
3. Science, mathematics
4. Music, art
5. Athletics

Biographical information collected in the form illustrated above has had a long history of practical use and also some history of having played a useful part in research. Many have regarded it with skepticism, for reasons that still have to be considered, but the fact that it has had a long history of practical utility in the selection of various classes of employees has forced researchers to give it serious consideration. It is of interest to note that the first really successful use of the biographical inventory was in connection with the selection of salesmen, particularly life insurance salesmen. Such devices remain, even today, the main instruments that are used for this purpose. Of course, such devices were not developed on the basis of any particularly sophisticated psychological theory of selling. The point stressed here is that this work of practical importance demonstrated that biographical information collected in this form could be used for making predictions, and probably with more success than biographical information collected in narrative form. Of particular significance is the fact that biographical items related to factual material had considerable predictive significance, while those related to opinions and attitudes tended to be of doubtful value.

During World War II, some success was achieved in the use of biographical information blanks for the prediction of performance in flying training, and there were even indications that such devices could be used for predicting aerial combat leadership. These later inventories that appeared in the wartime program were much more sophisticated than earlier devices in the theory on which they were based, and this sophistication has been shown in work that has been undertaken since that time. A major development incorporated into more recent biographical information blanks has been an attempt to group items in such a way that they measure a number of distinct and separate influences in a person's background, or even a series of relatively independent traits that may emerge from such backgrounds. There has also been considerable interest in attempts to predict variables other than occupational success. For example, there have been many studies in which biographical information has been used to predict reaction to stress, and predictions of sufficient accuracy to be used have been achieved.

The clinician has never been particularly in sympathy with this approach to the matter of using biographical information. He has tended to feel that the very uniformity of the material included in a biographical information blank is a disadvantage. He points out that the unique event is often a crucial factor in the life of an individual, and the unique event would be missed by any standard inventory. The clinician has not proved his case in this matter, and the success achieved with biographical inventories may perhaps make him stop and ponder.

Summary

1. The observation of behavior in the classroom and in other complex situations usually requires the use of observation schedules.

2. Observation schedules should include no more items than the observer can remember and easily locate on the list. The schedule should usually refer to items of behavior that occur with fair frequency. It should also be easy to recognize when an item of behavior has, or has not, occurred.

3. Observation schedules should be based on a theory concerning the relevance of the items of behavior observed to the purposes of the study.

4. The student should be on guard against a procedure for selecting items that results in the selection of those that are highly reliable but rather inconsequential. A checklist type of schedule may be quite unsuitable for the purpose of assessing the more subtle aspects of classroom phenomena, and the latter may have to be appraised in terms of the general impressions of the observer. The latter is a practice that research workers have strenuously attempted to avoid.

5. An interesting proposal is that observation be directed toward the verbal communication that occurs in the classroom. Since most of the transactions that occur between pupil and teacher are undertaken in terms of words, it seems reasonable that the analysis of these words will provide significant information about events in the classroom.

6. In most observation schedules an attempt is made to measure certain dimensions of behavior, rather than merely to keep a record of how frequently this or that event happened. Research workers are still exploring the usefulness of various systems of dimensions that may be used for describing events in the classroom, and one cannot state at this time that one system is more useful than another for particular purposes.

7. Illustrations were provided of some observation schedules

which have been widely used. Such schedules differ from one another in the specificity of the observations recorded and in the extent to which observations are coded before being recorded.

8. A new trend in the observation of classroom events is found in interaction analysis. Classroom events have significance partly because they form a part of a sequence and especially because they form a sequence of pupil and teacher interactions. A number of different techniques have been developed for recording such interactions. The system developed by Flanders has the factor of simplicity to recommend it. A more elaborate system has been developed by Hughes.

9. Pupils have sometimes been enlisted as classroom observers, and schedules have been developed on which they can record their observations. Such schedules have the advantage of providing information concerning the way in which the pupil views the learning situation. The pupil's perception may well be different from that of an adult observer.

10. Information is available concerning the characteristic of persons who distort their observations. Even with the best selection of observers, training in the procedures to be used is generally necessary.

11. The critical incidents technique represents a special method for selecting observations in certain situations. The technique has certain difficulties associated with it, which should be recognized.

12. Techniques have been developed for systematizing the process of self-observation. These techniques include self-rating procedures, Q-methodology, and personality inventories.

Some Problems for the Student

1. Attempt to build a list of *rewarding* behaviors manifested by teachers toward the children in a classroom situation. This checklist is to be used as a means of recording classroom observations of teachers.

CHAPTER 10

SURVEY METHODS

SURVEYS are conducted to establish the nature of existing conditions. A school survey is commonly conducted in order to determine what services the school can render its community, and perhaps to compare these services with those that are provided by other schools.

A distinction must be made between a survey and sample survey. In a sample survey, data are collected about only a portion of the events with which the surveyor is concerned. The design of the sample survey is such that the events examined provide data from which inferences can be made about all of the events. Thus an examination of one hundred rural high schools within a particular state may permit the making of inferences about conditions in the other five hundred.

The survey method represents research at a primitive level. It builds a body of fact that is usually of only local significance. The facts collected may contribute to the solution of immediate problems, but rarely do they develop a body of knowledge that can be used in solving future problems. Thus the technique tends to be a one-shot method.

The survey approach to educational problems is one of those most commonly used. It is followed in studying local as well as state and national problems. It is the commonest method used by principals to obtain information about certain problems. Most surveys result in the analysis of verbal responses, such as those given when an interviewer asks a question and obtains a reply. Similar methods may also be applied to the survey of concrete objects or other types of conditions and events. The Research Department of the National Educational Association has devoted a great deal of its effort to the survey of such matters as school transportation, size of classes, and various aspects of the physical facilities of schools. There is, however, a second type of survey conducted in a school or a school system, which is rather different from the type of survey that has been considered. This is the type of survey conducted by a consultant who has been called in to cast an expert eye over a school system and to advise on the points where the school or system needs to be improved. In this type of survey, the expert collects a great range of facts about a single school or system. He is interested in every phase of it, and no detail escapes his regard. He is concerned with putting together these details in order to provide a total picture as seen by an objective outsider. His approach is qualitative and does not lend itself to statistical treatment, for it is not built around hypotheses that can be tested by typical statistical methods.

The events or conditions that may be enumerated or measured during surveys include a great range of phenomena. The popularity of the public opinion survey as a newspaper feature makes one think of attitudes and opinions as the main source of data in surveys, but this is not necessarily so. Various classes of events that may form the central core of an educational survey must be given brief mention here.

Physical conditions related to learning. Many characteristics of the physical environment may be measured, such as the floor space per pupil in different schools, the number of books per pupil in the library, the intensity of the natural illumination on the pupil's desk, the mean temperature or humidity, and the like.

Many school surveys devote considerable effort to the measurement and evaluation of such characteristics of a school program, and on the surface they would appear to be on a solid foundation, for it is clear that the *measurement* of these variables is objective and does not involve the judgment of the investigator. These measures have satisfactory reliability, and thus their weakness is not at first apparent. The inadequacies of the procedure are a result of the fact that its usefulness depends upon the choice of suitable environmental variables—that is to say, variables that are genuinely related to the effectiveness of learning of the pupil. But very little is known concerning the relationship of such variables to learning processes in pupils. If the student looks back over research in the area, he is likely to find, not only little positive evidence to help in the selection of variables, but much negative evidence indicating the apparent lack of relevance of many variables he might choose. Such studies may have failed to demonstrate the relevance of some of these physical variables because any effect they may have is perhaps long-term and not sufficient in magnitude to manifest consequences over a period of a few weeks or even a semester. Long-term studies of the effect of these physical conditions are rarely feasible.

Behavior of teachers and other behavioral conditions related to learning. Surveys related to the behavior of those who control the educational process are sometimes undertaken, but they involve difficulties of which the prospective researcher must be aware. Many of these surveys pertain to the problem of assessing teaching effectiveness and are based on the assumption that particular characteristics of the behavior of the teacher facilitate learning in the pupil. Rabinowitz and Travers (1953) studied this problem. They pointed out that it is quite obvious that such a simple relationship cannot exist—even the casual observer in the classroom must have observed that some teachers are aggressive and tend to induce fear, while the same aggressiveness in other teachers, combined with other different qualities, produce enthusiasm and high motivation for work. It also seems probable that teachers are effective in different ways. Some are effective in explaining and demonstrating, while others have special skill in organizing socialized activities.

The recent trend in the conduct of surveys of teacher behavior is to set the modest goal of using the survey as a search for measurable characteristics of the behavior of teachers in the classroom. This trend is a result of the realization that those surveys of teacher behavior which attempt to study the effectiveness of teaching are overambitious in terms of present knowledge. Ryans' (1960) study of the characteristics of teacher behavior is an example of a survey which has such modest goals. From his statistical analyses of a vast amount of data pertaining to the behavior of both elementary and secondary teachers there emerged three major characteristics of teacher behavior:

Pattern X_0—Warm, understanding, friendly vs. aloof, egocentric restricted teacher behavior

Pattern Y_0—Responsible, businesslike, systematic vs. evading, unplanned, slipshod teacher behavior

Pattern Z_0—Stimulating, imaginative, surgent vs. dull, routine, teacher behavior

Such a study, and the results flowing from it, represents a first step in the investigation of the relationship of teacher behavior to pupil learning. Whether relationships will be found between variables such as those developed by Ryans and measures of pupil learning is an unanswered question. A study by Heil and Washburne (1962) came out with the odd finding that the extent of pupil achievement could not be related to measures derived from teacher observation, but it could be predicted from scores on a personality test. The implication of this finding is that observers have not yet learned to discern relevant teacher characteristics. This may well be so.

Pupil learning abilities. The surveys that are most likely to reveal facts of importance for educational administration are those provided by the pupils themselves. Such information has a direct relevance to the control and study of the learning process which the other classes of facts do not. Under this category surveys may be made regarding the reading achievement of pupils or their achievement in other so-called basic skills. Sometimes surveys of the information of the pupils may be made, as when a school determines what the pupils know or do not know about their local community, about health practices, about contemporary affairs, or about some other matter judged to be of significance in the educational program. Such surveys need not be confined to matters of student knowledge but may also include events in the attitudinal field.

Much survey research conducted in this area has a public relations value; that is to say, it serves the purpose of providing information that will ease tensions in the community. For example, a school may conduct a survey of reading skills of its sixth-graders in order to demonstrate that the children have learned to read as well as those in communities where more traditional methods of teaching reading have been used. However, such attempts to build understanding in the community may involve the school in technical difficulties, for the pupils whose achievement is to be studied may be naturally more rapid or slower than those in the other communities with whom reading skills are to be compared.

Surveys of factual information designed to satisfy particular pressure groups also present dangers and may result in the modification of the curriculum in undesirable directions. For example, the well-meaning citizens of one state have forced on the schools a curriculum that requires that the history of the state be studied every second year for all twelve years of public schooling. This has been the result of rumored ignorance on the part of pupils of particular details in the history of the state, and no doubt a survey of the achievement of the pupils would show up some ignorance in this respect. However, it is extremely probable that no change in this situation would occur if the time devoted to state history were halved or doubled. It is probably similar to the situation revealed by Joseph Mayer Rice who found near the turn of the century that it made little difference whether pupils spent one hour or five hours daily on spelling; in either case the achievement of the pupils was the same.

An ambitious attempt to study pupil attitudes by survey methods is the Purdue Public Opinion Panel, which conducts an opinion poll in cooperating high schools, mainly at the junior and senior levels. Schools that participate pay a very small fee to help cover expenses and in return obtain a report on the responses of their own students as well as on the responses of a wider sample of pupils. Surveys conducted in this manner are usually related to matters of rather widespread interest, such as the attitude of pupils toward various aspects of the curriculum or toward their parents. The results serve the purpose of stimulating thought rather than that of solving specific problems.

Much of the material collected about pupils by means of surveys is collected through the medium of paper-and-pencil devices, but information about pupil behavior can sometimes be collected by other means. It is possible, for example, to obtain records of the number of books borrowed by each pupil from the library if a survey of reading is being made. The consumption of foods in the cafeteria may provide some evidence of eating habits in relation to health. Absentee rates are of considerable interest. Artistic products and other products of the pupils' hobbies may provide evidence of how leisure hours are spent. There is a wealth of objective pupil data that can be incorporated in a survey, data that do not derive from verbal responses of the pupils.

Data collected about the pupil is likely to have a relevance to the planning and development of education that data derived from the other two categories do not have. Its directness does not make it necessary to invoke questionable assumptions to justify its application to the solution of real problems.

Levels of Complexity in Surveys

Survey studies are mainly of the "what exists" type; that is to say, they are designed to determine the nature of an existing state of affairs. They may be considered to be research in that they result in the accumulation of a certain type of knowledge, although their scientific status may be questioned. The reason for this is that scientific knowledge must consist of an organized body of generalizations that will permit the prediction of events which have not yet occurred and which are not predicted on the basis of what might be called common sense. The survey does not aspire to develop an organized body of scientific laws but provides information useful in the solution of local problems.

A genuine science of behavior in educational systems could never be based on surveys, but this should not necessarily deter the student from undertaking work in this area. Such surveys not only may solve problems of immediate importance but also may provide data that will form the basis of research of a more fundamental type. As an introduction, it may be pointed out that surveys vary greatly in the level of complexity of the problems they attempt to investigate. The simplest surveys attempt only frequency counts of events; the more complex may seek to establish relationships among events.

The frequency-count survey. In this type of survey, the sole purpose is to determine the frequency of occurrence of a particular type of event or condition. The best-known surveys of this sort are those designed to determine the number of persons in a group who expect to vote in a particular way at a forthcoming election. Schools may conduct surveys to determine how many children have received immunization shots of various kinds or how many teachers have M.A. degrees. Such surveys necessarily provide limited but often highly useful knowledge. However, they cannot be said to contribute in any way to an organized body of scientific knowledge about education.

The interrelationship-of-events type of survey. In many surveys, much more than a mere frequency count is sought; in addition, an attempt is made to find the interrelationship among events. Familiar studies of this type are those published by Dr. Gallup in which are shown tabulations of the voting preferences of adults split according to their socioeconomic level. Such surveys are usually based on some kind of theory concerning the interrelationship of events, and indeed should not be undertaken unless they are based on some fairly definite theory. It would be quite ridiculous to conduct a survey to discover the interrelationship of the physical characteristic of red-headedness and voting behavior. On the other hand, it would be quite reasonable to study the relationship between religious preference and party preference, for it is easy to see numerous reasons why there should be such a relationship. The study of such relationships is unlikely to provide direct evidence concerning causal relationships, and indeed they are extremely difficult to interpret. Although religious affiliation, for example, may be related to preference for one of the major political parties, it is clearly unreasonable to conclude that affiliation with religion *causes* the individual to vote for, say, Republican candidates. Yet it is clear that such a relationship, if well established, must be a result of complex causal relationships that may produce both phenomena. The survey itself is unlikely to establish the nature of these complexities and is thus likely to leave the pollster with little except the bare facts, which form only a basis for speculation.

Surveys that approach experimental conditions. Under certain conditions, surveys may acquire many of the characteristics of experimental studies. For example, a researcher may be interested in the effect of hunger on drives and motives, and if he is fortunate, he may be able to obtain volunteers who will fast for varying lengths of time. He may find evidence of the relative strength of food, water, sex, and other drives and motives by studying the fantasies and dreams of his subjects as starvation progresses, and perhaps he might attempt the use of projective techniques for this purpose. The experimenter would also use a control group fed a normal diet, and comparisons would be made between the fasting group and the control group. The fasting and the fed groups would be carefully matched on the basis of relevant characteristics, or subjects would be assigned at random to one or the other group. In describing this experiment, it would be said that the experimenter *manipulated* starvation; indeed, in experimental studies it is customary to manipulate one of the major variables.

A rather similar purpose can be achieved through a survey technique. If the scientist could select groups already exposed to starvation by the natural course of circumstances and compare the fantasies of this group with those of another group that was well fed, he would be reproducing many of the features of the experiment just described. As a matter of fact, it has been possible to do this through the reports of persons who were exposed to extreme conditions of starvation in concentration camps in Germany during World War II. Such studies have provided some evidence that as starvation proceeds all motives tend to become progressively more depressed except for those related to the obtaining of food.

There is, nevertheless, a major difference between the survey technique and the experimental technique. In the experiment described, a control group would have been included as well as an experimental group, and subjects would have been assigned to one or the other group in some way that could not systematically bias the results of the experiment. By contrast, in the survey technique in which a comparison of starved and fed persons is made, there is no assurance that these two groups did not differ systematically in some way that would affect the experimental results. Only when the assignment of persons to the starved and fed groups is under the control of the investigator—and this is true only in the case of the experimental procedure, only then is it possible to be moderately certain that some irrelevant influence is not systematically biasing the experimental results.

SURVEYS OF BEHAVIORAL PHENOMENA

The surveys of the conditions that constitute the environment of the school child, particularly the surveys of the physical conditions, do not manifest the complexities that surveys of behavioral phenomena may involve. True, school surveys involve difficulties of their own, but much useful data may be obtained by straightforward objective techniques, which can be applied only rarely to surveys of behavioral phenomena. The transitoriness of most behavior that is directly observed, including verbal behavior, presents difficulties of observation and recording that a school building, a library, or a teachers' college transcript does not.

Surveys of behavioral phenomena within a school system may be concerned with the behavior of pupils, teachers, parents, superintendents, school boards, or other persons connected with the educational process. Such surveys may be concerned with verbal behavior, such as the expression of opinions or desires, or nonverbal behavior, such as whether parents do or do not spank their children. They may also be concerned with determining the distribution of relatively enduring traits such as intelligence, authoritarianism, schizophrenia, and a host of other attributes. Less enduring traits, such as attitudes and interests, may also be surveyed. Public opinion polls represent surveys at an even more transitory level. There are almost endless possibilities for surveying human behavior.

Desirable Characteristics of Behavioral Data Collected in Surveys

Little, if anything, is to be learned from a survey that seeks to collect a few items of information from a population that is selected merely because it happens to be at hand. While surveys of behavioral phenomena are limited in what they can produce because of the nature of the technique that they involve, they do not have to be as limited as this. In addition, they do not have to be just a process for collecting a large array of disconnected items of fact. The collection of masses of disconnected facts runs counter to the very first principle of survey design— namely, that the items of information gathered should be interrelated within a plan or framework.

It is of particular importance in most educational surveys to avoid phenomena that are transitory. This is of special importance in the behavioral area. Observations that refer to physical conditions do not usually refer to events that are of only transitory significance. When they do, it is so obvious to the researcher that it cannot slip by unnoticed. In conducting a school survey, it is evident that the number of works of fiction in the library is a matter of more than transitory significance. True, it will change as time goes by, but only slowly. The square footage of floor space per pupil is also a matter of some permanence, despite changes in birth rate and in local sociological conditions. On the other hand, classroom temperature at a given hour on a particular day would probably be of only the most transitory significance and might provide little evidence of the quality of the physical conditions. Such a measure is quite clearly not one that could serve any useful purpose in a survey, and on this account it would be rejected immediately by any competent researcher.

In the case of behavior measures, it is much easier to overlook the fact that a measure may represent only an incidental phenomenon. For example, if a survey is made of the likes and dislikes of pupils for various school subjects, it is quite possible that the expressions of the pupils in this regard may be solely the product of the personalities of the teachers involved. The likes and dislikes of junior high school students for particular school subjects may not represent in any way a fairly permanent structure in their personalities, although at higher levels (from what is known) they may well be considered to be so. The same is true in the planning of public opinion polls. It is useless to ask for opinions about matters concerning which the public has not formed a well-crystallized opinion. Opinions given about matters that are new, and for which there has not been sufficient time to think through the issues and form opinions on a solid foundation, are not generally appropriate matters for surveys. Opinions given on the spur of the moment are likely to be prompted by incidents that would have little weight after the subject had been given careful consideration. This is a matter that must be taken into account not only in the survey type of study but also in studies involving instruments of the psychological inventory type. Interest tests commonly suffer from the defect of requiring the student to express his like or dislike for an activity in which he has never engaged and in which he has never considered participating. It seems reasonable to hypothesize that preferences thus expressed may reflect only what are commonly called snap judgments.

The fact that the behavior elicited by the surveyor's questions refers to a relatively stable response should not be taken as a guarantee that the responses can be used to make inferences of the type that the investigator wishes to make. An example of this is shown by responses to a question that has been included quite frequently in public opinion polls. This question as asked is, "Do you favor labor unions?" (Sometimes it is stated in the form, "Do you believe in labor unions?") Responses to this question show, almost invariably, that even groups that are known on other bases to be antagonistic to labor unions give high percentages of "Yes" responses. There is every reason to believe that these responses are highly consistent even over a substantial period of time, and that they therefore represent enduring qualities rather than transitory phenomena. Despite this fact, these responses cannot be taken to represent underlying structures in the personality the assessment of which would permit the prediction of behavior in situations that involve labor unions. Indeed, the response seems to reflect a common stereotype of behavior and to reflect the fact that to be in favor of labor unions is to occupy a socially desirable position. Nearly everybody is in favor of labor unions, just as nearly everybody considers himself a good citizen. For similar reasons, individuals like to call themselves *liberals,* and even those who might be more adequately described as conservatives may prefer to use the term *middle-of-the-road liberal.* Such stereotyped responses yield little information, except possibly the frequency of occurrence of such stereotypes. However, it is extremely difficult to identify cases where such clichés are operating.

The Role of Theory in Conducting Behavioral Surveys

Surveys of behavioral phenomena need to be most carefully planned if they are to yield useful data. The information-gathering process should be based on some theory of the nature of the phenomenon that is being investigated. In most cases this is likely to be a fairly complicated matter, and it may require very extensive information if answers are to be found to important questions. A classic case of a behavioral survey based on well-developed concepts and calling for a large number of items of information is the Kinsey study of sexual behavior in the human male. In this study, several hundred items of information were collected about each male included in the sample. The purpose of obtaining such extensive data was to be able to check and crosscheck a number of hypotheses concerning sexual behavior. The type of survey conducted by Kinsey contrasts with that conducted by Gallup and others whose data are published on a nationwide basis through the newspapers. The latter type of survey collects a very limited amount of data about a matter of vital concern to the public. It is not designed for the purpose of developing understanding concerning the nature of voting behavior. Its usual purpose is to predict a particular event, such as the outcome of an election, and although the pollsters have come to realize that some understanding of voting behavior may contribute to the accuracy of prediction, this is a secondary and minor goal. In contrast, Kinsey was not concerned with keeping a newspaper column going. His interest was a scientific one, and its goal was that of providing an organized account of certain aspects of human behavior, with some attempt to discover interrelationships.

The contrast that has been presented between the public opinion poll and the survey that has scientific purposes has had the purpose of pointing out to the student of educational research that polls published in daily newspapers are inappropriate models for the conduct of research. If educational research is to derive useful information from surveys, it is necessary that they be conducted at a proper level of complexity and based on well-thought-out concepts.

The theoretical framework used as a basis for a survey should, as far as possible, be stated as a theory, in the way outlined in earlier chapters. The limitation on this arises from the fact that surveys are commonly conducted in situations in which not much is known about the phenomena concerning which inquiry is made, and some of the data-collecting may be analogous to the grasping of a blind man in a new environment. The result of such grasping is the acquisition of information that will help him in developing a concept of the way in which his environment is arranged. The analogy does, of course, represent an extreme case, and the fact is that researchers, at least in their early years of development, would be most unwise to explore entirely unknown territory. They would be more likely to achieve positive results and to have a profitable learning experience if they were to conduct an inquiry into an area already partially explored and in which earlier workers had already developed concepts for use in understanding.

Where limited surveys are conducted, the theory involved may be stated in the simplest terms and often may consist of no more than a single sentence. Perhaps a good beginning for the development of a conceptual framework is to recognize that a survey that accumulates data by asking questions and recording the answers is not just an easy process of obtaining information.

The matter of stating questions and obtaining answers is far from being the simple one that it is commonly believed to be. Perhaps all who have used this technique for collecting data during the past twenty years have shown a surprising naïveté in this respect, and we owe a debt to J.W. Getzels (1954) for calling attention to our lack of sophistication.

Getzels has pointed out that, while numerous studies have been conducted to show that all kinds of conditions affect responses to visual patterns, no parallel research exists to describe conditions that affect responses in question-and-answer situations. He has borrowed a number of concepts from the field of perception to build a model that attempts to account for variations in the answers given to the same questions as the situation in which the question asked is changed. According to the model provided by Getzels, the asking of a question first produces an internal response, which is not verbalized. This immediate response is, in a sense, an answer to the question, and it is described as the "personal hypothesis" in this theory. Second, responses are made to various aspects of the situation in which the response occurs.

This is referred to as the stage in which the demands of the situation are sized up in terms of the individual's personal adjustment to that situation. Third, the individual formulates a response that will facilitate his adjustment to the total situation.

According to this theory, there would be a tendency for the respondent to reply to a question in such a way that his answer reflects what he perceives to be an appropriate response to that situation—that is to say, he answers in the way that he believes is expected of him.

The point here is that a theory to be used as a basis for a survey involving verbal responses must take into account the adjustments that are made between interviewer and interviewee. This complicates considerably the theory requirements for this type of work and recognizes at the outset that data thus collected cannot be taken at face value.

At a minimum level of development, a theory must postulate the ways in which the phenomena can be measured. If various methods of measurements are possible, then there should be some statement of how these measures are related to one another. For example, if a survey is being made of parental disciplinary actions in the home, one might postulate that the parents' account of frequency of disciplinary action should be related to the child's account. If the two accounts are unrelated, then the data are quite probably worthless. One might also postulate that a more truthful answer would be given if a parent were asked to indicate what he thought would be the best way to handle a common behavior problem than if he were asked how he would handle his own child.

A theory on which a survey is based must usually postulate the relationships of the phenomena investigated to possible causes. In the case of the disciplinary behavior of parents, a survey would be a barren and dull affair if it stopped at the point of finding out how frequently parents inflicted different types of punishment on their children. The investigator would almost certainly want to know something about the characteristics that differentiated parents who punished frequently from those who punished rarely. To do this, it would be necessary to construct a theory of the determinants of punishing behavior. This theory would then form the basis of the inquiry.

A theory on which a survey is based must have something to say about the specificity or generality of the phenomenon that is to be surveyed. If the behavior of parents is being surveyed concerning the extent to which they attempt to exercise control over the behavior of their children, it is important to know whether the phenomenon is a general one; that is to say, it is important to know whether a parent who exercises extensive control in one area of child activity also tends to exercise control in other areas. If no information is available concerning this matter, then the survey must be conducted so that it samples the various areas of parental control and provides information concerning them. Unless such information is given, the results of the survey will have little meaning.

A basic question to answer in the planning of a behavioral survey is, "What is the section of the population in which the phenomenon is to be found?" If the survey is to be concerned with an educational problem such as the existence of certain kinds of reading disabilities, the surveyor should know whether he is to be concerned with sixth- or twelfth-graders. The determination of this fact alone might have a desirable limiting influence on the scope of the investigation. Although it has been pointed out already that breadth is a most desirable characteristic of surveys, it is better to make an extended survey of reading disabilities of eight-year-olds than it is to collect less data about the entire population of school age. If the survey is to be strictly descriptive, the surveyor will proceed to determine what characteristics of reading skill are to be studied, in whom these characteristics can be most meaningfully established, and what are the sections of the population for which breakdowns are to be reported. It is probable that, if the reading skills of eight-year-olds are to be surveyed, the results would be reported for different socioeconomic levels, by sex, and by school. These would represent three variables that previous research has already established to be associated with the development of reading skills. A survey that does not yield such breakdowns is a nebulous affair, providing an impressionistic type of picture that lacks any detail.

Types of Data Collected in Behavioral Surveys

The data collected in surveys may vary in the degree to which they represent directly the phenomena in which the surveyors are interested. The collection of data directly about behavior relevant for an educational survey is difficult to achieve. Examples of such data are found in many studies—as, for example, those in which pupils' food choices in the school cafeteria have been studied. This can be done by direct observation, and such a procedure is obviously much superior to that of asking the pupils what they will eat or have eaten. Spelling behavior may be surveyed by the inspection of samples of pupils' work. There is some evidence, incidentally, that the latter procedure provides information superior to that which can be derived from spelling achievement tests. Such data, however, represent only the most fragmentary records of a person's behavior in a particular area. It is possible, if not probable, that deplorable deficiencies manifested by pupils in their choice of food in the school cafeteria may be justified in terms of their diet over an entire day. This sample of behavior, like most samples of directly recorded behavior, is too restricted and narrow to provide much useful information concerning the total eating habits of the pupils. Most surveys that attempt to obtain data directly without resorting to the collection of verbal reports suffer from this defect. This does not mean that observational techniques of the types previously discussed cannot yield valuable data and form the basis of worthwhile research, for they can. The implication is only that they are not well adapted to research needs in those cases in which surveys are being conducted.

A second source of data for surveys about behavior is found in existing records. Previous school grades and test records are examples of such data. Comparisons of the performance on tests administered at the same level but ten or twenty years apart represent a particularly interesting use of this technique. There is a very substantial body of data in most school systems about pupil personnel and teacher personnel, which may form the data of useful surveys. A word of caution should be injected here. Such data often include gross inaccuracies due to clerical errors made at the time when they were recorded. Further discussion of this matter will be presented later.

Since the collection of data about behavioral phenomena for the purpose of conducting surveys must involve mainly a question-and-answer procedure, it is necessary at this time to discuss the matter of formulating questions. The design of the questions to be used has come to be recognized as a matter of crucial importance in the planning of surveys. Suggestions for the design of questions can now be found in many sources. The reader is referred to sources such as Cantril (1947) and Parten (1950). Some texts on educational measurement, such as that by the author (1955), also offer suggestions to follow in the design of questionnaires.

It would be inappropriate to attempt to discuss here at length the design of questions to be used in surveys, since this is a subject about which there is an extensive technical literature. Nevertheless, it is necessary to provide a brief orientation.

First, note that the design of effective questions is much more than a matter of writing out clearly what one wants to ask. It is much more than a matter of the effective use of English. The question should be regarded as a stimulus to which there is a relatively stable response. If there is not a stable response or set of responses, then there is little point in asking the question, for responses to it will lack what is ordinarily termed reliability.

Second, the questions should be such that the responses are made to the questions themselves rather than to other aspects of the situation. For example, questions asked in a survey about the pay of teachers are likely to elicit a very high frequency of response to the effect that they are underpaid. Yet the same individuals who state that teachers are underpaid are likely to vote against increased state and city budgets that would make increases in their salaries possible. In answering the survey questions, these individuals are responding to the social pressures of the situation as much as to the question itself. Such responses are commonly referred to as stereotyped responses.

Third, the questions should draw responses that can be elicited with some uniformity. This is really saying that the procedure should have reliability and be reproducible. This is clearly not a sufficient condition to make a question useful, because questions to which there are stereotyped responses provide high consistency but little else.

Fourth, the questions must be such that inferences can be made from the responses to responses in other situations. This may not seem obvious when it is first considered, but it is precisely what is wrong with the question that elicits a stereotyped response—one given in the particular situation but presumably not given in other situations. If a survey is made to determine how the electorate will vote in a certain election, it is important to be able to assume that behavior in answering the survey questions will be related to behavior in the voting booth. If these two aspects of behavior are unrelated, the survey ceases to have any purpose. All questions asked in the survey method must be such that it is reasonable to assume some generality of the response. The reader is reminded that the relationship between verbal behavior and other aspects of motor performance is complex, and that a simple one-to-one relationship can rarely be expected.

The trend in collecting behavioral information about populations of individuals has been to standardize the questions asked by the interviewer. The opinion poll as it is commonly conducted represents a series of brief but standardized personal interviews, in which interviewers always ask the same questions and in which the responses of those interviewed are generally restricted to a few categories. It is possible to remove restrictions on the behavior of both the interviewer and the interviewee until the point is reached where a relatively free interview takes places, perhaps restricted only to the topic to be discussed. However, in surveys the difficulty of quantifying the data based on free interviews is such that they are not practical. The most that is likely to be done in departing from the situation in which both the question and the responses are restricted is the elimination of restrictions on the response. Such open-ended questions provide a range of responses that must ultimately be tabulated and codified.

The problems of collecting data by interview methods have been considered in detail in other parts of this book, and they cannot be considered further here. Despite the defects of interview techniques that have been noted, they must still be considered as the primary methods of collecting survey data about behavior.

Direct-Mail Questionnaire Methods

The last twenty years have shown a transition in survey techniques from the use of questionnaires sent through the mail to quite elaborate interview techniques. It is unfortunate that the same trend has not been apparent in educational research, where direct-mail techniques are still commonly used.

The central difficulty in all direct-mail techniques is that the percentage of returns is small. A questionnaire of some interest to the recipient may be expected to show only a 20 per cent return, even when conditions are favorable. If nonrespondents are contacted a second and a third time, the return may be increased to 30 per cent. Only rarely does it reach the 40 per cent level. Attempts may then be made to contact personally the final group of nonrespondents, but if this is done, it might be as well to perform the entire operation by interview.

A considerable amount is now known about who does and who does not respond to mailed questionnaires. At one time it was felt by many that it was largely a matter of chance whether a person did or did not respond to a questionnaire sent to him through the mail. If it arrived at a convenient time, he would respond to it; if it did not, he would not respond. Research has shown that this is not the case at all. A study by Wallace (1954) is particularly revealing in this respect.

Wallace sent four questionnaires at intervals to the same group. Some failed to return any, while others returned as many as all four. The tendency was for a person who returned one questionnaire to return all four. In other words, there are those who, by and large, tend to return questionnaires, and there are those who do not. Insofar as these groups differ in relevant respects, the results achieved with direct-mail questionnaires are likely to be biased.

Wallace's study also throws some light on the characteristics of those who return direct-mail questionnaires and those who do not. Of particular importance is the fact that those who return them show a marked tendency to have a college education, while those who do not have relatively less education. Since differences in education are related to a host of other variables, it is hard to find an area in which questions are not likely to elicit a different response from a well-educated group than from a less well-educated group. Thus the returns may be considered to be biased by an unknown quantity. It is of some interest to note that, while the returnees and nonreturnees differ in education, they differed little in the Wallace study in socio-economic status. Wallace states that the safest rule in deciding whether or not to use direct-mail questionnaires is: Don't.

Surveys of Behavior in Simulated Situations

A new approach to the problem of conducting surveys of behavior is found in a very large-scale research by Hemphill et al. (1962). The basic purpose of the study was to discover some of the dimensions of administrative behavior in elementary schools and also to obtain assessments of how teachers and superintendents regarded and evaluated each aspect of administrative behavior. It is not a study of administrative effectiveness as such but rather is it a study of what administrative behaviors occur and who considers them desirable or undesirable.

While there would be merit in studying principals in the actual job situation and in finding out how they handled the many situations that arise during the course of a typical school day, such an approach is not feasible. An observer would hardly be permitted to sit with the principal, listen to conversations often of a confidential nature, record the statements made by visitors, review the daily correspondence and the replies to it, and so forth. In the Hemphill study this problem was avoided by bringing principals from the schools into artificially constructed administrative situations. The principals were invited in groups of twenty, to the centers conducting the research. There, they were told that their name was "Marion Smith" and that they were the principal of the Whitman Elementary School in the town of Jefferson. They were then given an orientation to the community and school by means of a sound movie, filmstrip, personnel files, handbooks, a school survey, a school census, test scores of pupils, and other information. After the fairly lengthy orientation session, each principal was then taken to what was to be considered the school office. There they were told to imagine that this was the office on Labor day and that they were to prepare for the first day of school. The in-basket on the desk was filled with items which needed immediate attention. One of the tasks was to go through the in-basket and take appropriate action on each of the documents it contained. Another task involved the observation of three teachers still on a probationary status. The latter observation was undertaken by viewing kinescopes of teachers in classrooms. In addition, an attempt was made to assess the speaking abilities of the principals who were required to prepare and deliver a speech to the Whitman Parent-Teachers Association. In a second social situation a group of the principals were brought together by a mythical "Mr. Davies," the business manager for the district, with the object of selecting a new principal. The situation permitted observers to record relevant aspects of the participants behavior.

A major outcome of a study of this kind is a set of variables which can be used in subsequent research. Before studies can be undertaken which attempt to find means of predicting administrative behavior, a set of measurable characteristics of administrative behavior must be established. The study of the principals served this purpose and fifteen major characteristics of administrative behavior were identified. These are described in general terms as follows:

A. General Ability to Reason and Understand
B. Superiors' Over-all Impression
C. Concern for Human Problems vs. Conventionality
D. Gregarious Friendliness vs. Independent Initiative
E. Involvement with Others in In-basket Work
F. Effective Participation in Group Interaction
G. Anxiety vs. Emotional Maturity
H. Analyzing the Situation
I. Directing the Work of Others
J. Job Performance Values
K. Complying with Suggestions (Residual)
L. Teachers' Impressions
M. Age and Experience
N. Preparing for Decision vs. Taking Final Action
O. Instructional Awareness

The list of variables given above does not include many characteristics which one would expect to appear. For example, there is nothing included in it which covers such behavior as "improves working conditions" or "backs up staff." Another category which is notably absent is that of "delegates authority." These absences do not represent deficiencies in the appraisal procedure but simply reflect the fact that the principals studied showed an almost complete absence of these behaviors. The same is true of other categories which authorities on educational administration agree to be important but which do not emerge from the study.

The point which has just been made brings out one of the major values of the survey. It can serve to identify characteristics which show a sufficiently wide range of values that individual differences can be reliably assessed, but it also serves to identify those characteristics which have not been developed and to which training programs should give special attention.

The identification of variables that can be measured provides a basis for future research. In a sense, the kind of survey under consideration provides a foundation on which future research on the prediction of administrative performance and on the training of administrators can be built. Too many studies are undertaken without the ground having been thoroughly explored and cleared by a study such as this one. A too hasty attack on problems of training and prediction of success leads only to failure.

Checks on the Data-Collection Process

It is apparent from what has been said that the collection of verbal survey data is likely to leave the investigator with feelings of insecurity concerning the meaning of the information collected. It is usually recognized that empirical errors have been introduced into the data, and the size of these errors needs to be estimated if the results of the survey are to be interpretable. The experienced survey researcher will build into his study empirical checks that will provide him with information concerning the meaningfulness of his results.

Of primary importance are checks on the adequacy of the data-collection process itself. The early organizers of surveys of consumer preferences discovered that paid interviewers sometimes omitted the important detail of actually conducting interviews and adopted the shortcut process of filling out the interview schedules at home. Many ways have since been devised for checking on the honesty and accuracy of interviewers. One of these is to include on the interview schedule questions such that the distribution of responses in the population to be interviewed is known. Another common procedure is for interviewers to obtain the name and address of each interviewee and for a sample of these interviewees to be followed up independently.

Certain types of errors, known as *response errors,* are particularly difficult to estimate and control. Those who respond to interviewers are likely to show a tendency to overestimate those characteristics that are highly esteemed. Estimates of education and income are likely to be inflated unless they are preceded by questions that ask for such details as make subsequent falsification of answers hazardous. For example, if it is desired to determine a man's income, it may be well to start by establishing his place of employment, his grade within the organization, and the base rate of pay for that grade, before direct questions pertaining to income are asked. The early questions in such a series provide data against which subsequent responses can be checked.

The internal checking of responses is probably the simplest and commonest way of testing the consistency of data. A person's given age can be verified against data such as the age of his oldest child and the age of the person when the child was born. The latter two questions can be separated from one another by other material and also separated from the original question on the topic. Sometimes a question on birth date can also be included as an additional check. It is possible for a respondent to be consistent in answering all these items yet provide a completely false record, but the likelihood of this is small.

A type of check that has been used extensively for determining the trustworthiness of responses to personality test inventories has also been used in the conduct of opinion polls. The technique is simply that of asking a question to which the reply itself provides some estimate of the extent to which the respondent is providing trustworthy answers. If a person is asked, "Do you ever tell lies?" one may suspect that he is not telling the truth if he answers "No!" There are few, if any, who never tell lies. It is possible to introduce a series of such questions, which may be used to provide a so-called validating score. Nevertheless, the technique is not without its pitfalls. The reader should take note of the fact that such questions, if they are answered honestly, usually place the respondent in a rather bad light, and for this reason the tendency to falsification may be much greater than would be the case with more innocuous items. The answers to such so-called validating items, or scores derived from them, cannot be unequivocally interpreted at this time.

If checks based on internal consistency are used, it is sometimes possible to determine the adequacy of these checks by separating from the population a group that may be expected to` have an unusually high consistency of response. For example, if questions are asked school personnel about the behavior of individual pupils, one may expect principals to be less consistent than teachers, simply because principals have fewer opportunities to observe pupils. If a check showed that the principals were more familiar with the pupils than were teachers, the data would be open to suspicion.

The information given by internal checks provides evidence mainly of the internal consistency of the data. This is information related to reliability rather than to the trustworthiness of the data as a basis for inference. For this reason most opinion polls include checks whereby a part of the data collected are compared with equivalent data from some other source. A rich source of data in the educational field, which may be used for making many such comparisons, is that collected by the Purdue High School Opinion Poll. Other sources in the educational field are limited, and for this reason difficulties are encountered in the application of this method of checking the data. Hence a second and much less satisfactory method is commonly used; it involves the collection of observations additional to those ordinarily gathered in survey interviews. We are referring here to observations made by interviewers concerning the forthrightness or evasiveness of those interviewed and such behavior as may indicate whether or not trustworthy responses are being given.

The Identification of the Sample to be Surveyed

In solving strictly local educational problems, surveys are commonly conducted to cover every member of the designated population. In such cases we have no sampling problems, but there is also no population to which the results can be generalized. For example, in one state a survey was made of the attitude of members of the state legislature toward a particular educational proposal. Seventy per cent of the Republican members and 60 per cent of the Democrats were favorably disposed toward the proposal. Can a test of significance be applied to determine whether the one party differed "significantly" from the other in attitude toward this issue? The question is not a meaningful one so long as the total population has been polled, for a test of significance would attempt to answer the question as to what was the probability that such a difference existed in the total population if certain differences were found to exist in a sample. If the members of the state legislature can be considered to be a sample of, say, future and past legislatures, then a test of significance may be appropriate. However, we might have great difficulty in defining a population of which the members of the present state legislature could be considered to be a sample.

Sampling becomes a problem when it is desired to make a generalization from a sample of a specified population, either to other samples not yet drawn or to the population itself. The problem of sampling arises simply because it is desired to make a generalization.

There is an important distinction between a random sample and a representative sample. A *random sample* is one drawn in such a way that each member of the population has an equal chance of being included. Therefore, a random sample is one drawn without the guide of relevant variables in terms of which the sample should match the universe, and drawn in such a way that it is not systematically biased by the procedure in one direction or another. Of course one random sample will be expected to differ from another random sample; and, other things being equal, the larger the two random samples, the less will be the expected differences between their means on the characteristic sampled. On the other hand, in a *representative* or *stratified sample* cases are selected in such a way that the characteristics of the sample are similar in important respects to the characteristics of the universe. Thus, in polling the public on their choices in forthcoming elections, it is common practice to select a sample so that it is representative of the entire voting public with respect to certain characteristics that are related to voting behavior. For example, since voting behavior is related to income, it is important that the distribution of income in the sample be similar to the distribution of income in the universe. A similar control may be exercised over numerous related variables if the characteristics of the universe are known. This process of matching the sample to the universe permits greater validity of inference from the sample to the universe and from the sample to other variables than when the sample has been selected at random.

The researcher should avoid preparing an alphabetical list of names and then proceeding down the list until he has included a sufficient number in his sample. It is well known that some letters of the alphabet include more names from certain European groups than others, and this may produce bias in a sample selected on the basis of name alone.

In order to avoid the difficulties that are likely to arise from sampling an alphabetical list, a good plan is to select every fifth or sixth or tenth name, or whatever interval will yield the needed number while still distributing them over the entire list. Those who are absent on the day when the data are collected should be included as soon as possible thereafter. Substitutes should not be sought for these subjects, since it is possible that absentees have relevant characteristics that the substitutes do not have. Also, there should be as little delay as possible in the testing of the absentees, for in any interviewing period the characteristic that is being measured may change. The researcher should also avoid the practice of depending on volunteers as a basis for selecting a sample, since volunteers are likely to be differently motivated from nonvolunteers. In the latter connection, the author can recall an instance where volunteers were compared with nonvolunteers on the Rorschach. The main difference between these two groups was that the volunteers came to the testing situations determined to reveal as much as possible of their inner lives, while the nonvolunteers wanted to reveal as little as possible. Related influences may well affect scores from achievement tests.

Problems of sampling in educational surveys at the local level can often be completely avoided by including the entire universe of possible cases in the "sample." If a high school principal wishes to conduct a survey of the reading skills of the twelfth-grade pupils in his high school, it may be possible for him to include every one of them in the survey. In most high schools this would be a practical matter, but in large city high schools where enrollments may be as great as ten thousand, it becomes quite unnecessary to test every pupil in the senior class in order to obtain the desired data. The decision concerning which of the pupils to include in the survey is greatly facilitated by the fact that there is available a complete list of the names of all cases in the universe from which the sample is to be drawn. When such a list is available, major difficulties associated with the problem of sampling are eliminated. Nevertheless, there are certain errors that the researcher should avoid.

Another common error in sampling school populations is to sample by seating position in an assembly hall. This would happen if the first four rows in an assembly were retained for a brief period to fill in a questionnaire while the others were dismissed at the end of the meeting. If the pupils were free to seat themselves in any way they wanted in an assembly, it is likely that those who chose the rear of the room would be different in many respects from those who chose the front of the room.

Difficult problems of sampling arise when it is not possible completely to identify the universe to be sampled. The typical public opinion poll, the results of which are published in newspapers and magazines, faces this difficulty. If a representative sample of the adult population is desired to determine public attitude with respect to some issue, there is no way of locating and identifying in advance of the poll the names of those to be questioned. This fact makes it difficult to insure that the sample is representative of the universe, or that it has not been selected in some way so that a systematic bias has been introduced. Fortunately, most populations that the educator may wish to sample have been inventoried for him, as is the case with populations of pupils and parents. However, when he wishes to extend his inquiry outside of these groups, he runs into the difficulty of identifying the population that is to be sampled and therefore has difficulty in recognizing the cases that are to constitute the sample.

The problem that this situation presents is a difficult one, and we must pause here to consider some of the historical solutions and their weaknesses. The oldest method of all was that of merely avoiding the problem and including in the sample just those cases that could be easily located or that volunteered. The disastrous *Literary Digest* straw ballot on the outcome of the 1936 Presidential election was run on this kind of a basis. Millions were included in the sample—indeed, it was one of the largest ever included in a ballot—but circumstances beyond the control of the investigator caused the sample to be biased, and inferences made from the sample about the universe were unjustified, as the results clearly showed.

The public opinion pollsters who followed immediately after this debacle recognized that some control needed to be exercised over the characteristics of the sample. It was also recognized that those who volunteer opinion, as in the *Literary Digest* poll, may be so different from the total electorate that it may not be possible to select from these cases a sample that could be considered representative of the total for the purpose at hand. A similar bias would occur if a principal polled those attending the P-TA and assumed this to be a sample of all parents of all the children in the school.

The trend in the 1930's was to distribute the group included in public opinion samples geographically and to instruct interviewers, who were also distributed geographically, to obtain interviews with certain specific percentages of individuals in each economic structure, each race, each sex, and so on. For a long time this appeared to be a satisfactory procedure, and more by good fortune than anything else the predictions of the outcomes of national elections enjoyed a decade of apparent accuracy. However, it eventually became clear that the procedure of letting interviewers select those to be interviewed results in a bias in the sample thus selected. Interviewers tend to select interviewees who are rather like themselves. Thus, if the interviewers belong to an upper socioeconomic group, they are likely to include too few individuals in the lower income brackets. Interviewer bias is now a well-known and well-established phenomenon.

Some adjustment also had to be made for the fact that only some of those polled voted, and those who failed to vote represented a biased sample of the electorate. In addition, some last-minute changes in opinions were likely to occur, and not necessarily such that the proportions in each voting category remained unchanged. These adjustments were usually made on the basis of judgment based on past experience, and for many years this was a successful process. However, it is well known that in the 1948 Presidential election a failure occurred in the making of these adjustments, and the resulting predictions were notoriously inaccurate. Since that time, those concerned with the conduct of surveys have become more cautious in making such adjustments and have also worked on improved methods of obtaining samples for this purpose.

One of these newer approaches is referred to as *area sampling*. In this technique, highly detailed maps of the regions to be sampled are used and the area is systematically sampled. If, for example, a particular small area is to be included in the sample, then all persons living within that identified small area are included in the sampling. The sample thus selected is largely independent of the whims, likes, and dislikes of the persons collecting the data. Nevertheless, the method is not as simple as it seems, and difficulties are encountered in tracking down the persons identified. There are also definitional problems. If a person has residence in a particular locality, it does not necessarily mean that he lives there, and decisions have to be made about such matters.

In some localities, samples may be identified in advance of the process of collecting data by obtaining complete lists of residents. Here again, the procedure appears to be highly satisfactory on the surface, but difficulties arise in its application. Lists of residents are often inaccurate because of faulty methods of collecting the data on which they are based. An even greater source of difficulty arises from the time lag between the collection of data for making lists of residents, publication, and subsequent use for survey purposes. In many areas, a lag of only a year may render such lists quite unsuitable for identifying any kind of sample. On the other hand, other areas may show a high population stability.

Special problems arise when follow-up surveys of school graduates are made. Studies of these groups are commonly undertaken in order to determine the successes and failures of the graduates so that the program of the school may be improved. In these follow-up studies, it is easy to obtain a complete list of the names of the population to be studied—the difficulty arises in locating these individuals. Young groups are particularly mobile, but fortunately their parents represent a population much more stable in terms of home address. Many graduates can be contacted through their parents' homes, but in some localities it may not be possible to do this, since entire families may move to different parts of the country. If the survey is a follow-up of college graduates, then the alumni organization may be of great value in locating individuals. Classmates may also be consulted to determine addresses of cases that cannot otherwise be located. The investigator must be resigned to the fact that, in the educational follow-up survey, it is likely that a substantial fraction of the cases to be included in the sample will not be located despite intensive efforts on the part of the investigator.

Sometimes in conducting follow-up studies, one can check on the extent to which the sample collected is representative of the total population included in the study. For example, if the school files still retain the scholastic records of the population, it is possible to determine the extent to which the sample is representative of the universe that is sampled with respect to scholastic achievement. This would be an important fact if scholastic aptitude could be considered to be related to the phenomenon under study. If, in this case, a serious discrepancy existed between the sample and the universe, questions might be raised concerning the validity of inferences from the sample to the universe.

In the development of follow-up studies of graduates of particular educational institutions, a special problem occurs in the choice of specific classes to be sampled. Suppose that the purpose of the study is to obtain information concerning the adequacy of the curriculum for preparing pupils for the future. Perhaps it is considered that a sample of sufficient size can be obtained by including 50 per cent of the students from a single graduating class. In such a case, the investigator probably might become concerned with the problem of selecting a typical class, so that the results could be generalized to other graduating classes. The investigator would soon find that this task presents some real difficulties. He would note that recent graduating classes would be inappropriate for the purposes of the study, since the students would have been out of school too short a time to permit inadequacies in their school experience to reflect themselves. He might therefore consider including in the study a class graduated several years earlier. This plan might look good to him, until it is pointed out that these earlier classes had fed most of their male students into the armed forces, since the students graduated at a time when the military establishment was being built up to meet a war emergency. These students faced situations that later students did not face. Still older graduates also had unique experiences of their own, since they were thrust on a labor market where unemployment faced many. The investigator would soon be forced to accept the fact that no graduating class could be considered "typical," because education takes place in a changing world.

However, one presumes that there must be at least some uniformity running through the varied environmental conditions that present themselves to graduating classes. At least, one may expect that most members of all graduating classes ultimately face the problems associated with earning a living. Insofar as the graduating classes show such a common core of experience, it is feasible to make inferences from data derived from one class to other classes.

Sometimes the researcher may arrive at the conclusion that no class and no sample will provide the information needed. No survey is a panacea. The investigator nevertheless will exercise great caution in making the inference that the results derived from one graduating class can be generalized to other classes. Even though all graduates face the problems of earning a living, economic conditions vary from class to class. One class may graduate in times of depression, another in times of prosperity, and the resulting problems and difficulties may be entirely different. Indeed, one might even be forced to the unsatisfactory conclusion that the curriculum needed to prepare pupils for prosperity might be different from that necessary to prepare pupils for depression conditions.

Some Misuses of Survey Methods

The survey as it exists today within the framework of educational research finds its greatest misapplication in the local study of the type that educational institutions usually undertake for the purpose of justifying their existence. The difficulty with such surveys is that they are designed to answer questions that really cannot be answered at the present time by means of any data that one can conceive of collecting. For example, the author has watched the development of a study designed to provide an evaluation of selected aspects of teacher education. Some of the questions that those conducting the study proposed to answer were truly answerable, such as, "What has been the effect of state aid on the program?" Such a question can be answered mainly by consulting the budget office and by determining just how the money has been spent. However, an answer is likely to add but little to what is already known through the channels of common gossip. Most of the answerable questions posed by the committee running the survey were of this character. However, it was the questions that were much more difficult to answer, if they could be answered at all, that dealt with the problems of central importance to this survey; for example, "Does the institution graduate students who can teach successfully?" and "What are the weaknesses and strengths of the teacher education program?" Such questions, unfortunately, cannot be definitively answered by any means at present available.

Now in the case of the particular survey, those who asked the questions soon realized that there was no satisfactory way of answering them. They saw that there was no way of determining whether the teachers produced by the program could teach successfully. Thus an alternative question was formulated: "Are the principals who employ the graduates of the college satisfied with these graduates as teachers?" In order to answer this question, a questionnaire was sent to the principal of each school employing one graduate or more. This questionnaire asked for information concerning the extent to which the graduates were satisfactory as teachers. As one might well expect, those principals who did reply rated the teachers trained in the particular institution almost always as satisfactory, or very satisfactory. This, of course, meant absolutely nothing. A person inclined to make a derogatory report would probably make no report at all. Thus such "data," if one may excuse this misuse of the term, were quite valueless for answering any significant questions that might be asked about the teacher education program.

SURVEYING THE CONTENT OF THE CURRICULUM

The Analysis of the Content of Communications

In the previous section consideration was given to the problem of identifying the content of curricula. The analysis of such content is a further problem which may be involved in a research project. If the content of a curriculum has been broken down into an ordered set of propositions, those propositions and their order represent the verbal knowledge to be communicated to the students. Analysis of such communications is undertaken by techniques similar to those which have been evolved for the analysis of other forms of communication made under different conditions. Sometimes the assumption may be made that the content of a curriculum is specified by the particular textbook used, and that the analysis of the curriculum can be made through the analysis of the propositions contained in the text.

Curriculum Analysis: The Problem of Identifying Content

Content analysis refers to a group of techniques which have been designed for the analysis of verbal communications. The techniques are appropriate for the analysis of a great range of communications, including those to be found in textbooks, lectures, informal teacher-pupil interactions, written compositions of pupils, and other sources. Although the problems involved in the analysis of the content of a curriculum are of central concern to education, they represent an area of content analysis which has hardly been explored yet. Nevertheless, the significance of the analysis of the content of curricula is such that it will be given first place in the discussion of the area.

In recent years, emphasis has been placed in curriculum planning on the "content" aspects of the curriculum. Some courses are believed to contain more "content," or more worthwhile "content," than others and, hence, have been given a place of greater importance in the school program. Other courses which are alleged to lack "content" have been squeezed into a smaller amount of school time, or have been excluded from the program. Just what constitutes "content" is rarely defined, and the term remains an obscure one with respect to curriculum planning. The definition given here is one which the author finds convenient, even though it may not be universally accepted.

His position is that a teaching area has "content" insofar as that can be represented by an organized set of statements or propositions. These statements or propositions would include definitions, statements of fact, and generalizations and principles.

The propositions representing the content of an area always have organization, but the organization may differ from field to field. In the case of geometry, for example, the propositions are organized within a logical structure beginning with certain propositions referred to as axioms, which are essentially definitions, to statements which represent complex relationships in space. The content of physics has a somewhat similar structure. The structure of the content of history is different from either of these two in that the statements and propositions representing the knowledge in this area are organized in time. Some historical events occurred before other historical events and their sequence in time must be understood in order to understand history. The content of other subject-matter areas is much less clear. Consider, for example, English, the content of which is organized into a number of different structures. On the one hand there is the structure represented by grammar, which is a system of rules describing the customs which have evolved with respect to the use of words. But the teaching of English also involves the use of other structures within which the propositions representing the fields are organized. Since some of the content of English courses is historical, it involves the use of time sequences and a time structure similar to that involved in history. The reader may pause at this point and think of other systems in terms of which knowledge in the area of English is structured.

Research on curriculum problems is very likely to involve the study and analysis of the content of the curriculum, and this, in turn, involves both the determination of the propositions which represent the content and the nature of the structure within which the propositions are organized. It involves the development of knowledge about the structure of knowledge. Such a knowledge about the nature of knowledge is called a *metaknowledge*. Both curriculum planning and curriculum research require the development of such a metaknowledge but this is a matter which has not been widely discussed in educational literature outside of the writings of B.O. Smith of the University of Illinois, who has been largely responsible for calling attention to the problem.

Content is rarely defined. In most areas of knowledge the only available definitions of "content" are vague general statements found in curriculum outlines or in the material included in a syllabus. Euclid's system of geometry is one of the few areas in which the propositions defining the content can be easily identified.

There is also much learned in most subject-matter areas which is outside of content, as it has been defined here. Many motor and perceptual skills are not reducible to organized sets of propositions. In learning a foreign language, for example, skill acquired in pronunciation is not reducible to a set of propositions which encompass all aspects of the pronunciation. Pronunciation must be learned largely by imitation. While physical education has content in the sense defined here, a physical education major also acquires skills related to physical education activities which cannot be represented as a set of organized propositions. A course in literature may have as one of its major purposes that of providing the student with the aesthetic and emotional experiences which accompany the reading of a great work. That such a course provides knowledge of a kind cannot be denied, but it is not knowledge reducible to a set of precisely stated propositions. These aesthetic and emotional experiences cannot be communicated to others by the same means as would be used for communicating physics or philology. That such experiences play an important part in the educational process cannot be denied, but they do not represent content as the term is used here. Literature is not the only area of study in which experiences other than that of assimilation content, as such, play an important role. Most areas of study call for the exercise of thinking skills; and they may serve many different objectives, including that of assimilating the content. The historian may ask his students what the historical consequences might have been if a certain decision of the Supreme Court had been the opposite of what it actually was. Such a question and the thought it inspires on the part of the student may help him to assimilate the content under discussion and to develop skills in the utilization of the content. Indeed, the assimilation of content without the operation of such processes seems unlikely.

A final point to be made is that any work on the analysis of the content of a curriculum or a subject-matter field requires an understanding of the organization of the content as well as of the content itself. A precise definition of the content would require the listing of the propositions that represent the content, although this might require much more labor than is feasible. For most practical purposes, curriculum research must settle for something far short of such a complete list—but it does not have to settle for so little as the broad general descriptions typically used in the past.

Content Analysis in Communication Research

The history of content analysis, particularly in communications research, has been summarized by Bernard Berelson (1952). Some of the earliest studies pertained to the development of scholarship. Analysis of scientific writings produced at different times in the past has shown the changing interests of scholars in particular fields and the growth and decline of particular emphases. Other early studies in this field attempted to show the extent to which particular newspapers gave coverage of the news. This was accomplished by defining what was meant by "full coverage" on particular days by listing the events to be covered. The newspapers were then analyzed to determine what percentage of these topics were covered. Similar studies were also undertaken to compare the reporting of news in different countries, and the analysis of radio broadcasts became an area of military intelligence research. From this there developed a whole area of systematic intelligence research based on analyses of enemy publications, statements by prisoners, and the like.

While the trend in content analysis has been to develop quantitative methods, the possibility is still open that qualitative methods may have some merit. The clinical psychologist considers that a broad overview of the case he is working on may give him hunches which cannot be derived from the measures of personality he has at hand. The person making an analysis of intelligence data may believe that he can obtain hunches from looking at the data as a whole. The curriculum analyst may, for the same reason, hold the opinion that a broad overview of the content is important. These are matters which still have to be demonstrated—they are mentioned in order to indicate that although little attention can be given here to qualitative methods, they cannot be disregarded. Quantitative methods, on the other hand, are well developed and have had a long history of success. They have had a long history in the hands of scientists working in many different disciplines, including linguistics, sociology, and psychology.

A recent volume edited by Pool (1959) brings together much of the current knowledge concerning techniques in this area which have been evolved by workers in the several disciplines. He discusses the procedures under the paragraph titles which follow.

Intensity. Measures of intensity are attempts to indicate the emotional emphasis given a particular aspect of a communication. In the analysis of the content of a newspaper, emphasis may be measured in terms of the size of the headlines devoted to a particular topic, the number of words devoted to it, the number of pictures which accompany it, or the number of emotionally loaded words, and so forth. In the case of journalism such measures have often been used to reflect the bias in reporting. The emphasis given to one political party may be compared with the emphasis given to the other. Considerable skepticism has been expressed concerning the value of such measures despite their widespread use in studies of propaganda.

Frequency. The traditional method of undertaking content analysis is that of counting the number of times that particular ideas or words are presented; for example, one might attempt to determine the emphasis a textbook gives to the understanding of democracy by counting the number of times that the words *democracy* and *democratic* are used. Such a measure is not likely to fare very well. One can see this clearly when he realizes that such words might have a high frequency of occurrence in a speech by, say, Hitler, but with a derogatory connotation. The main fact which recommends frequency measures is that they are simple to obtain and comparisons of the frequencies derived from different sources may be compared. For these reasons frequency counts continue to be used.

Contingencies. This form of analysis hardly appeared before 1950, but since then it has come into considerable prominence. This approach can be illustrated by referring back to the example given of the occurrence of the word *democracy* and related words in printed materials. The frequency count could be made in the way described or it could be made by tabulating separately the cases in which it was coupled with the implication that democracy was being rejected. On this basis the counts would clearly differentiate between the usage in an American high school text and that in a speech by Hitler. Contingency analysis takes into account the *context* in which particular words or ideas are expressed. In this way the content analysis is more likely to represent the materials from which it is derived than is a simple frequency count.

Many aspects of content analysis have not yet been well standardized, and each research worker must to some extent establish his own. One problem, for example, is the size of the units to be used as the basis for the analysis. The morpheme is generally considered to be too small a unit for content analysis, although it is sometimes used. A "unit of meaning" is sometimes considered the most appropriate unit for analysis, but there is some difficulty in deciding what is meant by a "unit of meaning." Despite the fact that on the surface the selection of a unit of suitable size appears to be an important problem, there is some research to indicate that the unit may be varied within wide limits without making too much difference in the result.

The categories to be used in content analysis must be appropriate to the particular problem under consideration. In many areas, sets of categories have been prepared which can be used by subsequent workers. This proliferation of systems of categories is unfortunate for, as Pool (1959) points out, what is needed are standardized sets of categories which can be used for research in much the same way as standardized intelligence scales have been used in research on achievement. In certain areas, such as those involving the use of projective tests of personality, the value of standardized categories has been demonstrated.

Content Analysis in Educational and Psychological Research

In certain areas of educational and psychological research, the procedures of content analysis have had considerable impact. Some of the more important of these must now be given brief consideration.

A special case of content analysis which needs studying is that involved in the analysis of tests, particularly objective tests. The problem is a common one. Suppose a teacher or research worker wishes to use a published test for some specific purpose. He may be interested in making an analysis of the test to determine its relevance. In this connection, one group of educators (Bloom, 1956) has suggested that all test items of intellectual achievement be classified into a list of standard categories, which might then become generally used. Examples of the categories they employ are the following:

1.11 Knowledge of terminology
1.12 Knowledge of specific facts
1.21 Knowledge of conventions
1.22 Knowledge of trends and sequences
1.25 Knowledge of methodology
2.10 Translation from one level of abstraction to another
4.10 Analysis of elements
4.20 Analysis of relationships

This list gives just scattered examples from this attempt to categorize test items in terms of the achievement they are designed to measure. In the source from which these were abstracted, every effort has been made to define each category both in terms of general description and in terms of actual test items. However, despite the care with which this has been done, it is doubtful whether any two educators would show substantial agreement on the classification of items. The reliability of the process of classification needs to be determined experimentally.

This matter is closely tied up with the whole problem of determining the content validity of an achievement test. The term *content validity* is here borrowed from current usage. It is really inappropriate, since it refers, or should refer, to the objective properties of a test item. The so-called content validity problem is generally stated as that of determining the extent to which a group of test items can be considered to be a representative sample of a universe of items. This can be determined only if the dimensions of the universe are known. This problem of sampling is important in all fields of content analysis.

An aspect of content analysis that has had great significance for educational research is that related to the appraisal of the comprehension level of printed material. A whole series of readability formulas have been developed, but there is still much controversy concerning their appropriate uses and limitations. The earliest attempts to measure this characteristic of printed material used the simple expedient of determining the percentage of difficult or easy words in terms of a list giving the frequency with which words appear in certain types of published materials. Those who undertook these early measurements were aware that this simple procedure was inadequate for handling the complexities that even the most straightforward prose presents. It soon became evident that these simple methods had very little use, but not until the mid-1930's had sufficient research been undertaken to permit the construction of more useful methods. Gray and Leary (1935), who pioneered in this field, published a complex formula for measuring readability, based on five characteristics selected from a list of eighty-two assumed elements. Nearly a decade later, Lorge (1944) developed a similar formula based on only three characteristics— the number of "hard" words (as determined by a standard word list), the number of prepositional phrases, and sentence length. Other formulas appeared at about the same time as the Lorge formula; they included the Flesch formula (1951) and the Dale and Chall formula (1948).

There seems to be considerable agreement that the characteristics measured by these formulas are not entirely satisfactory and that the formulas cannot be applied to all kinds of materials. A formula that is quite satisfactory for measuring the readability of grade-school material may provide ridiculous results when it is used for assessing the readability of technical writing. A central difficulty is that the formulas do not take into account some of the more subtle aspects of style, which may have enormous influence on the difficulty level of reading material. An author may write in simple words, but his material may be difficult to read because he makes use of unusual analogy and innuendo in a way that conveys a richness of meaning through its overtones. No formula at present available takes into account this aspect of reading difficulty.

Reading difficulty is also a complex function of a person's previous experience. An elementary textbook in physics may be very difficult for a student before he has taken a course in physics, but easy once he has mastered the vocabulary and concepts of the field. Relatively slight differences in life histories may produce marked changes in readability of material. This fact illustrates the weakness of readability as a concept. When readability is being measured, the scientist is not actually measuring an objective property of certain stimulus material; rather, he is making a prediction of how individuals on the average will respond to this material. He is measuring, in effect, a response-inferred stimulus property, which is a rather weak variable to fit into a matrix of scientific ideas.

Measures of readability have many applications, both in school problems and in the broader field of public education. They provide an objective means of determining the suitability of materials for various age groups and for various levels of pupil ability within these groups. They provide a means of adjusting existing materials to a more suitable level of readability. Many works of classical literature that are quite inappropriate to the current reading level of pupils have been adapted to make them suitable through the medium of readability formulas. In addition, such formulas have been used to measure the readability of announcements and other materials designed for public education programs such as are sponsored by various health and safety organizations.

Content analysis of the type thus far considered presents special problems of sampling, because it is not usually feasible to make an analysis of all of the material available. In the preparation of word lists indicating the frequency with which various words appear, the problem is acute. The purpose of such counts is to measure the "difficulty" of words, but the term *difficulty* has meaning only when it refers to a particular individual or group. A word is "difficult" if it is difficult to understand or if its meaning is understood by only a fraction of the members of a group. Thus if the difficulty of words for a particular group is to be estimated from their frequency in reading material to which the group is exposed, it is necessary to know what this group reads and to sample it. It may happen that the members of the group differ greatly in what they read, in which case it is necessary to assume that at least some of these various materials are equivalent. Of course care will be taken to insure that all the materials on which word counts are made are not by the same author, because individual authors often have their own favorite vocabularies. The difficulty of words assessed from a representative sample of specified materials may not provide a useful estimate of difficulty of words for other groups that have different reading habits. The common practice in this area is to sample so-called popular reading materials, such as the *Saturday Evening Post,* in the hope that the results can be applied to a wide range of groups, but this method of identifying the sample to be analyzed has always been criticized.

Content analysis at more complex levels than that of word difficulty ceases to be an entirely objective matter. In the analysis of printed materials, the analyst is faced with a series of black marks which he must interpret. The interpretation process involves the same subjectivity as does the interpretation of pupil behavior in the classroom. There should be agreement among judges concerning the interpretation of materials before anything more than the simplest content analysis can be made. This is fairly easy when the analysis is at the level of counting words in different categories, since there is good agreement as to which words are to be classified as nouns, as adjectives, as verbs, and so on. Greater difficulty is experienced in separating fact from inference. Perhaps little reliability might be found if an attempt were made to single out from a total speech those remarks that reflected hostile gestures. We can think of a continuum that varies from one end of the scale, where there would be no agreement among analysts, to the other end of the scale, where there would be complete agreement. Under the latter conditions there is objectivity of measurement, a term meaning that there is social agreement. It is not unusual to find that those aspects of content analysis on which there is complete social agreement are the most trivial of those it is desired to measure. It is thus necessary to move further down the scale and to sacrifice some objectivity in favor of relevance.

As thus far considered, content analysis has not dealt with the classification of the *ideas* portrayed by written or printed materials. The latter type of content analysis has had a long history, but only recently does it seem to have taken a profitable turn. It finds its roots in some of the early free-association experiments, in which subjects responded to statements with the first word that came to mind. Attempts were made to classify and analyze the responses to obtain indications of interests, attitudes, the nature of repressed ideas, and a host of other conditions. These early attempts were not particularly successful, and indeed they were sufficiently negative to discourage a generation of psychologists from further pursuit of the method.

Reference is made here to the type of free-response test that has become known as a personality test, in which a stimulus is provided and the response is scored in some way that is believed to be relevant to the broad description of behavior. Such attempts to measure personality have a long history. Tests in which responses to ink blots are scored have a history that goes back before the time of Rorschach. The tendency in the early days was to score in terms of content categories, such as animals, plants, tools, structures, and buildings, and so on. The failure of these categories to produce useful results tended to discourage investigators from using this approach. Word association tests also produced disappointing results. In their pioneer attempt to score objectively free associations to words, Kent and Rosanoff produced a method of classifying single-word responses, but the instrument with its complicated scoring system failed to achieve the practical results expected of it.

The early period of discouragement with content analysis of the responses to personality tests was replaced by new hope through the work of Rorschach and his followers, who realized what others had not—namely, that the analysis of responses could be made along numerous dimensions. They saw that it was not necessary to stay with subject-matter categories, but that other aspects of the response could be scored. Interpretations of ink blots could be scored in terms of whether they referred to the blot as a whole, a major part of the blot, or a minor detail. They could be scored in terms of whether they were responses to shading, to color, or to the outline of the blot. They could be scored in terms of whether they referred to stationary objects or to moving objects. Rorschach himself seems not only to have had ingenuity in the setting up of such categories but also to have realized the importance of basing them on a rationale. Whatever success the Rorschach test may have had seems to have been largely a result of his talent in selecting scoring categories with a rational relationship to the categories of behavior they were designed to predict. The difficulty, of course, has always been in the establishment of the relationship between response category and the aspect of behavior that it is desired to predict. However, although the actual evidence available for such a relationship is slender, clinicians have felt that the Rorschach categories offer promise, and largely on the basis of their opinions, categories of this type have become widely accepted as perhaps the most promising method of content analysis yet devised.

The types of categories used in scoring the Rorschach became a prototype for scoring projective tests for a period of nearly twenty-five years. Recently, however, there has been a revival of interest in the scoring of responses in terms of categories of objects or events. This newer emphasis may be traced mainly to the developments made in the late 1930's by H.A. Murray of Harvard and his associates, which sparked a whole series of important developments that are now beginning to yield results of great importance. Murray postulated that human motivation could be measured in terms of a set of needs, such as need for achievement, need for sex, need for autonomy, and need for affiliation with a group. He also postulated an idea extended and developed at a later date by his followers; namely, that such needs could be measured through projective tests. The immediate outcome was a test known as the Thematic Apperception Test, which consisted of a series of pictures deliberately drawn so that the situations portrayed were somewhat ill defined and the human figures were vague and ephemeral creatures. The pictures were shown to subjects, who were asked to interpret them, and since they presented indefinite stimuli, the interpretation had to be a structure imposed on the picture by the individual describing it. The structure could be considered to some extent a product of the personality of the observer, reflecting his needs, motives, salient characteristics, and so forth. The Thematic Apperception Test, which became known as the T.A.T., never yielded a satisfactory system of classifying the responses in terms of their content and thus never yielded a satisfactory scoring system, at least not until parts of it were adapted by McClelland and his associates and a new notion of idea analysis was introduced.

The derivation of objective measures from instruments such as the Thematic Apperception Test presented problems that it has taken the best part of two decades to solve. The protocols derived from the test presented a range and richness of material that for a time seemed to defy objective categorization. Most of the early attempts to score such material resulted in elaborate systems that proved to be much too cumbersome to be of any real practical value, either in the development of research or in the assessment of personality in practical situations. The Tomkins (1947) method of scoring may be reviewed by the student as an illustration of one technique that is as ingenious as it is complicated.

The first major step in overcoming the difficulties involved in the scoring of such material seems to have come with the important observation by McClelland and Atkinson (1953) that subjects deprived of food for periods of one, four, and sixteen hours showed increasing numbers of references to food, food-getting, and hunger in the imaginative stories they were asked to produce. The observation is to some extent a repetition of that made nearly twenty-five hundred years earlier by Buddha, who observed that fasting failed to clear the mind of worldly things so that it could dwell on higher values. To the contrary, he found that the well-fed state is most conducive to the study of philosophical and ethical problems. The reader will note that this is the basis for presenting Buddha in statuary as a well-fed figure, if not as one who has eaten well beyond his physical needs.

The rediscovery that deprivation of whatever satisfies a need results in an increase in the amount of imagery related to that need opened a new era in projective measurement. McClelland also realized that it was desirable not to use just any picture in the arousing of imagery related to a need, but what was required was a stimulus object that would facilitate the arousing of such imagery. Thus the pictures used in the original Thematic Apperception Test did not appear to be particularly appropriate for measuring need for achievement, in which McClelland was interested, and he found it necessary to construct pictures more appropriate for this purpose. One of these shows a boy seated beside a table (or desk) on which there are a number of books. The boy is leaning his forehead on his hand and looking upward as if in reverie (the author hopes he is not projecting too much of himself into the interpretation).

The person who takes the McClelland test is asked to answer four questions about the picture:

1. What is happening? Who are the persons?
2. What had led up to this situation—that is, what has happened in the past?
3. What is being thought? What is wanted? By whom?
4. What will happen? What will be done?

The answers to these questions may vary from a few words to what amounts to a long essay. But it is not the volume of material produced that is of interest to the psychologist, and scoring systems should not be related to mere quantity.

The trend in the scoring of such material is to score each statement in terms of a number of categories. One category commonly used is the *desire for a goal*. If the subject writes, "The boy in the picture is determined to get a high grade," the achievement imagery represented by this response would be scored in this category. If the same subject were to have written, "The boy is thinking through his work carefully to get the highest grade he can," it would have been scored not only in the *desire for goal* category but also in the *goal-directed activity* category. Other categories that have been used are those referring to *expectation of success, expectation of failure, desire to avoid failure*, among others. A purpose of scoring each recorded item in several categories is to derive as much information as possible from the material provided, thereby to increase the reliability of particular scores.

The type of approach that McClelland has opened provided a means of scoring a great range of material. For measuring achievement and affiliation motivation, French (April 1956) developed an instrument that used a closely related scoring system but applied it to somewhat different material. Her test consisted of a series of brief descriptions of behavior, such as "Ray works much harder than most people," and "George will usually volunteer for a difficult task." The subject is asked to indicate why the person described behaves as he does, and the material is presented as a test of insight into the behavior of others. Since one cannot know the underlying cause of the behavior described in the test, the interpretation given must be largely a projection of the individual's own motives.

These scoring procedures have been successful in producing variables of consequence; that is to say, the variables lead to the making of some predictions and produce at least low-level laws that are consistent with other knowledge and with expectation. They represent definite advances over earlier procedures. The scoring of the Thematic Apperception Test type of instrument has taken nearly twenty years to evolve—a slow process, but scientific advances typically are slow. Perhaps the moral to be drawn is that the essential element for the development of any sound measuring instrument is a sound theory concerning how and why a particular procedure will evolve a useful device. If the theory is sound, it is probable that a useful measuring instrument will result.

The chief disadvantage of this type of measuring instrument is that the scoring procedures are extremely laborious. For this reason, the procedures must be considered as tentative, and they will probably be replaced ultimately by a measuring procedure much less laborious. This usually involves the substitution of checking procedures for free-response procedures. So far, no successful substitution of this kind has been made in the case of projective techniques.

While the projective devices just considered have been and continue to be the basis for a large volume of research, there are disconcerting inconsistencies in the data that have emerged. In addition, many attempts to reproduce some of the more striking studies have not been successful. There are even instances in which two carefully developed sets of instruments, both designed to measure the same needs, have been administered to the same group of subjects and no correspondence has been found between the two sets of scores. Travers *et al.* (1961) attempted to relate the needs of teachers measured by such a device to their performance in the classroom and could find no significant relationships, but the device they used yielded scores which were almost unrelated to scores derived from a picture interpretation test which purported to measure the same teacher needs.

Projective techniques and the content analysis needed to derive scores from the material may be specially adapted to the study of educational problems. For example, Figure VI represents an interesting approach to the study of teachers' concepts of their role in a classroom. Teachers were asked to draw a picture of a teacher with a class. It is believed that the products indicate the teacher's own concept of how he should behave in a classroom, and there is some evidence to substantiate this point of view.

SCHOOL SURVEYS

The development of methods for undertaking surveys has been intimately related to the development of accreditation procedures. This is hardly surprising, since the accrediting associations represent the major enterprises that engage in school survey work, although professors of education, educational consultants, state and local superintendents, and others also engage in surveys of schools to varying degrees. Accrediting associations, however, have had to enter into the business of conducting school surveys with a certain amount of system to their methods since they are open to public criticism.

Procedures for the evaluation and accreditation of schools and their programs should not be confused with educational research. They are procedures for setting standards and for helping schools improve their programs. However, programs for the accreditation of schools have had an intimate relationship to research in that many of the procedures involved have been the products of major research programs. In addition, accreditation procedures provide data collection facilities which have been used in the past by research workers and may be used more extensively in the future. This section is designed to give the reader some un-

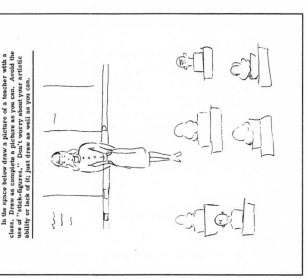

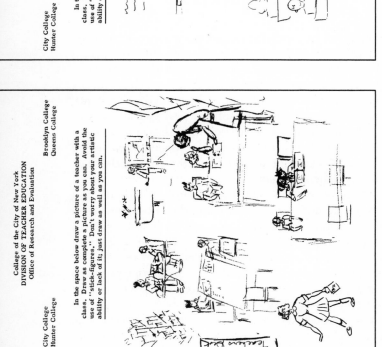

FIGURE VI. *A projective technique for studying concepts of teaching. Students of education and teachers were asked to draw a picture of a teacher with a class. This illustration presents two strikingly different concepts of how a teacher should behave in a classroom, and also how a classroom should be organized.* (Illustration by courtesy of Dr. William Rabinowitz, and collected as part of a research study at the Office of Research and Evaluation of the Division of Teacher Education, Municipal Colleges of New York City.)

derstanding of the data available in this connection and the instruments which have been and are being used for their collection.

The development of methods for evaluating schools by inspection has been closely linked with school and college relationships. In this process, the early stage was marked by the admission of students to college by examination, a procedure that is notorious for its tendency to standardize the high school curriculum in terms of college admission requirements. The recognition of the fact that cooperation between secondary schools and colleges was a necessary prerequisite to the development of secondary and higher education led to the founding of the New England Association of Colleges and Secondary Schools in 1884, the Association of Colleges and Secondary Schools of the Middle States and Maryland in 1887, and the North Central Association of Schools and Colleges in 1895. The latter grew out of the Michigan School Master's Club, which held an annual meeting at which secondary school and college teachers discussed problems of mutual interest. The members of this organization believed that it might be profitable to bring together teachers from a wider area, and thus the North Central Association of Schools and Colleges was formed. However, the early college and school associations were primarily devices for bringing together individuals to discuss and solve common educational problems, and it was not until 1901 that any activities were undertaken to develop a system of accreditation. In the latter year the Commission on Accredited Schools was established to investigate this matter. The Commission was given broad authority to set up standards for high school courses that would be accepted for credit by colleges, and to set up standards for accreditation in general.

Parallel with the work of the North Central Association was that of various state departments of education, which were concerned with the problem of accreditation from the standpoint of setting up minimum standards at which all schools should aim. Since that time, the function of accrediting secondary schools has been shared by state universities and state departments of education, which in many states have performed this function co-operatively and at times interchangeably.

While the initial interest in this area was in the accreditation of specific courses, the procedure soon broadened out to include a multitude of matters, such as the length of the school year, the number and length of the periods given each week in each subject, the training and experience of the faculty, the size and scope of the library and other physical facilities, and other matters too numerous to list here.

A study by McVey (1942) pointed out that the North Central Association of Schools and Colleges has been a powerful influence in the establishment of standards for secondary schools by the various states. He goes on to point out that this is partly a result of the fact that influential members of state departments of education have often been members of this association and have attended meetings where standards have been established.

The basic problem in the development of procedures for accrediting schools is to establish a basis on which schools are to be judged. Clearly it is insufficient to turn loose an observer in a school. Observation must be restricted to certain aspects of the school and its program that are considered of central importance to the effectiveness of the program. The essential characteristics observed during the accreditation procedure are referred to as *evaluative criteria*. The remainder of this section attempts to describe the general nature of the evaluative criteria that have been used in the accreditation of schools and colleges; that is to say, it describes the types of schedules that have been developed for guiding observers who are sent out to obtain information about schools by inspectional procedures.

The Accreditation of Secondary Schools

The most comprehensive attempt to draw up a guide for the evaluation of schools was an outcome of the Cooperative Study of Secondary Schools Standards, first organized in 1933 by the representatives of six major regional accrediting associations. The results of this study appear in numerous scattered publications. The purposes were the following:

1. To determine the characteristics of a good secondary school.
2. To find practical means and methods to evaluate the effectiveness of a school in terms of its objectives.
3. To determine the means and processes by which a good school develops into a better one.
4. To derive ways by which regional associations could stimulate and assist secondary schools to continue growth.

The same study also provided a series of schedules for evaluating secondary schools in the following areas:

Agriculture	Physical Education for Boys
Art	Physical Education for Girls
Business Education	Science
English	Social Studies
Foreign Languages	Progress of Studies
Health and Safety	Pupil Activity Projects
Home Economics	Library Service
Industrial Arts	Guidance Services
Industrial Vocational Educational Core Program	School Plant
Mathematics	School Staff and Administration
Music	

Furthermore, the volume on evaluative criteria (1950) derived from the study includes a schedule for evaluating individual members of the faculty. Various statistical and graphical devices for summarizing the data thus collected are also included. In addition, schedules are provided for determining the extent to which the school is meeting the educational needs of youth and for determining the nature of the child population served by the school.

Each one of the schedules for the evaluation of work in specific subject-matter fields organizes the evaluation into the following areas:

1. Organization. This covers such matters as how the curriculum is developed, whether there is continuity in the organization of studies in the area, and the like.
2. Nature of offerings. This category explains itself fairly adequately, but it does include such matters as whether the courses provide opportunity for student responsibility and leadership.
3. Physical facilities. This covers such matters as furniture, visual aids, and general classroom conditions.
4. Direction of learning, divided into the four areas given below:
   a. Instructional staff. This covers preparation, background, organization, and the like.
   b. Instructional activities.
   c. Instructional materials.
   d. Methods of evaluation.
5. Outcomes. This covers assessments of what students have learned in the program, though few hints are offered as to how the assessments are to be made.
6. Special characteristics of the program in the area.

Under each one of these areas a checklist is provided against which a mark or other symbol is entered according to the following system:

++ Provision of the condition is made exclusively.
+ Provision of the condition is made to some extent.
X Provision of the condition is very limited.
M Provision of the condition is missing but needed.
N Provision of the condition is not desirable or does not apply.

On the basis of all the evidence in any one area studied, an over-all evaluation is made of the effectiveness or worthwhileness of that aspect of the operation. These evaluations are summarized on a five-point scale, on which the points are as follows:

Scale Value	Interpretation
5	Excellent: the provisions or conditions are extensive and are functioning excellently.
4	Very good: (a) the provisions or conditions are extensive and are functioning well; or (b) the provisions or conditions are moderately extensive but are functioning excellently.
3	Good: the conditions or provisions are moderately extensive but are functioning well.
2	Fair: (a) the provisions or conditions are moderately extensive but are functioning poorly; or (b) the provisions or conditions are limited in extent but are functioning well.
1	Poor: the provisions or conditions are limited in extent and are functioning poorly.
M	Missing: the provisions or conditions are missing and needed; if present they would make a contribution to the educational needs of the youth in this community.
N	Does not apply: the provisions or conditions are missing but do not apply or are not desirable for the youth of this school or this community.

The items listed under each heading of each evaluation sheet vary in specificity. Some are highly specific, and many ask whether staff members have had specific types of experience— one item, for example, asks whether home economics teachers have had actual work experience in this field. Others are so general that it seems almost impossible to determine whether or not the condition exists. For example, it may be almost impossible to answer, in terms of the categories provided, whether the program of a school "is based upon an analysis of the educational needs of youth," for it is not clear whether the answer is to be based on systematic investigation. Also, it is not clear what is meant by "the educational needs of youth"—are these to be needs they have already experienced, or needs in terms of the problems they will face later in life? The term *need* is one with a multitude of meanings. As another illustration of the same difficulty, one may wonder how it is possible to determine whether a program "encourages enlargement and enrichment of the pupil's scope of interests."

The lists of evaluative criteria display no pretensions of being comprehensive, and indeed spaces are provided on the schedule for the addition of items that are relevant to the specific situation in which the evaluations are made but may not apply outside of those situations.

Any criticism of the schedules prepared in the cooperative study of school standards must take into account the purposes for which they were prepared and the background of thinking on which they were based. A superficial examination of the schedules reveals that while they bear some resemblance to orthodox psychological and educational measuring instruments they do not meet customary standards of acceptability. This criticism is not entirely fair, even though it may be pointed out that the end result of the use of the schedules is a single numerical rating based on a series of evaluations of a number of important elements in the situation. In addition, it may be pointed out that the ratings thus arrived at are produced by a highly subjective process and cannot be appraised in terms of norms because no norms are available. Finally, the measurement expert might point out that no evidence is given concerning the reliability of the assessments provided by the schedules, nor is there any evidence concerning the validity of these assessments. These criticisms are not entirely logical, for the following reasons:

First, the history of school inspection and accreditation during the last fifty years has illustrated a trend away from the use of quantitative data and a return to qualitative standards. Therefore the schedules that represent a recent stage of thinking in this area do not represent a series of measuring devices to be used in a standard way; rather are they guides to the thinking of the person who is undertaking the evaluation. They present a series of topics that *may* be given consideration in the total assessment procedure, and it is recognized that some topics may be irrelevant in some situations and that some relevant ones may have been omitted from the list. Some guide to thought is better than none.

Second, numerical norms of the type provided by most publishers of achievement tests would be largely meaningless in the assessment of secondary schools, since different schools must be assessed by different standards. The curriculum provided by a large secondary school serving an industrial population must differ in some ways from that of a small school serving an agricultural community. The failure of schools of the latter type to meet the needs of an agricultural population is the most common criticism professional visitors level at them, an entirely different criticism from that directed against schools in industrial communities.

On the other hand, the criticism concerning the lack of evidence of the reliability or validity of the recorded assessments cannot be passed off lightly. If individuals cannot show substantial agreement with themselves or with others in the entries made on the schedule with respect to a specific school, then the schedules and the records made on them have no value. Evidence of reliability would be fairly easy to obtain, and the only real excuse for its lack is the large amount of money that such an undertaking would probably involve. Evidence of the validity of the end products of the schedules must also be produced. No escape from this problem can be offered by any argument that the schedules are valid by definition, for the condition of validity by definition does not exist.

The *1950 Evaluative Criteria* represented an important step forward in the preparation of schedules for the study and appraisal of secondary schools; but schedules, like tests, require empirical tryouts and revision on the basis of the information thus collected. During the decade that followed the introduction of the standards, data were collected from visiting accreditation committees and from school faculty and administrators on the problems that had arisen in the application of the schedules. The resulting revision of the standards, incorporating the following among other important changes, appeared in 1960.

1. The schedule used in the statement of the philosophy and objectives was considerably modified since the original schedule appeared to determine the entries made by the school. It is, of course, difficult to remain relatively nondirective in such a schedule while trying at the same time to elicit the desired responses.

2. Some items were found to penalize a school which was justifiably different. Thus the schedule should not be such that it penalizes a school for being unusually progressive or conservative in its approach to education. Some items were eliminated because they did not differentiate among schools or because they dealt with peripheral, rather than central, educational problems.

3. A number of new schedules were added to cover such areas as health services, distributive education (i.e., marketing and merchandising), driver education, and religion. The criteria emphasize that the inclusion of these schedules should not be interpreted as placing pressure on any school to provide for these areas in their programs.

4. Considerable changes were made in the procedures involved in the evaluation of teachers. In the 1950 edition of the *Criteria*, teachers were asked to rate themselves and these ratings were reviewed by visiting committees. This procedure was abandoned. In addition, the evaluation of teachers which had to be made after a relatively brief period of observation was eliminated.

5. Considerable expansion of some of the explanations given in the manual was undertaken in order to clear up ambiguities. The manual also urges local accrediting organizations to develop additional procedures and to try out new ideas. Most of the changes and additions seem to be in the right direction, but a solid basis of research on which to base revisions of the standards is lacking. Complaints and criticisms may result in some improvement, but radical departures must be based on a sounder foundation.

Accreditation of Colleges

The need for developing a system for accrediting colleges arose from a different source than that which stimulated the development of machinery for accrediting secondary schools. Zook and Haggerty (1935, 1936) reviewed this matter and concluded that the movement for the establishment of standards for the accrediting of colleges arose from a need for exercising some social control over higher education, which expanded so vastly during the first half of the present century. These authorities point out that although there are many ways in which public control may be exercised over higher education, control by accrediting associations offers the advantage of freedom from political pressure and controversy. Accrediting associations may honestly raise standards of education without political intrigue or influence.

The problems of establishing criteria and of establishing standards are quite distinct. Two different accrediting agencies may use similar criteria, and yet, because their standards differ, they may vary in the percentage of institutions inspected that they accredit. Strictly speaking, the establishment of criteria should precede the establishment of standards.

The development of procedures for accrediting institutions of higher education has had a history covering over fifty years, and contributions to these procedures have been made by numerous individuals, many accrediting associations, divisions of the federal government, state departments of education, the American Council on Education, and other organizations and individuals. However, an overview of the situation would indicate that many of the major developments in the procedures have come from the North Central Association of Schools and Colleges, which has sponsored some of the few systematic studies in this general area.

In 1934, after many years of deliberation, the Association published a manual to be used in the accreditation of colleges and a series of schedules on which the data relevant to the accrediting procedure were to be recorded. In addition, a series of monographs published in 1935–36 provided extensive data on the use of the criteria described in the manual, and even went so far as to provide some normative data for some of the measures used in the accrediting procedure.

The manual provides criteria for evaluating each one of the following aspects of a college:

Faculty	Student personnel services
Curriculum	Administration
Instruction	Finance
Library	Plant
Induction of students	Institution's study of its problems
Intercollegiate athletics	

Each one of the areas to be evaluated is broken down into elements. Consider the matter of evaluating the faculty. This is first broken down into the areas of (1) faculty competence, (2) faculty organization, and (3) conditions of faculty service. For the first of these three, criteria for determining the degree of competence are listed. Some of these criteria are:

Percentage of total staff holding an earned doctor's degree.
Average number of years of graduate study of the staff.
Average number of years of experience in teaching and administration in institutions of higher education.
Number of scholarly books and monographs produced per staff member.
Number of memberships in national learned societies per staff member.
Number of places on national programs per staff member.

The criteria listed in the 1934 edition of the manual were tried out over a period of several years, and in 1941 a revision of the criteria was published. In the revised manual a substantial amount of normative data is provided to assist in the interpretation of data collected during the accreditation process. The normative data are based on the institutions of higher learning accredited by the Association. As an illustration of these data, with reference to the percentage of the staff holding an earned doctoral degree, average values are given respectively for junior colleges, teachers' colleges, liberal arts colleges, and universities, and in each case separate data are given for publicly and privately controlled institutions. In another table, data are presented showing the average number of books, monographs, and articles published per faculty member in each of these types of institutions.

The inadequacy of the evaluative criteria both at the secondary school and at the college level is well recognized by the Association in its reports, which frequently emphasize the fact that the program of a school must be evaluated as a whole. It is also recognized that there seems little possibility at the present time that qualitative criteria can be replaced by quantitative criteria, and that fundamentally the process of accreditation must depend on subjective judgments. Frequent cautions are given that the criteria outlined should be considered more as a guide to thinking than as a series of basic dimensions along which assessment must be made. The emphasis on caution gives recognition to the fact that the process of assessment in this area is still in the earliest stages of development.

Criticisms of Evaluative Criteria
Used in Accreditation

A number of important criticisms of the evaluative criteria discussed in this chapter must be considered, but these criticisms must be reviewed in the light of the fact that this type of measurement is relatively new, about as recent as the development of tests of intelligence. Nevertheless, these forms of measurements have not had as much concentrated thought bestowed on them by so many people as have intelligence tests. Work on accreditation procedures has been largely the spare-time activity of relatively few individuals.

First, it may be noted that there is no experimental basis for the evaluative criteria commonly used in the inspection of schools and colleges. There is general agreement that the main ultimate criterion of the effectiveness of an educational program is the extent to which it produces desirable changes in the pupils. Evaluative criteria for use in accreditation are based on the judgments of educators that certain characteristics of a school do have an effect on the extent to which the objectives of learning are achieved. It is assumed, for example, that it makes a difference in the amount of learning accomplished whether a faculty of a secondary school does or does not have professional education training in the courses provided by departments in education. As far as the author knows, there is no evidence that teachers with professional training of this type are more effective than those who do not. One would assume that it would make a difference (all teacher training is based on this assumption), but many assumptions made by educators in the past have been shown to be unjustifiable on the basis of scientific experimentation.

Second, the attempt to achieve rigorous standards of measurement may prevent the assessment of the outstanding characteristics of an institution. This is a problem well recognized even by those who have developed the evaluative criteria for the North Central Association. A secondary school may be performing a first-rate job even though its faculty has had limited training and the plant is poor. Desire to do a professional job may overcome deficiencies of formal training, and ingenuity may make up for deficiencies in the plant.

Third, normative data may have relatively little value since they do not set minimum standards but only show how one institution compares with others. On the norms provided, one institution appears to be low and apparently inadequate because others are higher on the scale, although the fact may be that all the institutions are inadequate.

Fourth, the normative material provided was developed during a period of great educational change, which included times of oversupply and undersupply of teachers. These changes would make it difficult if not impossible to use norms of the types provided, because by the standards provided, institutions would show great changes even from year to year.

Fifth, the system of evaluative criteria does not take into account the fact that single items may be crucial. A school that has a program quite unrelated to the needs of its students should not be accredited even if it is adequate on all of the other dimensions listed. A rural school that fails to take into account the fact that most of the pupils will eventually enter agricultural pursuits is inadequate, even if it achieves high scores on other variables.

One may assume that eventually all of these criticisms will be met after careful studies have been made of the extent to which the various factors are related to the degree to which the objectives of learning are achieved. Before this can be done, it will be necessary to develop valid measures of a great number of outcomes and to measure the outcomes of teaching under a variety of conditions. The problem is complicated by the fact that, different institutions have different objectives, and consequently the achievements of the pupils in one place may not be comparable with those in another.

An Overview of Accreditation Procedures

Survey procedures for assessing the effectiveness of schools and colleges in achieving particular objectives must be considered relatively crude methods of appraisal. They are all based on numerous assumptions, some of which are open to question. Although the validity of these procedures may be questioned, the process of inspection has certain intrinsic values that may justify it regardless of validity. First, accreditation and inspection procedures are becoming more and more a service; that is to say, they are designed to help schools and colleges improve themselves rather than to act as a threat. Accrediting agencies now often make available the services of special consultants to help schools with special problems. For example, the University of Michigan functions as the accrediting agency for the secondary schools of Michigan, and as a part of its function it provides consultants in a great many different areas.

Second, accreditation procedures encourage schools to examine themselves. This is always a healthy process, and a well organized accreditation agency can perform a valuable function by encouraging schools to do this.

Although accrediting agencies may use the most primitive methods of assessment and measurement, that they are useful when their power is exercised with wisdom cannot be questioned.

Summary

1. Survey research methods as they are currently employed by educational organization represent research on educational problems at a rather simple level, undertaken mainly to solve problems of local significance only.

2. Surveys conducted in educational research are commonly undertaken as efforts to determine the nature of the physical conditions related to education. Sometimes surveys are made of the behavior of teachers or pupils. A further type of survey attempts to establish the achievements of pupils.

3. Surveys may merely enumerate the frequency of occurrence of some type of event, or they may study the interrelationship among events.

4. Surveys may attempt to undertake studies that could be undertaken by experimental methods, but they do not provide the same certainty of knowledge that experimental procedures might provide.

5. Surveys of behavioral phenomena should not represent a mere effort to collect a set of unrelated facts. The information gathered should be interrelated within a plan or framework.

6. Surveys should avoid obtaining information about transitory behavioral phenomena. They should also avoid questions likely to produce a mere stereotyped response that the respondent feels to be appropriate for the occasion.

7. A survey should be based on a theory of the nature of the phenomena that are to be surveyed. Since surveys are often conducted in areas where relatively little is known, it is often difficult to develop an adequate theoretical basis. All surveys that involve a question-and-answer approach should be considered as studies involving a complex social interaction between a questioner and a respondent. The theory should specify the general nature of the phenomena to be investigated, the methods through which aspects of them can be measured, the conditions that produce them, and the population in whom the phenomena are to be found.

8. The direct observation of behavior in naturally occurring situations has limitations as a survey technique. It usually represents a highly selected sample of the total daily behavior of the individual. Surveys conducted through the administration of tests or through an examination of pupil products have had a long history of utility.

9. Problems and difficulties involved in the design of questions for surveys have been extensively explored by research workers, and the person who undertakes a survey involving the asking of questions should be familiar with what is known about the preparation of such materials.

10. Direct-mail questionnaires should be avoided unless no other method is available for obtaining the desired information. Those who return questionnaires delivered through the mail tend to be a more educated group than those who do not.

11. Surveys of behavior are sometimes conducted in artificial situations which simulate a realistic set of conditions.

12. In any survey, checks should be built into the data-collection process itself. The main type of check used is an examination of the data for internal consistency.

13. Since sample surveys are designed to obtain information from a sample that can be applied to a universe, it is most important that the universe to which the results are to apply should be specified and that the method of obtaining the sample should be an appropriate one.

14. The research worker who conducts a survey should be sure that the resulting data will be meaningful. Too often the results of surveys provide biased information to support some person's prejudices.

15. The analysis of verbal communications is known as content analysis. Curriculum analysis is a special application of content analysis. The content of the curriculum is that aspect which can be reduced to a set of interrelated propositions. The content of the curriculum, as thus defined, does not include all aspects of the curriculum. The content of the curriculum can be analyzed by the same procedures as are used for the analysis of other materials.

16. Two main approaches to content analysis are found. These involve the counting of frequencies and the counting of contingencies. The analysis by means of contingencies is generally considered to be a more advanced technique than the analysis of frequencies. The procedures which these techniques involve have not yet been fully standardized so the research worker must use his own judgment in the analysis of material.

17. Content analysis procedures have been widely used in educational and psychological research. One of the most notable of these is the attempt by Bloom and his associates to provide a basis for the analysis of objective examinations involving a set of standard categories. The difficulty level of reading material also involves the use of specially developed techniques of content analysis. A particular interest at the present time is the application of techniques of content analysis to the responses made to projective tests. While these techniques represent important technical advances there are many problems connected with their use which have not yet been solved.

18. The development of school survey techniques has been intimately connected with the development of accreditation procedures. In this connection, the North Central Association of Schools and Colleges has played a leading role.

19. The characteristics of a school that are observed during the accreditation procedure are referred to as evaluative criteria.

20. The Cooperative Study of Secondary School Standards was a comprehensive attempt to provide a guide for the evaluation of schools. This guide provided a system of rating scales through which the observations made concerning a school could be quantified.

21. The trend over the last half-century has been away from the use of quantitative standards, which have come in for serious criticism. The main difficulty in using such standards is that different schools have to be assessed along different dimensions.

22. Similar attempts have been made to provide quantitative criteria for the evaluation of colleges.

23. The numerous criticisms that have been leveled against present systems of evaluative criteria indicate that there exists here a fruitful field for research. There is a real social need for a continuing program of research in the area. The assumptions underlying the use of current accreditation procedures need to be investigated.

Some Problems for the Student

1. As a result of a school survey, an attempt was made to obtain a score indicating the qualifications of each teacher. This score was derived by adding together the number of years of teaching experience, the number of semester hours of professional training beyond the bachelor's degree, and a rating of "teacher effectiveness" provided by the principal. What assumptions are made in adopting this procedure?

2. It has been planned to determine by means of survey methods the number of those trained for teaching who remain in the profession after five and after ten years, and the reasons for attrition. Develop a theory that accounts for losses to the profession over the ten-year period. Suggest procedures that might be used for determining the rate of loss, and identify the assumptions on which the procedures are based.

3. A superintendent of a large city school system is aware of the existence of extremely low morale among the teachers. He

realizes that there is widespread mistrust of the administration of the school system, but he wants to obtain information that will provide him with a basis for making decisions that will right the situation. He can obtain a substantial sum of money to conduct a survey but is afraid to proceed lest his intentions be mistaken. What approaches might be adopted in conducting a survey so that the full cooperation of the teachers would probably be maintained?

4. Outline a procedure for conducting a survey of the arithmetic skills of the fifth grade children in a large city school system serving a community having a population of half a million. Assume that only 25 per cent of the pupils are to be sampled. What meaningful norms or standards could be used in the interpretation of the data, which are to be used for public relations as well as normative purposes?

5. A superintendent has requested his research department to interview all teachers leaving the system in order to obtain information that might help in retaining a greater number in the future. The request is specifically for an interview, and a questionnaire cannot be used. Plan a structured interview to collect information about this problem, basing it on a theory concerning the reasons why teachers leave. Suggest internal checks that might be introduced in order to estimate the validity of the data obtained. Suggest other sources of data that might be used to check those obtained in the interview.

CHAPTER 11

PREDICTION STUDIES

Research on Problems of Prediction

SURVEY research at its simplest level attempts to determine the nature of a particular universe of events. "What is the state of affairs that exists?" is the type of question that surveys most commonly attempt to answer. Inferences are sometimes made from the sample that is examined to the universe that is sampled, and occasionally predictions are made of future events, such as election results. The major purpose of surveys as they are conducted in educational research is not the prediction of events in the future. However, a great many educational research studies are carried out with the primary object of developing methods of making predictions. This type of study and problems attending its execution are considered in this chapter.

Prediction studies within the domain of educational research may be sociological, economic, or psychological. Attempts may be made to predict enrollments at some future date. Predictions may also be made of the future teacher supply and demand, and of funds to be available for teachers' salaries from direct taxation.

Other methods may be developed for forecasting the success or failure of pupils in different curricula. Sometimes attempts are made to provide predictions over a relatively long period of time —for example, studies that attempt to develop methods of predicting college success from tests given in junior high school. These studies are concerned with problems of the greatest importance, for the assignment of pupils to a proper curriculum in high school must depend on the ability of school personnel to predict how the pupil's talents can best be used at a later time in his career.

The Pseudo Science of Predicting Something from Anything

A word must be said about the type of educational study that involves predicting *something* from *anything*. Usually both the *something* and the *anything* are rather vague. Many such studies begin with the graduate student's dissatisfaction with current procedures for predicting scholastic success in some field of study in which he is interested. Such a student may have been a high school teacher of accounting. Greatly concerned with the fact that a rather large fraction of students who enter accounting courses fail to achieve satisfactory grades, he may feel there is a need for building a test that will eliminate those applicants who are almost certain to fail. Various tests have been tried out, but none has proved to be particularly useful. He decides to collect a number of new tests and administer them to students of accounting in the hope that one will turn out to be a good predictor of grades. This might be called a shotgun approach, and it has disadvantages with which the graduate student should be familiar.

First, it is a departure from the type of scientific methodology that has yielded so much in the past and represents a return to a much more primitive method of achieving knowledge. It is a return to the kind of prescientific technique practiced by the medieval physician, who tried whatever herbs and techniques he had at his disposal in the hope that something would be found to help the patient. Occasionally this approach worked and the patient was cured, and in this way there accumulated a considerable amount of unconnected items of information that had their uses in the primitive practice of medicine. Such scraps of lore did not make medicine a science. Neither will large numbers of correlations between test scores and measures of performance in handling life's daily problems of work and play constitute a science of behavior. Only when these apparently disconnected facts are integrated into a system is there any hope that they may form the rudiments of a science.

Second, even if a correlation exists between a test and the *something* it is desired to predict, there is always a real possibility that the correlation may be due to some irrelevant aspect of the *something*. For example, one might find that ratings of personal attractiveness of female college students correlated with grades in college. He might certainly suspect that this correlation was generated by the fact that male college professors might have a tendency to overestimate the academic achievement of outstandingly attractive college women. Such a hypothesis would be much more reasonable than to suppose that personal attractiveness has a genuine relationship to academic achievement.

Third, since it is a hit-or-miss procedure, it is necessary to include a great many potential predictors—unless, of course, a theory is available that permits the more accurate predictors to be selected in advance. Many studies of the predictive value of brief biographical items of information have been carried out by administering several hundred such items to groups whose behavior it was desired to predict, then selecting the items that had the greatest predictive value. Such procedures are laborious, require extensive statistical treatment of the data, and are costly. They are most appropriate where useful results must be achieved rapidly regardless of cost.

John Dewey (1910) elegantly compared the relative merits of the empirical and the scientific methods of prediction in the following statement:

While many empirical conclusions are, roughly speaking, correct; while they are exact enough to be of great help in practical life; while the presages of a weather-wise sailor or hunter may be more accurate, within a restricted range, than those of the scientist who relies solely on scientific observations; while, indeed, empirical observations and records furnish the raw or crude material of scientific knowledge, yet the empirical method affords no way of discriminating between right and wrong conclusions.[1]

Statistical Empiricism

A few would raise their voices to defend the viewpoint that, since the laws of behavior are statistical laws, statistical methods should be the primary basis for discovering such laws. This statement means that the ultimate purpose of educational research is to derive a set of statistical relationships between conditions and the consequent behavior of the individual. The end product of the behavioral sciences, then, could be represented by something like a dictionary listing sets of conditions (both internal and external) and the probability of occurrence of each of various consequent behaviors. Perhaps the end product of the behavioral sciences may be such a handbook, but this product would be quite unsatisfactory to most with a scientific turn of mind. Perhaps the advanced stage of knowledge reflected by such a handbook may have appeal in contrast to our present ignorance, but it is easier to see it in its true light if we consider the possibility of developing a similar product in other fields where it is not so difficult to be objective. Consider, for example, the problem of weather forecasting. At one time, weather forecasts for a particular locality were made by keeping records of *what followed what* in the sequence of weather conditions. Thus a high southeast wind in a particular locality might be taken to indicate rain, since rain followed more frequently than anything else on the tail of such a wind. Nobody

[1] From *How We Think*, by John Dewey, copyright © 1910 D.C. Heath and Company. Reprinted by permission.

knew why this was so. The probability of the occurrence was well established, but so long as nobody knew, there was no way of improving the accuracy of predictions. However, such a system of forecasting has been abandoned, because its accuracy could never be improved beyond that permitted by the data previously collected. The present system, which has replaced the old statistical system, is based on a knowledge of how weather conditions are produced. It is based largely on air-mass analysis and thermodynamics, and permits much more accurate predictions than the older statistical method. This does not mean, of course, that mathematical methods are not used for making predictions today, for they are. However, their function is to use data in accordance with some complex theory of weather prediction. Modern weather forecasting has in fact become highly mathematical, and introduces the help of electronic computers in order that complex mathematical functions may be computed at a relatively rapid speed.

There are two ways in which one may properly speak of statistical laws. First of all, the laws of physics are, in a sense, statistical laws. The statement that the pressure exerted by a gas on the walls of the vessel in which it is contained is uniform at all points, assumes that atoms of the gas moving at different velocities are moving in all directions in roughly equal numbers, so that the force exerted by these atoms of the container is uniformly distributed over the wall. If this were not so, the pressure on one part of the wall would be greater than on another part of the wall. Since there are large numbers of atoms or molecules of the gas involved, the probability is extremely small that all or most of them will happen to bounce off one small area of the vessel wall at one time and thus raise the pressure at that point and lower it at other points. In fact, this probability is so small that it is disregarded in the formulation of the law. This is one meaning of the term *statistical law;* but when it is said in educational research, that all laws of behavior are statistical, a somewhat different concept is usually involved.

When reference is made to *statistical laws* in educational research or in other research in the behavioral sciences, an entirely different concept is usually being considered. It is the author's impression that this concept signifies a tendency toward regularity in the sequence of events. Such tendencies may vary from complete regularity to regularities just above what one would expect on the basis of chance. If these so-called statistical laws were referred to as tendencies toward regularity in events, any respectability that is derived from the use of the word *statistical* would be eliminated.

Tendencies toward regularity may vary from those in which there is no knowledge concerning the laws of the observed tendency to those in which there is fairly complete knowledge. Mere tendency to regularity, or what appears on superficial examination to be a tendency to regularity, is often the point at which the scientist starts his work, and at this starting point one cannot say that there is anything that at all resembles a scientific law. Once the scientist has established the variables functionally related to the tendency to regularity, he has acquired useful knowledge that goes beyond that provided by a mere statistical relationship.

Empiricism and Research on Problems of Educational Prediction

Research on problems of predicting educational achievement has not usually been scientific in the sense in which the term has been used in this volume. Inevitably this has been so, for the urgent need for making accurate educational predictions has prompted those concerned with the problem to grasp whatever facts were available. In addition, in the partial solution of urgent problems that are complex in character, it is often much more feasible to try out a large number of possible solutions and see which will work rather than to develop a program of research along systematic and scientific lines. At least three types of empirical procedures have been adopted in this setting, and the merits of each need to be considered.

Method I. The miniature-situation approach. This is a procedure for developing methods of scientific prediction that really involves no research at all, but simply requires the educator to reproduce a miniature and abbreviated situation in which a subject can be given, so to speak, a trial run. The experimenter hypothesizes that performance in the miniature situation will reflect quality of performance in the larger situation in which it is desired to predict behavior. Thus, in the development of algebra prognosis tests, an attempt has been made to introduce into the test situation some of the learning activities that the pupil will have to face in his first course in algebra. Language prognosis tests use a similar technique. One such test measures the ability of the student to learn a small amount of Esperanto. It has been shown that the ability to learn small amounts of this artificial tongue is related to the ability to learn large amounts of other languages.

This technique is generally a successful one. The major condition that may mitigate its use is that which occurs when learning in the early stages of an activity involves abilities different from those involved in learning in a later stage. Such changes in the determinants of behavior as learning progresses have been shown to occur in certain instances, but these changes have not been particularly striking and probably are not sufficient to prevent the use of a miniature learning situation for selecting pupils most likely to succeed. However this may be, activity directed toward the development of such a technique for a particular purpose cannot be said to make a contribution to scientific knowledge. The product is a technique that in no way adds to available organized knowledge.

From the point of view of developing guidance practices, the miniature learning situation does not result in a product that fits well into current procedures. It is clearly quite impractical for the guidance counselor to administer as many miniature learning situations as there are situations in which one may desire to predict behavior. The guidance worker needs a short and comprehensive battery of tests that overlap as little as possible. A battery of miniature learning tests would show substantial overlap, with resulting inefficiency in the testing procedure. Guidance batteries that are currently widely used do not include the miniature learning situation type of test.

Method II. The hit-or-miss approach. This method has already been discussed, and it is briefly mentioned here in order to contrast it with other methods. This approach to the problem of prediction involves the administration of a wide range of instruments in the hope that one will be found that predicts successfully. This statement is a little exaggerated, in that the investigator is unlikely to try out just *any* instrument; rather, he will select those that appear to have at least some connection with the phenomenon to be predicted. The technique finds support in the fact that it has had a long and fairly successful history of application. A strong point in its favor is that many a time an unpromising variable has turned out to be the best predictor. Once this has occurred, it is nearly always possible to find a good reason why it should be so. On the negative side, there are several points to be noted.

The method involves a great amount of work on the part of those administering the tests and on the part of those taking them. There are real questions as to whether anyone is justified in taking so much of another's time. *Careful thinking through of the problem might result in the tryout of a much more limited battery of instruments, with less time lost by all.* This gain must be balanced against any loss that may result from unlikely variables turning out to be good predictors.

In addition, the variables likely to be selected are those that have some superficial relationship to the phenomenon that is to be predicted. If an analysis of the prediction problem is made in terms of current psychological knowledge, it is probable that only a few likely predictor variables will appear, but these may not have any relationship to the predicted variable obvious to the layman.

Method III. The scientist's approach to the problem of prediction. A third method involves the development of a theory concerning the nature of the phenomena to be predicted, and, on the basis of that theory, the derivation of methods hypothesized to predict. The author at one time attempted to develop a theory that could be used as a basis for prediction studies in the achievement area. It was built around the concept that the predictor variables in prediction studies were intervening variables and that they had certain specified relationships to one another. The author does not hold any particular brief for the theory he developed, and urges the student to develop his own miniature system.

So little has been done to develop prediction studies on the basis of this method that it is difficult to discuss the problems that it presents. The primary difficulty most certainly lies in the theory-construction phase itself.

The time factor in prediction. In experimental studies, the experimenter begins by specifying a certain set of conditions existing at the beginning of the experimental period; then certain experimental variables are manipulated for a given time, and the resulting changes in initial conditions are assessed. Thus substantial control is exerted during the entire time during which data are being collected. In contrast, in the type of prediction studies considered here, there are long periods during which occur events that are relevant to the outcome of the study but during which no control is exercised over existing conditions. This lack of control during long periods of time makes the results of such studies highly tenuous. The longer the interval between the prediction and the event to be predicted, the smaller are the chances of making a successful prediction.

Conditions necessary for effective prediction. Many prediction studies end in failure that could have been avoided if the researcher had considered the problem carefully in advance. In many such cases, a careful consideration of the problem in the first place would have led to the realization that the prediction made was not a feasible one. The discussion that follows is designed to help the student determine what is and what is not likely to be a feasible variable to predict.

In order that a phenomenon may be predictable from a given point in time, it is necessary that the determinants of that phenomenon exist in an identifiable form at that time. If one accepts the principle of universal causation, it follows that the conditions existing at any moment must include all the conditions necessary for accounting for all subsequent events. However, these determinants may exist within such a multiplicity of events that they may not be identifiable by any means at present conceivable. When such is the case, it is simply not feasible to attempt to undertake prediction.

This discussion may perhaps be abstract to the person who has not spent long years struggling with problems of predicting behavior so it is desirable to expand on the matter by way of a concrete example. Consider the problem of predicting the number of teachers who will resign from a large school system during each year for the next ten years. This is no trivial problem, since the long-term training of teachers requires that candidates be trained to replace those resigning from the system as well as to take other positions that will have to be filled over the course of the years. Large numbers of resignations may leave gaps that cannot easily be filled unless there has been long-term planning.

The time when it is necessary to make the prediction of whether a given group of teachers will or will not resign is four or five years before resignations actually take place, since this is the time required for recruiting and training new teachers. This is a considerable span of years over which to make predictions but many educational forecasts are made with a useful degree of accuracy over this period.

An immediate suggestion about how the prediction should be made is that data be obtained from the past and applied to the future. It certainly would be possible to obtain data on resignations over a long previous period, say twenty years, and to work out an average resignation rate. On the surface, this may appear to be a good method, until the data are closely examined and the discovery is made that most of the resignations occurred during a rather short period during the war. The reason for this was that teachers then were offered wages in industry far above those that could be obtained within the educational system. If this condition did not recur within a comparable period of time, one would not expect that the previous resignation rate would be comparable to the future resignation rate. However, even if such a period of high wages for ex-teachers did occur, school districts in the future might be willing to offer teachers a bonus or other financial incentive to stay on in the system, in which case the resignation rate might be held at a low and constant level. Insofar as the resignation rate depends upon unpredictable economic conditions and international tensions, it is not predictable by any technique at present available. At least, economists and political scientists have not yet succeeded in predicting such events and conditions.

An alternative approach can be taken if the the problem is redefined. In place of stating the problem as that of predicting the percentage of teachers likely to resign in a given year, it may be redefined as that of identifying those who are most likely to resist the temptation to resign. Stability could be given to a teaching body if it included only those who are likely to stay with the system indefinitely. It seems reasonable to assume that the personal characteristics of those who remain might be different from those who resign. One might suspect that those would stay who have a deeper interest in teaching and a more favorable attitude toward the activities it involves than those who would leave for economic reasons. (One might perhaps hypothesize that those who stay might tend to be less ambitious, and perhaps less intelligent, than those who leave.) Conceivably, a study could be designed to discover ways of identifying teachers who would not resign for economic reasons. At least some of the necessary conditions for practical predictions exist when the problem is stated in this way. However, it must be pointed out that the usefulness of a study of this kind might well be questioned. It would be hard to imagine an acceptable teacher-selection procedure that would permit the rejection of those who did not present characteristics making for long years of service. Indeed, such a procedure might well eliminate some of the ablest teachers— those who might come to provide leadership for the system. However, it must be pointed out that the problem of creating a stable body of teachers should be attacked realistically by making economic adjustments, for economic conditions are clearly a major determinant of resignations, and attempts to solve the problem by selection would not attack at its roots.

From what has been said, it is clear that, for a phenomenon to be predictable, the determinants must exist in some well-identified and measurable form at the time when the prediction is made. If partial predictions are to be accepted, and they must be because perfect predictions cannot be made, then only partial determinants need exist in an identifiable form. Since the determinants of political events remain largely obscure at this time —for we have had little success in predicting events in the social and economic sphere—prediction studies in the behavioral sciences must direct their energies toward the use of individual characteristics as variables. Many successful procedures for making predictions have been evolved through studies based on this approach. An excellent example is found in studies in the prediction of college success. As a result of studies conducted over the last quarter of a century, useful tests have been developed for identifying students who will later withdraw from college because of poor grades. This prediction can be made because the differences in grades are determined mainly by conditions within the individual. Such of these conditions as are related to differences in ability can be measured, but those related to differences in motivation cannot be adequately measured at the present time. The reader should note that although predictions in this area are quite accurate in terms of the level of precision one may expect in the behavioral sciences, they nevertheless leave much to be desired. The reasons for the rather large imperfections in our predictions must stem to a great degree from the existence of external conditions that affect grades. For example, such matters as whether the student is assigned to an instructor who has a personality compatible with his own, whether illness does or does not strike him, whether he falls in love or does not fall in love—all these and many others are unpredictable circumstances that introduce error into our predictions.

Another condition that must be established before a prediction study is undertaken is that the phenomenon to be predicted must be homogeneous in its causes; that is to say, that it always has the same causes. An example of a condition that it has not been possible to predict because of the multiplicity of possible determinants is delinquency. It is obviously most desirable to predict which children are most likely to become delinquent, so that the clinical psychologist and social worker can get to work to prevent this from happening. The difficulty is that there are many major determinants of delinquency. Some delinquency is a product of lack of intellectual insight into what is happening. Other causes include the effects of associates, the home background, and various pathological psychological conditions, to mention but a few. Under these conditions, there is no single effective way of identifying the potential delinquent. This problem is discussed at greater length later in this chapter.

An additional important condition for prediction is that the condition to be predicted must represent a well-defined phenomenon, and, if possible, that it represent a measurable variable. A much discussed variable such as teacher effectiveness does not meet the necessary standards of clarity. On the other hand, if specific and well-defined aspects of teacher effectiveness are used in prediction studies, then there is danger that the researcher may be able to predict only the trivial. The discovery of a significant and well-defined variable to forecast is often the major difficulty in the development of a prediction study.

Research designed to evaluate the effectiveness of counseling frequently suffers from the fact that the condition to be predicted cannot be described in terms of a single variable. Although we may talk in generalities and point to, say, *adjustment* as the condition to be predicted, there are many ways in which a person may adjust, and these cannot be compared to one another easily, if at all. In the face of this difficulty, many quite ridiculous criteria of the success of counseling have been evolved. For example, in one study the success of the counseling procedure was evaluated in terms of whether the counselee returned for more. A somewhat better solution might be to classify those who come for counseling into groups in terms of the type of adjustment to be made or the problem to be solved. Within any one group, it may be possible to distribute success at making the desired adjustment along a single and meaningful scale. Partitioning of groups into relatively homogeneous subgroups is often a solution to the problem of simplifying the conditions of prediction to the point where they are manageable.

Prediction Studies of Behavior as Studies of Enduring Traits

From what has been said, it is hardly surprising that most prediction studies deal with aptitudes of types that are known to be relatively enduring. Alternatively, they may be studies of biographical factors presumed to have an enduring effect on behavior. In any case, it is assumed that the uncontrolled events intervening between the time of prediction and the time of occurrence of the behavior it is desired to predict do not affect the magnitude or character of these traits. This is justified to a considerable extent, for it is known that the rank order of a group of children on an intellectual ability, such as that measured by a vocabulary test, does not change appreciably over a period of as long as a year or more. This property of long-term stability has resulted in the extended development and widespread use of such tests, for their predictive value is partly possible because of their stability over time. Studies of aptitudes have revealed a relatively small number of such traits in the intellectual field in the aptitude area that it seems profitable to measure. These are the variables that are commonly measured in aptitude batteries; beyond these there does not seem to have been much success in the measurement of highly stable intellectual variables.

As to nonintellectual attributes commonly referred to as personality traits, little success has been achieved in using them for prediction purposes. This may be a result of their instability. There is, of course, considerable evidence that the amount of many social traits that a person manifests depends to a considerable extent on the situation in which he is placed. At a cocktail party he may be a warm and genial character, quite the reverse of what he is at the office. Insofar as traits vary with the situation, satisfactory conditions for long-term prediction do not exist unless the situation to which predictions are to be made can be carefully described.

Difficulties in predicting also exist when the trait to be measured and to be used for predictive purposes is capable of extensive modification through experience. One may suppose that many social traits show progressive learning through the years of schooling. Unless the rate of learning is known, it is not possible to predict future behaviors from these traits, and the rate of learning is almost certainly likely to be an unknown.

Finally, consideration must be given to the problem of using biographical data for the making of predictions. The use of such data is based mainly on the assumption that the exposure of the child to certain environmental conditions results in the development of particular attributes that later become determinants of behavior. Difficulties in the use of such data arise because of the problem of identifying just what happened in the individual's past. There is little difficulty in determining *what he himself thinks happened,* but this may be quite different from what actually happened. Also, what *he thinks happened* will probably change from time to time, while what actually happened will not change. For this reason, among others, the predictive value of biographical events as they are reported has been found to be small.

The Availability of Appropriate Conditions

In the case of many prediction studies that students suggest, the difficulty of carrying them out lies in the unavailability of the conditions necessary for executing them. This is true of most of the studies of teacher effectiveness that are proposed. The misfortune is that so many of these are pursued under conditions that do not permit the production of meaningful results.

One could fill a volume describing the prediction studies that have been attempted, only for the researcher to discover that the conditions necessary for making the study did not exist or could not be found. Most studies related to the long-term predictive value of tests used in guidance are of this character. Only rarely is it possible to follow up those who have been tested at an earlier date. Studies of the prediction of leadership qualities from test scores also rarely can be followed through to a successful conclusion, if only for the fact that leadership is not a single behavioral dimension but a conglomeration of perhaps unrelated characteristics.

Studies designed to predict teacher effectiveness present some of the best examples of attempts to forecast phenomena under conditions that do not permit prediction. Such studies usually are based upon the assumption that an observer can spend a limited time in a classroom, perhaps an hour or two, and on the basis of what he sees can make a valid judgment of the effectiveness of the teacher. This, in turn, assumes that teacher effectiveness is a single dimension along which all teachers can be measured and compared. The realities and complexities of the teaching situation are such that these assumptions are nothing short of nonsense. One of the few definitive statements that one can make about the classroom situation is that it presents phenomena involving a great number of variables. Undoubtedly, observer characteristics enter into the selection of items from this complexity and result in many of the peculiar properties of ratings of teacher effectiveness. This, however, is not the only problem encountered in studies of teacher effectiveness. A large number of other conditions must also exist before such studies can be made profitably. In order to bring to the attention of the reader the range of circumstances that must exist for a study of this kind to be successful, it is worth reviewing here one of the better-conceived studies in this area.

The study referred to here is one by Morsh, Burgess, and Smith (1955), who were concerned with the extent to which student ratings of instructors could be used to predict the extent to which the objectives of a particular course were achieved. Unlike most of their predecessors, these investigators were able to find a situation in which this prediction problem could be studied. The situation was that presented by a group of 106 instructors who were *all teaching the same course* in hydraulics at an Air Force installation. It was also possible in this study to obtain the cooperation of two successive classes for each instructor, each class consisting of about fifteen students. Students were assigned to instructors at random, but, as one might expect, these groups differed considerably in their ability to learn the particular type of technical subject matter. Students were given both a pretest and a post-test of the subject matter taught in the course, and these tests were carefully tried out on an independent group of students. On the basis of the data thus collected, the tests were revised and improved in order to increase their internal consistency. It was assumed in this study, and the assumption was justified, that the effectiveness of the instructor could be measured in terms of the extent to which the objective of the course was achieved. The latter was the acquisition of subject matter, and it could be measured in terms of the achievement tests. On the basis of the student's previous grades and measures of his academic aptitude, a gain score from pretest to post-test was predicted for each student. However, the pretest was made extremely easy, and the gain score was not simply the difference between the pretest and the post-test scores, but the numerical value of the post-test score corrected for differences in initial knowledge of the subject matter as indicated by the pretest. The post-test scores were also corrected for differences in the learning ability of the students as measured by another aptitude test and by previous performance in school. Thus the gain score was the post-test score corrected, as far as possible, for differences in the learning ability of the students.

Unlike their predecessors, Morsh *et al.* were able to demonstrate that the average gain score shown by the class of a particular instructor was something more than a transitory phenomenon. Successive classes given by the same group of instructors showed similar gain scores; that is to say, an instructor who produced a high gain in one class tended to produce a high gain in a subsequent class, and vice versa. Thus it was established that differences between instructors produced differences in gains in knowledge that were consistent from class to class. As far as the author knows, the latter item of important information has not been positively established in any previous study. This does not mean, of course, that similar consistent gains would be found in the classes of other instructors whose teaching was in a different subject-matter field or directed toward different objectives. As a matter of fact, the author is aware of at least one other study in which the gain scores showed no consistency from class to class, and where its value as a variable to predict, therefore, rested in the shadow of doubt.

Morsh *et al.* clearly established that they were concerned with something more than a transistory phenomenon in the use of gain scores before they went on to study some of the conditions associated with high or low gain scores in particular classes. These investigators were able to establish that certain types of ratings of the instructor made by the student could be used to predict the corrected gain scores, but they were not able to establish relationships between particular aspects of instructor behavior and corrected gain scores. This seems to indicate that relevant aspects of teacher behavior that promote learning were not incorporated in the study. For the most part, such aspects of teacher behavior have not yet been identified.

The Morsh study represents a good beginning in the area, but only a good beginning. Advancement will be impeded by the fact that few researchers are likely to have available to them situations in which a large number of instructors are working toward identical goals and with students assigned to their classes at random. Even if such a situation presented itself, it is doubtful that most researchers would have the financial support necessary for preparing testing materials in quantity or for the employment of trained observers to obtain data concerning the behavior of the teachers in the classes. However, even if a favorable situation for studying problems of predicting teacher effectiveness existed, there is no guarantee that techniques for measuring aspects of teacher behavior are sufficiently advanced to permit extensive developments of knowledge. It is quite possible that investigations may not be able to proceed beyond the groundwork laid by Morsh and his associates.

The point stressed here is that the existence of a situation favorable to the making of a particular study may not insure success in advancing knowledge. The invention of high-powered microscopes did not permit the study of microorganisms. Although these miscroscopes had sufficient power, they could not be used for examining microorganisms until the additional technique of staining these organisms had been developed. Most complex problems—and most educational problems are complex —become amenable to study only after a multiplicity of techniques have been developed for handling various aspects of them.

Morsh *et al.* were able to take advantage of a unique situation that permitted the undertaking of a study that probably could not have been undertaken in most other educational situations. The latter do not ordinarily provide particularly favorable situations for the conduct of educational studies. In most cases, it requires all the ingenuity that the researcher can muster to adapt a proposed inquiry to an available research situation and to adapt an educational situation to the purpose of an inquiry, so that the study can be undertaken in a way that yields meaningful results.

This study has been discussed in some detail in order to bring to the attention of the reader the range of conditions that sometimes must exist before a meaningful prediction study can be made. The student should list carefully the conditions that he must find in order for him to carry through a prediction study in which he is interested, and then check to see whether such conditions actually exist in the facility where the study is to be undertaken. If the necessary conditions do not exist, the study should be abandoned. Too commonly in the past, researchers have proceeded with their prediction studies despite the fact that the results could not possibly be meaningful.

Fractionating Populations to Increase
Accuracy of Predictions

A number of interesting cases have been found in which it has not been possible to make predictions for an entire group, but in which predictions could be made within a section of that group. For example, it has been found in studies of achievement motivation that in some situations this variable shows little relationship to performance when an entire group is involved. On the other hand, when it is possible to separate from the total group those who see the task to be performed as a challenge, a marked relationship exists between achievement motivation and performance within this small group. This is not surprising, since achievement motivation can hardly be expected to operate in situations in which the individual does not feel a need to do his best.

In almost every area of educational research, one can think of situations in which it is necessary to partition a population of events in order to establish relationships. Where relationships are to be found between the qualifications of teachers and the characteristics of the curriculum, one would expect different relationships in urban schools than in rural schools. Sometimes it may be necessary to separate boys from girls in order to make a meaningful prediction. Sometimes it may be necessary to separate cultural groups. In other cases, relationships may apply to only certain types of economic conditions. A careful thinking through of most studies is likely to reveal the possibility that some of the relationships expected are more likely to occur in certain sections of the population than in others. It is of considerable interest to determine whether such hypotheses are sound.

Clustering of Variables to Increase
Accuracy of Predictions

It happens frequently in educational research that a large number of variables are included as potential predictors of a particular phenomenon. These predictors may show irregular but low correlations with the variable it is desired to predict. It would be possible, of course, to compute a combination of the variables that will best predict the particular independent variable. If this procedure were followed, and if the researcher were concerned with many predictions, he would be likely to find that a combination that maximized the prediction would provide what appeared to be an accurate prediction, but that when the same combination of best predictors was applied to a new sample, the prediction would shrink substantially. This is the well-known phenomenon of *shrinkage* that has dealt a fatal blow to many studies that were promising on the surface.

A second approach to the problem of building up predictions does not suffer from this hazard. It involves, first, the clustering of those predictor variables that belong together in terms of their intercorrelations. This can be accomplished by means of factor analysis or by the related method of cluster analysis. Variables that cluster are then combined in some way. Such composite variables may generally be expected to have the merit of having higher reliability than the relatively low-reliability elements of which they are composed.

In the clustering of such variables, a group should be constituted of elements that belong together, not only statistically but also according to a rationale. Unless this is done, any prediction made from the cluster is unlikely to contribute systematically to knowledge; rather is it likely to represent only an odd but perhaps useful relationship.

Just as variables within the predictor group may be clustered and then combined in the hope of improving the accuracy with which predictions may be made, so too may groups of independent variables be clustered. For example, an investigator concerned with the prediction of teacher behavior might have observed a group of teachers for the frequency with which they perform various acts, such as raising their voices, threatening to punish, offering rewards, asking for suggestions, encouraging a pupil to pursue a matter further, offering help, and so on. The investigator would probably find that only the poorest predictions could be made of the extent to which a teacher manifested any of these categories of behavior. However, it is quite likely that a correlational analysis would show that some of these behaviors tended to cluster together. It would certainly be expected that all behaviors representing expressions of hostility would represent a cluster of correlated measures of behavior. When measures of all of these behaviors are added to form a measure that might be described as the tendency to manifest hostility—from what has been learned about such a variable from other sources —one might expect this characteristic of teacher behavior to be reasonably predictable from test scores.

An example may now be given of a case in which both the dependent and independent variables in a study consisted of composites. In this study, a series of tests of creative ability was administered in order to predict the creative aspects of public speaking. The test scores were combined into composites on the basis of a previous factor analysis, and the composites had considerably greater reliability than the original scores. In order to increase the possibility of obtaining the greatest amount of predictability, the measures to be predicted were combined into similar groupings. Thus all measures related to high-level originality were combined, both among the predictor variables and among those to be predicted. The resulting composites might be expected to be related. It should be noted that this method does not have some of the disadvantages of the multiple-regression method of combining variables for maximizing predictions, and that the relationship is unlikely to shrink when it is tried out on a new sample.

Clinical Versus Statistical Prediction—A Problem
in the Validity of the Direct Observation
of Behavior

In recent times, there has been considerable controversy concerning the relative merits of clinical predictions and so-called
actuarial predictions. What is meant here by a *clinical prediction*
is a judgment arrived at by a psychologist after considering a
certain body of data. An *actuarial prediction* is made by combining quantitative data to derive a score, which is used to make
a prediction. Clinical psychologists have generally maintained
that it is possible to make more accurate predictions through the
exercise of clinical judgment than could be made by the statistical treatment of data alone—at least insofar as it is treated by
the methods at present in common use. The problem is an important one in the current connection, because it implies that
the data processing method of the researcher is inferior to that
of the machine.

Various approaches have been taken to the study of this problem. One has been to compare the actuarial prediction with the
prediction of the clinician made on the basis of the same test
scores.

Meehl (1954) has reviewed studies made prior to 1954 in
which the accuracy of predictions made by clinicians using test
scores are compared with the results achieved by statisticians
using objective methods. The results seem to vary considerably
from one study to another, depending on the nature of the condition to be predicted. In no clear-cut case did the clinicians
predict more accurately than the psychometricians. One suspects
that the psychometrician who has a well-developed procedure
for predicting a particular type of event or condition will do
better than the clinician, but if he does not have such a procedure, the clinician may possibly do better.

Just what can be concluded from the comparison of the statistician's predictions and the clinician's predictions made from

the same data is hard to understand. It would indeed be immensely surprising if a clinician could improve upon a testing and statistical procedure that had been developed and refined over the years for making a specific type of prediction.

Conceivably the clinician is better at making predictions than the statistician in certain situations, but the statistician may be more accurate in others. If, for example, it were desired to predict what the author will be most likely to do next Sunday, test scores would be a very poor basis for making a prediction. However, what he is likely to do can easily be predicted from a knowledge of his habits. It would seem that, whenever the behavior to be predicted is based upon well-established individual regularities of behavior, the clinician is almost certainly likely to do a better job than the statistician working with test scores. It is highly doubtful that a test could be made that could successfully identify the major habit patterns of the individual.

Tests are not well designed for predicting how a person will perform in particular situations of brief duration. Rather do they predict general characteristics of behavior over a period of time. It is generally much easier to predict how a student will achieve in courses over a four-year period than it is to predict how he will achieve in specific aspects of courses.

Problems of Multiple Prediction

So far in this chapter, consideration has been given to the problem of predicting a single criterion variable from one or more predictor variables. There are, however, more complex prediction situations that must also be given consideration here. A common problem of multiple prediction is that of validating vocational guidance batteries for predicting vocational success. It clearly would not be practical to develop data for predicting success in each and every occupation, for it may be presumed that occupations can be grouped together into categories that call for similar combinations of abilities. The same may be true for predicting success in vocational training programs from this same battery.

The basic question in the problem that we have just considered is how many categories should be used in the classification of aptitudes for vocational skills. No very satisfactory answer can be found, because for two training programs to be classified in different categories it would mean that persons exposed to both would have to show a performance in one that was quite unrelated to performance in the other. Such a fact is almost impossible to establish at the present time, because it is not feasible to submit the same individuals to two extended training programs one after the other. Even if this were possible, difficulties would arise in maintaining motivation, and thus evidence would not be obtained of the relationship between achievement in these two learning situations. For this reason, certain indirect approaches to this problem have been proposed. One of these is to determine whether persons who successfully complete the two courses of training can be differentiated in terms of a battery of aptitude tests administered prior to training. If no such differentiation can be made, then the two programs are considered to belong to the same classification. This conclusion is based upon the assumption that all relevant aptitudes have been measured, which may not be the case at all.

The latter situation may be represented diagrammatically, as shown in Figure VII. In this figure, the aptitude scores of successful members of two occupational groups are shown with respect to two aptitudes, A and B. The members of one group are indicated by circles and the members of the other group by crosses. Neither aptitude alone provides a good discrimination between the two groups, but the two groups can be well discriminated by a function of the two aptitudes represented by the line YY'. This function, when it is the best possible one, is referred to as a *discriminant function*. A person's score with respect to this function can be used to indicate whether he is more likely to belong to the one group or the other.

When more than two groups are involved, there may be more than one way in which it is possible to discriminate one group from another. In such a case there will be more than one discriminant function. This is illustrated in a study by Tiedeman, Bryan, and Rulon (1953). In this study scores on seventeen tests were obtained for airmen in eight different Air Force jobs. The problem was to determine the extent to which the test battery as a whole permitted the discrimination of the men in the different occupational groups. Two discriminant functions, each representing particular combinations of scores, showed some capacity for discriminating between the groups. One of these was a combination of scores that represented a variable differentiating me-

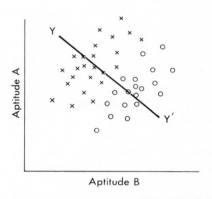

FIGURE VII. *Graphic illustration of discriminant function.*

chanical and nonmechanical occupations. The other involved a differentiation in terms of the degree to which the occupation involved intellectual requirements. This illustration shows how more than one discriminant function may be found when many groups are involved.

It has often been considered that the discriminant-function procedure represents a desirable model for educational classification. When this is suggested, it is often forgotten that the mere fact that it is possible to discriminate between two groups does not mean that the basis for discrimination is necessarily one that can be used for future classification. An illustration may help in understanding this point. In a certain research organization with which the writer is familiar, nearly all the research workers are men and nearly all the clerical workers and laboratory assistants are women. From these facts it is clear that sex may be used to make an almost perfect discrimination between the research workers and the assistants, but it is also clear that it would be most hazardous to classify future applicants for jobs as research workers if they are male and as clerical workers and assistants if female. Discriminant functions may be such that they are based on characteristics wholly irrelevant for purposes of subsequent classification. Many occupational groups may be discriminated from other occupational groups by accidents of history. The mere fact that a variable discriminates is not a sufficient basis for using it for subsequent classification. It is a necessary but not a sufficient condition for use in classification.

Most of the problems of prediction that have been considered up to this point are likely to resolve themselves ultimately into problems of selection. Thus we may seek to establish methods of predicting the classroom behavior of the teacher, but the ultimate justification of such studies stems from the fact that they contribute to an organized body of knowledge that will improve methods of teacher selection, and will enable us to discriminate between teachers who behave in accordance with some prescribed pattern that is considered desirable and those who behave in some manner that is inconsistent with this pattern. The usefulness of prediction studies in their contribution to selection and related guidance procedures has fully justified the extensive effort that has been channeled into them.

The Outcomes of Research on Prediction

The outcomes of research on the type of problems of prediction that have been considered in this chapter very largely represent contributions to the technology of education rather than contributions to an organized body of scientific knowledge. Nevertheless, when the outcomes of such studies are successful, they are likely to result in techniques for forecasting in situations where it is very important to make accurate predictions. Tests for the selection of college students were developed through prediction studies of the type discussed here. Although these studies, which were extended over nearly a decade, did not result in any major contribution to knowledge, they did provide useful measures of certain aspects of scholastic aptitude. Nothing was discovered in these studies concerning how students learn.

Viewed from another light, and using Kenneth Spence's terminology, it may be said that in such studies the relationship between a response in a test situation R_1 and a response in a learning situation R_2 is discovered. Such relationships R_1—R_2 represent a low-level type of law that does not involve any direct functional relationship between R_1 and R_2. Whatever relationship exists is based on a complex ramification of events which are not understood at all by the discovery of the R_1—R_2 relationship. It is obscure relationships of this type that are unearthed and rendered useful by such prediction studies as have been considered in this chapter.

The Phenomenon of Shrinkage

It is necessary to bring to the reader's attention a phenomenon that is discussed extensively in books on statistics. This is the phenomenon of *shrinkage,* which is most easily understood through an example.

A researcher was interested in the personality traits that distinguished the most popular pupils from the least popular in the twelfth grade of a large high school. By means of a sociometric technique he was able to select two groups of one hundred pupils each. One group contained only pupils rated high by their peers in the matter of personal popularity, while the other included only pupils rated low. The researcher then administered a battery of sixty tests to both groups and computed the mean standard score of each group on each test. The five tests that gave the largest significant difference between the two groups were then considered to be those that could be used to discriminate between the two groups. However, on repeating the experiment in the following year, the differences in mean scores between similarly selected groups of pupils had *shrunk* to negligible proportions. This example illustrates the shrinkage phenomenon, but it needs to be interpreted in order to be understood.

What has happened is this: Suppose that the experiment were to be repeated one hundred times and that, on the average over the entire series, scores on Test X differed negligibly for the two groups. Even if this were so, it is highly probable that in some of these experiments there would be found substantial differences between the groups in their average scores on Test X. This is the kind of thing that may have happened in the study involving the administration of sixty tests to the two groups of one hundred pupils.

In the illustration given, it is probable that the five tests selected as the most discriminating were those that happened to show a particularly large difference between groups on that particular sample. For this reason one can expect shrinkage of these differences on successive samples. The assessment of the true value of this difference could be made with some accuracy only by taking a very large sample of the two types of student. The fact that a large and unexpected difference occurs with a rather small sample is no basis for believing that it will turn up with another sample. The problem arises because the large number of variables involved permits the selection of those that happen to show particular "errors" in the study in question.

Just as differences in means may show shrinkage when an experiment is repeated, so too may other statistics show shrinkage when they are selected for extremes of magnitude and an experiment is repeated. Suppose that it were desired to predict success in shorthand courses in high school. A large number of tests might be given to beginning students in the hope that some of these might be correlated with later shorthand grades. If the tests that *happened* to have the highest correlation with shorthand grades were chosen as those most suitable for selecting shorthand students, the experimenter might expect to be disappointed when the tests were actually used for that purpose. Correlations of these "high predictors" with shorthand grades might be expected to shrink on subsequent samples. The reason for shrinkage in this case is exactly the same as in the previous example. Even if the tests when administered to a very large sample did not correlate with shorthand grades, on a small sample the correlations of these tests would be scattered over a wide range of values. The largest of these correlations would be large through the operation of chance circumstances that would be unlikely to be reproduced in subsequent samples.

A special and important case of shrinkage is manifested when multiple regression or multiple correlation techniques are used. Such techniques involve the determination of the best method of combining two or more measures in order to predict a criterion. The best combination for a particular sample takes advantage of any peculiarities that make one set of weights more effective than another. Now when these same weights are applied to another sample that has different peculiarities, their effectiveness in predicting the criterion measure is reduced. Thus one commonly finds that when a multiple correlation coefficient is calculated on a particular sample, and the same regression weights are then applied to a new sample, the new multiple correlation has shrunk.

An example of the difficulties that may arise when the phenomenon of shrinkage is not taken into account is illustrated by a common technique of test construction. In the building of an aptitude test to predict a criterion, such as passing or failing a course in engineering drawing, it is common practice to administer a great number of different test items to a group that is to complete the course, and then to select from this pool those items that are the best predictors of grades in the course. Under such conditions one may expect the predictive value of the items to shrink when they are used for predicting grades in future samples. If the number of items above a certain level of significance is equal to the number that might be expected on a chance basis, the selection procedure should be rejected as worthless.

Studies should be designed so that the hazards of shrinkage are minimized. If possible, the procedure should involve a method of estimating shrunken values. This can be done by a number of procedures:

1. Simple cross-validation procedure. This is the procedure that has been traditionally used. For example, in developing a test to predict a particular criterion, such as success in algebra, test items that seem likely to predict success are administered to a large group, say one thousand cases. The data are then partitioned into two sections with five hundred cases in each. Sometimes the partitioning is undertaken so as to make the two groups unequal, in which case the larger of the two groups is used in the first analysis. On the basis of the first sample of data, the items most successful in the prediction of the criterion are selected. The hypothesis that the selected items will truly predict the criterion is then tested on the second sample of items. When the discriminating power of the selected items is determined on the second sample, the values will be found to have shrunk from what they were when derived from the first sample, but the shrunken estimates of discriminating power will show considerable stability when applied to subsequent samples.

The problem of shrinkage is particularly acute when multiple correlation techniques are used. In most studies one should provide independent samples on which the original values can be checked.

2. Double and multiple cross-validation. In the design that has just been discussed, the values derived from Sample A are checked on Sample B. An alternative procedure is to derive two original sets of values, one from Sample A and one from Sample B. Those derived from Sample A are then checked on Sample B, while those from Sample B are checked against Sample A. In the case of an item-selection project it may be wise to choose for the final version of the test that is being built only those test items that stand up under both procedures. This double cross-validation method makes fuller use of the available data than does the simple cross-validation method.

3. Statistical methods of handling the shrinkage problem. For several decades statisticians have attempted to devise methods for estimating the amount of shrinkage that will occur on cross-validation. This problem has been most extensively studied in the case of multiple correlation techniques. The problem has not been solved in any satisfactory way, but it appears that certain iterative methods of computing multiple correlations offer some promise.

Nonlinear Relationships

Most prediction problems that are investigated within the domain of educational research are based upon the assumption that the relationships between the variables involved are linear. A *linear relationship* is simply one in which equal increases in the predictor variable are accompanied by equal increases in the variable to be predicted. It is generally quite acceptable to assume that any relationships that may exist are linear, for rarely have nonlinear relationships been found in the educational field, even when they have been actively sought. This is hardly surprising, since most measuring instruments are constructed in the first place to be such that they have a linear relationship with certain criterion variables. Thus the approach usually taken to instrument construction results in the lack of curvilinear relationships between the instrument and other variables. In addition, those engaged in the study of individual differences have developed a wide range of statistical techniques based upon the assumption that relationships are linear. These techniques include those associated with factor analysis and such techniques as those of simple and multiple discriminant analysis, canonical correlation, multiple regression, and association procedures. By means of these tools the study of problems related to individual differences has been pursued. Such techniques are limited in the types of relationship that they can be used to study, and they are ordinarily quite unadapted to the study of nonlinear relationships. The adaptation of these methods to the study of nonlinear relationships usually results in the generation of functions that are extremely complex and require very elaborate arithmetical operations for their solution.

The problems of studying nonlinear relationships have been discussed to some extent in the section that pertains to profile analysis and pattern analysis. The latter techniques would be used when a relationship between two variables is not linear but the actual nature of the relationship is not known. The difficulties and impracticalities of utilizing most pattern-analysis techniques were noted, and it was also pointed out that they are likely to occur only when the researcher does not really know what he is expected to find. If he does know what to look for, then he can adopt techniques that look for this expected relationship and no other, and his task becomes a relatively simple one. Comprehensive pattern analysis looks for each and every type of relationship that might possibly exist; and since the possibilities are numerically large, the technique is correspondingly elaborate. The need is for studies that look for a few specific expected relationships, and then, perhaps, curvilinear relationships may be found.

Some Problems of Predicting Rather Rare Events

Meehl (1955) has pointed out that even though a measure may have predictive value for a given purpose, it may still happen that fewer errors may be made by *not* using it than by using it. Until it is understood, this paradox appears to present a situation filled with contradictions. Consider the problem of identifying persons who will become involved in delinquencies during a given year. Suppose that a test has been developed, which, it has been demonstrated, has value in identifying future delinquents. Let us also suppose that this test was given to 10,000 high school children, and that 200 were identified as likely to become delinquent. At the end of several years, it would be possible to determine which of those identified as probably delinquent actually were delinquent. A table similar to Table 3 could then be drawn up.

One additional statement must be made in order to interpret these data, namely that the delinquency rate for this group is 10 per 1000. This is referred to as the base rate. With this fact in mind, the table indicates that the test does have some success in identifying those who become involved in delinquencies. However, by using the test on the group of 10,000, altogether 240 incorrect decisions were made (170 + 70). If no test had been

TABLE 3. Hypothetical Data on the Identification of Those Expected to be Involved in Delinquencies

	Number Actually Involved in Delinquency	Number Not Involved in Delinquency
Those predicted to be involved in delinquencies	30	170
Those predicted *not* to be involved in delinquencies	70	9730

given and if all of the group had been classified as nondelinquent, one would have expected only 100 incorrect decisions to have been made, which would have included all the cases that became delinquent. Thus fewer incorrect predictions are made by avoiding the use of the valid test than by using the test. Is it desirable to avoid the use of predictors where similar circumstances exist?

The answer to this is not a simple matter. Note that in Table 3 the test does identify correctly 30 of those later involved in delinquencies, but problems are created by the fact that it has erroneously identified as delinquent 170 cases who were not so. What has to be determined is whether the advantages gained by identifying the 30 delinquents outweigh the disadvantages of incorrectly identifying 170 as probably delinquent. If the testing requires an elaborate procedure and the help of many technicians, the losses may outweigh the gains. Also, financial and social problems may be introduced by identifying as potential delinquents those who are not.

The problem that has been discussed in this section becomes particularly acute as the base rate of the characteristic to be identified becomes very small. Attempts to identify rare talents, rare diseases, or any rare phenomena present situations such that selection devices are likely to provide a very much larger number of misclassifications than are provided by failure to use the instrument. This problem is most easily avoided when the base rate is near the 50 per cent mark. In addition, as the value of the test for selection purposes increases, the number of misclassifications is also reduced.

Summary

1. Studies designed to develop methods of prediction in education are of great practical significance but do not necessarily contribute to scientific knowledge.

2. There are three general approaches that may be taken to the problem of predicting educational achievement, which are as follows:

   a. The development of test situations that are miniatures of the learning situation in which it is desired to predict behavior.
   b. The administration of a wide range of instruments in the hope that one will predict.
   c. The development of a theory of prediction and the development of methods on the basis of that theory.

3. An event can be predicted if all of the conditions that ultimately lead up to that event can be observed or measured at the time when the prediction is made.

4. A major difficulty in predicting behavior is that one does not know the precise nature of the situation in which behavior is to be predicted.

5. The event to be predicted should represent a well-defined phenomenon.

6. Most prediction studies of behavior are based on the assumption that personality consists of a complex of relatively enduring and permanent traits. While stable intellectual traits can be measured, the same cannot be said of the field of personality.

7. A major difficulty in conducting many types of prediction studies stems from the fact that the conditions necessary for research on the prediction problem simply do not exist. This is particularly true of most attempts to predict teacher effectiveness. An example of a unique situation in which this problem could be studied with meaningful results was discussed at length.

8. Sometimes it is feasible to make a successful prediction in one section of a population but not in another.

9. A common method of improving predictions is to cluster variables that are related. Sometimes it is possible to cluster the criterion variables as well as the predictor variables.

10. Numerous studies have been made that attempt to contrast the relative success of the statistician and the clinician in making predictions from test scores. However, these studies do not compare the accuracy of the clinician in making predictions through clinical techniques with the accuracy of the statistician making similar or other predictions through psychometric techniques.

11. Many problems of prediction involve the determination of how many predictors are to be used for classifying persons into a number of groups such as occupational groups, and also how many of the occupational groups form a reasonable system for the classification of occupations. Research is only beginning to explore such problems.

12. In most prediction studies the phenomenon of shrinkage is likely to occur, and the studies should be designed so that it is possible to estimate the effect of shrinkage or to eliminate it.

13. One cannot always assume that the relationships between variables will necessarily be linear.

14. The fact that a variable has predictive value in a particular situation does not necessarily mean that it can be used profitably in that situation. Meehl's paradox occurs when the base rate for the occurrence of a particular event is low.

Some Problems for the Student

1. List some major assumptions that must be made in order to predict college enrollments fifteen years hence.

2. Identify some of the major difficulties involved in predicting the number of elementary school teachers that will be available for placement ten years hence.

3. One of the few skills taught in high school for which there are no satisfactory aptitude tests is typing. What hypotheses can be suggested to account for the failure to predict grades in typing classes from aptitude tests administered prior to training?

CHAPTER 12

STUDIES OF DEVELOPMENT

STUDIES of development, unlike most of those that have been considered up to this point, are concerned primarily with time trends; that is to say, with changes that occur as a function of time. Survey studies and prediction studies are occasionally concerned with time trends, but their techniques are not primarily directed toward the study of such phenomena. This chapter on developmental studies is included for two reasons. First, there are difficulties inherent in the conduct of such studies, which the student of education should know. Second, studies of development are of such far-reaching consequences for education that research of this type must assume a place of great importance in the future even if it has not in the past.

Some of the most important problems of education involve time trends, for education itself is concerned with personal change and with the control of learning as it occurs in the pupil. While the classroom teacher is mainly concerned with change over a relatively short period of time, such as a semester or a school year, administrators and those concerned with policy-making at a high level may be concerned with change over a much longer period, such as a decade or a lifetime. Classroom examinations given at the end of a semester are virtually limited studies in which increments in an area of intellectual skill are studied over a short period of time, perhaps without recognizing that change may not be permanent but will undergo a period of waning as well as waxing as time goes by. The latter type of problem has become of increasing importance as educators have extended their interest in educational problems from the childhood years to the entire life span. Studies of the intellectual functions in the later years are largely studies of decline.

Developmental studies may be quantitative or qualitative. Pioneer studies, such as those by Arnold Gesell on the development of motor and perceptual skills in young babies and those by Jean Piaget and his associates on the higher mental processes, have been essentially qualitative and descriptive in nature. Both have attempted to describe the nature of certain changes that occur in children as they grow. Little attempt has been made to measure these changes in these studies, but rather has the purpose been that of description. Perhaps it is necessary to begin developmental studies at the descriptive level, for then the investigator is able to obtain a "feel" for what is important to measure and what is trivial. Until the researcher knows what variables are of genuine importance, he is not really in a position to conduct quantitative studies.

While the value of descriptive studies is not questioned here, they might not be considered appropriate for a thesis or dissertation. Quantitative methods play such an important part in modern scientific methodology that the student may be expected to acquire some familiarity with them when he works on his thesis or dissertation. In addition, descriptive studies that do not involve measurement can so easily lead to false conclusions that they should be reserved for the experienced research worker. One is reminded of the astronomer Lowell, who thought he saw the canals on Mars as double lines rather than as the single lines earlier observers had described. For many years thereafter, astronomers confirmed Lowell's observation, but today it seems to be well established that the supposed doubleness of the lines was a figment of his imagination. Such are the hazards of qualitative observation. Perhaps it may be well to point out a few of the sources of these hazards.

First, the observation and description of behavior at various age levels permit the observer to see what he wants to see—and even the best observers tend to some extent to see what they want to see.

Second, the observer faced with the innumerable events that constitute the flow of behavior is likely to be bewildered by the richness of the material. He may be overwhelmed with the abundance of fact and feel that he does not have the kind of genius that can fit this bewildering array of events into a meaningful framework. As a result, he may direct his efforts to recording masses of material that he does not know how to handle.

Studies of short-term development related directly to the learning process will be considered first, since they are practical ventures for the student of education working toward a master's or doctor's degree. Later in the chapter, consideration will be given to the classical type of long-term study of development that finds its roots in the qualitative descriptions of development of the nineteenth century biologists. A few such long-term studies do attempt to relate environmental conditions to learning, but the difficulties of doing this are substantial.

STUDIES OF DEVELOPMENT OVER SHORT PERIODS OF TIME

A great many studies have been undertaken that attempt to measure development over relatively short periods of time—perhaps as short as a few days. These studies of development are particularly significant for education because of the emphasis that they place on learning phenomena such as occur in schools. There studies relate measures of development to environmental conditions and learning conditions on the one hand, and to pupil characteristics on the other. They are designed to find out who learns what and under what conditions. In such studies, learning is conceived in the broadest sense. Not only are skills such as reading considered to be learned, but so too are thinking, judgment-making, and decision-making skills. Characteristics of personality are also presumed to be learned and subject to the influence of the school environment, and hence developmental studies of such characteristics as they emerge under different conditions constitute an important field for educational research workers.

Theoretical Basis for Short-Term Studies

Of all the branches of psychology, the one which has shown the most sophisticated development in terms of theory construction is that of learning. Since the turn of the century many of the greatest leaders in psychology have devoted their efforts to the construction of theories of learning. With this historical fact in mind one might well expect that, of all educational research, the area having the most adequate theoretical basis would be that of classroom studies of learning. For many historical reasons, this has not been the case: studies of classroom learning have more often than not lacked any theoretical basis.

The author has reviewed elsewhere (Travers, 1963) research on classroom learning conducted in the early part of the twentieth century. This research was exploratory in nature and generally related to such practical problems as whether the teaching of Latin did or did not train the mind. The innovations which Thorndike introduced into the schools at this time followed from his laboratory research and generally had little relationship to classroom experimentation. Most of his innovations were based on the concept that frequency of association was an important factor in learning and, hence, effective learning results when an association has been made a sufficient number of times. For example, in the design of elementary school readers, new words must be introduced over and over again before the child acquires the capacity to recognize them on sight. Readers for older children should be designed to include mainly words to which the child had already been frequently exposed. Only much later were studies undertaken which attempted to validate these new procedures. Almost the only area in which Thorndike conducted classroom studies was in the area of adult learning and that mainly for the purpose of determining whether or not older persons learned less rapidly than younger learners.

The 1930's brought new theoretical developments, notably those of gestalt psychology. This new approach to problems of learning, with all of its elegance and sophistication, did little to provide a theoretical basis for classroom research on learning. Gestalt psychology tended to emphasize the inborn characteristics of the learner and had almost nothing to say about how the environment should be arranged to control learning. While Thorndike had been concerned mainly with verbal learning, the gestalt psychologists were concerned with perceptual learning of a kind which tended to be remote from the classroom. But even if gestalt psychology had had direct and important implications for education, it is doubtful that it would have had much impact on classroom research—which by then had taken on an entirely new color. Research was seen as the weapon which was to protect progressive education from its opponents, and classroom studies were planned to determine if the new method did achieve the goals it had set for itself. In such an atmosphere there was little place for classroom research closely tied to an up-to-date framework of learning theory. Whatever tie to theory it had was to the broad educational theory espoused by the progressive education movement. Some contend that the theory of learning during that period had not progressed to the point where it could provide a sound basis for the conduct of educational research.

In the few years prior to World War II and in the years that followed, major developments took place in research on learning which began to have an impressive effect on educational research. The first was the attempt by Hull (1943) to state in precise and formal terms a learning theory which was to become the basis for a vast amount of research. The second was the introduction by Skinner of a number of concepts which gave freshness and new vigor to the field. Hull and Skinner are at opposite poles in the emphasis they give to rigid theoretical formulations based on research and modified by them. Hull has been the outstanding exponent of developing theoretical formulations, while Skinner considers that more significance should be attached to an empirical and experimental approach and advocates deferring the development of theoretical models until a rather late stage in the growth of a science. This does not mean that there are no postulates implicit in Skinner's work, for there clearly are. But he is against any attempt to formulate comprehensive theories of learning until the science of learning reaches a more advanced stage than it has today. Despite the fact that Skinner dubs himself "antitheoretical," he does not hesitate to derive postulates and generalizations from his work or to apply them to new fields, such as the design of teaching machines—an area in which he has shown vigorous leadership. He is only against ambitious and global theories.

A third influence which has had a significant effect on educational research has been the work of Kurt Lewin. His theoretical influence is seen in four areas of educational research, and constitutes those aspects of learning which they involve. These four areas are: (1) conflict, (2) self-concept, (3) level of aspiration, and (4) group process (which has become an area of sophisticated theory development in itself).

Mention must be made of the influence of Donald Hebb, who has provided evidence indicating the importance of learning in the preschool years. Through his influence, a large number of studies of perceptual and motor learning have been undertaken and the foundation has been laid for the systematic planning of learning in the early childhood years.

Today, most educational research which pertains to learning shows the influence of one or more of these four major sets of developments. A typical study of learning conducted today by a student of education will derive its basic postulates, if it has any, from one of these three sources. Rarely any more will such a study be based on a comprehensive theory of learning for such comprehensive theories are generally considered passé in the present climate of scientific research. Thus one finds numerous studies based on Skinner's basic postulate which he refers to as the *law of reinforcement*. Many of these studies are at the practical level: they attempt to determine what are the most effective reinforcers in the classroom. Many studies have been conducted on the effectiveness of adult approval, mechanical reinforcers such as a bell or a light, material reinforcers such as are supplied by trinkets or candy, negative reinforcers such as an electric shock or the word *wrong*, and so forth.

Other reinforcement studies have investigated the effect of delay on reinforcement. This is clearly an important educational problem for the common practice is for reinforcement to be delayed after the completion of an assignment. The effect of this delay on the learning process has been studied. While the general rule is that reinforcement is most effective when it follows directly the response to be strengthened, under some conditions a delay in reinforcement may take place without any loss of effectiveness. How reinforcement should be distributed in order to provide the most rapid acquisition and the most efficient retention represents another problem which research in this area has attempted to explore.

While research on problems of reinforcement in learning can be carried out without the experimenter falling into too many pitfalls, the same cannot be said for research in those areas of learning to which Lewin made major contributions. Consider, for example, some of the problems involved in conducting research on the relationship of the self-concept to learning. Most of those who conduct studies in such an area are likely to have the personal bias that the self-concept is an important determiner of the individual's capacity to learn. However, the mere fact that one can demonstrate that learning difficulties tend to be accompanied by inadequacies in the self-concept does not necessarily support that position. An inadequate self-concept is just as likely to be a result of learning difficulties as learning difficulties are likely to be a result of an inadequate self-concept. Wylie (1961), who has made a thorough and exhaustive review of research on the self-concept, concludes that the research as a whole is plagued by difficulties which make it almost impossible to interpret the data. He who wishes to conduct research in this interesting area would do well to study Wylie's book carefully, since it is recognized as the most comprehensive and scholarly review of the area that has yet been made.

STUDIES OF PERCEPTUAL LEARNING

While gestalt psychology represents a comprehensive and programmatic approach to problems of perception and the role of perceptual processes in learning, it failed to attract the younger generation of research workers. Research on problems of perception in relation to learning and to education was to continue, but under the sponsorship of persons with a wide variety of backgrounds. For this reason, research on the area as a whole does not show any particular unity in approach, and few studies have been undertaken on the basis of a comprehensive theory of learning. Perhaps this state of affairs is an advantage at a time when a vast number of striking experimental results are being reported and new techniques for research in the area are being explored. Premature attempts to order these facts might have a stultifying effect on these exploratory activities. Certain striking lines of research which appear to raise questions about current educational practices will be mentioned here briefly to suggest to the student avenues which he may wish to explore further.

First, brief consideration must be given to the work of Donald Hebb on perceptual development and sensory deprivation. Hebb has demonstrated, with data derived from both human and subhuman subjects, that normal intellectual and emotional development is highly dependent upon exposure of the organism to appropriate stimulation during the period of growth. Deprivation of opportunities to use the sense of vision, for example, results in an inability to undertake the simplest visual perceptual tasks—such as shape and form recognition—even though the eyes may be in perfect functioning condition. Extensive practice with the tasks involved in visual perception over a period of years rather than months, seems necessary before such skills as reading can be undertaken. Deficiencies in sensory experience produce difficulties in learning which are extremely difficult to remedy. One of Hebb's favorite examples of this phenomenon is the young adult who has been blind from birth and who suddenly gains vision. Such a person is able to enjoy the beauty of color immediately, but the simplest visual task baffles him. Learning to discriminate between a square and a triangle, as simple a visual discrimination as one could imagine, may take months of practice. Learning to read is out of the question before extended perceptual training has been undertaken. In short, years of perceptual training are required before the person can use vision intelligently. Similar results have been achieved in experiments on other sensory areas, in which animals have been used as subjects and deliberately deprived of some particular aspects of sensory experience.

Evidence is accumulating that appropriate early training in children of preschool age may well make it possible for the child to master many skills years before they are ordinarily mastered at present. An interesting overview of such educational possibilities is provided by Fowler (1962), who has accumulated evidence that precocity is often the result of early and extensive perceptual training.

A second important area of research, related to that which has just been considered, is the tracing of the development of perceptual phenomena and the conditions that affect them. Those involved in elementary education have been particularly interested in studies related to the development of a concept of the self and the extent to which the statements made by the adult about the child influence this phase of development. There is also considerable interest in the extent to which children's percepts are realistic or involve fantasy and in the role of experience in such behavior. Solley and Murphy (1960) provided a useful summary of research on these problems.

A third research frontier which has implications for education is the study of the relationship between the individual's needs and values and his capacity to perceive. While this area presents a series of fascinating problems, the research worker is likely to encounter many pitfalls. An informative illustration is provided by the early researches, which supposedly showed that anxiety-producing words (*punishment, illegitimate, accuse,* and the like) were less easily recognized than words which do not produce anxiety. Later research showed that the main reason for this was that anxiety-producing words are less common and less frequently encountered than words which do not produce anxiety. The next step was for research workers to prepare lists of anxiety-producing and non-anxiety-producing words which appear with equal frequency in print. The technical difficulties which such research involves are considerable and the beginner must be sure to familiarize himself thoroughly with what has already been accomplished before designing his own study.

Related to research on perceptual learning are studies of concept formation, an area in which important advances are being made. A presentation of this approach, which has major research implications for education, is found in a work by Bruner, Goodnow, and Austin (1956). The argument presented by these writers is that man is able to cope with his environment because he is able to group together and categorize events and discriminate these from other events or other categories of events. Thus man has classified colors into a few categories which are given names such as *red, yellow, blue,* and so forth. Thousands of colors that can be discriminated from one another can be classified under this simple system of names. A category is simply a class of events that are all treated as if they were equivalent. Much of human learning consists of acquiring the ability to discriminate between what should be included and what should not be included in particular categories, such as *dog, cat,* and so forth. According to this theory, when a person is able to discriminate between events that should belong and events that should not belong in a particular category, he has achieved *concept attainment.* The studies by Bruner *et al.* are concerned with the conditions related to concept attainment.

In order to develop further the presentation of this type of theoretical development, consider the case of a child who is learning to discriminate between those moving objects that adults categorize as *dogs* and those moving objects that are categorized as other than *dogs*. On seeing a moving object, the child makes a tentative prediction or *decision* whether or not the object is a dog. The decision is found to be correct or incorrect when he names the object and an adult indicates approval or disapproval. This is the *validation* of the decision. The consequence of a decision is referred to as the *payoff*. The decision and the test of the decision provide potential information concerning the attributes that can be considered as predictable of belonging to the category *dog*. As this information accumulates, it progressively limits the possibilities of what is to be included in the category. The child might go about this by first attempting to make the discrimination in terms of color and by calling all moving *brown* objects *dogs*. This would be referred to as a *strategy*. In other words, the sequence of decisions through which information is acquired is called a *strategy* or a *sequence of strategies*. The strategies adopted depend on the requirements of the problem situation, and they are retained or changed as they are successful or unsuccessful.

This discussion is presented to bring to the attention of the reader the fact that a well-developed theoretical framework exists for conducting developmental studies of many aspects of the higher mental processes. Such studies conducted within a framework of theory will probably replace the purely descriptive studies that have been characteristic of past research.

RESEARCH ON ADULT LEARNING

While most developmental studies related to formal training and learning have been undertaken with children of school age, some interest has also been shown in limited places to problems of adult learning. This is an important and worthwhile area for fruitful studies and one which has been influenced by many preconceived notions, as is illustrated by the commonly heard statement, "I am too old to learn."

Pioneer studies in the field of adult learning and in the problems of teaching adults were conducted by Thorndike (1928). His general findings were that the older adult in his fifties has about as much capacity to learn as the youngster leaving high school. But there appear to be differences in motivation: the older adult expects to learn too much in too short a time and becomes impatient with the slowness of his pace; the younger adult is much more accepting of the fact that learning is slow. Such motivational differences have not been adequately investigated as yet, although they are important from many standpoints. An understanding of these differences would have direct application to the rehabilitation of the adult who must train for a new job because disease prevents him from pursuing his old one or because a changing industrial economy has eliminated his occupation. Research in this area would also have many other important practical applications.

A new area of adult training is that directed towards developing leadership and improving leadership skills. Research on leadership behavior has been conducted for over a quarter of a century in psychology, but research on the behavior of administrators in schools has appeared in any quantity only in recent years. Research on problems of leadership and administration emerged because psychologists saw the practical implications of laboratory studies which they had conducted and saw the possibilities of extending their work into a practical domain. Perhaps the most influential single study ever undertaken which appeared to have significance for the exploration of administrative problems was that by Lewin, Lippitt, and White (1939), later reported in full by White and Lippitt (1960). This study is so well known that it is only necessary to remind the reader that it involved the use of three types of leadership—described as *authoritarian, democratic,* and *laissez-faire*—each of which was studied in relation to the behavior and work output of groups of Boy Scouts. Considerable differences were found in the behavior of the different groups under the three types of leadership. This study and others led Lewin to become interested in problems of leadership development and the dynamics of groups. From Lewin's work there developed a field of research and training activity which has emerged as a force of considerable strength in our culture. A strong sponsor of leadership research which helped focus attention on problems of leadership and administration was the military, which did much to encourage such research in the postwar years. All branches of the service have realized that efficient weapons are not enough and that quality in leadership is a necessary component of an effective fighting force.

In the civilian area the work of Lewin was carried on after his death by many psychologists, including a group which was first attached to M.I.T. and which later moved to a research center at the University of Michigan where their group remained relatively intact. Research conducted by this group has explored the processes occurring in social situations and also the problem of training individuals in sensitivity to group processes.

Extensive possibilities for training and research on problems of group sensitivity are provided by the National Training Laboratories, which are operated by the National Education Association for these purposes.

Research on group processes and the dynamics of leadership has become such a specialized area in itself that the brief space devoted to it here can do no more than to acquaint the reader with the fact that such research, with its important implications for education, has already been developed at a sophisticated level. Those who wish to engage in research on administrative problems should familiarize themselves with the work already conducted on group process and leadership problems. Of particular importance are a series of studies conducted at Ohio State University mainly by Stogdill and Hemphill. Another source of information is a work by Thielen (1954). For a discussion of the problems of conducting work on leadership research in education, the reader may consult the relevant chapters in a volume edited by Halpin (1958).

Short-Term Studies of Personality Development

Studies of the development of interests and attitudes have had a long history. The preliminary excursions into the field of personality development and the educational conditions that affect it were probably stimulated by the existence of instruments for the measurement of personality characteristics. L.L. Thurstone, who developed the first well-designed attitude scales, also initiated research on the role of various pupil experiences in the development of attitudes. Throughout the 1930's, large numbers of studies relating attitude changes to educational experiences appeared in the literature. Such studies showed again and again that curricular materials designed to change attitudes did so in terms of responses to verbal attitude scales. There is as yet little evidence to show that the changes in attitudes measured by these scales are associated with corresponding changes in other phases of behavior. In recent years there have been some attempts to remedy this basic defect through the introduction of disguised attitude scales, which are designed in such a way that the person taking them is unaware of the purposes for which they are given. Scales of this type must still be considered to be experimental in character, and the relationship between behavior on such scales and behavior in other areas still needs to be established. There is also another question that must be raised about such studies: Are the changes produced just changes in superficial characteristics that have little deep value for the child? Changing a child's expressed attitude toward a racial minority by showing him a film may mean only that for a little while he will repeat the sentiments expressed in the film rather than those he has heard elsewhere.

Social psychologists have long struggled with the problem of developing a theory of attitudes. Clearly, attitudes are complex phenomena and their relationship to verbal behavior is not a simple one. An attempt by Katz and Stotland (1959) comes near to providing a theory which appears to have usefulness in the conduct of educational research. Katz and Stotland recognize that attitudes are complex and define their three major components: the *cognitive,* the *affective,* and the *action* components.

The cognitive component is that aspect of attitude that is related to knowledge. Attitudes toward political, religious, or racial groups, and so forth, are based to some extent on what the person "knows." The information involved in this "knowledge" may be correct or incorrect, but in either case it functions as a foundation on which the attitude is built. It forms what is referred to as the *cognitive basis of attitude.* The cognitive component, in the case of some attitudes, may be very weak. A person who is prejudiced against a particular religious group he knows little about has an attitude with a very weak cognitive component.

The affective component is that aspect of the attitude which involves what are commonly referred to as *feelings.* This component is what the typical attitude scale attempts to measure. There may be a strong affective component, as when a person has strong feelings about an object although he has little knowledge of it.

The action component represents the extent to which the attitude has habits of action associated with it. Some attitudes may have strong cognitive and affective components but almost no action component associated with them. A person who belongs to a particular church may know much about the church in terms of its history and theology, but he may still not attend services. His attitude toward the church thus lacks any appreciable action component.

Such a theory of attitudes accounts well for the fact that the typical attitude scale is a very poor predictor of what a person will do. It cannot be otherwise, for such a scale merely measures his feelings and provides no information concerning the strength of action components. If the Katz and Stotland theory is sound, it also suggests that much of attitude education in schools is futile since it limits itself to the development of the cognitive and the affective components alone.

The account of the Katz and Stotland theory presented here is an abbreviated version which necessarily omits many of the important concepts which it introduces. The aspect presented here was selected because of its importance for educational research and planning.

The guidance area is another in which educators have made a concentrated effort to produce personality changes of real consequence, and it is hardly surprising that this area has attracted many research workers interested in determining the changes that guidance programs produce. Early studies in the area were largely unsuccessful because of the lack of sensitivity of the measuring instruments available, and also because of the lack of a useful theory concerning the changes to be expected. When the author (1948) reviewed such studies, he could find no reported evidence that personality changes produced by guidance procedures were measurable. Recently, research methodologies have been developed that offer promise of measuring personality change resulting from guidance. Since 1948 considerable progress has been made in this area as a result of the bringing together of the theoretical position of Carl Rogers and the technical research skills of William Stephenson. These two men together evolved methods of studying the effects of counseling that have had great success in demonstrating personality changes resulting from the process. Stephenson, through the application of what he termed *Q-methodology*, was able to provide a technique for measuring important outcomes of counseling within the framework of the personality theory developed by Carl Rogers. This technique, unlike those previously used, was sufficiently sensitive to demonstrate changes occurring during counseling. This in itself constituted a major advance. Emphasis should be placed on the fact that successful developments in this area of research resulted from the bringing together of a theory and a technique through which the theory could be successfully explored.

THE DESIGN OF TRANSFER OF
TRAINING STUDIES

Research on the study of transfer of training has evolved distinct designs to handle the investigation of the problems involved. Most transfer experiments involve two learning tasks which are commonly designated *Task 1* and *Task 2*. The general purpose of such an experiment is to determine the effect of learning one of the tasks on the learning or retention of the other task. Two basic experimental designs are involved; these are known as the *retroaction* and the *proaction* designs.

The problem of generalization of learning, or transfer of training as it has been commonly called, is—from the educational standpoint—one of the most important areas of learning and development that can be investigated. If school learning were conceived to be the accumulation of isolated items of information, the expected consequences of education would be extremely limited. Fortunately this is not the case, for school learning is conceived largely as the learning of techniques, skills, principles, and methods that can be applied to a vast range of problems outside the school. This is possible because the solutions to some problems learned in school can be generalized to certain other problems outside school.

The retroaction design involves the following experimental procedure:

Transfer group: Performs Task 1—Performs Task 2—Performs Task 1
Control group: Performs Task 1—Rests or performs some unrelated task—Performs Task 2

This is referred to as the retroaction design since the backward effect of Task 2 on Task 1 is studied. In this design there is always a problem raised concerning what to do with the control group while the transfer group is performing Task 2. Just to allow them to rest is not satisfactory since this may give the control group some advantage over the transfer group. On the other hand, to engage the control group in some supposedly irrelevant task might conceivably raise or lower their subsequent performance on Task 2.

The proaction design is rather different and can be represented in the following way:

Transfer group: Performs Task 1—Performs Task 2
Control group: Rests or engages in irrelevant activity—Performs Task 2

In this design the purpose is to determine if the performance of Task 1 facilitates or interferes with the *subsequent* performance of Task 2. The task may be either a learning activity or merely a measure of performance at a particular level of learning. In most transfer experiments both tasks involve a learning activity.

Research on transfer at the beginning of this century typically involved learning situations similar to those which occur in schools, but the trend in recent times has been to use greatly simplified learning situations which bear only a remote resemblance to school learning. While the early studies were directed toward the determination of the amount of transfer from one school subject to another, more recent research has been aimed at the development of a theory of transfer. Thorndike's theory of transfer, known as the *identical elements theory*, held sway for over a quarter of a century. The inadequacies of this theory are now quite apparent. The problem is that of finding a substitute theory which can be of value in the designing of curricula and training programs.

Laboratory vs. Classroom Studies of Learning

The difficulties involved in the study of learning in the classroom situation have led many research workers to questioning the desirability of conducting experiments in the classroom—at least until much more knowledge has been acquired. There are two distinct points of view in this matter.

On the one hand, there are those who feel that meaningful experiments on learning are best undertaken in the classroom, since the realistic conditions under which learning actually occurs can be found there. This view is supported by the persuasive argument that it is usually unwise and often impossible to generalize from the laboratory situation to the classroom. In addition, children can be studied over a longer period of time in the classroom than is possible in the laboratory.

On the other side of the question, it is pointed out that the laboratory has produced many important findings about learning. It is proposed that learning phenomena be explored first in the laboratory, and—once positive results have been obtained—that an attempt be made to reproduce the results in the classroom situation.

No definitive statement can be made concerning which approach is likely to yield more information. The immense opportunities offered by each one of the two approaches suggest that both be explored. The research worker's disposition and interests —perhaps more than anything else—should determine which approach is taken at this time.

Some compromise between traditional laboratory approaches and direct studies of classroom phenomena is possible. For example, Van Wagenen and Travers, in a series of studies now in progress, are using what may be referred to as a *simulated classroom situation*. The studies are concerned with the effect of various reinforcing conditions on learning and require the use of an artificial eight-pupil classroom set up in a vacant room in an elementary school. The group meets for a given number of experimental sessions during which a trained adult performs the role of the teacher. Under such conditions one can compare the learning of pupils who are directly reinforced through interaction with the teacher with the learning of those who merely observe other children being reinforced. One can also experiment with other conditions related to reinforcement within this experimental situation. The "teacher" can administer reinforcements in different ways: by indicating whether the pupil is right or wrong, by indicating only when the pupil is wrong, by adding praise or reproof to the indication of right and wrong, and so forth. In such an artificially established classroom with an ad hoc group of pupils, experiments can be carried out which could not be undertaken in the typical classroom situation and control can be exercised over many important learning conditions. The situation also retains many of the important features of the classroom and thus reduces the hazards involved when generalization is made from experimental results to actual classroom situations.

STUDIES OF DEVELOPMENT OVER LONG PORTIONS OF THE LIFE SPAN

Some Traditional Approaches

Studies of development over the life span have their origin in the work of nineteenth century biologists. The study of life cycles had a prominent place in the curriculum developed by Thomas Henry Huxley for the training of biologists, and the influence of this curriculum is still evident today. The study of the development pattern as it was pursued by nineteenth century biologists involved the detailed description of changes in form and function as they occurred in the life cycle. This work had its origins in scientific curiosity, but, as often happens, important practical applications were soon found for the outcomes of this research. Information concerning the life cycle of small organisms became the means of controlling diseases such as malaria and yellow fever. Descriptive work on the development of organisms is still pursued because of the important impact it has on problems of public health.

The work of the biologist in the field of development has been mentioned here because it formed the foundation of the work that psychologists have pursued in this same area. The research of Jean Piaget is in the descriptive tradition of the biologist who has only very recently turned to experimental studies. Gesell's studies of the development of behavior in young children and Piaget's studies of the development of the higher mental processes are in the biologist's tradition of attempting to provide accurate records of changes as they occur in a living organism exposed to a particular environment. Figures VIII and IX pro-

FIGURE VIII. A study of the origin of number concepts. A girl, six years two months old, solving a problem involving the use of continuous quantities. (Photo by courtesy of Professor Bärbel Inhelder of the Institut des Sciences de l'Éducation de l'Université de Genève.)

vide illustrations of work in progress in Piaget's laboratory. The modification of development through modification of the environment represents a more advanced stage of educational inquiry. The fact that most long-term developmental studies in the educational field are of the descriptive type is no reflection on the research workers. It means only that they are still in the early stages of establishing a science. It is to their credit that they are pioneers.

Studies of development over short periods, such as six to twelve months, can be undertaken by most research workers who have had a reasonable amount of training and experience, but serious practical and theoretical difficulties arise when longer pe-

FIGURE IX. A longitudinal study of the development of geometrical concepts. A six-year-old boy in the process of solving a spatial problem and manifesting somewhat typical difficulties. (Photo by courtesy of Professor Bärbel Inhelder of the Institut des Sciences de l'Éducation de l'Université de Genève.)

riods of time are involved. This is particularly unfortunate, since all teachers and educational administrators must be concerned with the contribution that particular programs make to the life-time development of the individual. The elementary school teacher should rightly be concerned with the achievement of immediate goals such as the acquisition of reading skills, but he cannot forget to consider the effect of his teaching on behavior as far remote as that of adult life. One may hypothesize that the adult's attitude toward reading began its embryonic development in the elementary schoolroom, and that it underwent a prolonged and continuous period of growth. Although it may be hoped that the educational process itself shows continuity, there is not much evidence to show that this is accompanied by a corresponding continuity in the process of development.

Long-term studies of development may follow either one of two rather distinct patterns. In one type of study, an attempt is made to follow a group as it grows and moves forward through life, and every attempt is made to retain contact with all members of the original group. This is the hard way of conducting developmental studies. In the second type of study, no attempt is made to follow a whole group; instead, individuals at each one of several age levels are selected for study. This may be referred to as the *cross-sectional approach*. It has the obvious advantage of permitting the researcher to complete his developmental studies without waiting for individuals to grow up. This second technique has a long history. Its beginnings go back to the days of Francis Galton, who made the first systematic attempt to trace the growth and decline of human abilities. A brief review of one of his classic studies will be used here to reveal some of the weaknesses of the approach.

Galton's efforts to measure human characteristics and to trace their course of development not only represent pioneer attempts in scientific measurement but are also the first to cover the life span. The collection of data for these studies was made possible by the unusual circumstances presented by an international exhibition held at Earls Court, London, in 1884. Galton was invited to set up a booth at this exhibition, and he seized upon the opportunity of using it as a means of collecting data about a sample of persons whose ages spread across the entire life span. With this end in view, he set up a number of tests which covered such varied phenomena as height, speed of movement, the ability to make simple judgments such as those involved in bisecting a line or judging its perpendicularity, strength of grip, visual acuity, and so forth. The population on whom such measures were made consisted of those individuals who happened to visit the booth —people of the sort who typically visit exhibitions, some in almost every age group, but a preponderance of those in the younger groups.

Galton tabulated the data in order to arrive at a general impression of the curve of each of the abilities measured, and for more than a generation his data remained unique in the field. A curve derived from such data is presented in Figure X.

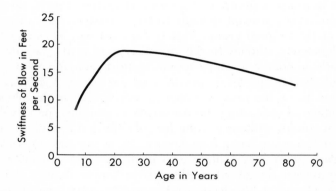

FIGURE X. Data illustrating changes with age. Relationship between age and swiftness of blow. (Data collected by Francis Galton in 1884 and later reported by Ruger and Stoessinger.)

A straightforward interpretation of data such as those presented in the figure just considered is not as sound as it might appear on the surface. The curve cannot be considered to represent the typical growth and decline that an individual might be expected to follow. The reasons for this must now be given consideration.

First, the older group in a population is always a selected sample of what was once a much larger population. A group born in 1970 will lose some of its members through death by 1980, and death is not an event that strikes at random. One can be quite sure that those who survive over the decade will be different in many respects from those who die. Among other things, the survivors will probably be living, for the most part, in more favorable economic circumstances than those who die. There will also probably be some selection for intelligence, in that the more intelligent will be more able to cope with the hazards of daily life. At the other end of the age scale there may well be selective survival for personality attributes that make for quiet and sober living. Thus in plotting the average of a given characteristic for each age group over the life span, one is plotting data for groups that are selectively changed at each age level. The data may be considerably different from those that would be obtained if the same group were measured at regular intervals through the years. On this account alone, the cross-sectional method of obtaining developmental data must be considered highly unsatisfactory except for the crudest purposes.

Second, if the cross-sectional method is adopted in a particular community, the results may be distorted by selective migration. For example, the author knows of a community on the northern border of the United States where in recent years there has been a tendency for the better-educated members of the young adult group to move south to the larger industrial centers. This migration has not affected either those in the upper grades of school or those in more advanced years. If an intelligence test were given to every member of this community and the average score for each age group were plotted against age, the result would be a curve which would show a rise up to about the age of twenty, then a decline, followed by another rise in the region of the early thirties. A graph of this kind could not possibly be considered to represent the rise and decline of intelligence in this population, because other conditions are operating to determine the shape of the curve.

Third, even if the problems that have just been discussed exist only in minimal amounts, there is another difficulty in the interpretation of data derived from the cross-sectional approach which must be considered. In the case of the individual there is doubt whether it is reasonable to expect that development occurs in the manner depicted by the smooth graphs resulting from the type of data collected by Galton. Functions such as height may show periods of acceleration and depression, which result from disease or particularly unfavorable or favorable circumstances in the child's environment as well as from changes in glandular functions. These important individual irregularities in developmental functions are obscured by the cross-sectional approach.

The longitudinal method of studying development is not without its difficulties. However, these are not related to the interpretation of the data but to the process of collecting them.

First, there is the obvious difficulty involved in waiting year after year for the data to accumulate. This difficulty is not necessarily insuperable, for many long-term studies have been made that require researchers to follow cases over a decade or more. Willard Olson (1949), for example, was able to follow the development of children on numerous variables as they progressed through school. He was not only able to plot individual curves for various functions, but he was also able to interrelate the different functions and to demonstrate that changes in development rate are related to many differing conditions. In addition, Olson was able to demonstrate a certain parallelism in the development of different functions, and he put forward the hypothesis that all development variables are functionally interrelated.

Second, there is the problem of attrition. It is not uncommon for a researcher involved in, say, a ten-year study to find that fewer than one third of his cases remain by the end of that period. If funds for travel are available, it may be possible to follow those who have left the community, but this is an expensive process. In planning follow-up studies, the researcher would do well to choose a community in which a highly stable population, without much emigration, is known to exist. Whatever procedure is adopted, attrition adds immensely to the cost of the study, if only because this factor makes it necessary to start with far more cases than are to be included in the completed study.

Third, there is the difficulty of sustaining the interest and cooperation of the subjects in the study. This is not too much of a problem when the subjects are "captive," as they are in experimental schools run by universities and colleges, but it is a problem when the subjects must be contacted at their homes and brought into the laboratory for study. Under such conditions, it may be desirable to reward the subjects with a knowledge of their performance and perhaps with money, too, if any is available. With adults, an effort may be made to keep the group informed of the purposes and progress of the study, but this attempt to stimulate interest will probably have appeal only to the brighter elements in the group.

The points raised here should indicate to the reader the time, money, and effort that are required for the successful completion of a longitudinal study of development.

A final point to be made is that a study could be designed in which the cross-sectional and the longitudinal approaches were combined. In such a study, the cross-sectional approach might be used as a preliminary check on hypotheses and those which were consistent with the data could then be rechecked in a longitudinal study.

NEWER APPROACHES: I. THE MANIPULATION OF CONDITIONS RELATED TO DEVELOPMENT

As scientists have become aware of the inadequacy of the concept that development follows a fixed pattern, attempts have been made to study the effect of modifications of the environment on the developmental pattern. Such studies can be made by two different procedures. Suppose that one were interested in studying the effect of lack of interaction with adults during early childhood on the subsequent social behavior of the school-age child. One way to go about such a study would be to find groups of children who, through circumstances, had little contact with adults and to compare their subsequent behavior with that of children who had had relatively high amounts of interaction with adults. The socially deprived group would probably be composed of children from foundling homes and orphanages, while children raised in typical homes (and whose mothers did not work outside the home) would constitute the high social-interaction group. An immediate difficulty stems from the fact that the two groups differ not only with respect to the amount of social interaction with adults, but also with respect to other important factors which may affect the results of the study. The foundling group is likely to come from genetically inferior stock. Many of the foundling children will have suffered from serious malnutrition and exposure prior to admission. In the foundling home they are likely to lack intellectual as well as social stimulation. These factors may well account for any subsequent social difficulties which such children display, and the lack of interaction with adults in the foundling home may be only a minor factor in the total picture. Similar difficulties are likely to plague all research workers who attempt to study long-term development through the study of selected groups.

A second approach is to manipulate experimentally the conditions which one may desire to study. One of the most famous examples of this procedure is found in the work of McGraw (1935, 1943), who conducted studies of development on twins. In these studies one twin was given special training in a skill, such as stair-climbing, while the other twin was deprived of both the training and the opportunity to acquire the skill until the age at which the skill typically appears. In technical terms, one would say that in these studies the condition experimentally manipulated was training. The results of Myrtle McGraw's experiments on training conditions in relation to development are well known. The effect of the special training on the course of the development of the skill was negligible. Once he was given the opportunity to learn, the twin that had had no special training rapidly acquired the skill and caught up with his specially trained twin. Deferred training was much more efficient than training spread out over a very extended period which began at much earlier age levels.

The general results are mentioned because from them emerged a number of educational doctrines which represented unjustified generalizations from limited scientific data. The general conclusion which tended to be drawn from such studies was that learning should be posponed until maturation reached the point at which learning could occur rapidly and efficiently. This conclusion does not follow from the data provided by studies such as those of McGraw. Indeed, the results have to be interpreted today in a way entirely different from that in which they were originally interpreted. Consider, for example, the case of twins, one of whom was trained in stair-climbing while the other was not. The assumption is made that the one not given special training did not have relevant learning experiences, but such was almost certainly not the case. A young child who had never seen a staircase would still have had extensive opportunity to learn the components of the skill of stair-climbing. Merely pulling himself to his feet and then climbing on a chair would involve all the component skills involved in stair-climbing. Thus, the twin given special training in stair-climbing may have had only a negligibly greater amount of experience than the other twin. Much of what were considered to be the effects of maturation in such experiments were more probably the results of learning by daily experience and bear a close resemblance to what Hebb has referred to as "early learning." Of course, some of the skills involved in such developmental studies are motor functions closely allied with inborn mechanisms in the nervous system that would minimize the effect of special intensive early training.

A review by Fowler (1962) serves to point out that the generalization from early developmental studies which emphasizes the role of maturation was an unjustified conclusion. He marshals ample evidence to show that in the area of conceptual and perceptual development early training may have dramatic results in producing precociousness. Many of the studies he cites, which describe effective training in the first few years of life, need to be repeated. For example, he cites a study by Davidson (1931) in which children in the three-to-five-year-old range were given training in reading ten to fifteen minutes a day with remarkable results. Although many of these children were of average ability (as measured by an intelligence test), they made substantial progress and two of the three-year-olds completed the equivalent of a first-grade program and were well on the way to becoming fluent readers. Such studies need to be repeated for, if they are reproducible, they have enormously important implications for the planning of education. A perusal of other sections of Fowler's review will reveal many other exciting studies which need to be reproduced and which could well form the basis for a thesis or dissertation.

Although variables related to the development of intellectual and motor skills can be manipulated and controlled by the experimenter, there are some conditions that cannot. The relationship of the mother to the child is considered to be of the greatest importance to the development of personality, but mothers cannot be trained or persuaded to handle their children in particular ways for the sake of a scientific inquiry. For this reason, many studies relating important environmental conditions, such as child rearing practices, to personality development of the child must be undertaken by other means. In such a case, the study has to be conducted by finding parents who display different child-rearing practices and then relating these practices to the characteristics of the children. Sears *et al.* (1957) provide an example of such a procedure. In this study an investigation was made of both the child-rearing practices and the behavior of the children, and some effort was made to relate the two. Such a procedure is not as sound as the experimental approach and is likely to yield less information. To illustrate this problem it may be pointed out that child-rearing practices are to some extent related to social class; hence one cannot be sure that a particular effect on the child is due to the child-rearing practices, as such, or whether it is a result of some other aspect of social class. Experimental procedures avoid this difficulty in those cases in which they can be applied.

NEWER APPROACHES: II. RESEARCH ON THE DEVELOPMENT OF INDIVIDUAL DIFFERENCES

In recent years a new type of study has appeared which is designed to throw light on the development of individual differences. Textbooks on educational psychology published as far back as the first decade of this century noted the fact that there is great uniformity of behavior at the beginning of human life. As the child grows, there is a constant increase in the amount of differentiated behavior that appears, and individuals show an ever-increasing range of differences in the responses they manifest to a given situation. Thurstone was so much impressed with this fact that he proposed that a convenient zero of intelligence might be established at that point at which individual differences vanish.

Most measures of intellectual ability indicate a tendency for individual differences to increase as age increases. Some caution should be exercised in the interpretation of this fact, since the change in the spread of scores may be as much a product of the measuring instrument as it is of the function that is being measured. Instruments available for measuring intellectual skills may be such that they do not measure individual differences adequately at the lower levels. In other words, individual differences at all age levels may be identical. This interpretation is generally not considered acceptable, for it does not fit the common observation that young babies show little in the way of individual differences, their repertoire of behavior being limited to a small number of responses that all (or very nearly all) babies show.

A new approach to this problem has been taken in recent years through the extension of factor-analytic methods to this area. The reader is undoubtedly familiar with the fact that most batteries of aptitude tests that are administered to adults can be considered to measure a limited number of factors—the verbal factor, the numerical factor, the deductive reasoning factor, and so forth. It has been postulated by many workers that tests given in the lower grades do not manifest the existence of a series of underlying traits represented by these factors, but, rather, that they appear to demonstrate only the existence of a single general intelligence factor. The differentiation of behavior that occurs as education progresses is accompanied by the appearance of the distinct abilities that are measured by typical aptitude batteries. The procedure for studying this problem has been to administer batteries of similar tests at various age levels. The batteries used must be such that the tests differ in difficulty but not in content. Thus an arithmetic reasoning test would be one in which the problems at all levels involve reasoning with quantities, but differed from level to level in the complexity of the reasoning process involved. The computations involved should be of the same order of simplicity at all levels, since the computation aspect measures a factor different from that measured by the reasoning aspect. After such batteries have been administered to a series of different age groups, factor-analytic procedures are applied in order to determine whether the same underlying structure of abilities appears at the different age levels. While the evidence derived from such studies remains somewhat ambiguous, it does nevertheless tend to support the hypothesis that factors emerge in the structure of human ability as the individual grows up.

Looking Backward: A Technique for Developmental Studies

There are limited possibilities for conducting developmental studies by searching in the records for data that have already been collected on individuals. For example, many school systems administer intelligence tests at regular intervals through perhaps as many as twelve grades. The researcher may look back through the records of the system and trace the development of particular individuals who have passed through it. With these data and a little patience, it may be possible to trace their subsequent development and hence to have a record that covers two or more decades.

A major difficulty in following this procedure stems from the fact that school records rarely contain the material in which the researcher is interested. Also, school records in the matter of tests are far from being the reliable sources of information that one would like them to be. Too often, the records show the entry of an intelligence quotient without giving any indication of the test on which it is based. It is well known that intelligence quotients based on different tests are not comparable; hence such data must be considered to be largely uninterpretable. The professional staff of schools should not be blamed for this situation, since they often are fully aware of its existence but unable to remedy it because of lack of the clerical help needed for the keeping of adequate records.

When data are available that adequately document the tests given as well as the scores, another problem arises. This is a result of the fact that different tests are often given at different times in the school program. If these data are to be used, it is necessary to convert the various test scores to a common base. The data for doing this may or may not be available. At best, such converted scores are far from being as satisfactory as scores based on comparable tests. The conversion process itself tends to weaken the data because it involves the use of constants that are only imperfectly estimated.

An unusually novel approach to problems of development has been evolved by D.R. Miller and G.E. Swanson (1958). These investigators were initially impressed with earlier studies that had demonstrated that some social and economic groups manifest a higher incidence of certain mental diseases than did other groups. For example, the lower socioeconomic groups produce more than their fair share of schizophrenics. Now, while this is an important empirical finding, it does not indicate *why* this relationship exists. Miller and Swanson set themselves the task of investigating this and similar relationships for the purpose of determining the variables in the background of the individual that have important effects on certain aspects of later personality.

The general procedure adopted was that of identifying a sample of subjects to be studied, obtaining information about the child-rearing practices to which they had been exposed early in life, and then determining the response of each to a number of situations in which conflicts of motives had been aroused. In order to limit the number of variables operating, the selection of subjects was narrowed by confining the group to white Protestant boys who had been born north of the Mason-Dixon line. Additional restrictions included were that they had to be within one year of the average grade of boys of their age, emotionally stable, above average in intelligence, and from stock that did not come from northwest Europe. Those from broken homes were also eliminated. The application of all of these criteria resulted in retention for the study of only 1 per cent of the boys available. The extreme care exercised over the selection of subjects should emphasize to the reader the importance of this phase of a well-planned series of studies.

The mothers of all the boys included in the study were interviewed. In order to determine the way in which the boys responded to conflict situations, projective tests related to such conflicts were administered. These tests were all of the story-completion type and were designed to determine the way in which the individual responds to a situation involving a conflict of motives. The tests were also administered after the individuals had been exposed to a realistic situation in which the same conflict of motives was likely to occur.

The technique employed by these investigators is likely to be a productive one, and some of the relationships discovered are of considerable interest, even though they should not necessarily be accepted at face value. For example, they found very definite relationships between the type of maternal discipline exercised and the way in which the subject expressed aggression. However, maternal discipline is not related to the severity of guilt feelings or to the development of defenses against these feelings. Time of weaning was found to be related to severity of guilt about death wishes (wishing someone were dead), about stealing, and about disobedience.

A major difficulty in the interpretation of the results of this series of studies stems from the possibility that the background conditions studied may not be the ones that are really producing long-term effects on behavior. It is possible, for example, that age of weaning may be related to a whole host of important attitudes on the part of the mother. These attitudes, in turn, may have important consequences on child development. Thus it may be that attitudes rather than time of weaning are producing the particular effects. The chief strength of the studies stems from the fact that the results fit rather well a widely held theory of the Freudian type.

The technique is essentially an historical one. An attempt is made to reconstruct past events on the basis of documents and reports. Such reconstructions are always difficult to undertake, particularly when they involve the human memory over a span of many years. Historians, who have learned to exercise great caution in the use of evidence, might well discard as useless the kind of evidence which psychologists sometimes use in developmental studies when they try to reconstruct what happened in a particular home twenty years earlier.

Studies of Changes in the Later Years

Considerable interest has been manifested in recent years in research into changes in intellectual functions and personality characteristics in the later years of life. Much of this interest stems from the fact that during the 1930's the country was faced with the probability that the mean age of the population would show a steady increase as a result of the low birth rate. The implication of this fact was that there would be an increasing number of older workers, many of whom would need retraining for new jobs in a rapidly changing technology, and that there would be other problems of the utilization of the time of this section of the population. These problems of education, counseling, and recreation seemed to provide a new and intriguing field for research, although perhaps it must be said that they attracted the sentimentalists rather than the mature and established research workers. The poor quality of much that has been done in this area in the last fifteen years is probably accounted for by this fact. It has also been responsible for the endless array of questionnaires that have cluttered the field.

A central problem of considerable scientific and educational interest that has been studied in this area is that of the extent to which different abilities show decline during adulthood. There has been much speculation concerning the over-all changes in the functions of the nervous system over the entire life span, and Hebb (1949) has attempted to build a theory concerning these changes. Hebb's book is a fascinating effort to coordinate and make sense out of a conglomeration of data, and it should be read by all who are concerned with changes in intellectual functions over the years. However, Hebb's theory does not provide a useful conception of any differential decline that is to be expected in the later years of life.

Empirical studies of the decline of abilities are extremely difficult to undertake for reasons that have already been discussed, such as differential mortality among different ability groups. There are also problems in testing older individuals, for such persons may be very poorly motivated in the testing situation and may fail to show any enthusiasm for finding out their abilities. Insofar as this is so, the decline in measured ability may be at least partly a function of declining motivation. Just what abilities should be measured in the older adult in order to appraise his continued capacity to make a contribution to a community is also problematic. In the case of the young, it is common to study development in terms of those abilities that are known to be related to educability in the academic sense of the term, but one does not know whether these same abilities are related to the educability of the older adult. The problems in this area represent an important field of educational research, but one that should be approached with the greatest caution, for the difficulties involved in making genuine advances are immense.

A related problem is the determination of the age at which man reaches his peak performance in particular activities. The importance of this problem to education becomes clear when it is pointed out that education should be planned so that the years of maximum ability are not those primarily occupied with course work. This may be the case at present, for the tendency is for the doctoral degree to be completed in the late twenties, while in many areas the period of maximum performance may well be the early twenties. The subject is not without problems from a research viewpoint. While the usual techniques have involved the determination of the average age at which the great men of history produced their finest works, one cannot deduce from the evidence that this age truly represents a peak of performance of the nervous system. Perhaps this peak of performance is mainly a product of the cultural conditions under which the persons involved happen to work.

Contrasting Empirical Data on Development with a Theory of Development

Most of the discussion of long-term development studies up to this point has been concerned with the problem of tracing the course of development as it occurs in contemporary society. This information is of only limited value, because it provides no indication whatsoever concerning the conditions that must exist in order for particular aspects of development to be maximized. Perhaps there is some value in knowing what is the typical pattern of growth, for then it is possible to know whether some observed behavioral phenomenon is unusual for a particular age group. The parent is then able to know much about the behavior to expect of a child at each age level. However, despite this information, the parent would still not know how to handle deviations from the expected pattern, for data do no more than describe typical patterns.

It has been stressed that the merely descriptive represents only an initial step in scientific work. A science on which educational procedures are to be based would have to provide information concerning the relationship of various environmental conditions to development. How this aspect of a science of education is to be built cannot be clearly seen from the present vantage point. Similar children cannot be subjected to different environmental conditions *over long periods* in order that the effect of these conditions on development can be studied. It is true that children can be found who have been exposed to different conditions, but there can be no certainty that any differences are the product of those conditions, for the children may have inherited dissimilar characteristics before they were exposed to these conditions.

Summary

1. Studies of development are concerned with time trends and behavior. The early studies in this area attempted to map out changes in behavior that occurred as the child advanced in years and were little concerned with the influence of the environment on behavior.

2. The early studies also tended to be qualitative and descriptive and were therefore limited in what they could achieve. The introduction of quantitative methods has vastly increased the value of the knowledge which studies of development can yield.

3. Studies of development over relatively short periods of a few months are generally concerned with the effect of learning conditions in school on the behavior of the child. Most of these have had to be restricted to intellectual development because of the limited techniques available for studying changes in personality.

4. Research on learning in school has been conducted within many different theoretical frameworks. Present research on learning shows the influence of four main trends. First, there is the influence of Hull and a drive-reduction concept of learning. Second, there is the influence of Skinner, who emphasizes the importance of collecting large quantities of data so that the general nature of learning phenomena can be mapped out. Third, there is the influence of Lewin, who introduced such concepts as *conflict, self-concept,* and *level of aspiration,* and who recognized the importance of certain types of group processes in relation to learning. Finally, there is the influence of Hebb, who has been notable in his emphasis on the importance of the early stage of learning.

5. Extensive research on the role of reinforcement in classroom learning is now in progress. Some of this consists of laboratory studies, but some research is also undertaken in the classroom itself. Other research has stressed personality factors in learning and a large body of literature exists on the role of the self-concept in learning. However, there are still many unsolved technical difficulties with respect to research on the self-concept.

6. Research on perceptual learning has shown substantial growth in the last decade based on a multiplicity of different theoretical frameworks. Particularly important for the planning of education are the studies of Hebb on early perceptual learning. A second area of importance is the study of conditions that facilitate and interfere with perception. A third is the study of concept formation.

7. Research on problems of adult education go back to studies by Thorndike, who became interested in the extent to which older persons could learn as well as younger ones. In recent times there has been much interest in research on leadership and group processes because of the concern for training persons for administrative positions.

8. Substantial research has been undertaken on the development of attitudes and interests. Much of the research on the effect of teaching practices on attitude development conducted in the 1930's came before understanding of the complex nature of attitudes had been achieved. While objectives of education usually assume that attitudes will have action components, typical attitude education may do almost nothing to develop such action tendencies.

9. Special designs have been developed for the study of transfer of training. At present, studies of transfer generally are not undertaken in schools; they require simplified laboratory settings.

10. One cannot say at present whether laboratory studies are superior or inferior to classroom studies. Probably both should be undertaken if an understanding of the problems of learning and teaching is to be achieved.

11. Much of the early work on the study of human development was an attempt to produce accurate descriptions of the develop-

ment process. The assumption was that many features of the behavior of the growing organism were relatively independent of training or that the environment was sufficiently uniform from child to child that individual differences in the features studied would not occur.

12. A more advanced approach to problems of development is found in studies which attempt to assess the impact of some aspects of the environment on development. One procedure for doing this is to use twins: one twin is given special training while the other is not. The approach is not limited to the study of twins.

13. Many studies undertaken in the 1930's supported a maturationist point of view, for little effect was noted when special training was given during infancy. These conclusions, however, cannot be generalized to conceptual development.

14. While some research on the development of aptitudes and individual differences has been undertaken, the picture which emerges is far from clear. The role which adequate opportunities for early learning play in the development of aptitudes needs to be explored.

15. Some developmental studies which involve an enquiry back into the life history of the individual have been undertaken. Such studies encounter all the difficulties historians encounter in their attempts to reconstruct history.

Some Problems for the Student

1. In recent years some businessmen have advocated a technique known as *brainstorming* as a means of obtaining new and original approaches to their problems. A group that "brainstorms" a problem first holds a session in which there is a free flow of ideas, and no idea is ever criticized during this session. The production of wild ideas is encouraged, and no critical evaluations are allowed. At a later session the ideas are evaluated and sifted for merit, with the purpose of isolating those that have practical value. The advocates of brainstorming claim that through this technique everybody can become creative.

Design a study in which an attempt is made to determine whether training in brainstorming techniques results in increased production of new ideas, and, if such an effect is found, whether it will transfer to areas of thinking other than that in which training has taken place. Assume that it will be possible to introduce training in brainstorming in high school classes.

2. A research worker was interested in determining whether curves of the development of different functions tended to be parallel; that is to say, whether an increase or decrease in one function was accompanied by a corresponding increase or decrease in other functions. He was able to administer tests of vocabulary and arithmetic reasoning to pupils who were starting the ninth grade, and administered parallel forms of the same test to the same pupils at the beginning of each subsequent grade in high school. The height and weight of the pupils were also measured when they returned to school each year.

What characteristics must the tests possess in order that the data may be used to test the hypotheses in which the scientist was interested? What units would be satisfactory for plotting curves for all functions for a single individual on the same sheet of paper? After the data, which had been plotted on graph paper, had been examined visually for the expected phenomena, what other methods could be used for examining the data?

CHAPTER 13

EXPERIMENTATION IN EDUCATION

Terminology

There are certain terms used in experimental research in the behavioral sciences with which the reader should be familiar. The person or other living organism whose behavior is studied in an investigation or experimental inquiry is referred to as the *subject,* or sometimes simply as *S.* In the literature of experimental psychology, *S* may stand equally well for a rat, a monkey, or a human being. It is an impersonal term denoting the living organism that is the center of the study. The person who conducts the investigation or manipulates the experimental conditions is the *experimenter,* a term commonly abbreviated as *E.*

THE MEANING OF LABORATORY EXPERIMENTATION

The word *experiment* has many different meanings. Scientists of the past have generally used it in a broad sense to cover explorations which cannot be considered to involve rigorous testing of hypotheses. Many of these experiments are explorations in which the scientist has no clear hypothesis but only at the back of his mind the thought: "I wonder what would happen if I did this?" Some important examples of this kind of experimentation can be found in current literature. For example, Hebb (1945) exposed chimpanzees to a number of different stimuli in order to determine the nature of those that evoke fear responses. Such an exploration may produce definite hypotheses which can be tested later in specific experiments. Much of the research which sparked the development of the physical sciences was of this character. The work of Michael Faraday at the Royal Institution, and his manipulations of wires and magnets and solutions, fits this pattern, and so too does the work of Mendeleyev, who "experimented" with different ways of ordering the elements until they fell into the pattern of the periodic table. This kind of experimentation was successful in the hands of a Faraday or a Mendeleyev, but these were men who ranked among the greatest of their generation. Such exploratory activity without a clear goal in mind is rarely successful when undertaken by the inexperienced, let alone by those who lack the acme of creative genius. Yet the fact is that such activity has been characteristic of a majority of those who laid the foundation of the physical sciences. To the examples of Faraday and Mendeleyev one may add Cavendish, who, burning hydrogen, discovered that the product was water; Magleigh, who conducted experiments on the polarization of light; Boyle, who mixed acids and alkalies to produce compounds with properties different from those of their original constituents; and numerous others. These exploratory demonstrations or experiments, as they have been called, form the very cornerstones of physics and chemistry.

In this chapter consideration will be given to experimentation in the narrow sense of the term rather than in the broad meaning discussed in the previous paragraph. In this narrow meaning, *experimentation* refers to a situation in which some condition or conditions are deliberately varied in order that the effect of this variation may be studied. In classical experimentation, a single variable is studied; but in some of the more modern experimental designs the effect of several variables may be studied within the framework of a single experiment. The reason for restricting our discussion to this kind of experimentation and excluding the exploratory type of experiment is that the latter appears to be quite unsuited to the beginning research worker—unless he is a rare genius.

Just as there is no clear-cut line of demarkation between the carefully planned laboratory experiment and the demonstration or exploration, so too is there none between field studies and laboratory experiments. In a school that has a cooperative administration, one may divide third-grade pupils into two groups by random assignment. One may then determine the relationship between spelling ability and differing amounts of daily drill in spelling (given over, say, a two-month period). The researcher would have to arrange for the teacher in the one group to give, say, five minutes a day of drill in spelling and for the other teacher to give, say, fifteen. In order to take into account the fact that teachers differ in their ability to teach, more than two teachers and more than two groups would have to be involved in such an experiment. In this case the school is used as a laboratory and a variable—the quantity of drill—is manipulated.

A very similar study might have been conducted on a field study basis without manipulating the variable quantity of drill.

The scientist might have selected fifty classes approximately equal in spelling skill at the start of the third grade. He then might have obtained a measure of how much time was devoted to spelling drill in each one of the classes during a three-month period and, at the end of that time, he might have measured the spelling skill of each pupil in each class once more. Thus an estimation could be made of the relationship between spelling skill and drill, but the knowledge thus achieved would be much less certain than that derived from the experiment previously discussed. It is possible that those teachers who provided the greatest amount of spelling drill were those working in districts where parents were concerned about spelling and were giving their children help in this skill in the home. Thus, in the field study, classroom drill in spelling might be augmented by help in the home, and the observed gains might as easily be a product of that help as a product of drill conducted by the teacher. For reasons such as this, the laboratory type of study—wherever it can be carried out—is likely to yield more useful and more certain information than the field study.

In the case of many studies to be conducted in school situations, it is not possible to manipulate those variables it is wished to manipulate. When this occurs, if it is still desired to conduct the particular experiment, it becomes necessary to do so in the laboratory or in special buildings or facilities set aside for this purpose. When this is done, it is often necessary to simplify greatly the conditions that occur in the classroom, and the experimenter may decide to conduct his experiments with one pupil at a time rather than thirty.

There are those who raise the cry "Artificiality!" when the proposal is made that studies be conducted under the grossly simplified conditions of the typical laboratory experiment. This criticism should be evaluated in terms of the fact that most of our knowledge of the highly complex events of the physical world has been derived from the study of simplified events that the scientist has studied in the laboratory. The study of simplified phenomena under artificial conditions has been a highly successful technique in developing useful knowledge.

The term *experimental school* should receive comment at this time. Sometimes such schools are also called *laboratory schools*, but in actual fact they are not experimental in the sense in which the term is used here. Neither do they provide laboratory conditions—that is to say, conditions under which carefully controlled experiments can be conducted. The term *experimental* in this context refers more to the *novel* character of the curriculum and to the fact that something new is being tried out rather than to experimentation in the technical sense of the term. In this chapter, we are concerned with controlled experimentation in the laboratory sense rather than with the uncontrolled study of curricular innovations.

Experimentation may occur within the laboratory or outside it. Laboratory studies usually require relatively small numbers of subjects and the careful control of many factors that cannot be controlled in other situations. When experimentation requires equipment or complex apparatus, it may be necessary to work within the laboratory. Of course the laboratory itself introduces variables which it may be desirable to control but which cannot be controlled easily. For instance, human subjects who are introduced into a laboratory expect to behave in a certain way, or at least feel that the situation calls for certain kinds of responses.

Experimentation is likely to be conducted in classrooms when it is desired to use fairly large groups and when it is considered necessary to study pupils in what might be termed their natural habitat. Of course, if it becomes known that an experiment is being conducted, this knowledge affects the behavior manifested by pupils and others. There are real difficulties in manipulating conditions outside the laboratory, and some of these are considered in other parts of this chapter.

There are a great many situations other than the laboratory and the classroom in which experimentation may be undertaken. Indeed, any situation in which relevant conditions can be manipulated may be considered as potentially one in which experimentation may be carried out.

The Need for a Cautious Approach to Experimentation

Experimentation is the most powerful method for deriving knowledge that has any certainty of validity, hence, it should be vigorously pursued. Nevertheless, experimentation is one of the more difficult of methods to pursue successfully. It is therefore necessary to consider in considerable detail all the common difficulties that experimental studies are likely to encounter. This is likely to give the student the impression that the difficulties of experimentation are so many and so widespread that the new researcher should simply avoid experimental studies. Such an inference should not be drawn; rather, the reader should take the approach that once he is forewarned of the difficulties commonly encountered, he is well equipped to design productive experimental studies.

Before considering the difficulties involved in experimentation in education, brief consideration will be given to the role of experimentation in the development of any science. While it is commonly said that experimentation is the path by which a science advances, this should not be taken to mean that it is the only one. Most of the major figures who have advanced science in the last hundred years have not been notable as experimentalists. Einstein never carried out a major experiment, and neither did Darwin or Freud. While experimental workers have checked many of the deductions of Einstein, these experiments followed rather than preceded major advances. To a considerable extent, experiments serve to consolidate advances already made rather than to make advances in and of themselves. Priestley's experimental studies of combustion served to demonstrate to the scientific world what he already was sure was true. Much classic experimentation serves the purpose of demonstrating to the world at large what the scientist already knows to be the case. The moral to be drawn is perhaps summarized by the statement that while thought without experimentation may be productive, experimentation without thought is futile. In other words, when the student embarks on an experiment, it is assumed that he is checking some aspect of a well-thought-out theory, which may be his own or somebody else's.

Let us now face squarely some of the major difficulties encountered in developing experimental studies, realizing that well-designed experiments can be carried out by the student who is aware of the common pitfalls.

CONCERNING DIFFICULTIES IN MANIPULATING EXPERIMENTAL CONDITIONS

Some variables can be successfully and easily manipulated in experiments with human subjects, while others cannot. Most of the experimentation that has been undertaken in the field of education has involved the manipulation of learning conditions—perhaps because these are the most readily manipulated. Unfortunately, much of this work fails to meet the standards of good experimentation because in reading an account of the experiments one cannot determine just what was the nature of the variable manipulated. When one reads that one group of classes was taught by progressive methods and one group by traditional methods, one has little basis for inferring just how the two groups of classes differed in the learning conditions provided. They probably differed in numerous unspecified ways.

The first rule to follow in designing an experiment is to be sure one knows exactly how conditions are to be varied among the experimental groups. This is much more than a matter of attaching labels such as "progressive" or "traditional." If such categories are to be used, then a clear set of specifications must be drawn up to establish just how these two sets of learning conditions are to differ. Such a set of specifications would have to indicate the characteristic behaviors of teachers and their interactions with pupils under these two conditions and also any other teaching events which distinguish one method from the other. In addition, some provision would have to be made to collect data in the classes in order to determine whether the conditions actually differed in the way in which they were supposed to differ in terms of the experimental design. But even if all this were done, the experiment would still not be worth undertaking as a scientific endeavor for it would involve a jumble of variables and no clear-cut conclusion could be drawn concerning the relationship of particular learning to the achievement of the pupils. Experiments which make significant contributions to knowledge involve the manipulation of much simpler conditions. While the chapter on development gives consideration to some of the variables which can be profitably introduced into learning studies, consideration will be given here to the extent to which some of these variables represent manipulable conditions.

Conditions related to the presentation of information. Some of these variables have been extensively studied in connection with the use of new educational media. For example, many studies have been undertaken which compare the relative effectiveness of visual and aural presentations of content. On the surface such studies appear to be easy, but they involve all kinds of difficulties. One can readily present information by means of movies or by lecture, but there are difficulties in insuring that the same amount of information is presented through the two media. Furthermore, the visual medium may present the information in pictorial form or in written form. If the written form is used, the outcomes of the experiment may be determined by the fact that reading rate is generally more rapid than speech—which gives an advantage to the visual presentation. A comparison of the effectiveness of different media may not make too much sense at this time. Perhaps a more important problem is that of determining the particular techniques which can be effectively used with each medium. In addition there are important problems to be studied concerning the value of transmitting information through more than one sensory channel. Many major projects which involve the development of movies for instructional purposes have implicitly assumed that the use of ears *and* the eyes is better than the use of either alone and that both sensory channels should be used simultaneously. This assumption is probably unwarranted and suggests a whole area for research.

Conditions related to feedback. While Thorndike stressed the importance of knowledge of results, this is still a neglected though promising area for research which permits the manipulation of important variables. Research already indicates that the manner in which a teacher marks and comments on the papers of the students may make a substantial difference in their learning rate, but as yet relatively little is known about the value of various classes of reinforcement. Insofar as the feedback of information calls for behavior on the part of the teacher, difficulty may be experienced in exerting experimental control. However, feedback provided by written comments and by various ways of enabling a student to check on his answers when workbooks are used are clearly amenable to experimental study. Perhaps such studies are more easily carried out in classrooms run along traditional lines than in those with a more modern atmosphere. In the classroom run along more progressive lines, much of the feedback is provided by peers in informal ways and little control can be exerted over it.

One of the conditions related to feedback which has produced interesting and consistent results is failure, which has generally been demonstrated to have a depressing effect on intellectual processes. However, most of the studies of this problem have been laboratory studies and much more needs to be learned about the effect of failure in a classroom situation.

Conditions related to classroom management. The experimentally-minded educational research worker is likely to be tempted to manipulate conditions of classroom management. Studies which attempt to compare one condition of classroom management with another are generally referred to as *studies of teaching methods.* The experimenter simply does not have the control over this class of variable needed to undertake much in the way of systematic experimentation. Much the same thing may be said of experiments with administrative conditions. The administrator is not able to change or modify his pattern of administration at will. One might hazard the generalization that experiments in which humans are required to produce a change in their own behavior as the variable manipulated are not likely to be very good experiments.

Some further consideration must be given to this problem. Suppose that a student desires to study the effect of certain aspects of teacher behavior, such as the number of rewarding statements, on specific aspects of pupil learning. Teachers may be quite willing to cooperate and to provide a specified amount of praise for pupil accomplishment, but some teachers will be much more convincing than others when they praise a pupil. If an experiment has been set up involving a group of teachers who administer much praise and a group who administer little praise, the experimenter can be sure—however well he has trained and rehearsed the teachers in their respective roles—that some teachers will deviate markedly from the prescribed course of action. Whenever behavior is the condition to be manipulated, we cannot expect to conduct experiments with clear-cut results. Even more complicated and unsatisfactory are experiments in which the co-operating teachers are personally involved in the outcome and hence are likely to be influenced in their behavior by their own desires. Most experimental demonstrations of the merits of progressive methods in education suffer from this limitation, particularly because they usually require teachers who believe in so-called progressive methods to adopt, for experimental purposes, methods that they believe to be unsound. What happens under such conditions is that the teaching methods with which the progressive methods are to be compared are presented in a way that can be described only as a caricature. The results of such studies obviously cannot demonstrate any useful principle.

The main source of difficulty in controlling teacher behavior stems from the fact that, while the experimenter may wish to control the behavior, much of it is actually controlled by the teacher's own motives and by his desire to see one outcome of the experiment rather than another.

However, there is another source of difficulty, which is the inability of certain teachers to assume certain roles. It is just no use asking some teachers to attempt to teach by methods that require them to act as authority figures. These teachers simply cannot assume that kind of a role because it is inconsistent with their personalities and life goals, and because they do not have the repertoire of responses needed for playing the part. For similar reasons, other teachers are capable of playing only an authoritarian role in the classroom and would feel threatened by the classroom situation if they could not maintain full control of it. Since this experimental difficulty is not always recognized by researchers, many experiments are undertaken in which the results depend more on the personal makeup of the participating teachers than on any other factor.

There is a final matter to be considered in classroom experimentation, and that is what may be called the personal bias of the pupils. To some extent, pupils will behave in the way in which they believe they are expected to behave. If they know that the class, or the teacher, is being observed, they are likely to cooperate with the teacher, since cooperative behavior is considered most desirable for children. This pupil phenomenon is most pronounced, and even teachers who have serious problems in maintaining class control may have no trouble when they are being observed.

Conditions related to motivation. While motivation is widely considered to be a major factor in determining rates of learning, not too much success has been achieved in establishing the conditions in the classroom which raise or lower motivation. McClelland *et al.* (1953) have based their work on the assumption that motivation can be aroused by the introduction of appropriate cues, such as telling a person that his performance on a particular task indicates his worth. Numerous studies have now been conducted in which such cues have been manipulated by the experimenter, but the results have often proven to be very difficult to reproduce. The student is cautioned against considering undertaking a study in this area because of the high probability of obtaining negative results.

A particular cue that has been extensively used in experimental research on learning is threat. Sometimes the threat may involve a physical consequence, as in research in which subjects are threatened with an electric shock. More often threat is designed to have psychological consequences, as when a subject is told that he is doing miserably or that "nearly everybody does better than you have done." In most of the research in this area, threat is introduced as a motivational cue and is designed to produce internal stress in the subject. The effect of threat and the resulting internal condition of stress vary from situation to situation and also, no doubt, with the characteristics of the subjects involved. Nevertheless, research in this area continues for it is important to find out more about the relationship of threat and stress to learning but there is the additional important educational problem of training individuals to meet stressful situations and handle them effectively.

Although threat and stress, which is the response to it, are an important area for research, the results of studies have not been particularly profitable. The products of experimentation in one laboratory can rarely be reproduced in another laboratory. So inconsistent are the results that often when the same experiment is reproduced in the same laboratory, the data may lead to opposite conclusions. The reasons for this were not apparent when researchers first embarked on experimentation in this area, and not all of them have yet been identified. However, there are some that seem to be sufficiently clearly recognized at this time to permit a brief discussion.

First, there is the difficulty presented by the fact that persons who visit a laboratory as subjects realize that no real harm will come to them, and that whatever threats they face will result in only transitory unpleasantness. On this account, whatever must be suffered by the subject may be accepted in much the same spirit as thrills and fears are accepted by those who visit the side shows at county fairs. The threats introduced by the laboratory situation may produce entirely different responses from those introduced by life situations.

Second, it is possible that most of the stress situations that it is desired to reproduce in the laboratory are not those that result from single incidents; rather are they those resulting from conditions existing over a relatively long period of time. There is at least a little evidence that neurotic conditions derived from childhood experiences are not the results of a single dramatic episode, but that they stem from recurrent situations that disrupt because of their frequency rather than because of their severity.

Third, the experimenter is limited for ethical reasons to the manipulation of certain mild threats. One cannot assume that responses to mild threat are the same as those to severe threat except in degree. It is quite conceivable, and in some cases we know it to be a fact, that the response to severe threat is quite different from the response to mild threat.

Fourth, in the laboratory situation the goals of the subject may be quite different from those in other situations where similar stresses operate. Unless some control can be exercised over these goals, the effect of stress on performance cannot be studied in any meaningful way, so the control of this aspect of the situation is crucial.

Fifth, experimenters are so limited in the stresses they can reasonably and ethically induce that serious questions may be raised as to whether it is worth even attempting to experiment in this area, despite its obvious educational importance.

Finally, stress, threat, and related variables can probably be studied most easily in the classroom situation as it ordinarily occurs. It is not difficult to find classrooms where threat is frequently used and where the pupils live in a continuous state of tension. Such conditions probably represent much more severe threat and stress than the experimenter would ever dare introduce into any experimental situation.

On the Importance of the Availability of Experimental Techniques

A student may decide to conduct an experiment on a significant problem before establishing whether suitable experimental techniques are available. This error is very common among graduate students. Since the development of experimental techniques is a painstaking endeavor often requiring long and sustained effort, such students are likely to find themselves engaged in a project requiring much more time than the thesis or dissertation ordinarily demands. The graduate student should choose an experimental research in an area in which well-worked-out techniques already exist.

The history of experimental studies shows that the development of an experimental technique for the study of an important problem has often sparked a long train of related studies. For example, when Ebbinghaus developed a series of experimental techniques which involved the use of nonsense syllables, he made it possible to study problems of memory which had never been amenable to study before. The approaches he used are still the basis for much research. A recent book by Underwood and Schulz (1960) reports a long series of researches which use techniques very similar to those developed a century ago by Ebbinghaus and which are still yielding significant scientific information. Even in those sciences which have had a longer period of rapid advance than has psychology, a single important technique may have had an equally significant long-term effect. For example, the development of the diffraction grating at the end of the last century opened up new approaches to the study of interference phenomena of light and provided techniques which are still widely used in physics laboratories.

Many other examples of the development of experimental techniques which have laid the foundation for important advances in knowledge could be provided. Much of the knowledge available about learning had its origins in the maze and in the experimental procedures which developed around the device. At the human level one can point to the valuable techniques introduced by Bruner, Goodnow, and Austin (1956), which have opened up new paths to the study of the conceptual development of man.

The student who is conducting his first research and who is intrigued by experimental approaches to problems would be wise to choose an area for study in which there are already well-developed laboratory techniques. Although his time would be well spent on the development of a new technique, such an enterprise is not generally considered appropriate for a dissertation or thesis.

Trial Runs as Explorations in Measurement

One of the major functions of a trial run is to determine what is and what is not measurable in terms of available instruments or new instruments that it is feasible to develop. Quite commonly an experiment or investigation is planned, but attempts to execute part of it demonstrate that the suggested procedure could not possibly yield any results because of the crudeness of available measurement procedures. The need for such preliminary trial runs to establish the meaningfulness of results as well as the feasibility of obtaining measurements of adequate accuracy has not been properly recognized by educational researchers. It would be easy to point to large educational investigations that have been pursued over many years at a cost of hundreds of thousands of dollars and that have produced no results of any consequence; these investigations would never have taken place if a few preliminary studies had been conducted. Such is true of most ambitious studies in teacher personality.

A common type of problem raised by a preliminary study is the lack of individual differences in the field in which measurement is to be made. If all measures made have the same numerical value, then there is little point in the application of measurement, for measurement is a procedure designed to indicate how much phenomena differ from one another. Another type of failure is due to the unreliability of a particular measuring instrument in the particular situation in which it is to be used. If it is a verbal instrument, it may be found to be incomprehensible to the particular group to which it is administered, and there may be little hope of modifying it while still retaining its original purpose. However, more frequent than any of these difficulties is the discovery in the preliminary trial that the phenomenon to be measured eludes measurement, even though attempts are made to adapt all available devices that seem appropriate.

Laboratory Analogs and Paradigms

Most experimental sciences advance knowledge about commonly observed phenomena by introducing into the laboratory simplified versions of these phenomena. Galileo wished to study the laws of falling bodies but found that their high speed under natural conditions made it almost impossible to study them, and also that natural bodies fell under such varied conditions that systematic study was difficult. For this reason he proposed to study bodies moving down an inclined plane. Such bodies move relatively slowly, and their laws of motion can be studied with relatively crude instruments. History has fully justified this practice, for the laws discovered through the use of such laboratory analogs or paradigms have been found to be a sound basis for making inferences about bodies falling under free conditions.

When Count Rumford observed that the boring of cannon generated great heat, his inference that the heat generated was proportional to the work expended was one that could be tested only in a laboratory setting and with equipment other than cannon-boring machinery. Man's curiosity about lightning had to be satisfied almost entirely through the study of small quantities of electricity manifested by sparks in the laboratory. Cavendish could never have determined the density of the earth except through a laboratory technique that permitted him first to work out a value for the universal gravitational constant. The reduction of natural phenomena to laboratory-size paradigms, or analogs as they are called, has been almost universally the main basis of scientific progress.

When Galileo decided to study falling bodies by means of bodies moving down inclined planes, he had a logical and rational argument underlying this procedure. He argued that the less the slope of the inclined plane, the less would be the force producing motion in the object. If the angle of incline of the plane was θ, then the gravitational force acting down the plane would be g sin θ, and the force acting at right angles to the plane would be g cos θ. On this basis, a simple mathematical function was provided to relate events in the inclined-plane situation to events in the free-falling-body situation. In contrast, in the behavioral sciences in general and in the educational branch of these sciences in particular, such well-established relationships between the laboratory phenomenon and the out-of-the-laboratory phenomenon do not exist. Such relationships as do exist can be expressed in words that are vague in comparison to the mathematical relationships characteristically found in Newtonian physics. Because the relationships thus expressed in words are vague, the generalizations derived from such laboratory studies lack the certainty of applicability to other phenomena that is characteristic of Newtonian types of generalization.

This means that the procedure for applying the laboratory generalizations of the behavioral sciences must involve much more caution than is necessary in the physical sciences. This does not mean that the physical scientist is never wrong in his applications, for he is, but because of the rigorous nature of his deductions he is less likely to be wrong than is the behavioral scientist. The rationale of the physical scientist can be wrong, and it often fails to take into account factors that influence large-scale phenomena but do not influence events in the test tube. For this reason, large-scale plants are sometimes failures although the small pilot plant was a success.

The results of laboratory experimentation with educational problems should be applied first to limited situations where careful appraisal can be made concerning the effects produced. Only when it can be shown that laboratory results can be at least partially reproduced in real-life settings should any widespread application be planned. At this point, great difficulties may often be encountered, for the real-life situation may not permit the quantitative appraisals needed to give credence to the results of a field trial.

In spite of the risk that generalizations derived from laboratory experiments may not be applicable to real-life problems, many scientists feel that this should not deter us from experimentation with educational problems on a laboratory basis.

Apart from the obvious advantages of laboratory experimentation that have been discussed, there is the fact that many phenomena simply are not amenable to study under the conditions in which they are ordinarily observed. This does not mean that all educational phenomena can be studied with advantage under laboratory conditions, because many are not amenable to such investigations. For example, if the researcher were interested in the effect of neurotic behavior of the teacher on pupil behavior, he would not use a laboratory approach, because psychologists would generally hold the opinion that the main effect of the teacher's neurotic behavior is observed after pupils have been subjected to it over substantial periods of time. In the laboratory, we could not and would not expose individuals to neurotic behavior over several months or years. Such matters must be studied in educational situations as they occur.

Some Difficulties in Undertaking Experiments

Problems of experimental design are now studied by mathematical statisticians as a comprehensive area of inquiry. The problems studied by this group are considerably different from those that are considered in this chapter, for they revolve largely around the efficiency of experimental design. This concept of efficiency is related to the matter of so planning experiments that the maximum amount of information is obtained from a given number of observations. Problems of experimental design in this sense of the term will be given brief consideration in the chapter that follows, which is planned to make the student of education sensitive to such problems and to perhaps encourage him to study further.

It is important that the student also be sensitive to certain difficulties in experimentation in the behavioral sciences that are largely a product of the type of events studied. These difficulties are rarely discussed in books on experimental design because such works are usually written by statisticians who are unfamiliar with common flaws in the mechanics of actual experimentation. It requires experimentation in the field to become aware of these difficulties which are not necessarily a product of the logic of the design.

In the pages that follow, flaws that the author has commonly observed in experimentation in education are discussed. Undoubtedly there are many others that occur with less frequency.

Deficiencies in design due to failure to include a control group. This is the most elementary of all deficiencies in experimental design. A principal wished to find out how much progress his fourth-graders made in social studies as a result of the curriculum offered. He was able to find a published test that seemed to measure the achievement of objectives of social studies stressed by the fourth-grade teachers, and he administered the test at both the beginning and the end of the school year. He was pleased to find that the group made as much progress as that shown by the norm group described in the manual for the test. What the principal did not know was that pupils who did not study material related to the content of the test made just as great a gain in score over the year as the pupils whose achievement was being evaluated. Experimental design always involves the establishment of conditions such that a comparison can be made between the effects of two or more conditions. Where the second condition is absent, the results become uninterpretable.

Deficiencies produced by the experimental procedure generating a variable. This deficiency is somewhat similar to that previously discussed. One should make sure that the experimental procedure itself does not introduce increments in score that can be carelessly attributed to the experimental treatment. An example is necessary in order to illustrate this error in experimental design. Ballard (1913) performed a well-known experiment in which he assigned school children the task of learning poetry. At the end of the learning period, the children were asked to write out as much as they could remember of the poem. Next day Ballard returned to the school and asked the children to write out once more all they could remember of the poem. He was surprised to find that on the second occasion, the children were able to recall more of the poem than they had on the first occasion. This apparent increment in learning after formal learning had supposedly ceased became known as the *phenomenon of reminiscence,* and for forty years it was described in textbooks on education and learning as a genuine phenomenon. However, information now available indicates that reminiscence is probably a product of faulty experimental design. The error lies in the fact that the procedure used to measure retention immediately after the learning session is itself a learning experience, which increases the scores achieved on subsequent measures of retention. Ammons and Irion (1954) performed an experiment in which groups were given poetry to learn. Some were tested according to Ballard's procedure, while others were tested only after an interval of time. Only those groups that were tested immediately after learning showed the apparent phenomenon of reminiscence. The groups tested after an interval of time produced average scores no greater than the average of the groups tested immediately after learning. This study suggests strongly that the supposed phenomenon of reminiscence is a product of faulty experimental design.

Various designs that can be used routinely have been suggested to take care of this hazard. One that has been suggested makes use of four experimental and control groups and can be used generally for determining the effect of a particular learning condition. It is especially suited to the type of study in which a pretest is administered to determine the state of learning at the beginning of the study, then a learning period, and finally a post-test to determine the state of learning at the end of the experiment. The four groups used in this design, denoted by the letters A, B, C, and D, are exposed to four different schedules as follows:

Group A—Pretest, learning experience, post-test
Group B—Pretest, post-test
Group C— learning experience, post-test
Group D— post-test

Only Group A is administered the entire series of tests and learning experience. The remaining groups are administered only varying portions of the schedule. In this way the experimenter can determine whether some irrelevant aspect of the experiment is producing any increment from pretest to post-test in Group A.

Deficiencies produced by contamination of data. Many experimental designs give spurious results because correlations are generated by spurious elements. For example, a scientist was interested in discovering the abilities related to talent in a course in creative writing. As a part of his study, he administered a battery of tests of creativity to the students at the beginning of the semester and planned to study the relationship between these test scores and measures of the characteristics of their written products during the course. The tests were scored, and the researcher discussed these scores with the instructor in the course in order to obtain cues concerning the relationship of the tests to creative talent—but this was an entirely unfortunate mistake. What it did was to open the possibility that the instructor's evaluations of the students' writing might be influenced by his knowledge of their test scores. The data provided by the instructor concerning the students and their creative product was contaminated by his knowledge of their scores on the tests of creativity. In another example, a doctoral student of education was interested in comparing two methods of rating pupil performance but decided to perform both types of rating himself. Both ratings were contaminated by his personal opinions about the persons being rated.

Contamination is by far one of the commonest of the errors of educational research design that render data uninterpretable. Such contamination is often difficult to identify and may pass unnoticed. One of many reasons why research plans should receive independent review is so that such factors can be identified.

Designs that make unwarranted assumptions about the nature of the scales used. The commonest examples in education of designs that manifest this error are those involving the use of growth scores. For example, a researcher set up the hypothesis that teachers who introduced into their classes rewarding comments (such as, "That's good, Billy") produced greater gains in pupil knowledge of social studies than those who did not. This study was to be conducted in sixth-grade classes in a large school system in which the teachers follow a rather rigidly prescribed social studies curriculum. The general plan of the study was to administer equated forms of a social studies test at the beginning and end of the sixth grade, and to correlate average gains in scores for each class with the observed frequency of rewarding comments occurring during visitation periods. If the researcher were not aware of the central defect of this design in the early stages of his work, it would probably become apparent in the later stages, when it becomes evident that some classes had greater knowledge at the beginning of the sixth grade than others had at the end. While some increased their average scores from, say, 30 to 50 correct items, others increased their average scores from 55 to 75. These two increases are numerically equal and according to the design of the study should be treated as equal, but the equality of these two increments must be considered an unjustifiable assumption. As a matter of fact, there may be reasons for believing that the one increment is much more difficult to achieve than the other in terms of the time and effort required. Also, the two increments may differ qualitatively, in that the one may be achieved by bright students while the other is achieved by the dull. The two increments cannot be considered comparable, and studies assuming that they are should not be designed. Such studies will provide results that are uninterpretable.

Deficiencies that result when relevant variables are confounded with irrelevant variables. This is one of the more obvious errors of experimental design. Both the error and the meaning of the term *confounded* can perhaps be best explained by means of an illustration. A researcher wished to study the effectiveness of flash cards in the teaching of reading. In order to do this, sixty first-grade pupils were given a reading readiness test. They were divided into two matched groups such that for each pupil in one group there was a corresponding pupil in the other group who had the same reading readiness score and who was of the same age and sex. Both groups used the same readers and workbooks, but the teacher of one group devoted time to the use of flash cards each day while the other teacher did not. At the end of six months the reading skills of both groups was measured, and the relative achievements of the two groups compared. However, this comparison was quite meaningless, because any advantage attained by one group over the other might as easily have been a product of difference in teachers as a product of difference in method (flash cards vs. no flash cards). It could be said of this situation that differences in teachers were *confounded* with differences in method, so that any differences in the two groups could not be attributed to the one or the other. It is imperative that such confounding of the main conditions be avoided. This could have been done in the present case by extending the experiment to other groups and other teachers. Duplications such as this are referred to as *replications*.

Deficiencies resulting from sampling by groups and not by individuals. Somewhat related to the error described above is this sampling problem. Consider the spurious design involved in a study in which the effects of two methods of teaching reading were compared. In this study, the researcher selected from one school six second-grade classes that agreed to use Method A, and from another six second-grade classes that were to use Method B. The researcher drew the unjustified conclusion that the results showed that Method A was superior to Method B on the basis of the fact that, although both groups had closely similar initial scores on a reading test, the final scores for Group A were substantially larger than those for Group B. The conclusion was not justified because there might have been differences between the two schools other than those in teaching methods. Differences in socioeconomic level or social status of the two school populations might alone lead one to anticipate that differences in rate of learning to read would be found. What has happened in this experiment is that differences in treatment in which the researcher was interested have been confounded with other differences. This is similar to the deficiencies previously discussed, but it can be remedied without adding additional cases.

The basic defect in the design could have been remedied by the simple procedure of dividing the six classes in each school into two groups, one of which would have been exposed to Method A and the other to Method B. In this improved design, it would be possible to estimate differences between methods within each of the schools and to estimate the differences between schools regardless of method. Assigning individuals at random to treatments rather than groups to treatments will always avoid this flaw.

Deficiencies resulting from failure of designs to take transfer of training into account. Most books on experimental design written in the Fisherian tradition fail to note a phenomenon, unique to the behavioral sciences, that complicates the problem enormously. This is the effect of transfer of training. Many educational experiments cannot be conducted by the efficient types of experimental design found in books on the subject because of this effect. An example of this difficulty is presented in a study by Thomas *et al.* (1956) concerned with the problem of predicting trouble-shooting ability. Two examples of each of two types of mechanical problem were constructed, and it was hypothesized that performance on Type A problems would be related to measures of rigidity because of the unexpected nature of the required solution, while problems of Type B would not. The data were consistent with this hypothesis when Type B problems were presented before Type A problems, but when the reverse order (AB) was used, then performance on the first Type B problem was also correlated with measures of rigidity. What appeared to happen was that when a Type B problem was encountered after Type A, the subject was set to look for an unusual solution. Under these conditions, a commonplace solution acquired the property of becoming unexpected.

Deficiencies due to insufficient cases. One of the most elementary errors in experimental design results from failure to include a sufficient number of cases, but no simple rule can be given to guide the student in this respect. Part of the difficulty stems from the fact that when very small differences between groups exist (in relation to their internal variation), more cases are needed to demonstrate the difference than when relatively large differences are involved. Much also depends on the nature of the experimental design used, for some designs are much more sensitive than others in identifying small differences.

However, quantity can never make up for quality in the collection of data. The researcher is always better off with a few carefully made observations than with large quantities of observations made under varying conditions and of doubtful reproducibility.

If very large numbers of observations have to be made in order to obtain a reasonably accurate estimate of a difference, then it is doubtful whether a difference of that particular magnitude is large enough or consequential enough for the researcher to spend his time in further studies of the phenomenon. The author's own prejudice, which he follows in his work, is that if a difference between two treatments is not clearly apparent when each treatment is applied to fifty cases, then the phenomenon is one of small consequence. Certainly phenomena for investigation that provide more clear-cut results of the type sought can be found quite easily.

Deficiencies in design due to failure to take subject bias into account. In most situations, there is a tendency for human subjects to behave in a way that they feel is expected of them. Thus in a classic experiment in which a group was singled out for observation in a factory, it was found that any variation in the conditions of work produced an increase in output, which remained even after the original conditions were restored. Groups singled out for study in schools are likely to learn more than groups not thus identified. For this reason, in any educational experiment where there is an experimental group and a control, both groups should feel equally singled out, or better still, both groups should be unaware of the fact that they are participating in an experiment. For this reason, in experiments with drugs, one group receives the drug to be tested while the other receives a placebo which looks and tastes exactly like the drug. Both groups are kept in ignorance of the fact that some received the drug and some did not.

Deficiencies introduced by the observer because he knows the treatment to which a subject or subjects have been exposed. In many studies in the behavioral sciences, the data are collected through human observers who must exercise judgment in the recording of their observations. These observers, much as they may try to act in accordance with the ideals of the scientist, have their own preferences concerning the way they would like to see an experiment come out. These preferences are likely to influence the data as it is recorded if this process involves any element of judgment. The best way of overcoming this source of error is to design the experiment in such a way that the observer does not know which human subject has been exposed to each treatment. This is not always possible, but in its absence serious reservations must be held concerning the way in which the results can be interpreted. This kind of difficulty is commonly encountered in the studies of progressive vs. traditional types of classrooms, in which it is difficult, if not impossible, to hide from the observer the general nature of the school program. The observer has to look only at the paraphernalia available to know whether the school expects the teacher to run a "traditional" or a "progressive" type of classroom. This setting is likely to prejudice the observer into interpreting what he sees in a manner that will match the interpretation to the setting. This is a type of error to which even an observer who is aware of the problem is likely to be prone, and it is one that renders useless many attempts at systematic inquiry.

Deficiencies due to planning studies in which rare events form the crucial aspects of the data. An experimental design is not likely to be feasible if it is built around a rare type of event. An example from outside the field of education provides an illustration of a type of problem familiar to the reader. During the early days of the development of antipoliomyelitis serums, experiments were carried out in an attempt to determine the value of various experimental serums. In some of the first experiments, approximately 20,000 pupils were randomly assigned to two groups. One group was given the experimental serum while the other was administered a placebo. At the end of the season, when the incidence of polio in the general population had fallen to its lowest ebb, the number of cases of polio in the two groups was counted. In such an experiment, it might have been found that in the innoculated group there had occurred six cases and in the placebo group ten cases. Now, although this difference is numerically large, it can be accounted for in terms of the differences one might expect if many samples of 10,000 cases each had been administered the placebo. In the conduct of such research, it soon became quite obvious that what appeared to be large samples were inadequate for the purposes at hand; and it was necessary, as the reader will remember, ultimately to use samples of as many as 300,000 cases in both the experimental and the control group.

For example, suppose it were planned to introduce a safety program into the elementary schools of a small city. It might be proposed that steps be taken to evaluate the effectiveness of the program by excluding half the elementary schools from it and then by comparing the traffic-accident figures for these schools during a semester with those for the schools which had the safety program. The weakness of the design is that too few children are likely to be involved in traffic accidents for the comparison to be statistically meaningful.

Deficiencies in design resulting from the experimental procedure itself affecting the conditions to be observed. A serious difficulty in educational research results from the fact that the process to be observed is often changed beyond all recognition by the mere process of observation. The description and recording of events within the classroom presents this problem in an acute form. We can no longer accept the notion, based on wishful thinking, that the introduction of an observer into the classroom does not affect events therein, for clearly it does. Indeed, some have suggested that it just may not be possible to study the events in the classroom under the conditions that ordinarily prevail. They have likened the situation to the Heisenberg principle in physics, which states that the position and the velocity of certain particles cannot both be determined at the same time. These difficulties of conducting classroom studies seem to be insuperable at the present time, but it must not be assumed that they do not exist. One should at least speculate on the effect that this difficulty may have on the result of studies.

The Availability of Appropriate Experimental Conditions

The preceding sections of this chapter emphasize the negative side of experimentation, what not to do; but mere avoidance of pitfalls does not insure that the resulting experiment will be even mediocre in value. In the literature can be found reports of study after study that are flawless in technique of design but otherwise completely inconsequential. Ingenious experimentation of the type that builds a science of behavior owes its contribution to the fact that it is built on a sound theory and that the idea could be developed experimentally under available circumstances. These two conditions need to be discussed further here.

A sound idea for experimentation in the behavioral sciences must find its roots in the current tide of organized ideas that constitute the present state of the art. Many ideas that appear sound from the viewpoint of the layman may not be sound from the point of view of current knowledge. The layman will always protest this statement, as he always has, for it is inevitable that he will conceive of himself as an authority on problems of education. This conflict between lay opinion and scientific opinion is not new and has occurred in fields other than the psychological. The layman's emphatic belief that the earth was flat or that it was the center of the universe are illustrations of common sense being wrong while the scientist was right. Today it is not uncommon for the student of education to base the ideas about which he wants to experiment on lay opinion as well as on his professional background. This is a real handicap, but it is hard indeed for a person who has spent the first twenty or thirty years of his life thinking in terms of the layman's conception of behavior to change and to think in terms of the scientist's conception. Early habits of thought are probably never entirely discarded.

OBSERVATIONS DURING EXPERIMENTATION

Many experimentalists have pointed out that the careful surveillance of the collection of data is vital for successful scientific research. This is not just a matter of watching to see that the experimental procedure is carried out with care. Incidental observations made during the course of an experiment may often provide valuable data. One does not have to go far to find discoveries of the utmost importance which have been made as a result of incidental observation during the course of some other investigation. A classic example is the discovery by Fleming which led to the discovery of penicillin. Fleming noted that staphylococci died in certain dishes which had become contaminated from outside sources. While many research workers would have written off this phenomenon as an experimental nuisance, Fleming saw that it suggested a means of destroying staphylococci causing infections. Roentgen's discovery of X-rays was also the result of an incidental observation made during the course of an inquiry into the nature of certain kinds of radiation.

One cannot tell the experimentalist what to look for, but only that he should be forever vigilant. When he sees something of particular interest he would be well advised to stop and investigate. Many scientists have said that a research worker is fully justified in dropping everything in order to explore an unusual event which has caught his attention. While systematic investigation is most desirable, it does not mean that the scientist should be compulsive about following his plans through to the end and shutting out all distracting phenomena.

An example of what is meant here may clarify matters for the reader. The author at one time observed some of his associates experimenting with a problem of teacher personality. The approach was that of introducing the prospective teacher into certain situations that showed systematic variation in such factors as the amount of stress, number of persons to be supervised, and so on. The assumption was made that a person is what he is and will show the basic core of his personality in whatever situation confronts him. Another assumption was that the traits manifested in these experimental situations would be the same as those manifested in the classroom. This reflects a number of common conceptions (or perhaps one should say misconceptions) concerning the nature of personality. These conceptions are quite inconsistent with many phases of modern psychology, and particularly with those that recognize that behavior changes as the goal changes. Since the goals of the teacher in the classroom may be quite different from those of the same teacher in the experimental situation, it may be expected that behavior will correspondingly vary. Unfortunately, not enough is known at the present time to predict behavior in the teaching situation from behavior in the experimental situation, at least if one's point of departure is the layman's variety of trait theory. There appear to be wide individual differences in the ability to assimilate current technical theory into one's thinking and to utilize it as a basis for experimentation in education.

The point was made earlier that the effective experimentalist must have vision enough to see what can and what cannot be accomplished under possible experimental circumstances that present themselves. The difficulties of manipulating some conditions, such as those related to teacher behavior, have been discussed, as also have some of the problems of laboratory experimentation that limit greatly what can be done. The shrewd experimentalist will not disregard these difficulties and proceed as if they did not exist, rather he will design experiments that circumvent them and permit the emergence of a clear-cut answer to the question asked. This aspect of experimental design, almost as much as that of finding a problem appropriately oriented with respect to theory, calls for great ingenuity and makes the design of experiments a pursuit that calls for high intellectual power. There is no routine way of setting up experiments. Genuine contributions to scientific knowledge are not made by the application of well-tried formulas to be found in textbooks, but rather do they require at least some small creative effort.

A final word of encouragement. Finally, the student is again urged not to be overwhelmed by the difficulties of experimentation. Rather, he should feel that he is now familiar with the major difficulties commonly encountered and that he is now in a position to plan well-designed studies. Since most flaws in experiments arise simply because the novice in research is unaware of their existence, the reader at this point should feel prepared to try his hand at designing experimental studies. The great value that this approach offers to the development of a science of behavior in educational situations is a factor that should urge him to use experimental methods whenever they are feasible. The more ambitious doctoral student may well deliberately choose these most powerful of all methods of collecting information.

Summary

1. Experiments constitute a group of activities undertaken by scientists. Some experiments are essentially demonstrations. Some represent explorations conducted by the scientist without knowing quite what to expect. In recent times the tendency has been to reserve the term *experimentation* for those inquiries in which a study is made of the effect of manipulating one or more variables.

2. Just as there is no clear line of demarcation between demonstrations and systematic attempts to study the effect of manipulating a particular condition, so too is there no rigid line between field studies and experiments.

3. While the term *experiment* is used with a diversity of meanings in educational circles, the chapter is concerned with a narrow interpretation of the concept. The term *experimental school* does not refer to any phase of experimentation as it is considered here.

4. There are many difficulties involved in the manipulation of conditions in educational experiments. An error of past generations of educational experimentalists has been the attempt to manipulate complex conditions such as progressive and traditional approaches to education. Experiments involving such complexes of variables do not generally produce results of value. Of the various conditions that are likely to be manipulated in classroom experiments, those related to classroom management present the greatest difficulties.

5. Trial runs and exploratory studies are important steps in the development of the experimental studies. They serve the purpose of determining whether the planned research is feasible in terms of the proposed techniques.

6. Laboratory studies are usually simplified versions of the phenomenon in which the scientist is interested. This approach can be justified in terms of the immense success it has achieved in the past. However, it may be much more difficult to generalize

from laboratory studies in the behavioral sciences than from studies in the physical sciences.

7. There are certain common deficiencies in the design of experiments, which recur with such frequency that they should be familiar to all who undertake research in education. These are deficiencies resulting from:

   a. The failure to include a control group when one is needed.
   b. The experimental procedure itself generating a variable.
   c. The contamination of the data.
   d. The making of unwarranted assumptions about the nature of the scales used.
   e. The confounding of irrelevant variables with relevant variables.
   f. Sampling by groups and not by individuals.
   g. The failure to take into account transfer of training.
   h. The failure to include a sufficient number of observations to provide the precision needed.
   i. The tendency of subjects to favor one outcome rather than another.
   j. The human observer being biased in the making of his observation because he knows which subject or group has been exposed to which particular treatment.
   k. The failure of the experimenter to recognize that he is dealing with a rare type of event.
   l. The experimental procedure itself affecting the conditions to be observed.

8. Sound experiments are based on sound scientific theory. The mere fact that a design is statistically sound does not mean that the experiment is sound.

Some Problems for the Student

1. An educator was interested in determining the relationship between intelligence test scores and grades in a certain school subject. In order to avoid contamination of the data, he himself administered an intelligence test and then kept the unscored

answer sheets stored in a locked file until the grades were handed in. However, his data could still be considered as contaminated. Why?

2. One sixth-grade class was given no spelling drill during a semester, while another in the same school was given thirty minutes daily of spelling drill. Differences at the end of the semester were measured on a standardized spelling test to determine the effects of the two procedures. List the sources of inadequacy of this design and then redesign the study.

3. A principal interested in safety education kept careful records over a number of years of the absences due to accidents among the pupils in a five hundred-pupil school. One year he decided to introduce a concentrated program of safety education, and at the end of the year he compared the record with those of previous years. Why would his data probably yield little of significance?

4. A research worker was conducting a study in which reading speed was to be measured under two different conditions. Under Condition A the pupil knew the precise purpose of reading the material. Under Condition B he was instructed to study the material because it contained information that would be of value to him later. The purpose of the study was to determine the effect of the specificity of goals on the amount of learning taking place. In order to carry out the study, all eighth-grade teachers were asked to release pupils for it over a two-month period. The pupils were sent to the experimenter one at a time. The teachers made the decision concerning which pupils should be sent. The experimenter first ran all subjects under Condition A and then all subjects under Condition B. What are the errors in this procedure?

CHAPTER 14

PROBLEMS OF RESEARCH
DESIGN

THE preceding chapter discussed the practical problems of experimentation, with particular reference to the feasibility of undertaking various types of experimentation. The extended discussion reflected psychological as much as statistical flaws in design. In this chapter the mechanics of design will be discussed, but the reader should keep in mind that designs that are methodologically sound from the statistical viewpoint may be applied to trivial problems and may even be based on assumptions inconsistent with those that the use of the particular data require.

Terminology of Design

In order to understand research design methodology, it is necessary to understand certain terms that are commonly used in the discussion of designs. The knowledge derived from a research is generally derived from a *sample* of a *universe*. The *sample* might be all eighth-graders in Chicago whose birthday fell on the first day of any month, and the *universe* might be all eighth-graders in Chicago at the present time.

The researcher is sometimes interested in the effect of the presence or absence of some conditions on behavior, such as the effect of drill on spelling achievement, or the effect of knowledge of results or lack of knowledge of results on computational skill. Differences in the conditions in which the researcher is interested are referred to as differences in *treatment*. In the simplest type of educational study, differences between the presence or absence of a particular condition are studied, and this would represent a comparison between two levels (presence or absence) of a particular treatment. In more complicated experiments, many different treatments may be involved and the interaction of these treatments may be studied. For example, one might study formal drill vs. no formal drill in the teaching of mathematics, and the teaching might be undertaken by either extravert or introvert teachers. Extravert teachers might be more successful with drill methods than with nondrill methods, and the reverse might be true of introvert teachers. Designs that permit the estimation of the effect of each treatment can be adopted within a single study.

Sometimes the research worker is concerned with the characteristics of the individuals involved in a study, especially in relation to some aspect of performance. Thus in studies of the results of different teaching methods, the researcher may wish to take into account pupil differences in ability because he may believe that some methods are better for bright pupils and others better for the dull. The characteristics of the population studied that are taken into account in a design are referred to as the *population characteristics*. These may be physical characteristics or psychological characteristics such as are measured by tests. They may also be derived from the person's background and represent the type of experiences to which he has been exposed.

It is not the purpose of this book to familiarize the student with the statistical problems underlying advanced designs and their merits. Such matters are well taken care of in textbooks devoted to mathematical problems. However, it is believed that complex experimental designs are only rarely appropriate in education. They seem to have had their most extensive application in fields in which there is a large and well-developed body of systematic knowledge. Agricultural experimentation is such a field. Much is known about the effects of various fertilizers, and there is a large and growing body of verified empirical information that provides essential background information for advanced agricultural experimental design. Most applications of complicated research designs in education are related to matters of practical interests rather than to matters of scientific importance. Rarely are they seen in researches that attempt to contribute to organized scientific knowledge about behavior in educational situations. It is important to emphasize this point, since there seems to be a growing belief among educators that the best way to turn out graduate students who can undertake research is to give them a course in experimental design of the type based on recent advances in statistics. Such courses may not only teach the student about designs that are largely unsuited to research in the behavioral sciences but they may also fail to familiarize the student with some of the more important shortcomings of experimental design that are unique to the behavioral sciences. Too often the student of education leaves such courses intent on applying what he has learned but finding that the chief application is to routine studies, such as those that attempt to partition differences in pupil achievement among such factors as school size, rural vs. urban differences, age groupings, sex groupings, ability groupings, and so forth.

There is some division of opinion among those engaged in educational research concerning the utility of complex designs that take into account a large number of different variables, except in areas where much knowledge has already been acquired. Those who design studies involving numerous variables claim that this is necessary if useful results are to be achieved. The argument is that many variables are involved in most behavioral phenomena, and hence these should be taken into account in any study that is planned. On the other side of the argument it is claimed that the research worker usually does not know what these variables are, and guesswork rather than sound theory is likely to be the basis for including those that are included. Only rarely do elaborate designs give the impression of being firmly rooted in theory. Skinner (1956), who has participated in this controversy, has pointed out that most of the important facts of science were discovered long before complex designs had ever been invented. In addition, it is true that important facts in the behavioral sciences continue to be brought out by workers in educational research using the simplest type of experimental designs. Many fine studies may illustrate the use of complex designs, but it seems likely that simple designs will serve a useful purpose for many years to come.

Functions of Statistical Methodology

It would be inappropriate in this book to provide any extended discussion of statistical methods, since these require intensive study on the part of the student of education who is preparing himself to engage in educational research. The student will always be limited both by what he knows and by what is known in the field of statistics in the planning and execution of studies.

At this time it may be of value to review the major functions of statistical methodology as it currently impinges on educational research. Present methods serve the two broad purposes of testing hypotheses and imposing a structure on observations. The latter function is really an extension of that performed by descriptive statistics, which served primarily the purpose of describing groups of observations in terms of certain characteristics of that sample of observations. An example of the application of descriptive statistics is the summarization of the heights of a group of children in terms of the mean height of the group and the standard deviation of the heights. If the distribution of heights is known to approximate normality, then the mean and the standard deviation will specify and summarize the distribution of all of the scores. This function of summarizing large masses of data is still an important one, and it is used by all agencies that collect massive amounts of data for various purposes. In the last two decades, these methods have developed far beyond the simple methods and concepts involved in the example just given and have entered a realm of great complexity. While the classical problems of descriptive statistics commonly involved the description of measures of a population with respect to a single variable, modern developments present multivariate problems, that is to say problems involving many variables. A battery of twenty tests may be administered to a population of high school seniors. It may be found possible to describe the data provided by these twenty scores in terms of a much more limited number of factor scores. Factor analysis serves this type of descriptive function and permits the summarization of numerous scores in terms of a few. In a sense it is possible to say that this procedure structures the data, and of course in a sense it does. By establishing certain hypothetical variables referred to as factors, it is possible to "understand" the remaining scores in terms of these factors. The factors do not necessarily represent any underlying reality that has greater significance than the variables directly involved. Indeed, they may be strictly hypothetical entities introduced for convenience, and there may be no actual phenomenon that they may be said to represent with any directness. This should not be taken as an attempt to belittle the use of techniques that have been developed to give structure to data, for they have been of immense value in the development of the applied technology of testing and measurement.

Procedures that give structure to data have become progressively less and less acceptable as the core of doctoral dissertations in education and in the behavioral sciences. Part of the reason for this is that the procedures can be mechanically applied, but it is generally agreed that a thesis or dissertation should require the student to solve a problem at least partly by concentrated personal effort and reflection. There is little educational value in grinding out a study by mechanical means.

A second purpose of statistical methodology concerns the justifiability of inferences made from data, or, in other words, the confidence that can be placed in particular inferences. While it may be necessary to find a convenient structure for data in the early stages of an inquiry, as when ratings are combined to produce factor scores, the later stages involve the testing of hypotheses and the making of inferences from data. Tests of significance vary in the degree to which they are efficient. Some do not make proper use of all the information provided by the data, while others do. The validity of the tests, if they appear to be appropriate, depends upon the extent to which the assumptions on which they are based are satisfied by the situation in which they are applied. If a statistical test depends upon the assumption that the universe from which a sample is drawn is normally distributed, it may not necessarily provide correct information concerning the confidence that can be placed on a particular inference in connection with which it is used, if the universe is otherwise distributed. Usually we know only that the conditions required by most tests of significance are only partially satisfied, but some comfort can be found in the fact that, in the case of most tests of significance, empirical trials have shown that considerable departures from the assumptions called for can be made before the statistical test becomes substantially biased.

The graduate student of education is most likely to be mainly involved in statistics that serve the second major purpose; namely, the testing of hypotheses. Through such methods a science of behavior in educational situations is likely to be produced.

General Characteristics of a Well-Designed Experiment

First, it is necessary that the data of the experiment be free from bias. In testing the relative efficacy of two methods of teaching reading, it is not sufficient to choose two groups of schools that appear to be equal and to assign one method to one set of schools and the other method to the other set. Suppose these two sets of schools were the Southside Schools and the Westside

Schools, and that the researcher decided to assign reading Method A to the former and reading Method B to the latter. In making this decision, he may have been influenced by certain quite unconscious biases. For example, he may have been convinced in his own mind that Method A was superior to Method B. He might also have given his prejudice weight in deciding to assign Method B to the Southside Schools, forgetting that previous test results showed that their pupils were generally slower learners than pupils in the Westside Schools. In such an event, the conditions of assigning teaching methods to schools were such that the data resulting from the experiment would inevitably show a bias in favor of Method A. It is just this kind of bias that a well-designed experiment is designed to avoid. This is accomplished by eliminating the influence of personal choice in the assignment of treatments to schools. If it were administratively necessary to treat each set of schools as a block, then the methods could be assigned to the schools by tossing a coin. However, to treat each set of schools as a block would be highly unsatisfactory. What is needed is to assign the methods to each school by use of a table of random numbers or by some other means free of personal bias. Some specific instances of introducing bias into data were discussed in the preceding chapter.

Sometimes in the collection of data, bias is introduced by the fact that treatments are assigned on the basis of conditions over which the experimenter had no control. For example, the author was at one time confronted with the problem of determining the effect of the use of diagnostic reading tests within a school system where some schools used these tests and others did not. Those that used the tests made some effort to interpret the profile of scores attained by each pupil and to plan a program of work designed to overcome the deficiencies thus revealed. It was suggested by the school authorities that a simple method of studying the problem might be to measure the reading proficiency of pupils in the two sets of schools, and to determine whether the pupils in schools that used the diagnostic tests were superior in reading to the pupils who did not have the supposed advantages of the diagnostic tests and the related remedial training program. However, the results from such a study would almost certainly be biased. In the situation under consideration, it could be shown that the pupils in the schools using diagnostic tests came from more favorable home backgrounds than those in the other schools. This in itself would probably produce differences in level of reading in the two sets of schools and make the results of the proposed study uninterpretable.

This would probably not have been the only source of bias in that study. The schools in which the diagnostic tests had been introduced might have had better trained facilities than the other group of schools, and this superiority would have reflected itself in teaching and in the resulting level of reading skill. Perhaps this discussion may not only illustrate the problem of eliminating bias but also point up the advantages of an experimental method in which treatments are assigned to cases by a bias-free method.

Later in this chapter, consideration is given to a variety of errors that may introduce bias into an experiment. But the warning should be given here that bias has a way of creeping into experiments even when it is least expected. Some of the ways in which it can sneak up on the experimenter are discussed in later sections of this chapter.

Before leaving the topic of bias, some further explanation is needed. Students commonly ask the question, "Does the elimination of bias mean that if the effect of differences in treatment is zero, then differences between treatments will be zero?" The answer to this question is "No." If such is the case, then the observations based on the two treatments must be considered as samples from the same universe of observations. The means and characteristics of the two samples will vary from one another, as would be expected on the basis of sampling theory. Lack of bias means that they would not differ in any *systematic* way.

Second, the experiment must be designed in such a way that it is possible to determine the magnitude of the differences that might be due to sampling alone. This may be stated in another way; namely, that the experimental data must yield an estimate of error. This condition could be overlooked in most of the experimentation conducted by the physicist or chemist, because in such experiments errors of measurement are extremely small and data tend clearly to support or reject the hypothesis under consideration. It is only when the experimenter enters fields where errors begin to be large in comparison with differences between treatments that the concept of estimating error becomes a matter of prime importance. Many experiments of great significance were performed before the statisticians' concept of estimating error was introduced, but the scientists who undertook those experiments were not oblivious to the idea. They relied upon their knowledge of errors of measurement that their equipment and materials involved. They were able to make judgments concerning the significance of their results with a rashness that the modern behavioral scientist cannot generally afford. Nevertheless there are some excellent experiments in psychological literature where no systematic effort has been made to estimate error. The phenomena of stimulus generalization has been explored largely through studies in which there has been no attempt to estimate error, but here again, the results have been so clear-cut that the experimenter's knowledge tells him that errors are extremely small compared with experimental effects.

Third, the experimental design must insure that there is sufficient precision for the data to be able to provide answers to the questions that are asked. In an experiment known to the author, students of education in their sophomore year were divided into two groups. One group was given extensive opportunity to visit school classrooms, while the other devoted an equivalent amount of time to additional academic work. It was hypothesized that those who had the school experiences early in their course would be able to profit more from the academic work and would be able to see its implications for classroom practice more clearly. The criterion for the success of this procedure was to be found in terms of the effectiveness of the student's performance in practice teaching. The experimenter was careful to divide the twenty-four sophomores by random assignment to the classroom visitation and the academic work groups, and fortunately all twenty-four stayed with the program long enough to complete student teaching. The students were rated during student teaching by the regular classroom teachers to whom they were assigned, on the basis of their over-all effectiveness as well as on more specific aspects of performance. For the purposes of this study, the over-all rating of performance was used and an attempt was made to determine the significance of the difference in the rated performance of the two groups that had been exposed to different educational treatments. As one might expect, the results were negative, since the difference between treatments was small and the error term was extremely large. The experiment lacked the precision to answer the question that was asked.

What can be done to increase the precision of such an experiment? One answer, but perhaps not the most satisfactory, is to increase the number of observations. As observations are added to the original experiment, a more and more precise and stable estimate can be made of the difference due to treatments. In the present case, additional observations could be added by dividing the sophomores year after year into two groups and providing the differential training.

But this is not the only method by which the precision of an experiment can be increased. It is the one that should be used as a last resort and only after other means of increasing precision have been exhausted. The main alternative involves the removal of that which can be ascribed to the effect of identifiable conditions from the error variance. Thus in the study of student teaching that has been described, the main condition affecting a person's performance may be his own childhood experiences in the classroom. The sophomores might be divided into a group who had been to relatively progressive schools and a group who had been to relatively conservative schools. An equal number of each of these could be assigned to each type of educational treatment during the sophomore year. In the analysis of the results, it would be possible to subtract from the error term that fraction of the variance resulting from differences in type of school attended. This would reduce the error term and thereby increase the precision of the experiment.

Traditional experimentation in the physical sciences involved the manipulation of a single factor at a time. Indeed, textbooks on experimental procedures that are more than twenty-five years old stress this aspect as an essential feature of the experimental method. Largely through the initial work of R.A. Fisher and the later work of his students and associates, the concept has been developed of varying more than one factor at a time. The advantages of such multifactor experiments are numerous. First, they answer several questions within the framework of a single experiment. Second, each observation may contribute data to the answering of every question with almost as much precision as if the experiment as a whole had been designed for answering a single question. Third, through the multifactor experiment it is possible to answer questions concerning the effect of one factor on the other. This is a matter that was not easily investigated before Fisher developed his techniques, although the problem was familiar to many scientists. It thus may be possible to demonstrate that under certain conditions of work, incentives interact with the student's level of motivation, and thus it happens that the well-motivated student is the one who responds to the incentives for learning held out by the teacher. These interaction effects are probably extremely important in the behavioral sciences, although scientists are likely to remain preoccupied with more straightforward and less complex effects for the present.

Controls in Experimental Design

The design of research is closely associated with the use of what are called *experimental controls*. Although well-designed experiments and other forms of research have been undertaken for many hundreds of years, the use of the term by scientists goes back for only about one hundred years. Boring (1954), who has studied the history of the concept of control in experimentation, finds three common uses of the term, which have added confusion to writings on scientific methodology because they have been used interchangeably.

First, the term *control* is used to refer to a restraint on experimental conditions. Thus in the administration of a test to determine whether children who have had certain diseases suffer a hearing loss, it may be considered desirable to conduct the tests in a soundproof room in order that extraneous noises may not interfere with the results obtained by some pupils and not by others. Extraneous sounds are *controlled* so that the resulting conditions will be as uniform as possible.

Second, the experimenter exercises control over the variable that he is manipulating. In determining auditory acuity, sounds are presented that vary in loudness and pitch. It is important to control the pitch of the sound since some persons may have a hearing loss only for sounds of a certain pitch. It is known, for example, that as individuals grow older they begin to manifest a hearing loss for sounds of high pitch. Thus the experimenter *controls* the pitch as well as the loudness of the sound that is presented as a stimulus.

Third, there is a sense in which the scientist refers to *control* groups or *control* experiments. Boring introduces this meaning of the term by referring to Mill's method of experimental inquiry. Mill's first method is the Method of Agreement, which states that if A is followed by a, then presumably A is the cause of a. The word *presumably* is used advisedly, since it is obvious that A is not necessarily the cause of a even if it always has preceded it. In my home, eggs are always served after grapefruit at the breakfast table, but nobody would claim that the grapefruit causes the eggs. In Mill's second method, it is postulated that if A is always followed by a, and if the absence of A is always followed by the absence of a, then A can be asserted to be the cause of a. This method is an extension of the first, and it involves the introduction of the control consisting of *the absence of A*. It represents a very common method of educational experimentation. For example, it can be shown that children who have certain speech defects improve if they are given remedial speech treatment and do not improve if such remedial work is withheld. If studies of this problem had demonstrated *only* that those who had remedial work improved, it would still leave open the possibility that improvement was due not to the treatment but to the passage of time and to various unidentified influences. However, by showing that the withholding of treatment is associated with an absence of improvement, the experiment is enormously strengthened and the conclusion that the treatment produces improvement may be justified.

Mill's method of *concomitant variation* is really only an extension of the two that have just been discussed. If this method were applied to the problem of determining the effectiveness of remedial speech training, it would be necessary to establish not two groups, one with and one without treatment, but a series of groups with varying amounts of treatment. It would then be possible to relate the amount of treatment to the amount of improvement in speech. There are certain obvious advantages of the method of concomitant variation over the simple methods. In the example under consideration, it would permit the determination of whether increasing remedial work beyond a certain point yields worthwhile added increments in improvements. It is quite possible that the pupil can benefit from only a limited amount of remedial work and that additional increments have little or no effect.

The reader may ask at this point why it is that the method of concomitant variation is only rarely used in *experimental* studies of behavior. Experimental studies in the literature are almost always designed to include only an experimental and a control group. Rarely are groups established with varying degrees of a particular type of treatment. The reason is purely a question of time and money. It is usual for the investigator to find difficulties in stretching his limited resources to permit groups of adequate size for both the experimental and control series. Intermediate series would involve prohibitive amounts of both time and labor.

The extent to which controls (in the third meaning of the term) need to be introduced is always a matter of judgment. If a teacher of calculus administers a pretest to his students to determine how much they know about the subject matter of his course, and then administers a final examination, and if the content of both tests relates only to the course in calculus, one may infer that substantial increases in scores from the pretest to the final examination may be attributed to learning in the course. Indeed, if this mathematics professor were to introduce a control group who took both examinations but who received no training in calculus, his colleagues would probably speak of him as being unreasonably overcautious and too free in wasting the time of his students. On the other hand, the psychology professor who also gives a pretest and a final examination may well wonder whether increases in scores are a result of learning in his course. In this case, the increase may be a result of general reading, discussions with other students, and related materials learned in courses in biology, sociology, and other subjects that overlap with psychology. In the judgment of the author, it would be highly necessary to include a control group in the latter case in order to improve the possibility of attributing gains in score to the content of the course.

The student should also be aware of the possibility that a pretest may, in itself, be a learning situation. Although little knowledge of a field may be acquired through taking a test, the student may become familiar with the form of an examination and this in turn may facilitate the answering of questions on subsequent tests.

The Function of Replication in Relation to the Problem of Estimating Error

In the behavioral sciences, a single experiment in which a measurement is made on one subject exposed to experimental treatment and the same measurement is made on a control subject cannot yield meaningful results. The design of experiments that can achieve this end and that can be used to derive useful generalizations requires the introduction of what are known as replications.

The term *replication* is frequently used with reference to experimental designs, and it refers to the making of additional observations comparing two or more treatments. Some replication is obviously necessary if there is to be any experiment at all. This can be explained by an example.

Suppose that it is desired to determine the effect of a second-grade workbook on the development of skills. A very unsophisticated experimenter might start with two beginning second graders, of the same age and with equal reading skill. One of these two pupils might be given a particular workbook to use during the semester; while the other did not have a workbook. At the end of the semester, both pupils would be again tested, and let us say the pupil who had had the workbook made the higher score. Just what can be concluded from such an experiment?

The answer to this question is that no conclusion of any value can be drawn. If two pupils have equal scores on a reading test at the beginning of a semester, they will probably have different scores by the end of the semester—as a matter of fact, they will very probably have different scores if they are retested only a day later. The latter effect illustrates the fact that there are errors of measurement. Thus the pupil who achieved the higher score might have achieved this score without the use of a workbook. Also the child who had the workbook might also have had certain advantages, such as a parent who worked with him on his reading difficulties. All of these uncontrolled sources of variation in final test scores are collectively referred to as *experimental errors*. In order to estimate their magnitude, it is necessary to replicate the treatments (with and without workbook) with additional cases.

This matter may be considered from another point of view. If the score of the pupil in the one group is X_1 and the score of the pupil in the other group is X'_1, then the single difference $X_1 - X'_1$ cannot be evaluated for its significance because there is no standard with which it can be compared. If a second pair of cases is added to the data, a second comparison $X_2 - X'_2$ may be computed, but the added data also enable us to begin making an estimate of variability within each group through the comparisons of $X_1 - X_2$ and $X'_1 - X'_2$. As pairs of cases are added, it becomes more and more possible to evaluate differences between groups, because the data enable us to estimate what differences would be expected if both members of each pair were drawn from the same group.

The question is inevitably asked at this point concerning the number of replications that should be included in the design. This is not an easy question to answer. Sometimes it is possible to compute the number of replications that are needed to attain a particular level of precision. There is also a second procedure, which is particularly applicable to research in the behavioral sciences, where data are collected not at one time but in a series of separate sessions. When this is done, replications can be added until the desired precision is reached; that is to say, until conclusions can be drawn with a definite degree of risk that they are wrong. A procedure known as *sequential analysis* may be used at any given stage in the collection of data to determine how many additional replications are needed in order to obtain the desired degree of precision.

Replication is necessary in order that the variability of subjects exposed to a particular treatment may be estimated. However, the multiplication of observations may serve an additional purpose if more is done than merely adding cases randomly selected in pairs from the same populations. In the case of the study of the two reading methods, it would be desirable to draw samples exposed to both methods from different intellectual levels, and perhaps too from schools in different socioeconomic neighborhoods. If such a plan of investigation were pursued, it might then be possible to determine whether one method was superior to the other, not only for children in general but for children at different intellectual levels and for children from different socioeconomic backgrounds. An interaction might be found between method and intellectual level—that one method was better with the brighter children and one with the duller. If the design is properly planned so that it includes other factors, much more information can be derived from a single inquiry than if all replications represent only the addition of randomly selected observations from the same population.

More information will be supplied by a single pair of observations if factors other than that which is being studied (differences in teaching method) are controlled. This statement should be qualified to the effect that control is important only insofar as it affects the variable in which we are interested; that is to say, in the example under consideration, reading achievement. The procedure may be adopted of matching one member of each pair with the opposite pair on one or more relevant variables. If pairs could be matched absolutely on all relevant variables, the remaining difference between pairs would be attributable entirely to differences in reading method. This situation is, of course, a limiting condition that can never be actually achieved. Usually we do not know what all the relevant variables for matching the pairs should be, and many that can be identified cannot be measured.

There is, of course, no certainty that even in an experiment where subjects are carefully paired for exposure to the two treatments there may still be differences between the groups thus selected for study. This is why it is necessary to obtain an independent measure of experimental error. All that can be done is to assign subjects to the two treatments in such a way that there is equal probability of the subjects in the two groups being affected by these uncontrolled conditions.

Matching procedures increase the precision of experimentation; that is to say, they increase the amount of information that can be derived from a particular number of cases. Thus experiments with matched cases can be undertaken with a smaller number of subjects than when assignment is by a random procedure. Nevertheless, there are often serious difficulties in the matching of groups. Often relevant data are not available. Often there are not a sufficient number of subjects to permit the careful matching of several groups. This is clearly shown by the fact that educational literature is remarkably devoid of studies that have involved the use of carefully matched groups.

There is also a criticism of matching procedures arising from the fact that matching has often been accomplished only after large numbers of cases have been collected in both the experimental and the control groups. When this is done, it usually results in the very uneconomic procedure of discarding subjects, which means that time and energy are lost. Such loss of data is not a necessary part of a matching technique, for if only carefully matched subjects are used in an experiment that is tedious to undertake, it may be possible to reduce materially the time spent in experimentation.

Matching procedures have not been largely replaced by techniques that handle the problem by strictly statistical procedures. These procedures have also been an outcome of the work of R.A. Fisher, and they are known as *the analysis of covariance*. They are generally more efficient than matching procedures and do not make it necessary to discard cases, as often happens when matching procedures are used. While matching cases with respect to more than one variable is a difficult and cumbersome procedure, the analysis of covariance can be used to control differences on several variables, and thus it provides the experimenter with a powerful tool for exercising control over sources of error in his data.

Sources of Error

A basic problem in the design of research is the estimation of error. Without such an estimate, the results of a study cannot be interpreted. Little has been said about the sources of such errors, so a brief consideration of this matter is now appropriate.

A convenient classification of error is provided by Lindquist (1953). He divides sources of error into three types according to whether they are associated with *subjects, groups,* or *replications.* He refers to these three types of errors as S errors, G errors, and R errors, after the first letters in the words *subjects, groups,* and *replications.* These errors can be illustrated by a simple example. Suppose that sixty first-graders were to be used in an experiment to determine the relative effectiveness of two methods of teaching reading, and that they were divided at random into two equal groups. It is possible that one of these groups might have more than its share of bright pupils, and as a result that group would have an advantage in learning to read regardless of the method used. This source of error, which is due entirely to chance factors determining which pupils are to be exposed to each method, is referred to as an S-type error. However, even if the groups are perfectly matched, it is possible that one group might have advantages over the other group during the experiment itself. For example, it might happen that the one group had had a better teacher than the other. The errors introduced through such uncontrolled events are referred to as G-type errors, since they are attributable to differences in conditions to which the two groups are exposed. If the same experiment were repeated in another school, it is possible that the method of teaching reading found most effective in the first school might be least effective in the second school, and this phenomenon might be a genuine one. It is certainly conceivable that a method of teaching reading that is highly effective for teaching children from literary homes might be a poor method for teaching children in impoverished neighborhoods. Such differences between replications are referred to by Lindquist as R-type errors. Such an effect as that discussed could also be referred to as an interaction of socioeconomic background and teaching method. It is desirable to design studies so that errors resulting from all of these sources can be taken into account insofar as they are relevant to the outcomes of the study. Here it is only possible to familiarize the reader with these various sources of error.

Factorial Designs

Up to this point, our discussion, has been limited to simple, classical designs that are based mainly on the concept that an experiment is performed by keeping all factors constant except one. The essential principle that R.A. Fisher introduced to revolutionize experimental design was the concept that more than one factor could be varied within the structure of a single experiment. Such an experiment involving many factors may contain all the information and provide the same precision as a series of independent experiments involving each of the facts singly, and it will provide savings in effort and work on the part of the experimenter. An additional advantage of the multifactor design is that it may permit the estimation of the effect of the interaction of the variables.

The concept of interaction is a relatively advanced one in the history of the experimental sciences, and it has become particularly useful in the biological and social sciences. It has become a key concept in the biological sciences largely through the study of chemicals in the form of fertilizers and drugs. In the use of fertilizers, the interaction phenomenon is dramatic in effect. Nitrogen alone added to a deficient soil may produce little effect on growth, and the same may be true when phosphorus alone is added. However, when both are added the effect on plant growth may be remarkable. Under these conditions, it would be said that the variance of plant growth due to nitrogen alone, or to phosphorus alone, would be negligible, but variance due to the *interaction* effect of nitrogen and phosphorus would be large. Other well-known and important interaction effects are found in pharmacology, where the combined effects of Drugs X and Y are found to be greater than what one would expect to find from the effects of the two drugs administered separately. This effect is known as the *synergic effect*, and it is extensively illustrated by the well-known procedure of compounding several drugs into a single dose of medicine.

In the behavioral sciences, it is not possible to point to clearcut and well-recognized phenomena that illustrate the interaction effect, possibly because such interaction phenomena are not usually studied in most experiments. One reason for this is that it is only rarely possible to provide a rationale on the basis of which they may be studied. It is easy to see why plants do not grow in a deficient soil even if either nitrogen or phosphorus is added, for plants need both of these elements in an available form, and one can well understand why it is that both added together produce results greater than would be expected from the effect of each separately. Other interactions in the biological sciences are fully in accord with expectation, but in the behavioral sciences one is much less certain of what to expect. Perhaps at this point it may be well to pause and consider some cases in educational research where one may expect to find interaction effects.

One such situation is presented by the relationship of teachers to the type of curriculum in terms of which they can most effectively work. It has been suspected for a long time that the teacher who presents what has been called an "authoritarian" personality has great difficulty in working within the framework of a school program in which pupil initiative is encouraged. It is alleged that such teachers work most effectively within a traditional type of curriculum, where nearly all activity is initiated, controlled, and directed by the teacher. Such a situation does at least call for habit systems that are consistent with those one might expect to find in the so-called authoritarian personality. On the other hand, the teacher who feels secure in a classroom situation and who does not find activity initiated by the pupils threatening, might be most effective in a situation where there was no need to control every movement of the pupils and where he could function more as a counselor and guide than as a dictator. As far as the author is aware, it has never been demonstrated that there is this type of interaction between teacher and teaching program, yet it is reasonable to suppose that such an interaction may be crucial. If such a study could be undertaken, it should provide data important for the selection of teachers.

The above example is given just to indicate the interaction phenomenon in a meaningful context. Too often the interaction variances are measured and tested for significance without being given any particular meaning. Such a practice is not consistent with the development of a rational science of behavior in educational situations.

In the case of the comparison of the two methods of teaching reading, there were two methods which may be said to represent Factor A in the study, two socioeconomic levels representing Factor B, and two ability levels representing Factor C. Information might be obtained from this experiment concerning each of the following:

The effect of A on reading achievement
"   "   " B "   "   "
"   "   " C "   "   "

The interaction effect of A and B on reading achievement
"   "   "   " A " C "   "   "
"   "   "   " B " C "   "   "
The interaction effect of A, B, and C on reading achievement

The "interaction effect" of A and B refers to the effect of combining those two factors over and above the effect of the two factors alone. Thus if there are three factors (A, B, and C) there would be a minimum of 2^3 observations that would have to be made in order that each one of these effects could be evaluated, since each level of A would have to be combined with each level of B and each level of C. In actual practice, there would have to be a replication of the eight observations in order to increase the precision of the experiment to the point where it could yield useful information.

Where the number of factors in an experiment is 3, the number of observations needed, without replication, is 2^3. With n factors, it is 2^n. It can be seen that this becomes numerically large very rapidly as n is increased. With 10 factors, it would require 2^{10} observations, which is equal to 1024. This assumes that the effect of all of the interactions is to be computed. Replication would also be necessary in most studies in the behavioral sciences, and thus the number of observations to be made would be extremely large and might even be larger than the number that could be made with the time and facilities available. In such a situation it is not necessary to go back to the old system of varying one condition at a time, for the newer principles of experimental design offer certain compromises that reduce the number of experimental observations needed. In this latter type of design, application is made of a procedure known as *partial confounding*. In this procedure, a design is set up so that it is possible to estimate the effect of only some of the interactions. However, since most of the interaction effects cannot be identified with any known or hypothesized phenomenon, their effects are pooled in order to provide an estimate of error. The result of partial confounding is to cut down on the number of interactions from which an estimate of error can be made. The concept of partial confounding is extremely valuable in the development of efficient experimental design.

An important example of a partially confounded design is the Latin square, first introduced into agricultural experiments, where its meaning can be easily understood. Consider the case of the agricultural experimentalist who wished to compare four different fertilizers that varied only in the amount of phosphorus they contained. Let these fertilizers be labeled A, B, C, and D. This experimentalist had available a square plot of land, which he had divided into sixteen equal smaller plots, each one of which was also square. His next problem was that of deciding which treatment to apply to each plot. The plots are shown in Figure XIA.

A. Plot arrangement

1	2	3	4
5	6	7	8
9	10	11	12
13	14	15	16

B. Assignment of treatments

A	B	C	D
C	D	A	B
D	A	B	C
B	C	D	A

FIGURE XI. Illustration of Latin square design.

Any assignment of treatments to plots must take into account the possibility that the soil may show greater fertility on one side of the total plot than on the other, and the Latin square takes into account just this possibility. The assignment plan shown in Figure XIB represents the application of one of many possible Latin square designs that might be used to solve this problem. It should be noted that each treatment occurs only once in each row and only once in each column. There are many other Latin squares that satisfy this condition, and the one utilized should be selected at random.

An example of the application of a Latin square problem to education may now be considered. Let us reconsider the problem of determining the relative effectiveness of four methods of teaching reading, denoted by the symbols A, B, C, and D. It might be possible to set up four methods of instruction that differed in the techniques used. The research worker hypothesized that children in some school districts learned to read more rapidly than children in others, and that perhaps the workbooks used also made a difference. Thus it was planned to conduct the experiment in sixteen schools which varied both in school district and in workbook used according to the scheme shown in Figure XII. On

School Districts

		1	2	3	4
	Type 1	School 1	School 2	School 3	School 4
WORK-	Type 2	School 5	School 6	School 7	School 8
BOOK	Type 3	School 9	School 10	School 11	School 12
	Type 4	School 13	School 14	School 15	School 16

FIGURE XII. Diagram showing the selection of schools for experiment in terms of school district and workbook used.

the next page is Figure XIII, which shows a method as assigning the treatments to schools. The assignment is such that all four treatments appear in each school district as well as with each workbook. It is then possible, once the data are collected, to compare school districts, to compare schools that differ in workbook, and also of course to compare treatments.

It would be quite unthinkable to select a single case from each one of the sixteen schools, since our general knowledge of educational measurement would tell us that such an experiment would be so lacking in precision that little if any useful information could be derived from it. The researcher on this account would probably select as many as thirty pupils from each school, which would amount to having thirty replications of the Latin square design.

It should be noted that this design answers a very general question as to whether the methods can be considered to produce different results. It is not designed specifically to examine the question of whether one particular method is superior to the other methods, though such a hypothesis can be tested. The design is perhaps appropriate if a very general exploration is to be made of reading methods, merely to see if different methods do produce different results.

A	B	C	D
C	D	A	B
D	A	B	C
B	C	D	A

FIGURE XIII. Assignment of treatments to schools according to Latin square design.

In recent years considerable interest has been shown in the problem of testing the significance of particular comparisons within the Latin square once it has been demonstrated that there are over-all differences of significance among the treatments. Some of the methods for doing this involve quite elaborate assumptions, which should be fully recognized before these methods are embarked upon. The arithmetical procedures involved in testing the significance of particular comparisons, or sets of comparisons, are not as complicated as the student might fear them to be since tables have been prepared which eliminate much of the work.

If a first principle of design is that there must be a way of estimating the probability that an observed difference between treatments could have resulted by sampling from a single universe of observations, a second principle is that designs must be arranged so that known sources of variability can be separated from both the main treatment and the estimate of error. Thus Mitzel and Rabinowitz (1953), in an experiment on the social-emotional climate in the classroom, employed a design that permitted the estimation of differences between observers, differences from day to day in the performance of the same teacher, and differences between teachers, which was their center of interest. Consequently they were able to remove from their estimate of error variance the variance due to observers and the variance due to the daily variation in teacher behavior. Such a design is referred to as $2 \times 4 \times 4$ design, since there were two observers, four visits to classrooms, and four teachers.

Degrees of Freedom

An important concept is that of *degrees of freedom*, a concept derived originally from physics that has been used extensively in the area of experimental design. If a body can move only in a plane, it is said that the body has two degrees of freedom but is restrained on a third degree of freedom. If a body is restrained so that it can move only along a straight line its movement is said to involve only one degree of freedom. However, in statistics, the term has assumed a rather different meaning, which is related to the other only by analogy. Possibly the simplest explanation of the concept is to think of degrees of freedom as independent comparisons, a concept that needs to be amplified at this point.

For the sake of explanation, let us consider a grossly oversimplified case in which two pupils, X_1 and X_2, received one treatment (say in reading), while two other pupils, X_3 and X_4, were exposed to another. The comparison that it is desired to make between the reading scores of these pupils would be between the two treatments and might be represented by the term

$$(X_1 + X_2) - (X_3 + X_4).$$

An estimate of the variation to be expected from sources other than treatment would be provided by the two additional independent comparisons

$$X_1 - X_2$$
$$\text{and } X_3 - X_4.$$

These comparisons are referred to as independent comparisons because the numerical value of each one cannot be determined from the other two. However, if an attempt were made to introduce another comparison, such as $X_1 - X_4$, it becomes clear that this comparison can be calculated from the other three and therefore cannot be considered to be independent of them. The number of independent comparisons that can be made in a system of observations represents the number of degrees of freedom of that system.

Four observations permit three independent comparisons. Ten observations permit nine independent comparisons. In general terms, one may state that N observations permit $N - 1$ independent comparisons, which represent $N - 1$ degrees of freedom.

Now if the comparisons that it is desired to make are 3 in a particular experiment and there are 30 degrees of freedom in the system, this means that there are $30 - 3$ comparisons or degrees of freedom that may be used for the estimation of error. Designs must always be such that after meaningful comparisons are listed, a sufficient number of other independent comparisons are available to estimate the experimental error with the required degree of precision. If an experiment is restricted to ten observations, it would be meaningless to attempt to study nineteen comparisons, since this would provide no independent estimate of error.

There is a simple way of determining whether a series of comparisons are or are not independent. Consider the case of the comparison involving the four measures X_1, X_2, X_3, and X_4. We were concerned with the three comparisons that could be written out as follows:

$$X_1 - X_2$$
$$X_3 - X_4$$
$$(X_1 + X_2) - (X_3 + X_4)$$

The corresponding coefficients of these terms may be arranged as follows:

+1	−1	0	0
0	0	+1	−1
+1	+1	−1	−1

It should be noted that the sum of the coefficients in each row is zero, and also that the sum of the cross products of any two rows is also zero. Comparisons that satisfy these conditions are independent.

The Testing of Hypotheses

All that has been said in this chapter up to this point is based on the assumption that the experimenter has in mind certain clear-cut hypotheses to test. The methods of experimental design that have been discussed are such that they assist the experimenter in testing his hypotheses with the minimum amount of data for a given degree of precision, and sometimes they permit the formulation of generalizations that cover a wider range of circumstances than would be possible if the classical type of experimental design were used. It is common to formulate hypothesis in a form which is known as the *null hypothesis*. In this form the hypothesis states that no difference is expected. Thus if an experiment were to be carried out involving two methods of teaching reading, and reading skill was measured by a test at the end of the training period, the null hypothesis would state that the two groups would not differ. If a difference were found between the mean scores of the two groups, the next step would be to determine by appropriate statistical methods the probability that such a difference or a larger difference would occur by chance. If the chances are found to be quite small that such a difference or a larger difference would occur by chance, the null hypothesis is rejected. Since the testing of the hypothesis from the data involves the determination of the probability that such a difference or greater would occur by chance, there is a certain logic in stating all hypotheses in the null form. In the sense described, it is possible to test the null hypothesis, and if the chances are extremely small that the difference (or a larger difference) would have occurred by chance, we may be willing to accept the alternative possibility that the difference was a product of differences in treatment. The latter hypothesis cannot be proven in terms of the data, but it does become more and more plausible as the null hypothesis becomes less and less plausible.

The analysis of variance and related statistical techniques that are outside the scope of this book are the techniques used for testing the null hypothesis, and they always provide an estimate of the probability that a particular difference could have occurred as a result of variations produced by sampling. The probability value that must be reached before it is decided to reject the null hypothesis is a matter of judgment, but it will depend on the consequences of making an error. In this connection, two types of error have been distinguished and have become known as *errors of the first kind* and *errors of the second kind.*

In the particular experiment comparing the effect of two methods of teaching reading, the results might be presented in the form of the statement, "The probability that the observed difference or a greater difference would occur as a result of chance variations alone is 0.1." This means that if the two treatments had no differential effect, the results of sampling would produce a difference this size or greater in 10 per cent of all experiments. The experimenter might say to himself that this probability is small, and hence it is reasonable to conclude that the observed difference is generated not by chance variations in the sample drawn but by differences in treatment. If more thorough experiments were carried out later, substantial evidence might be collected to show that this conclusion was wrong. If this were the case, the experimenter would have made an *error of the first kind.* In this type of error, the null hypothesis stating that there is no difference between treatments is rejected when it should be accepted.

Errors of the second kind are exactly the opposite type of error. They represent the case where the experimenter accepts the null hypothesis when he should not have done so. It is not possible to say that these errors are more or less serious than errors of the first type, because everything in this respect depends upon the circumstances. Fortunately, in education, the result of committing either type of error is not likely to be catastrophic, but in experimentation in other fields an error of either type may on occasion result in the loss of human life. In the interpretation of experimental results, it is important to keep in mind the consequences of each one of these types of errors. If the penalties involved in committing one of these types of error are heavy, caution must be taken in arriving at a conclusion that may make these penalties take effect.

The Design in Relation to the Question Asked

The care that needs to be exercised in relating the design to the question asked is well illustrated in a study by Mitzel *et al.* (1953), which was developed to illustrate some of the problems that this may involve. The Mitzel study involved the use of data from an earlier study in which two observers made four visits apiece to each of four classroom teachers. From these observations, a climate index was derived. Thus thirty-two measures of this index were derived. Mitzel *et al.* noted that three major questions might be asked of these data, which may be stated as follows:

1. Did the two observers "detect differences among the four teachers' behaviors on the four particular occasions on which they were visited with respect to the . . . climate index?"
2. Is it reasonable to hypothesize on the basis of the data that, if other observers visited other teachers on other occasions, differences between teachers other than chance differences would be found?
3. If the two observers were assigned to observe other teachers in the population of teachers from which the four were drawn, would other than chance differences in the climate index be found?

The analysis involved in these three cases is considerably different. The particular question to be asked in this case depends much on what are the experimenter's future plans and what he intends to do with the results.

The first question is a rather trivial one. It is of interest only if we wish to know whether the same observers visiting the same teachers on different occasions would still be able to observe differences between those teachers. The answer tells us absolutely nothing about the differences that might be found if other teachers or other observers were used.

The second question leads to a much more useful answer, if it can be answered. The experimenter is likely to be interested in predicting what would happen if other observers were used with other teachers. In order to answer this question the four teachers must be considered as a sample of a universe from which other teacher samples could be drawn, and the observers as a sample of a universe of observers from which other observers might be drawn. We are interested in generalizing from our observers and teachers to other observers and teachers. If the results of the study are to be used by other research organizations, this type of generalization is necessary.

The answer to the third question is particularly useful if the study under discussion has been conducted as a preliminary to a more extended study using the same two observers. It indicates something about the results to be expected from these two observers.

Random Models, Fixed Factor Models, and Mixed Models

The choice of the comparisons to be used in the estimation of error is a complex matter, often involving judgment, which cannot be more than touched upon here. The matter is ultimately connected with the type of design that is used and the questions that the design is to be used to answer. Two major classes of experimental designs commonly considered in this connection are referred to as the *random model* and the *fixed factors model*. The fixed factors model is also called the *fixed constants model*. In addition, some designs include both sets of characteristics and are referred to as *mixed models*. Most research in education involves the use of mixed model designs.

First, let us consider briefly the random model design. An

example would be a study which involved the random assignment of pupils to six teachers selected at random from all sixth-
grade teachers in a school system. Inferences from such a study
would be made about the universe of pupils from which the
pupils were sampled and inferences could also be made about
the universe of teachers from which the teachers were sampled.
If, for example, it were found that differences existed between
the mean achievement of pupils in the six classes, one might want
to know the probability that such a difference or a larger difference would occur if another random sample of teachers or another
random sample of pupils were selected. This can be done with
the random model design. In the random model there is always
random selection involved from a universe. In practice, strictly
random models are rarely found in educational research and
tend to deal with rather trivial problems.

In the fixed factors model, a sample is not drawn at random
from a universe. Suppose that a scientist wished to study the
relative effectiveness of three new and different methods of teaching beginning algebra and that he had one teacher proficient in
the application of each one of the new methods. Now the three
methods are not random samples from a large number of different
methods that might have been selected; they may be the only
new methods that exist. The three methods are not in any sense
a random sample from a universe of methods. They represent
three distinct categories of teaching and represent fixed factors
in the experimental design. If the design were further elaborated
so that each method was taught by both male and female teachers, then sex would represent another fixed factor in the design.
Male and female cannot by any stretch of the imagination be
considered to represent a sample of two sexes from a universe of
sexes: All the sexes there are fall within the two categories.

Most designs include both random and fixed factors. Consider
an experiment in which two different methods of reinforcing
correct responses in pupils were used at three different grade
levels in a school system. The kinds of reinforcement used could
not be considered to represent a random sample of all the different
kinds of reinforcement that might be used. They represent fixed

factors in the design. On the other hand, the particular classes selected for the experiment might be selected at random from those at the appropriate level in the school system. Such a design, therefore, includes both fixed factors and random sampling.

While many designs call for a random selection of classes, the procedure adopted often violates this requirement. Practical difficulties often require that the experimenter use whatever classes are available. This may introduce bias into his results, for the selection may include only bright children, or only children from a superior economic level. Such a bias may make it unreasonable to generalize the results to other classes in the system.

Finally, we come back to the statement that the particular comparisons selected for the estimation of error will depend upon the type of design used. While the reader should be aware of this problem and of the difference between a random model and a fixed factors model, he should consult with a statistician in deciding how to estimate error.

Sampling and Problems of Generalization in the Design of Studies

The design of experimental studies and investigations in the behavioral sciences, as in the biological sciences, is intimately connected with the problem of sampling. The intention of the author cannot be to provide the student with an adequate background in theory of sampling; it can be only that of making the student sensitive to some of the problems in the area so that he can turn to more comprehensive works to learn about the details of their solution—at least insofar as these problems have a solution.

In the testing of almost any hypothesis by statistical means, an assumption is made that the observations recorded represent a sample drawn from a defined universe by methods that do not introduce bias. A universe from which a sample is drawn consists of all those cases that might be included in the sample. The term *universe* is a technical term and is used in a technical sense. Some of the factors that introduce bias into the drawing of a sample were already considered in the chapter on survey techniques, with particular reference to the problem of identifying a limited number of persons who are to be interviewed from an unidentified universe of persons. In this chapter, the more general problem of obtaining samples of specified universes will be discussed.

Suppose that the director of research in a large school system decided to survey the reading abilities of children who had passed their ninth birthday but who had not yet reached the age of nine years and six months. In this school system, a few less than 10,000 school children fell within this age range and these were distributed among twenty-five schools. It was clear that the director of research could not test all of these children on the particular test to be used. Therefore he decided to test a sample and to use statistical methods for making inferences concerning the total population from the scores derived from the sample. A member of the board of education immediately suggested that it would be administratively convenient to limit the testing to pupils in a single school, since these pupils could then be tested together in a single session. The director was quick to point out that it was a well established fact that one could not justifiably make inferences from the reading performance in a particular school to the reading performance in all schools, since average scores on the particular test in earlier years had been shown to fluctuate substantially from school to school.

Thus it is clear that the accuracy of the inference made from a sample to a universe will depend on the way in which the sample is selected. The suggestion of the member of the school board lacks merit because it introduces bias into the sample for the sake of administrative convenience. Whatever sampling procedure is used, it is absolutely essential that it not include any systematic bias. The simplest method of obtaining a sample from a population is that of obtaining a random sample, which is simply a sample in which every case in the population has equal chance of being included. By definition, the sample deliberately derived from one school could not be considered a "random" sample because cases from other schools would have no chance of being included in it. One way of obtaining such a sample would be to obtain a list of all such children, number them consecutively, and then select from this list by means of a table of random numbers. Such tables can be obtained from libraries. In using such a table, it would be appropriate to start by taking the first four digits and selecting the child who had the number corresponding to these four digits. The investigator would then take the next four digits and select the child whose number corresponded to these digits, and so forth. Thus each child in the population identified would have equal opportunity for being included in the sample to be studied. Under such conditions, well-established procedures can be used for making inferences from the sample to the population, and it is justifiable to neglect the fact that the population is not unlimited in size as such procedures require. The fact that the latter assumption is not fulfilled is not likely to affect our inferences appreciably when the number of subjects is as substantial as it is in the present case.

In this simple type of inquiry, it is presumed that the director of research is interested in estimating the mean reading score of the defined population from the sample. In the case of the random sample that has no systematic bias, the best estimate of the population mean is the sample mean. It is of course expected that there will be a difference e (e for error) between the sample mean and the universe mean, but since the method of drawing the sample introduces no systematic bias, if the inquiry were repeated with new samples one would expect e to be negative as often as it was positive.

In this very simple inquiry, much can be done to reduce the value of e to a minimum. If the investigation is efficiently designed, it will be possible to obtain an unbiased sample such that e is smaller than it would be with a random sample of the type discussed. In essence, what is done is to take steps to insure that the sample is as far as possible *representative* of the universe sampled with respect to important characteristics that are related to reading. For instance, it is known that girls show a tendency to be better readers than grade-school boys of the same age. Hence it would be desirable to insure that the sample included the same proportion of boys and girls as was included in the universe under consideration. Since neighborhood is also related to reading skill, it would also be desirable to insure that the schools were represented in the sample in proportion to the actual enrollment of the particular age group under study. Thus the sample would be stratified, and by making the sample more and more closely representative of the population, the tendency would be for the error term e to be steadily reduced.

Let us now consider a slightly more complicated problem of design in order to illustrate the relationship of problems of design to problems of sampling. Suppose that the director of research had been asked to evaluate a remedial reading program. In this program, approximately one hundred children in the elementary grades were given special remedial training in reading each year. The problem may be stated in this way: "If the reading skills of the pupils are measured at the end of the year of special remedial training, what is the probability that a random sample of children, similarly selected but without training, would perform as well or better than the trained sample?" It is therefore necessary to estimate the reading characteristics (mean and standard deviation) of the universe from which the remedial reading group was a sample, for the time at which the remedial group finished their special training. We may hope, of course, that the director of research did not find himself in the position in which many of his colleagues had found themselves—that of having no way of determining just what population had been sampled in the first place and then trying to remedy the situation by inferring the population from the sample. What he should have done was to exercise the most careful control over the selection of the original sample, so that he would know just what population had been sampled. Unless this had been done, the data collected at the end of the experimental year would have been of extremely limited value if not entirely worthless. The prevention of such common tragedies is a matter with which the student of education must become fully cognizant.

The director of research would do well to start by identifying the universe to be sampled. One way of doing this might be to administer a reading test to all grade school children at the beginning of the year. In each grade (or possibly in each age group), the lowest 10 per cent or 5 per cent might be considered to be the population eligible for remedial training in reading. Another method of identifying the universe might be to define it in terms of the cases recommended by teachers, but this method is likely to provide a highly variable population from year to year. Therefore, let us assume that the director of research identified his universe in terms of a cutoff on a distribution of test scores. His next step would be to select a sample to which should be administered the remedial training, and, at the same time to select a second sample that would also be followed up but would be given no remedial training. The latter sample, referred to as a *control sample,* would be used for estimating the population characteristics at the end of the year with respect to reading skills so that a determination could be made of the probability that the trained group could be considered a sample of the untrained population. The investigator will attempt to make both his experimental and his control group as representative as possible of the identified universe.

In all sound experimental design, it is important to start by defining the universe to be studied and then to establish methods for sampling that will maximize the information supplied. All too often the reverse procedure is undertaken. The author is aware of a book that describes the behavior of four cases of reading difficulty. These four cases are presented without any inkling of the nature of the population of which they may be considered to be a sample. The reader is thus left wondering about the inferences that can reasonably be made from the data provided by the sample of four. On the other hand, if it were known that these cases were every tenth case admitted to a reading clinic for eight- to twelve-year-old children in a large city public school system, it might have been possible to make certain statistical inferences from the behavior of the sample to the behavior of the population sampled.

This example illustrates the methodological error of studying a number of cases and then seeking a population of which the cases could reasonably be considered to be a sample. When such a population is believed to be found, an attempt is then made to draw inferences about the universe from what is known about the sample. This procedure is quite unjustified as a basis of statistical inferences. At best, one can make what may be termed "judicious inferences," keeping in mind that these are based on the assumption that the population considered is identical with that actually sampled.

The reader may ask at this point, "Would it not have been as satisfactory if the director had taken a group who had passed through the remedial training program and matched them on the basis of initial reading test scores with a group that did not have special treatment?" This question implies that a comparison would then be made at the end of treatment between the treated and the nontreated group. This procedure represents common practice in educational research, and its weakness is not apparent at first sight. But it leaves the investigator with a difficulty.

If it were found on the basis of a statistical test applied to the final reading scores that there was only a small probability that the two groups of scores could be considered as samples from the same population of scores, one would be led to expect that, if the experiment were repeated with a new sample, similar results would be achieved. The difficulty, however, is that we do not know just what population should be sampled in order to achieve the same experimental results. Those included in the original remedial reading sample may have been simply cases that had been chosen because they appeared to be those that could be treated with a high degree of success; or they might have been a group that for some unknown reason responded well to treatment. The reverse might also have occurred if negative results had been achieved, for the investigator would not know to what population the results could be generalized. It might also have happened that a group that responded particularly poorly had been selected. In the case of positive results, it would have been shown that there was some likelihood that positive results could be achieved by remedial training, but it does not tell us with what group positive results are most likely to be achieved.

The Error of Sampling One Universe and Generalizing to Another

While consideration has been given to the cardinal sin in experimentation of failing to identify the universe sampled, a still more grievous sin is commonly committed by those who attempt to utilize and to apply research results. This is the error involved when a specific and well-defined universe is sampled and the results are generalized to quite different universes. Writers in the area of mental health seem to specialize in this error. They find, for example, that the children who come to a particular clinic and are examined there display an inability to do schoolwork under pressure and have to be given reassurances of the teacher's support if they are to learn effectively. In numerous writings such data or similar data have been taken as a basis for inferring optimum classroom conditions for typical schoolchildren. The error is obvious but rarely pointed out. Here, the behavior of children sampled from a clinic population has been studied. The scientist may make inferences about the clinic population from the behavior of the sample, but there is no basis for making inferences about other populations of children such as normal school populations. While this example of false inference is commonly found in the writings of clinical psychologists and psychiatrists, a similar error is made by writers on education who specialize in areas other than the clinical. It is a very easy error to make. The student of education should be particularly on his guard when he comes to writing the last chapter of his thesis— the place, he feels, where he can bring out the full implications of his study for education. At that point he had better ask himself to identify carefully the population to which his results may be reasonably generalized and the assumptions that underlie that generalization.

Individual Differences and Block Design

Research designs of the block type, which originated in the work of R.A. Fisher, are unsatisfactory in the way they handle the matter of individual differences. This may be explained by means of an example. Suppose that a study were being conducted to estimate the extent to which differences in pupil satisfaction in different classes could be associated with teacher differences. In this study four high school teachers, who were each teaching four different classes of thirty pupils, were selected. Two of these teachers were judged to be the most intelligent in the particular school, and two were judged to be the least intelligent. The pupils in each class were also divided into the fifteen more intelligent and the fifteen less intelligent in terms of a well-known intelligence test. The experimenter had in mind the hypothesis that the ablest students derived satisfaction from the ablest teachers but not from the least able teachers, and that the reverse was true in the case of the least able students. Now the experimenter in this case was undoubtedly thinking in terms of a continuous distribution of the intelligence of teachers, and probably assumed that what happens in the case of the two extreme groups of teachers can be used as a basis of generalization to intermediate groups.

However, such a generalization is not justified. The relationships established with extreme groups may not represent two points on a linear continuum. The responses of pupils to the intermediate teachers may be quite different from what it might be expected to be on the basis of that assumption. This situation can be remedied to some extent by including intermediate groupings, but the inclusion of more groupings adds greatly to the complexity of the design. Correlational analysis of the type that has been used traditionally for the study of individual differences has advantages over block designs in many studies in which human characteristics must be incorporated.

Brunswick's Representative Design

Particular attention to the problem of generalizing from experimental results has been paid by Brunswick (1947). This writer points out that thinking in psychology is still influenced largely by classical experimental design, in which an aspect of some phenomenon is isolated and then studied under laboratory conditions. Thus in psychophysics, the aspect of the phenomenon of visual acuity that has been most closely studied is the ability to perceive two closely situated points of light as distinct points. The separation that such points must have before they are perceived as separate by a particular individual would be considered a measure of the visual acuity of that individual. In further classical types of experimentation with this problem, the relationships of numerous conditions to visual acuity, as thus defined, have been studied. The typical and nineteenth-century-approved classical design involved holding all conditions constant except the one that the experimenter was manipulating.

The major change that has occurred in the classical type of design is the one due to the impetus of R.A. Fisher, which has been discussed briefly in this chapter. However, it may not provide results that are any more generalizable than the results of classical experiments.

Brunswick points out that these designs have one central weakness that has been disregarded. While they are usually planned with the purpose of including a sample of cases representative of a particular population or subpopulation, they fail to sample the variety of conditions to which it may be desired to generalize the results. In a great number of psychological experiments, the results found under one set of conditions may not be reproducible under other conditions. Indeed, it sometimes happens that one laboratory is unable to reproduce the results of another laboratory. Even in a simple experiment in which visual acuity is to be measured and studied by means of two points of light, it is doubtful whether the results are satisfactorily generalizable to other situations. If the purpose is to obtain results that can be generalized to other situations, the results may be disappointing. A person who has relatively low visual acuity in the laboratory situation may do surprisingly well in other situations, for it is known that visual acuity is related to the general nature of the visual field, the intensity of surrounding illumination, the wave length of the light involved, the state of adaptation of the eye, and so forth. What Brunswick suggests is that we sample these conditions systematically in order to obtain results that, by and large, are applicable to these varied conditions.

Brunswick developed at least one example of a representative design that involved a problem of size constancy.[1] In this design, size constancy was measured under a great many different conditions, such as in a closed space like a room, outside the building, under different illuminations, etc. The purpose was to derive principles that could be applied under these varied conditions. Similar types of representative design are extremely difficult to undertake on matters of educational interest. For example, it would be valuable to be able to measure the expressed attitude of white children toward Negro children under varied conditions in order to predict related behavior under those conditions. Although the researcher might want to do this, the probability is that he would be able to measure such an attitude only under classroom conditions, and this would provide inadequate information for predicting what expressions and other evidences of attitude would occur under other conditions. Representative designs in the attitudinal area are rarely feasible.

The acute reader at this point may well ask why it is that a "representative" design is suggested. Would it not be simpler to list the extraneous variables that might affect the outcomes of an experiment and then incorporate them in a block design of the Fisherian type? When this can be done, it is of course the recommended procedure, but in research in the behavioral sci-

---

1. Size constancy is the tendency to see objects as being of a given size even though the distance between the object and the observer varies. Thus, a Cadillac appears to be a big car even though it is viewed at a distance of several hundred feet.

ences the conditions that affect a particular phenomenon are usually so numerous that it is not feasible to incorporate them in a block design, for an unwieldy number of blocks would be involved. In most cases, it would also appear that these incidental conditions, though numerous, each contribute only a small effect —probably too small to produce significant results in a feasible block design. In this type of situation, Brunswick suggests that a systematic effort be made to obtain representative samples of these conditions.

The concept of representative sampling that Brunswick has developed has come in for much criticism. One criticism that the reader will probably already have considered is that major advances have already been made in many areas in the behavioral sciences without resorting to the elaborate procedures Brunswick's system demands. The psychology of learning is an example. Most of the important facts and principles of human learning that are discussed in typical textbooks were derived from laboratory experiments. For example, the principle that knowledge of results is an essential condition for learning was derived from a consideration of learning as it occurs in the laboratory and was demonstrated with simple laboratory experiments. Yet it seems to have wide application in the field of teaching.

A second criticism is that it results in the production of probabilistic laws—that is to say, laws that state only that there is a certain probability of a certain event happening as a result of a given set of conditions. Because Brunswick's system permits prediction over a wide range of situations, it is inevitably limited in the accuracy it can achieve. On the other hand, the more traditional approaches, because they aim ultimately at establishing *all* of the determinants of a particular event, have the ultimate aim of perfect prediction.

Summary

1. Courses in experimental design provide the student with a limited range of techniques for planning studies. However, a well-planned study can still pertain only to trivia.

2. Statistical methods serve two main purposes: one of these is the testing of hypotheses; the other is the summarization of data.

3. Well-designed studies have certain characteristics: they are free from bias, which may be introduced in various ways, some of which are not easily discerned. They must provide some satisfactory way of estimating error. They must insure sufficient precision to provide answers to the questions that are asked. The design must also be such that it yields as much information as possible from the number of observations that are made.

4. The term *control* is used in a number of distinct senses. It may refer to the control of conditions that may interfere with the outcome of a study; it may refer to the control of the crucial variable that is being studied; or it may refer to the use of control groups or control observations.

5. Replication is introduced in order to increase the precision of a study; that is to say, to increase the accuracy with which the main effects can be estimated.

6. An alternative to replication for the purposes of increasing the precision of a study is to control some of the sources of error. The traditional method of doing this was by a matching procedure, which has now largely been replaced by statistical methods.

7. The multifactor design is becoming more and more commonly used. Not only does this design permit the estimation of the effect of more than one variable, but it also permits the estimation of the effects produced by the interaction of these factors.

8. Sometimes designs are adopted that will not permit the estimation of all of the interaction effects. In such designs some interaction effects are said to be "confounded" with other interaction effects. Such designs commonly are used when interest is centered on the main effects, and they result in economies in the collection of data. An example of such a design is the famous Latin square.

9. The extent to which results have to be clear-cut in order to permit acceptance or rejection of a particular hypothesis depends on the consequences that follow if a mistake is made. If the consequences are serious, it is necessary for the data to present

much more clear-cut results than when the consequences are relatively unimportant.

10. In checking the design of a study, it is important for the researcher to be sure that it will answer the questions that are asked, not merely closely related questions.

11. Brunswick has pointed out that experiments should be representative with respect to the situations they sample. However, the extent to which such a procedure should be adopted is controversial.

CHAPTER 15

DATA-PROCESSING AND REPORTING

Data-Processing

The plan for the processing of data should be made at the time when the study is designed. By this is meant the time when the final plan is evolved. Of course, some preliminary studies have to be undertaken to insure that the enterprise is feasible. This is a more important matter than it may seem to be on the surface, and perhaps its importance may be brought home by citing an example.

A student once approached the author with a proposed study of the effectiveness of two methods of teaching typing. The design of the experiment was a familiar one, with several pairs of matched groups assigned to the two methods. At regular intervals throughout the training program tests were to be taken by the students. These tests would require rather prolonged periods of typing, lasting for as much as an hour each. The experiment was to be conducted over two semesters. During the conference with the student on this matter, a rapid computation was made of the volume of data to be collected and the time it would take to derive the scores that would be subjected to analysis. As nearly as could be determined, the work would have taken about six months of the student's full-time attention. Also, the data would have consisted of sheets of typing and were such that it hardly seemed possible to design a device that would result in the quick scoring of the material. It would have been an unreasonable use of the student's time to spend six months in clerical work, since this period could be much better spent in training related to his professional goals.

Various devices may be used to facilitate the derivation of scores from the raw data. One of these is a stencil scoring device. Unless it is absolutely essential, never conduct research in such a way that the answers to a test are marked in a booklet. A separate answer sheet is a compact method of recording raw data. If the scores are to be converted to standard scores, then it is sometimes convenient to print the conversion table right on the answer sheet. If possible, the researcher should avoid having scores recorded on both sides of the answer sheet, since it is inconvenient to transcribe these scores onto rosters. Sometimes the separate answer sheet should not be used. Whenever speeded tasks of simple functions are involved, the operation of finding the appropriate place on the answer sheet and marking it may contribute more to the variance of the test than the function it is desired to measure. In such cases, it is obviously desirable to avoid the use of a separate recording system. What can be done in such a case is to print the problem right on the answer sheet above or beside the place where the answer is to be recorded.

An alternative to the answer sheet is a version of the IBM punched card. Such cards are familiar enough to the reader through their several common uses—as checks, as bills, and so forth. They may be printed so that they have spaces on them similar to those found on answer sheets. The cards are then marked with a soft pencil, just as would be answer sheets, but of course they cannot be scored with the usual test-scoring machine. Instead, they are run through a machine that converts the marks to punched holes. A computer can then be used to derive scores for each card.

Test-scoring machines can be adapted to the analysis of all kinds of data. At the present time the common type of scoring machine is one built by International Business Machines Corporation. This machine not only scores but also is fitted with an item-counter device. This device permits the counting of the number of answer sheets that are marked in a particular position. It is thus possible to run a number of answer sheets through the machine and to determine the number that chose the first answer to the first problem, the second answer to the first problem, and so forth.

The scoring machine just discussed will probably become obsolete within a few years. International Business Machines already has an experimental model of a greatly improved new machine. A new concept of answer-sheet scoring has been introduced by Lindquist, who has built a machine at the State University of Iowa that is capable of performing most of the scoring required in the United States at this time. This work can be performed at a highly competitive price. The advantages and disadvantages of a single and centralized scoring service are not known at present and still need to be explored. The reasonableness of the scoring charges of this monster machine will make many research workers consider undertaking larger projects than they might otherwise consider. A picture of the Iowa scoring machine is shown in Figure XIV.

If verbal material is to be quantified, it should be collected through the use of directions that require the individual to produce only a limited volume of words, unless of course this is inconsistent with the purposes of the research. If too much emphasis is placed on quantity, the product may be time-consuming to score. If much written material is called for, it should be divided into brief sections by means of appropriate directions. Sometimes instructions can be given to subjects to ask them to prepare material in outline form rather than as continuous prose.

Occasionally an experiment can be redesigned so that the quantity of data involved becomes more parsimonious. For example, one piece of apparatus designed for studying the problem-solving process required the subject to obtain information about the working of the machine before the problem itself could be solved. The apparatus was built so that the information-gathering pro-

FIGURE XIV. *The Iowa scoring machine. This large scoring machine developed by Dr. E.F. Lindquist and his associates at the State University of Iowa is capable of performing numerous scoring operations at high speed. It has the capacity for scoring most of the testing programs administered in this country at the present time, and its services are available to anybody willing to pay scoring charges.* (Photo by courtesy of the Iowa Testing Programs, State University of Iowa.)

cedure of the subject was recorded in detail, and from such records it was hoped that the relationship between different information-gathering procedures and success in solving the problem could be studied. Such studies would have involved the analysis of vast quantities of material recorded on tape. This could have been avoided by comparing the problem-solving ability of groups trained in different techniques of gathering information, in which case the data-gathering procedure would not have had to be recorded. The only information needed would be whether each subject did or did not solve the problem.

Some ingenious investigators have used a plan to reduce the clerical work involved in the handling of data, but one that is not endorsed here. The procedure is simply that of requiring the subjects to undertake the clerical work. Where responses are to be coded, the subjects perform the coding; where the tests are to be scored, the subjects score the tests. This is an undesirable practice, for two reasons. First, it introduces sources of error variance over which the researcher may have no control. This is to some extent true even when a simplifying device such as an answer sheet is used. At least some error variance is introduced through errors in marking the answer sheet, but this variance becomes particularly pronounced when a speeded function is involved. If a complicated recording procedure is used, substantial errors may be introduced by the process. Second, a problem of ethics is involved. The researcher may have some justification in asking for the time of persons for the purpose of advancing knowledge, but he must respect their time and ask them to do only what is essential. The researcher should not be guilty of exploitation. Of course the issue does not arise if the subjects are paid, except that it may be much more efficient to employ a few well-supervised, trained clerks than a large number of untrained persons.

What to do about missing values is a particularly perplexing problem to which there is no completely satisfactory solution. In studies involving the analysis of correlation coefficients, a missing value in a table of raw data is of little concern. It does not matter much whether the coefficients in a table are based on slightly different numbers of cases. In factor analysis and in many other mathematical methods that are used for structuring data, slight variations in the number of cases from coefficient to coefficient are of little consequence.

On the other hand, when block designs are being used as the basis for an experimental design or as a basis of any other type of research, the problem of missing values becomes acute, since the computational methods that have been developed and that form the basis of tests of significance require the use of all cell entries. If certain cells are disregarded, the net result is to introduce an unknown amount of bias into the test of significance. There is no point in applying a test under these conditions, since it will not yield any kind of answer to the question posed.

At one time it was commonly suggested that mean values be substituted for the values of missing observations. The argument was that the measures were presumed to be normally distributed, and in such a case the class interval that includes the mean includes also the most frequently occurring values. Thus the insertion of the mean is an attempt to substitute the most probable value for the missing one.

Another approach is to compute expected values for those missing from the other values provided by the data. Through the computation of regression equations, it may be possible to provide a least-squares solution to this problem. However, this procedure is likely to produce more internal consistency in the resulting data than they would otherwise have. It will also bias tests of significance to an unknown degree. This problem has been worked upon, and proximate solutions that attempt to eliminate bias in tests of significance have been developed for many of the commoner block designs. The reader is referred to Cochran and Cox (1950), who have provided excellent accounts of the usefulness of these solutions and who have summarized research on this matter.

Another problem that sometimes arises is that of whether to discard certain observations that for one reason or another fall far outside the range of the other observations. Such discards must not be made after a preliminary inspection of the data has shown that the discarding of certain observations would make the data more in accordance with expectation. Discarding *must* take place before the significance of the data has been examined, for if this rule is not rigorously observed, the tests of significance that are applied will probably be biased. On the other hand, if this practice is observed, there is no reason why the researcher should not set up rules for discarding observations. These rules must apply to all observations, never only to certain groups. An example may illustrate this point.

In the last few years substantial interest has been shown in eyelid conditioning, not because of any intrinsic interest in the phenomenon itself but because it can be used for studying a wide range of problems of learning. Eyelid responses are usually produced by a slight puff of air directed on the eyeball. However, only some of the responses appear to be true reflexes. On the contrary, some have a latency period, a delay in occurring, that makes many observers classify them as voluntary responses. In experiments that use eyelid conditions as the medium through which knowledge is acquired, it is customary to discard from the data those responses that occur more than a certain given time after the stimulus is applied. Different delays are permitted by different experimenters but each experimenter sticks rigidly to the rules that he has set for discarding observations.

The researcher should always be on guard lest the procedure established for discarding observations does not by some means affect tests of significance that are later applied. This can happen in many ways, but the basic effect is always produced by there being a greater number of discards in one group than in another. Reasons why this may occur should always be carefully scrutinized, but even when the greatest care is taken to avoid any bias of this kind, there is always a faint possibility that a bias may have been introduced. The best rule to follow is to avoid conducting studies that involve the discarding of observations.

Observations may be recorded on rosters or on cards with numbered spaces. The author's preference is for the latter system, since it provides greater flexibility and facilitates certain operations with data, such as the separation of groups of cases on which it may be desired to conduct special studies. The roster method of recording is highly inflexible, and even the correction of errors on rosters may present difficulties.

It is particularly important to check the accuracy with which all entries are made. The procedure is such a simple one that it often gives the false impression that it is just not possible to make errors on such a straightforward copying task. One very common type of error is the transposition of digits, such as occurs when a number is correctly read as 51 but incorrectly recorded as 15. Another source of error is the recording of digits in incorrect boxes on the cards or on the roster. All recordings must be checked with the most scrupulous care in order to catch such errors, for they may seriously affect the conclusions drawn from the data.

The processing of data presents certain problems that must now be considered. An important consideration in the data-processing procedure is that the scientist should *know* his own data. Unless there is a close personal contact between the researcher and his data, many important findings will never be made. Limitations may remain unnoticed unless close contact with the data is maintained throughout the processing procedure. For these reasons, there is at least some wisdom in performing a part of the data-processing by hand methods. This is no problem in the case of the student who is conducting research to fulfill the requirement for a master's degree, since the quantity of data is relatively small, and in any case it is probable that he will process all his data himself. On the other hand, if the quantity of data is large, it will be necessary to process all of it by machine methods, in which case it is difficult for the researcher to come to know his data as well as he should.

The student should be warned against the incorrect use of information derived from data. One such use is found in the researcher who gets to know his data well in order that he may derive from them hypotheses to be tested later by means of statistical tests. It should be remembered that statistical tests of hypotheses are not designed to test hypotheses derived from the data themselves. If such tests are applied to these hypotheses, they will produce answers that are biased.

The problem is perhaps better understood by considering an actual example. A research worker studying differences between delinquents and nondelinquents finds negligible differences between the two groups in all of the variables where he had planned to test the difference. However, a close scrutiny of the data reveals that the blue-eyed children who were unusually tall for their age showed a high incidence of delinquency, and this is advanced as one of the major conclusions of the study. The error made by the research worker in this case is that if one were to compare the two groups on a large number of characteristics, it would certainly happen that *in this sample* some combination of characteristics would be found that just happened to differentiate the two groups. There would be no reason for believing that the results would be repeated in a new sample.

What the student should do is to list, during the planning stages of the study, all of the *reasonable* hypotheses that he proposes to study. His data should be collected for the purpose of testing these hypotheses and no others. All subsequently developed hypotheses squeezed out of the data would be subject to the criticism that they are not firmly rooted in the theory on which the study is based, and any apparent positive results would probably be the result of chance peculiarities of the particular sample.

The Use of Data-Processing Machines

While the student of education of ten years ago would have processed his data with desk calculators or by hand methods and perhaps have spent many months in the process, the student of today should consider the use of high speed computers for this purpose. In most institutions facilities for the processing of data are available and advice is readily obtained on how to go about the undertaking. The brief information given here should enable the student to approach a computing center with the knowledge necessary to ask intelligent questions of those who operate the machines. If the school at which the student is studying for his graduate degree does not have a computer available, a neighboring institution will undoubtedly be willing to undertake the work for a modest fee. Privately operated computer centers which undertake contract work for business firms are generally not sufficiently familiar with research problems to be of much help to students of education.

High-speed computers generally consist of a storage unit in which the data to be processed and the directions for processing it are stored and a unit which performs the common arithmetical operations on the data in accordance with the directions. The machine will also perform certain other operations, such as comparing two numerical values and determining which one is larger. The set of directions is referred to as the *program*. A set of directions which compute correlation coefficients from data would be referred to as a *program for computing correlation coefficients*. Programs can be used over and over again once they have been prepared and libraries of programs exist in most computing centers so that common statistical operations can be performed without the writing of new programs.

Only a few years ago a program was a lengthy and cumbersome affair—even one for performing a relatively simple operation, such as the computation of a mean and standard deviation, might require as many as a hundred listed operations. In recent years shorthand methods have been developed for writing such programs. These shorthand methods have required the invention of suitable "machine languages." One of the machine languages used today for writing programs in a brief and concise form is *FORTRAN*, which stands for Formula Translating System. An example of a program written in *FORTRAN* for the computation of a test of the significance of the difference between two means is shown in Figure XV. As can be seen by the example, this machine language resembles English in many respects. But there is one important difference: the machine language must be written with the greatest precision, for the omission of even a period or a comma may result in a complete change of meaning. What this means is that the rules of syntax for a machine language are precisely stated and must be followed to the last minute detail. The learning of such a machine language is an excellent exercise in the precise use of language.

Short courses (lasting no more than ten class hours) in the use of machine language are given by many organizations. Such a class provides a useful background for anyone who has data to run on a computer. Such a brief course does not make a person expert in the use of the language, but it will permit him to read and understand a program and know what such a program involves. It will also help him with the preparation of his data for machine-processing.

```
        FORTRAN
        PROGRAM TO CALCULATE A T-TEST
        DIMENSION X(99,2)
      3 FORMAT ( I2,2F5.3)
      4 FORMAT (20F4.1)
      5 FORMAT (1X, I2,5F12.3,I3)
        READ  3 ,N,TO5,TO1
        READ  4 ,((X(I,J), J=1,2), I=1,N)
        FLN=N
        SUMD = 0.0
        SUMDSQ=0.0
        DO  10  I=1,N
        D=X(I,1)-X(I,2)
        SUMD=SUMD+D
     10 SUMDSQ=SUMDSQ+D*D
        DBAR= SUMD/ FLN
        VARD=(FLN*SUMDSQ-SUMD**2)/(FLN*)FLN-1.))
        STDEVD=SQRTF (VARD)
        SDDBAR=STDEVD/SQRTF (FLN )
        TOBSRD=DBAR/SDDBAR
        IF(TO1-TOBSRD) 15, 15 , 12
     12 IF(TO5-TOBSRD) 14, 14 , 13
     13 LEVELT= 111
        GO  TO  30
     14 LEVELT=555
        GO  TO  30
     15 LEVELT=999
     30 PRINT  5 ,N,DBAR ,VARD ,STDEVD, SDDBAR,TOBSRD,LEVELT
        CALL  EXIT
        END
```

FIGURE XV. Illustration of a program written in FORTRAN for applying a t test to determine the significance of the difference of means.

The program and the data are generally transmitted to the machine on tape, but the research worker typically transmits his data to the computer center on punched cards. The cards have to be punched according to a definite format prescribed by the particular machine that is to be used. The cards must be carefully verified after they are punched. The author can remember a case in which the key punch operator skipped a column on one card. The error was not picked up during verification, and the entire study had to be recomputed later.

Programs are available for nearly every operation that the student of education is likely to want to perform and he would do much better to search a few program libraries than to attempt to write a program of his own. This point is mentioned because several research reports have been published recently in which the writer has stated that he had written particular machine programs while the knowledgeable reader knows that such programs were available at the time that the research was conducted. Programs are available for analysis of variance, multiple regression analysis, and various factor analytic procedures, as well as for the preparation of tables of intercorrelations. The machines will also apply specified tests of significance to data.

When the student first sees a table of charges he may be overwhelmed by the thought of receiving a large bill. What he has to know in evaluating such charges is that the machines work at tremendous speeds and may perform vast amounts of work in a matter of minutes. Recently, one such machine undertook a task that would have taken two man-years on a desk calculator; the computer completed the work in seven minutes. A new and transistorized version of the same machine would undertake the same work in less than two minutes. Even a relatively high charge of five dollars a minute will permit large amounts of work to be undertaken for less than twenty dollars. In most universities students can obtain machine time either free or at a nominal charge.

The computations undertaken by the machine should be checked for over-all reasonableness. While a high-speed computer may not make an error for years, human operators do make errors and may feed the machine the wrong program or the wrong set of data.

The student should be warned against a practice that is sometimes observed. This involves the checking of only those statistics that do not appear to be in line with expectation or with other values that have been computed. This partial checking introduces biases into the results and makes them appear to conform to expectation more closely than would accurately checked results. The reason for this is that a complete recheck of all results often changes some of the results that conformed closely with expectation, so that these show greater departures from expectation. The numerical results of a study must be reported with the highest accuracy that it is possible to achieve.

All work that involves computation must be carefully labelled. Most inexperienced researchers have the feeling when they are working on data that they will easily remember them when they come back to them at a later date. When they return to the data in a few weeks or months, they invariably find that they cannot identify what was done, and much time is lost in determining just what the computations signify. Often data remain permanently lost because they cannot be properly identified.

The data, and the computations based on them, should always be retained for a considerable time after the final report on the study has been published. This is necessary because a critical reader may desire to check other hypotheses with the data, or may wish to check the same hypotheses by different methods or after certain corrections have been introduced. It is embarrassing when someone questions the validity of the analysis and the researcher is unable to produce the basic data so that the matter can be checked.

The Processing of Qualitative Data

Many of the data collected in educational research are qualitative. These present special difficulties when they are to be processed. In the early stages of acquiring information about a phenomenon, no attempt may be made to process carefully the facts that are collected. Freud's classic observations on the behavior of disturbed patients are examples of qualitative data collected and examined for the purpose of developing hypotheses, and the conclusions that he drew guided the research work of subsequent generations of psychologists. Early explorations are usually made in this way, but ultimately such observations must be analyzed systematically. The mere inspection of data without the aid of systematic analysis is a hazardous process, and there is always danger that the researcher will dream into his data elements he wishes to see there but that do not really exist. For this reason every effort must be made to reduce such data to a form in which they can be analyzed by appropriate methods. In this way personal prejudice can be eliminated from the interpretation of the material.

As a first step in the analysis of qualitative data, it is necessary to code the facts that are involved. This means simply that a number must be assigned to each class of fact. Thus, if the cumulative records of children are to be studied, it may have been determined that perhaps 80 items of information are to be coded. Those concerned with the coding operation might be asked to code all items of information on a sheet, a section of which might be as follows:

42. Progress through school   0 = never held back a grade
                                            1 = held back one grade
                                            2 = held back two or more grades

43. Absenteeism from all causes (average days per year over period of record)   0 = 5 days or less
     1 = 6–10 days
     2 = 11–15 days
     3 = 16 or more days

44. Speech   1 = no speech difficulties reported
     2 = speech difficulties but no action taken
     3 = speech difficulties and remedial work started

Through such a code sheet the qualitative information obtained in the cumulative record is converted into a set of numbers, which are then used for the analysis. Sometimes the numbers are entered directly onto the code sheet, if it is quite brief. If the code sheet is long, the code numbers are often entered on a separate sheet or card. The code numbers on the cards may then be punched into other cards if the data are to be analyzed by machine, or the cards may be sorted by hand if a hand analysis is to be made.

Certain precautions must be taken in adopting this type of procedure. First, it is necessary to conduct a trial run in order to determine whether the coding system involves any ambiguities. It might then be found that, for example, severe weather one year had closed the school for ten days. Since this eventuality had not been taken care of in the coding system, an additional rule would have to be introduced into the coding of Item 43; namely, that absenteeism is not to include days lost through the closing of schools. Additional rules of this kind almost always have to be introduced when a coding system is tried out.

Any set of rules established for the purpose of quantifying qualitative material should be tried out further by submitting the material to different coders in order to determine whether the rules can be applied with consistency by different workers. This tryout helps to establish the error resulting from differences in the judgment of different persons. The tryout may also result in the development of methods that eliminate these discrepancies. The reliability of such procedures should always be given in the report of the study, unless the procedures are such that it is clearly evident that *careful* independent workers can produce independent results. This might be true where the entire process of quantification required only the counting of the number of words written in documents produced by subjects.

Errors are commonly made in clerical procedures that involve the coding of data. These are usually referred to as errors of carelessness, but in actual fact they are probably caused not so much by the failure of the clerk to be conscientious as by the immensely boring nature of much of this work. The upshot is that it is essential for all clerical work of this kind to be rechecked independently by another clerk. It may not be necessary to lay down the standard that only perfect agreement is to be accepted, since this may be unrealistic, but some standard should be established. Scores that do not agree within one point, or two, or three —or whatever is considered reasonable—must be redetermined, preferably by another person. Clerks must work independently, otherwise this check would be quite meaningless.

WRITING THE REPORT

While the author imagines Heaven as a place where one can do research without ever having to write a report, the requirements of this world are that research be described in a written report. For many research workers, the preparation of the report is a particularly burdensome task. The report of a research may be thought of as a history of the research, and a history from which a reader may be able to reconstruct what happened. Let us consider some general points to note in writing this history.

First, the report should be written in a consistent style throughout. Table headings, footnotes, and appendix material should follow a consistent format. Editorial assistance is very helpful in producing such consistency. Many graduate schools recommend manuals to follow in the writing of theses and the student should familiarize himself with the style requirements of his school. He will probably have to set himself a few rules to follow. For example, some use the word *data* as a plural noun as it is in the Latin from which it is derived, but some recent writers prefer to consider *data* as a singular noun. A number of rules to follow in such respects may be noted.

Second, a scientific report must be written in clear and concise terms; there is little place in it for personal animosities, anecdotes, displays of wit, and the like. Recently, there appeared a report of a very interesting research project which was ruined by the overwhelming intrusion of the research scientist's personal whims, his hostilities toward colleagues, stories of personal experiences which had no relevance to the topic, and other inconsequential material. The reader of such a report reacts much like a teacher who has read through a term paper of a pupil which would have been outstanding were it not for an inexcusable boner in the last paragraph. His first impulse is to give the student a failing grade, but later, after his emotional reaction has subsided, he may change the grade to a C or even a B. Much the same is likely to be true of a reader of a research report who finds it spoiled by a display of personal prejudice and irrelevant humor. This does not mean that the report has to be written in a dull pedantic style. Enthusiasm may still appear between the lines and the report as a whole may convey the spirit of adventure, but the report should be a presentation of research, not a presentation of the personality of the author although the latter inevitably shows through.

Third, the tone of the report should be one of appropriate modesty. The scientist is a humble person who realizes that even the labor of a lifetime is likely to add but a small increment to man's knowledge of his environment. In writing a research report it is easy to let one's enthusiasm lead to an overemphasis of the importance of the findings. The scientist is rarely in a position to evaluate the significance of his findings in the total picture of knowledge. Only through subsequent history can such an evaluation be made.

Beyond these initial words of advice, the author finds himself treading on uncertain ground. He can recall journal editors who marked the margin of some of his most prized paragraphs "Not clear." After a few such experiences, he wonders whether any writer should ever try to give advice to another on how to present his ideas. Nevertheless, he has been asked so many times by students and researchers to advise on problems of reporting research that he realizes that the student also will demand a section in this book on the same topic. The section that follows repeats the advice that he has given to graduate students on many occasions, and also repeats the criticism he has made of these students' dissertations. Whether such advice can improve the student's writing is a matter about which the author cannot even speculate.

It is common for a dissertation to be written in at least two forms. The initial form presents the material to an examining committee. The second form is a condensed version that presents the material for publication. The initial version, like any other piece of writing, must be written with the nature of the specific audience in mind. It is to the student's advantage that he know personally those who constitute this audience and be able to write specifically for them. To some extent, he should write with their expectations in mind. If one of them is likely to ask the student to relate his findings to some particular theory, then he should be sure to do this.

In the case of writing for formal publication, the problem is much more difficult. The student would do well to start by reading articles in the journal that is being considered as a place of publication. From this overview, he should arrive at judgments concerning the nature, length, and organization of the articles that the editors favor. Editors, like any other people, have personal preferences, and these must be taken into account since they may be the deciding factors in determining acceptance or rejection of the student's product.

The Introductory Sections of the Report

The introductory sections usually begin with a statement of the problem. The author feels that in the reporting of most research studies at least the general nature of the problem to be investigated should be outlined in the very first paragraph of the report. The statement may not be in a full and precise form at this stage, since it may first be necessary to introduce the reader to a number of terms and concepts before the problem can be accurately set forth; nevertheless there should be a statement of the problem, even if only in a general form.

The introduction must also provide an appropriate theoretical orientation for the reader. This may involve a history of the problem and a review of related studies. In some cases, the theoretical framework of the problem may be so familiar to those who are likely to read the article that it may be quite unnecessary to state it except in general terms. For example, a student working on the problem of reinforced learning would obviously not review reinforcement theory, which has been described fully in so many other sources. On the other hand, if the research is concerned with a theory with which the reader is unlikely to be familiar, it is essential that the theory and its background be outlined in the introductory section. If the theory is the researcher's own, it is desirable that it be fully presented in terms of the procedures described in earlier chapters of this book.

In the preparation and execution of a research, extensive work is often undertaken on the review of previous studies in the area. If it is done by a senior research worker with broad experience in the field, this may constitute a major contribution in itself. When substantial effort has been devoted to this phase of the undertaking, it is possible that a separate article may ultimately be prepared and published to cover the outcomes of this activity. Such publications may form an immensely valuable contribution to the professional literature; but when such a separate contribution is made, it is necessary in the research report itself only to refer briefly to this article and to list it as a major reference, giving merely the major outcomes of this activity.

The review of the literature should lead up to the full and complete statement of the problem. If the introduction gives or implies the statement of a theory, as it should, the problem should be stated as a deduction or consequence of the theory. Earlier in the introduction, the student should have defined all the terms needed for understanding both the theory and the statement of the problem. By the end of the introductory section, the reader should be fully prepared for understanding the explanation in subsequent sections of how the problem was solved.

The Over-all Format of the Report

The research report is an historical record of what the researcher did. Like all good records of history, the research report should permit the reader to reconstruct what happened and without distortion. The research report typically follows a time sequence, beginning with an account of previous work, followed by a description of the research undertaken, and ending with ideas for future studies. There are many ways of providing a documentary record concerning what happened in a particular study, but the following outline represents a plan of presentation quite commonly found in research literature:

1. *Introduction*
   A. The problem
   B. Previous research
   C. Theoretical implications of previous research
   D. Relation of present research to the theoretical position stated in C
   E. Specific hypotheses to be tested
2. *Procedures*
   A. General procedure adopted in the research
   B. Equipment and other types of instruments used
   C. Directions given to subjects
   D. Selection of subjects and their characteristics
3. *Results*
   A. A summary of the data
   B. Tests of significance
   C. The testing of the hypotheses outlined in 1
   D. Conclusions
4. *Implications*
   A. Implications of the research in relation to the theoretical position previously taken
   B. Implications for further research
   C. Practical implications (if any)

The Description of the Procedure

The vital importance of the section that describes the procedure or method is often not appreciated by the novice in scientific research. The criterion of a well-written description of the procedure or method used is whether it provides sufficient detail for another researcher to reproduce the study. Too often the experimenter writes up his work only to find that insufficient detail is given for another even to begin to reproduce it. In the behavioral sciences, the writer faces real difficulties in deciding what are and what are not the important details to report in describing his procedure. It is clearly quite impossible to detail all of the conditions related to the undertaking of a study. For example, in describing an experiment, is it relevant to report that the experimenter was a woman, or that she was a blonde, or that she was born in Germany? The author knows of one study in which it was relevant that the experimenter was a woman, and the results probably could not be reproduced without a control over that factor. However, he does not know whether any experiment has been reported in which it was relevant that the experimenter was blonde or was born in Germany. In any event, the fact that a factor is important in one study does not mean that it would necessarily be important in another study. The decision has to be made in each case concerning what is to be reported and what is to be omitted. The fact that this decision must be based largely on judgment reflects our lack of knowledge about behavioral phenomena.

The description of procedures should include a reproduction of verbal directions given to the subjects. If these are lengthy, they may be relegated to an appendix, or a footnote may indicate where a complete set may be obtained. Minor differences in wording may have substantial effects on the outcomes of a study. Unfortunately, matters of intonation and emphasis cannot be accurately described, although these may have substantial effects on the results.

The description of apparatus is likely to be unsatisfactory unless the greatest care is taken. Since it is not usually possible to publish a blueprint, it is necessary to specify the essential details. However, the experimenter sometimes may not know what are the essential details. This statement may need some explanation.

The author was concerned some time ago with the replication of an experiment that involved apparatus. The piece of equipment specified was the Harvard tachistoscope, which is widely used in psychological laboratories and is readily available. The object to be viewed through the tachistoscope was illustrated in the original article, and this was easily reproduced by a draftsman. However, after some work with the equipment, it became evident that a crucial feature of the entire arrangement was the size of the object presented. This had not been specified in the original article, but the results could be reproduced only when the object was a certain size. The original experimenter had been unaware that this was an essential aspect of his experiment and had failed to report it. Unless there is a great deal of replication with variation, the experimenter is likely to be unaware of the essential characteristics of his apparatus.

One advantage of using standard apparatus can be seen when the problem of description arises. It simplifies matters greatly to be able to report that a Harvard tachistoscope or a Brush Model 392 amplifier was used, since this equipment can be duplicated by other experimenters. The home-grown type of equipment needs careful description.

Sometimes the research worker calibrates apparatus, in which case it is necessary to describe the method and technique used in calibration. Sometimes the equipment used in calibration is as complicated as the apparatus itself.

A common omission in studies of educational behavior is a failure to indicate just who was included and who was excluded from the study. This is the matter of specifying the sample that was included, or perhaps one should say what universe was sampled in selecting subjects for study. There is the same need for specifying the universe that is sampled when the objects are inanimate as when they are living. The student will realize that unless the researcher knows how his sample is drawn, he will not know to what his results can be generalized.

In describing the method used for selecting human subjects, sufficient information should be given so that the reader may know to what population the results may apply and also how he can obtain a similar sample and reproduce all the conditions of the study.

Reporting the Results and Stating the Conclusions

The results of a scientific study should usually be presented in a table for which there is some explanatory material; but, since many studies in education do not approach ideal standards, this method of reporting cannot always be attained. A distinction should be made between the results of the study and the interpretation of the results. By "results" is usually meant the summarized data and the test that is applied to determine whether they are or are not consistent with the hypothesis they were designed to test. In educational research some test of significance must usually be applied to the data in order to test the hypothesis. It is usual to describe this test in the results section of the report and to indicate the assumptions made in its application. Usually these assumptions will be approximated rather than completely fulfilled, as when it is said that distributions of scores can be considered to be samples of normally distributed universes. Sometimes, although the conditions required by the test of the hypothesis are not completely satisfied, empirical studies carried out elsewhere have shown that these departures will not affect the outcome. The results section should also describe any special and unexpected events that occurred during experimentation, as when subjects were unable to complete the schedule because of illness or other causes. The treatment of missing values should also be discussed in the results section.

As far as possible, the table or tables presenting the results of a study should be self-explanatory and should not require extended reading of the text in order to understand them. On the other hand, the material in the text should point out the important aspects of the data and draw attention to the relevance of the results.

Just how much tabular data should be presented is always a matter of judgment. As a general rule, only those statistics that are crucial to the testing of a hypothesis should be presented.

Detailed raw data rarely can find a place in a research report, except where they are of such unusual interest that their reproduction is definitely in the interest of science.

A common error in the presentation of results is the division of the results into too many separate tables. Many research reports can be improved by the consolidation of tables into larger units.

Some comment should be made on a special problem of reporting results that occurs from time to time. The problem is that of what to do with experiments that do not yield anything that can ordinarily be reported as results. Reference is made here not to experiments that yield negative results, which can usually be reported by the procedures discussed, but experiments which are prevented, by some technical hitch, from being carried through to their proper conclusion. These abortive efforts are not entirely useless in the information they provide. Indeed, if the problems they raise are never discussed in the literature, others will attempt similar experiments and end in similar difficulties. The difficulty of reporting such efforts stems from the understandable unwillingness of editors to accept articles about them. To the author, the way out of this dilemma is to report the results of abortive experiments in the introductory section of a report of a further experiment that was successful. One may preface a successful experiment with an account of the various avenues and approaches that were explored before it could be undertaken. Such an account can be brief, but it should be sufficient to warn others about the limitations of the alternatives that were explored.

This does not mean, of course, that weaknesses in the approach revealed during the course of the study should not be noted. Sometimes it is necessary and desirable to admit that the main knowledge derived from an experiment is how to design a more conclusive study. It also happens quite frequently that a study designed as a crucial and conclusive experiment turns out to be, on further examination, ambiguous in its results because of the various ways in which they can be interpreted. There are many well-known cases of such experiments that were designed by famous experimenters. For example, there has long been argument as to whether it is possible to have nonreinforced learning. Experiments have been designed in which animals, usually rats, have been provided with opportunity for learning without any apparent reinforcement. However, it has usually been possible for the protagonists of reinforcement learning theory to point to the possible existence of hidden reinforcing conditions which destroy the conclusiveness of the results.

The conclusions should state the extent to which the data are consistent or inconsistent with the hypothesis or hypotheses. They should be stated in the same order as the original hypotheses and should parallel the list of the latter. The statement of the conclusions should not be contaminated with implications or with other types of speculative discussion. There is no reason why they should not be stated in a fairly terse form.

A common error is made in drawing conclusions from research results. This error is seen in cases where an investigator collects data that reject a hypothesis and hence question the validity of the postulate on which the hypothesis is based. Under such circumstances, some investigators are inclined to turn around and seek reasons why the experiment was really not a crucial test of the issue it was designed to settle. The situation indicates either that the investigator had become too attached personally to his own ideas or that the test of their validity was inadequate in the first place. If the latter was the case, the question may be raised as to why the experiment was ever conducted. If the experimenter changed his mind during the research and began to question its utility, then he should have stopped his work and certainly not published his results.

Writing the Implications and Discussion Section

The creative research worker will inevitably speculate on the implications of his study that extend beyond his immediate purposes. He will also want to communicate his thoughts on such matters to a wider public. True, nobody is ever likely to treasure these thoughts as much as their creator; nevertheless some may be useful to other research workers, and a few may even be real gems. The section of the report dealing with implications may be used quite appropriately for setting forth these thoughts.

It is important that the section on implications be more than a splurge of personal notions. Whatever ideas are presented must be set forth in a well-organized form. Sometimes it is convenient to organize them around a few areas for which the implications have special importance. For example, in one study of mechanical problem-solving with which the author is familiar, the implications were organized around two topics; namely, the selection of mechanical trouble-shooters and the training of trouble-shooters. Good organization will develop in the reader of the report a better appreciation of the importance of the writer's ideas than will a poorly organized section.

Brevity in the implications section is also a very desirable characteristic. Most readers have only limited appetite for the speculations of others. A lengthy section may produce boredom and lead to the rejection of even the good ideas that are presented. While a discursive style may, at times, be extremely useful for driving home a point, a certain degree of crisp conciseness should be aimed for here, as in other parts of the written report.

The section on implications is also the section in which it is appropriate to give some indication of the future direction of the program of research of which the report represents a part. Perhaps it may be well to remind the reader again that if research is to be profitable, it must be programmatic. A research report should end, therefore, not with a note of finality but with some indications of the unfinished business that should be the next preoccupation of the researcher.

If the report has been introduced with the presentation of a theory that the research is designed to extend or modify, then the final section may well restate the theory in the light of the findings. This process may involve such radical changes in the original formulation that what is virtually a new theory has to be stated. Whenever the research results in the restatement of a theory, it follows that the research report should indicate how changes in the theory should modify current practices.

Use of Diagrams, Tables, and Figures

A common error in the writing of technical reports is the failure to use diagrams effectively. The author can remember more than one instance when he had to wade through ten or more pages describing a complicated piece of apparatus when a simple diagram and a page of description would have sufficed. The author also suspects that some readers are quite unable to translate verbal descriptions into visualizations of the equipment described. The medium used for communicating should be appropriate to the material to be communicated.

If diagrams of apparatus are given, and they are necessary if any apparatus has been used in the study, it is most desirable that they be prepared by an artist. This is not necessarily as expensive a procedure as it sounds. If an artist is provided with a good sketch, he is likely to produce a finished diagram with considerable speed. The author has had many such made for approximately ten dollars each.

The artist or draftsman will have to be informed of the size to which a diagram will be reduced on publication. Usually, he will draw it on a larger scale and his drawing will be reduced photographically.

Figures and graphs should be presented in such a way that they are self-explanatory. The headings and captions to figures and graphs should provide all the explanation needed. Discussion of what the table or graph demonstrates in relation to the hypotheses can be appropriately included in the text.

Typed manuscripts do not usually have an index, but if a dissertation or other research report is published as a monograph of substantial size, then an index is a most important feature. It is prepared during the page-proof stage, when final page numbers have been assigned to each portion of the text. A simple procedure for making the index is for the person who is reading the page proofs to have at hand a quantity of three-by-five index cards or slips of paper. Each time a technical term or name is encountered in the text, it is noted, together with the page number, on a card which is then deposited in a box. After the reading of the proofs, the cards are put in order to form an index.

In any larger work, an index is an invaluable aid to the reader and should be prepared with care and thoroughness. Its usefulness depends to a great extent on the appropriateness of the classification of concepts that it uses.

Other Points on Organizing the Research Report

When a research report is of such a length that it requires organization into chapters, it is most desirable to provide the reader with certain devices that will enable him to keep track of the argument and to find his way around in the mass of material. This can be done in several ways.

First, it is desirable to provide chapter summaries. These should help the reader to organize his thoughts by going over the highlights of what he has read and the conclusions and arguments presented. The summary should be strictly a summary; it should not include new material that happened to occur to the researcher after the report was written. It may well be organized into a series of numbered paragraphs, and these should be written in a concise form.

Second, a system of paragraph and section headings may well be adopted. Indeed, some writers like to begin by preparing a list of headings and then writing the sections and paragraphs in any order, working at any one time on those where they feel that their thinking has reached the point of maturity and where an organized statement can be put down on paper. Some writers prefer to use a system of major headings and minor headings, in addition to chapter headings, but this can be done only where the material lends itself to this type of organization.

Third, a good table of contents is a most desirable guide for the reader. Where paragraph and section headings are used, these should be listed in the table of contents.

Finally, brief mention must be made of style of writing in the report. He who tries to advise another on questions of style is treading on uncertain ground. When one sees how often literary critics have been wrong in predicting the acceptability of the works of writers, one realizes how unreasonably prejudiced one may be in one's preferences for style. Also, a person's style is dear to his heart, and suggestions that it be changed or even that it be criticized may arouse ire. Therefore the author, acting with a certain sense of self-preservation, will at this time point out only certain common features of technical writing that detract from its value in communication.

First, there is the error of using too difficult a vocabulary level. A writer should not select a word just because it is appropriate and because *he* knows the meaning of it. A necessary condition for the use of the word is that the reader also know its meaning. When unfamiliar words are introduced, the writer must remember that the reader will have to learn them. It is not sufficient that they be formally defined once and then used. This is like asking a person to learn a word by exposing him to it once. What one has to do in writing is to give the reader as much opportunity as is feasible to learn new terms. These must be not only defined but also used in contexts where their sense can be inferred from the general meaning of the sentence. The writer who introduces several unfamiliar terms and then fails to provide the reader with a learning experience is likely to find that most of his public does not read beyond the introduction.

A few technical writers have acquired the reputation of writing in a language familiar only to themselves. Such writers may have been careful to define their terms, but since these terms have not acquired general usage, readers have never learned them and much of the writing that uses this language is never carefully read. Hence, much of it is lost. For this reason, the reader should realize that new terms should be coined only when it is absolutely necessary to do so.

Just as unfamiliar words should not be used except where they are essential, so too is it desirable to avoid passing references to obscure theories with which the reader may not be familiar. If such a little-known theory must be mentioned, it is desirable to introduce it by presenting its main features. Such brief descriptions can be appropriately introduced as a part of the text. The nineteenth century practice of using lengthy and elaborate footnotes to explain any obscure point in the text is one that has become less and less frequently used in scientific literature.

Those who have not had previous experience in writing often manifest the error of unnecessary repetition. Some repetition is necessary in most writing, and the old adage applies that the teacher should start by telling his audience what he is going to say, then he should say it, and finally he should say what he has said. A report, as much as a lecture, is a learning experience for the audience and a teaching experience for the writer. Thus systematic repetition of the type described by the adage is a desirable feature of written presentation. The kind of repetition that should be avoided is that where the writer keeps on harping on a point or coming back to it.

A frequent error of style, particularly common in the literature of educational research, is that of writing out in extended detail facts that have been presented in a table in concise form. An example of this from a mythical report is given below:

The table under consideration shows the percentage of correct answers to the arithmetic problems given by various categories of college students. It can be seen that freshmen, sophomores, juniors, and seniors obtained on the average 32, 34, 43, and 44 per cent of the problems correct. When the same group of freshmen is divided according to whether they came from Type A, Type B, or Type C schools, the percentages are 29, 31, and 33. The corresponding figures for the sophomore group are 31, 32, 36; for the junior group, 41, 42, 45; and for the senior group, 43, 44, 45.

Drivel of this kind fulfills only the purpose of confusing the reader, who would have understood the data perfectly well had he been left to examine a well-constructed table. By contrast, a writer does well to point out the highlights of a table and also any important features which might otherwise escape notice.

A similar stylistic fault is seen when a writer is attempting to explain a mathematical operation that he has performed on data and does this by giving an extended account of the arithmetic involved instead of providing a brief account of the algebra or of the general purpose of the operation. An example of this kind of error of presentation is the following:

> The totals for each one of the horizontal rows were squared and from the sum of these values was subtracted the square of the grand total divided by 500. The result of this operation was then divided by 6 and the dividend was entered in Table X. A similar arithmetical operation was then performed with the totals of the vertical rows, etc.

What the writer should have done was to state that he performed an analysis of variance according to customary procedures. If he wanted to explain further what he was doing, a brief algebraic explanation would have sufficed.

Final Publication

Most theses and dissertations do not achieve publication beyond that provided by microfilm services or the reproduction of a summary in *Dissertation Abstracts*. This is usually not because the findings do not merit publication but because the author does not take the necessary steps to incorporate his findings in the professional literature. Most doctoral dissertations from a well-established graduate school contain enough of consequence to provide at least one publication, and some may yield several. They would not have been accepted in partial fulfillment of the requirements for a degree if this had not been so. True, a dissertation of no consequence occasionally slips by through some misunderstanding, as when everybody involved had become committed to accepting it before its worth had been properly evaluated, but such cases are exceptions. Failure to publish the results of a doctoral project is almost always due to the fact that the student failed to take the steps necessary to achieve this goal. Often this is due to lack of motivation, since the achievement of the doctoral degree represents the achievement of a personal goal and publication has little to offer to the student. In addition, he may have already revised his product so many times that any further revision is seen as a most distasteful and repulsive task. However, the doctoral student, though aware of these blocks and impediments, should recognize that he has to consider more than personal gain in deciding whether or not to publish. He also must consider that in the preparation of his dissertation he has occupied much professional time on the part of a faculty, and that he can repay this debt to society by making his findings part of the body of professional knowledge represented by published literature. If he does not do this, much of his time and the time of others will be lost, and later students may repeat his work without ever knowing that they are merely repeating what has already been done. Master's degree students have a lesser responsibility in this respect.

The most desirable place of publication is the professional journal that specializes in the field in which the student has worked. Many such journals publish without charge except for special materials such as tables and cuts. Less desirable as places of publication are those journals that require the authors to defray the cost. It is inevitable that the free-publication journals should be able to select the best contributions.

Most journal editors will provide considerable help in shaping an article so that it presents its material in the most effective way. Suggestions by editors concerning the revision of manuscripts should be given careful consideration. In such matters, the editor's experience is likely to provide a sounder basis of action than is that of the neophyte in the field. Editors are deeply concerned with making their journals into the best publications they can possibly produce.

New Methods of Distributing Technical Information

Twenty years ago it was a relatively simple matter to publish long articles that included substantial quantities of tabular material, but today lengthy scientific documents are extremely difficult to publish. This change is partly due to the large increase in publication costs that has taken place over the period, but an additional factor is the expansion of research in the behavioral and educational sciences, with the result that most journals receive many times as much material as they ever have space to publish. One partial solution for this problem is for journals to provide additional sections in which material may be published at the expense of the author. A few writers have been attracted by this proposition, and especially by the fact that it results in immediate publication and the usual long delay is eliminated. Nevertheless, the expenses of such early publication are high and beyond the economic circumstances of most young research workers, even if they are fortunate enough to have their article accepted.

Those who have thought about the problem of providing publication facilities, and hence of the problem of distributing scientific information, agree that traditional journal sources will become progressively even less adequate than they are at present. New methods of distributing scientific information must be found, and some are in the process of being developed.

One attempt to develop a new technique in this connection is represented by the American Documentation Institute, which is commonly represented by the letters ADI. It is a private, nonprofit organization that provides a special type of service.

When a research worker is faced with the problem of publishing a study that includes, for example, large tables of correlation coefficients or variances and covariances, he may write his article so that only the analysis forms an integral part of the article. The original table of correlations or other material on which the analysis is based may be omitted, but a footnote is included indicating that these materials have been deposited with the American Documentation Institute and giving the order number of the document. A reader who wishes to refer to the basic data underlying the analysis may write to the American Documentation Institute and, for a small fee, may obtain either a photographic copy of the document or a reproduction on microfilm. Charges for this service are very moderate.

Since the American Documentation Institute provides only photo reproductions, it is necessary that all documents transmitted to them be suitable for this purpose. Material should be typed with a heavy black ribbon that is quite new, and there should be no stray marks or messy erasures. It hardly needs to be pointed out that the name and location of the person depositing the document should be marked clearly on every document.

Documents deposited as a part of a study that is appearing in a journal should be submitted to the journal with the manuscript. This is done in order that the editor may better judge the entire manuscript and determine the relevance of the supplementary documents.

Brief mention may be made of an organization with the Department of Defense, which may represent a common method of the future for distributing scientific information. This is the Armed Services Technical Information Agency, usually known as ASTIA, which represents an attempt to provide a pool of well-organized technical information derived from the research agencies of the Department. The Agency prepares an organized list of titles, referred to as the *Title Announcement Bulletin,* or TAB, and this is distributed to using agencies. At the same time the Agency prepares abstract cards, which are distributed to those who need additional information about particular titles, and some users are provided with complete sets of cards in specific areas if they so request. If the information on an abstract card interests a user, he may request a copy of the complete document. The latter is provided either as a full-size reproduction or in some form of microreproduction. The copy is returned when no further need exists for its use.

The ASTIA program seems to the author to be in many ways a model for programs of the future. Perhaps it should be pointed out that Ohio State University took a step in this direction some years ago in preparing comprehensive bibliographies in the area of education and educational research, but the program was perhaps ahead of its time and did not blossom into a document collection and reproduction service. When the ASTIA system is applied to civilian problems of disseminating information, it is suspected that the present system of journal publication may become obsolete. Many problems will have to be solved in this connection, but a new system is surely needed.

Summary

1. The plan for the processing of the data should be drawn up at the time when the study is designed.

2. Data should be collected in a form convenient for processing.

3. If apparatus is used that records the desired data mechanically, it should be arranged so that it delivers data in a concise and manageable form.

4. Procedures for quantifying data should be written out in detail and should be given a trial run prior to actual use in the study. The reliability of these procedures should be reported if they involve judgment.

5. The problem of handling missing values should be discussed with a statistician if it arises. The discarding of observations may seriously bias the outcomes of a study unless the research worker knows how to handle this problem.

6. Clerical work should be checked for accuracy, since inaccuracies may introduce large errors.

7. The research worker must avoid the error of deriving hypotheses from the data and then testing the hypotheses from the same data.

8. High-speed computers are commonly used for the processing of data. In order for such machines to operate, they must be supplied with a set of data and a program which will instruct the machine concerning the operations to be performed on the data.

9. The program is generally written in the language specially designed for the purpose of communicating with machines. The program must be written with great precision and must follow rigidly the rules of syntax of the machine language.

10. Statistical work must be carefully checked. If the researcher checks only those statistics that appear to be out of line, he will introduce bias into his results.

11. The introductory sections of the report should always contain a clear and concise statement of the purposes of the research. These sections should also outline the background of the problem and the theory on which it is based. They may sometimes form the basis of an article for journal publication.

12. The section of the report that describes the procedure should be sufficiently detailed to permit reproduction of the study. This is not the easy matter that it may appear to be on the surface.

13. The results section of the report should contain statistical summaries and reductions of the data rather than the raw data. The conclusions drawn from the study should be clearly related to the hypotheses that were stated in the introductory sections.

14. The final section on implications should discuss the problem of "where do we go from here." The writer of such a section should avoid the temptation to throw in many wild ideas. The section should be a well-organized presentation of thoughts and concepts that emerge from the study.

15. Diagrams and tables should as far as possible be self-explanatory. Often they are appropriate substitutes for lengthy discussion.

16. The student should seek to publish at least an abbreviated account of his study so that the results are made available to the profession.

17. The American Documentation Institute represents a relatively new method of distributing technical information and one that may well supersede many of the functions formerly undertaken by journals.

CHAPTER 16

SOME FINAL

CONSIDERATIONS

IN THIS book, an attempt has been made to familiarize the student with some of the methods that can be adapted or that already have been adapted to the purposes of educational research. The author feels that this presentation may have left the impression that a knowledge of techniques placed at the command of a shrewd analytic intellect represents the essential ingredient of successful research. If this impression has been given, the author has been guilty of misrepresentation, so this final chapter has been written to impress the reader with the importance of other factors in a successful research enterprise. To some extent, this chapter must be speculative, for only a little is known concerning the personal and environmental conditions that are necessary for the production of creative research. Some of the available information will be given here, but an attempt will be made also to stimulate the reader's thinking concerning the problems of developing a creative research program.

Ability, Productivity, and Some Possible Reasons for Lack of Productivity

The conditions necessary for high-level creative work have been identified to only a limited degree. At present there is much speculation concerning this matter—and a little research, much of which is stimulated by the worthy hope that it will be found that a democratic type of organization is most favorable to the creative process. Corroboration of that view will be hard to find, if it can be found at all, without a radical reformulation of the problem. Certainly it will be many decades before sufficient information will have been acquired about this problem to advise the student concerning the environment he should seek out if he is to be creative in his research. Perhaps different students will have widely different requirements in this respect. However, there would be some agreement among graduate school faculties that certain students who seem to have all the intellectual skills necessary for creative talent often fail to produce original research, and that lack of productivity often has its roots in certain common causes that must be given brief consideration here. The student who is aware of some of these conditions may find means of avoiding them.

First, there is the problem of excessive ambition. Every graduate school is familiar with the student who cannot find a problem worthy of his consideration. He sees his fellow graduate students as persons willing to study trivia that are beneath his dignity. He is likely to spend time disparaging the efforts of his associates. It is most desirable not to be this type of student. Until a person has accomplished much in research, he is not in a position to criticize the simple-mindedness of his associates. Only accomplishment in research brings with it the right to criticize, except for the few who have established themselves as recognized critical reviewers. The behavior of the graduate student who is hypercritical of others is usually interpreted to be a symptom of defensiveness and of feelings of inadequacy. The student should be aware of this, and perhaps this awareness will help him avoid this error of the beginning researcher.

The foregoing remarks need to be qualified. Often the over-ambitious graduate student has the greatest potential as a creative research worker. The student who is content to study some commonplace problem that can be solved by routine methods is probably concerned mainly with obtaining his doctoral degree and then leaving research forever. He has neither the ambition nor the creative talent for a career in research, which takes high ambition and a willingness to undertake a search for knowledge as a pursuit worthwhile in itself. Perhaps, also, a successful scientific career requires a certain impermeability to criticism and a tendency to pursue courses of action that others think are unproductive.

The author also suspects that the graduate student who is most capable of generating novel research ideas is the one who is often least able to evaluate such ideas critically. This is hardly surprising, for critical abilities seem in themselves to inhibit the free flow of ideas. Those who have ideas may be expected to have many poor ones as well as many good ones, and they need help in sorting them into one category or the other. Such students need the help of faculty advisers who recognize worthwhile and researchable ideas and who praise the student for them. Too often such students are met with a barrage of criticism directed toward their poor ideas and do not receive credit for their imaginative talent.

Another source of lack of productivity is found when the researcher feels satisfied with his results only if they show high consistency with expectation. Part of this tendency is, no doubt, a fear of criticism. To present clear-cut results that can have only one possible interpretation places the scientist in a position beyond reproach and beyond criticism, but few experiments ever yield results of this kind. Most scientists in the behavioral area must be content with results that show some accordance with expectation but involve at least some small suspicion that the results could have arisen by chance. Difficulty in tolerating the ambiguity that such results provide has prevented many students from finishing well-conceived studies. Many completed studies remain unpublished for this same reason. This problem, insofar as it arises in a graduate school of education, is probably best handled through encouragement given by the faculty.

An interesting problem in this connection is posed by the work of Mendel, who, it will be remembered, counted the frequency with which smooth peas and wrinkled peas appeared in certain hybrids. Statisticians who have examined his results state that they manifest a much closer agreement with the frequencies that would be expected on the basis of his theory than are ordinarily encountered. Some have suspected that the Abbé may have seen that his results showed some departure from theoretical expectation and, fearing that his work might be rejected by the scientific body, made some adjustments in his data. Of course this is just a hypothesis, for we cannot possibly know with any certainty whether he did or did not tamper with his data. The moral to be learned is perhaps that even if Mendel did adjust his data, the theory that it was designed to substantiate was rejected by one of the world's leading scientific societies, and thirty years passed before it was accepted.

Another difficulty that seems to arise in the case of some research workers and that chronically limits their productivity is failure to communicate with others during the early planning stages of the inquiry. Such communication, with the resulting exchange of ideas, seems to be an important factor in the development of the research worker. It permits both the critical review of research ideas as well as the development of these ideas to the point where they are researchable. True, there are some workers who communicate little with their associates and yet produce research of real value, but such workers are generally persons who would be considered to be of the highest capability, even by graduate school standards. Most graduate students require substantial interaction with their associates as a part of their education and as a part of the process of evolving a researchable problem.

Difficulties of communication often permeate the entire research process. Some students show evidence of being able to conduct a well-designed experiment even though they do not seem able to describe it to others at the time or to write a presentable account of what they have done at a later date. Perhaps the administrative solution to the difficulties of such students might be to team them with some of their more communicative associates who are less adept as experimentalists. Graduate schools may have some difficulty in accepting such a solution.

The Importance of the Social Atmosphere in Creative Work

Historians agree that creative work has been produced in quantity by mankind only at certain times in history. For reasons that are largely unknown, these periods of creativity have usually followed great wars. The social climate seems to be an essential factor in releasing creative talents, for one may assume that the available talent is the same from generation to generation.

The author is inclined to believe that much the same is true of the graduate student who wishes to engage in creative research. The existence of a proper social atmosphere is important for undertaking creative work at the highest level at which he is capable of operating.

It is doubtful whether graduate schools of education have been particularly successful in providing a social environment congenial to the development of creative talent. Schools of education, like most graduate schools, are designed for students who are willing to conform to a mass of rules and regulations, who take and pass required courses regardless of whether or not they consider them worthwhile, and who are willing to develop a dissertation about a problem of interest to the faculty. As Benjamin Bloom and his associates have shown at the University of Chicago, the college professor is interested in developing students similar to himself. There is nothing wrong with this— except for the fact that there is now considerable evidence that the creative person tends to be a nonconformist and is somewhat insensitive to the demands of the community in which he lives.

Nonconformist students have always had their problems. One is reminded at this point that Oxford University was founded by a group of students from the University of Paris who did not like the way in which the latter institution was run.

Perhaps the nonconformist student who has never regarded himself as such may, by reading this, recognize the source of some of his difficulties and benefit by this insight. It is the writer's fond hope that some faculty members who read this may as a result develop softened attitudes toward students who find that bearing with the rules and regulations of a graduate school is distasteful. A sympathetic attitude toward the oddities that go along with creative talent would do much to generate in schools of education an atmosphere in which original research can thrive.

Another major difficulty in generating an atmosphere sympathetic toward research stems from the fact that few members of most schools of education faculties engage in research and thus do not regard it as an activity about which they can speak with enthusiasm. The young research worker should probably be developed in an environment where research is pursued with an excitement that can almost be described as breathless anticipation. This is not the kind of atmosphere found in most schools of education, though it does exist in a few. This situation has not been remedied by the development of bureaus of educational research, few of which conduct work that might be described as original research or research as it is discussed in this book. Most of these bureaus devote their efforts to rendering advisory services or to conducting surveys at a rather superficial level. They have an important public relations role, and if they do not contribute to new knowledge, they do at least facilitate the dissemination of the old. They provide an atmosphere that probably encourages the development of the administrator, but none has acquired a reputation for developing research workers.

The limited scope of such bureaus and institutes has been unfortunate. Although they may have provided service to local communities, they have contributed but little to the development of educational research as a branch of endeavor in the behavioral sciences. The result is that scientific research related to educational problems has had no sponsors, except for the few in major graduate schools who conduct research for their own satisfaction. There is a real need for research institutes of education that conduct research of the type which has been stressed in this book. Such organizations would provide facilities for producing a whole generation of educational researchers dedicated to discovery in the field. Education would indeed then have a body of professional research workers, much as other fields have, and would not have to rely upon research traditions being carried on by a few overworked professors who are able to eke out a few hours a week of research work.

Prolonged and Sustained Effort in Creative Work

A major difficulty faced by the graduate student in producing research that might be called original is that this requires prolonged and enduring effort. One can be misled in this matter by the well-known fact that many important ideas have come to famous scientists at times when they were thinking about something else. This is a rather typical phenomenon among high-level scientists. However, what should not be missed in this matter is that these important ideas did not appear in individuals who had never sought to discover them. In every case, they appeared in individuals who had struggled long to find a solution, and it happened that the solution came at a moment when they were concerned with other matters. There seems no doubt that the creative person spends extended periods of great conscious effort when all of his energies are devoted to the solution of a problem; indeed his energies may be so completely channeled that he appears to have almost a detachment from the other aspects of life, even to the point where associates may consider him to be callous or thoughtless. The absent-mindedness of the intellectual is just one symptom of this deep preoccupation. In this milieu of thoughtfulness the important ideas emerge, though often at a moment when the mind has turned to other things.

The graduate student, however talented he may be, is rarely able to devote his entire energies to the solution of a single problem. He has to be preoccupied with course work and with somewhat prosaic matters such as language requirements. It is probably for this reason that even the brilliant doctoral student rarely produces a brilliant doctoral dissertation. Conditions conducive to work of this quality are not provided for the graduate student.

What has been said up to this point fails to bring out the distinction between what may be termed "creative research" and routine investigation. Most master's theses and doctoral dissertations fall into the latter category. They are designed to test some fairly obvious hypothesis. They may be considered to develop, as it were, a territory that has already been well explored, but they are valuable, for it is the well-developed territory that yields riches. The graduate student as a researcher is a developer rather than an explorer. If he makes discoveries, they are minor if not a little prosaic. It is the explorer who makes the major discoveries, and for him too are reserved the special excitements of high adventure, the despairs of failure, and occasionally the thrill of genuine discovery. The developer's life is somewhat more tranquill and decidedly less venturesome. He knows a great deal about the territory in which he is operating. He knows with some certainty what will be the outcome of his labors. In contrast, the explorer is searching for something that he does not yet know except in the vaguest way, and like Columbus, he ultimately may not recognize what he finds. The reader will clearly recognize that this book is directed toward the developer rather than the explorer.

Ghiselin (1954) has described this aspect of the creative process in a way that is particularly appropriate. He refers to the creative person as one who is struggling to realize the unrealized, who wants to accomplish something still beyond anything he can as yet conceive but which is there in its vaguest outline at the periphery of consciousness. The creative person may spend a lifetime in struggling to find a medium through which he can realize this objective of peripheral awareness. Many never find it.

The characteristics of the research worker that have been noted in this chapter present a problem in the matter of developing educational research. The problem is generated by the fact that many schools of education require their faculty to have had public school teaching experience. This tends to select persons who are unlikely to have much of the disposition that one might hope to see in the researcher. A person who has a real interest in theoretical problems or in such abstract matters as represent the very roots of research can hardly be expected to show a deep interest in the activities of classroom management as a possible lifetime pursuit. The outstanding research worker, with his ability to detach himself from his environment, might even be considered a poor risk as a teacher in the public schools. Schools of education should come to realize that the talents required by personnel who operate schools are probably quite different from those required in research.

The argument has often been put forward that in order to understand educational phenomena, it is necessary to have had the experience of teaching in a classroom. The argument is extremely persuasive, but its attractiveness is thoroughly superficial. Its inadequacy is seen when it is extended to other fields. Does the physicist have to experience a free fall before he is prepared to study free-falling bodies? In the case of the behavioral sciences, personal experience in a situation often produces the actual disadvantages of being unable to perceive the situation with any objectivity.

The Financial Support of Research

Any course in educational research should leave the student with a concept of its cost and some idea of how it is financed. Most of those who take courses in educational research do not expect to make it a lifetime pursuit, but many may become administrators who perhaps will have some responsibility for sponsoring research projects and for obtaining financial support for them. In order to fulfill this function of fund-raiser and expediter of research, it is necessary to have a concept of both the cost of research and the nature of available sources.

There is no way of estimating how much is spent annually at the present time on educational research. Much, if not most, of the money spent is channeled into activities related to the collection of administrative information. This activity is usually referred to locally as "research," but would not fall within the meaning of the term as it is used in this book. There is no way of drawing a sharp line between administrative data-gathering and research, since there are all shades of intermediate activity. For this reason, one cannot obtain an estimate of current expenditures in educational research.

If the amount spent on educational research by large city school systems is examined, it is found to be relatively small. Annual budgets of $30,000 for research purposes are considered to be exceptionally large. In contrast, a major manufacturer of cameras will spend $100,000 on the development of a single mechanical innovation, simple because it is not possible to develop a new device for less. Manufacturers just do not expect to derive benefits by investing small sums in research, partly because a substantial fraction of all research does not result in a useful product. On the other hand, boards of education commonly expect useful products to emerge from a relatively small investment, and they often derive little return from the money invested because the investment was too small.

Bureaus of educational research in universities rarely have much financial support and are often staffed by relieving a professor of a course so that he can then devote forty or more hours per week to the venture. Such bureaus, as has been pointed out, tend to be overloaded with work of a nonresearch character. There are just a few bureaus that have established full-time research professorships, with no strings attached as to what the incumbent is to do in the position. This is a direct support of research in a way that is sorely needed.

It has been possible during the last ten years for a few bureaus of educational research to obtain funds by undertaking contracts for the U.S. Office of Education. Under this system, money is obtained for undertaking specific projects on which a proposal has been submitted. Such projects vary in size, but most are between $20,000 and $40,000. These may seem to be large sums, but the cash received does not represent the cash that is actually invested in research personnel. The institution itself is usually entitled to a fraction of the money to cover its investment in buildings and their upkeep and management costs. A research contract of $20,000 might involve a deduction of $3,000 for overhead charges, leaving only $17,000 for the research itself. The latter sum might be sufficient for the quarter-time services of a high-level project supervisor and two full-time research assistants and a clerk.

The value to an institution of developing a research program in this way has been a matter of controversy in the literature. Some institutions have felt that it has provided a real opportunity to develop a research program. Others have felt that it has not been a good method of expanding research because it means hiring temporary professional employees who cannot be given any guaranty of a permanent position.

Both major and minor foundations have provided some support for educational research, and they are sources from which additional help may be sought. Proposals may be submitted to foundations, which will have them reviewed by competent persons in the field. Since World War II, there has been a tendency for foundations to provide institutions with rather large sums of money for long-range programs of research. This is in accordance with the concept that research is best carried out along programmatic lines. An immediate consequence of this is that the individual researcher has only limited opportunities for raising relatively small sums for his own projects.

The author is a little unhappy about the policy that involves the donation of large sums to schools of education or bureaus of educational research to be spent within a relatively short period of time. This has been done, as in one case where an institution was given several million dollars for a five-year research project. On the surface this might seem to be a promising approach, for it does at least give recognition to the fact that productive re- . search costs substantial amounts of money. It does, however, neglect one important aspect of research that must be recognized if successful work is to be done; namely, that inquiry into a novel field is not likely to be accomplished successfully by persons who have not already spent much time thinking about related problems. The outstanding advances in the behavioral sciences seem to be made typically by scientists who have spent many years thinking about and working on a problem and who have developed a group of scientists with whom they work and who together have learned to speak a common language. It perhaps may have taken many years before the leading scientist in this group reached the point where his thoughts had become organized into a useful system.

After the last war, the United States government attempted to "buy" research in the behavioral sciences on a grand scale. This action was taken on the assumption that creative ideas could be bought just like any other commodity. Such a procedure seems to have had some success in the production of technological developments, but the author is unaware of any major scientific development that has been made in this way, and it would be surprising if any had.

Foundations expect a return for their money. For this reason, a foundation is likely to evaluate the person who submits an idea as carefully as it evaluates the idea itself. An idea may be a good one, but if it is submitted by a person who has little notion concerning how research should be conducted, there is no point in investing money in the project. For this reason, it is difficult for a person who does not have an established reputation to obtain a grant for original research. Some foundations do have small funds set aside for sponsoring those who are new in the research field, but such sponsorship is considered to be a long shot, with high chances that there will be no return on the investment.

Money for educational research is available, and perhaps one might say that it is available in quantity. What is lacking is a body of trained research workers with a broad scientific background who have the capacity for conducting programmatic research. The few who at present have these qualifications can utilize only a small fraction of the money that could be made available for educational research.

APPENDIX:

AN EXAMPLE OF A THEORY FROM

THE BEHAVIORAL SCIENCES

IT IS difficult, if not impossible, to obtain from an educational science of behavior illustrations of a fairly complex theory of behavior stated with some degree of precision. A handful of simple theories involving one or two postulates can be found, but these are relatively few and far between. It is therefore necessary to turn to the field of psychology to provide a good illustration of a fairly well-stated theory that has some complexity. The illustration selected here is one developed by Ammons (1954), and it is shown in Table 4. It should be noted that all terms that have any special technical significance have been defined with some care. The theory as it is presented here includes only four postulates, but it has been derived from a more comprehensive theory containing twelve postulates.

Once he had stated his theory, Ammons went on to look for situations in which he could test some of the deductions from it. In one case, he found a situation that seemed to provide a rough test of deduction 4a. In an essay examination in one of his classes, some students were given four questions, all of which were hard, while some were given four questions, two of which were easy. It was hypothesized that when the questions were all hard the "feelings" and drive of the students would be heightened and more error responses would occur. The data were found to be consistent with the hypothesis.

The reader should note that the theory may be described as a miniature system, and by this is meant that it is not a general theory of behavior but a theory of only a very limited segment of behavior. Ammons refers to it as a theory of error to indicate that it is concerned primarily with the prediction of error behavior. He has generally taken the stand that it is limited theories of behavior formulated with some precision that at present will serve best for the purpose of organizing knowledge of human behavior.

Much can be learned about the problems and difficulties of developing theories of behavior in education by examining this theory. First, note that the language of a scientific theory is rather different from the language ordinarily used for discussing behavior. The language refers to ideas and concepts that are quite different from those used generally in describing behavior. This is partly because the formulation of a theory requires that the phenomena with which the theory is concerned should be described as far as possible in terms of variables that can be measured. In the most advanced theories, such as those developed in the physical sciences, all terms are quantified and the postulates are represented by equations.

The advantages of stating a theory in terms of variables is obvious when we turn to a consideration of the next criticism that may be leveled against the theory presented. If the deductions from the theory are examined, it will be seen that they are not derived from the postulates in a manner that has any great rigor. They do follow from the postulates in a general sense, but they do not give the impression of following with absolute necessity.

The fact that most theories in the behavioral sciences are such that there is no rigorous method of making deductions from them results in much controversy over which theories are to be accepted and which are to be rejected. Indeed, it has happened

—although on rare occasions—that certain evidence is accepted by one school of thought as substantiating a theory and accepted by another school of thought as rejecting the same theory. Such conflicts are entirely the result of difficulties encountered in stating the postulates of the controversial theory in such a way that rigorous deductions made from them can be used to substantiate or reject the theory. As theories in the behavioral sciences become better and better formulated, this type of controversy will inevitably vanish.

Finally, it must be pointed out that the language used in decribing the theory is not the language ordinarily used for describing behavior in daily conversation. The language of the theory, which is referred to as the data language, is usually a technical language of its own. The language of daily living does not lend itself well to the development of theory in the behavioral sciences.

TABLE 4

Theory of a limited aspect of behavior drawn up by Ammons in terms of postulates, definitions of the terms used in the postulates, and some deductions derived from the postulates.[1]

Definitions

Error: A response other than that appropriate to the motor set present, where this response is appropriate to other parts of the stimulus complex.

Response: Observable striated muscular behavior by the individual.

Motor set: Bodily orientation for the performance of a given behavior, inferred jointly from the instructions given by the experimenter or subjet to himself and the physical orientation of the person. We can to some extent get at it by asking the subject what he intends or intended

[1] From " 'Errors': Theory and Measurement," by R.B. Ammons, in The Kentucky Symposium: *Learning Theory, Personality Theory, and Clinical Research.* Copyright © 1954, John Wiley & Sons, Inc. Reprinted by permission.

to do, or by setting up an objective criterion for determining whether or not the physical orientation would allow the performance of the task.

Appropriate response: The response which the individual says he intends or intended to make and for which he is physically oriented is the appropriate response to the motor set. Appropriate responses to other parts of the stimulus complex are those which would be most frequently made if those parts of the stimulus complex were dominant.

Stimulus complex: Various components which make up the stimulus such as stimuli from motor set, specific drive stimuli, and external stimuli. Any of these can be changed relatively independently, changing the stimulus complex.

Dominance of a component of the stimulus complex: A drive stimulus is more dominant as the drive becomes stronger. When the subject is asked to describe a situation, a particular stimulus component is dominant to the extent that it is mentioned earlier in his description.

Drive stimuli: Those stimuli characteristically noted by the human organism in connection with hunger, thirst, sex frustration, fear, anxiety, etc. One could infer the presence of such stimuli in terms of strength of drive.

Definitions

External stimuli: Environmental energies which affect the receptors of the organism.

Strength of the response tendency: Latency of the response, physical strength of the response, and probability of the response occurring in the presence of or closely following the presence of a given stimulus complex.

Stimulus similarity: Stimulus complexes are similar to the degree that they contain similar components and are relatively less separated along the various discriminable continua.

Strength of drive: Might be the self-rating of the individual or might be inferred from the past history of the individual with respect to the time since drinking, time since eating, number of times a pleasant or unpleasant consequence has followed a particular stimulus complex, etc. Thus drive stimuli can be associated with primary or secondary drives as conceived of by Hull. Emotions are considered to be drives.

Reward: The satisfaction of some need, goal-object consumption, or avoidance of noxious stimulation.

Postulates

Postulate 1: To any stimulus component or complex, there are a number of possible responses. The strengths of the response tendencies differ. Thus there is present a "strength" hierarchy of responses to any given stimulus component or complex.

Postulate 2: The more similar a stimulus component or complex is to another given stimulus component or complex which has regularly elicited a response in the past, the stronger the response of this kind now elicited by the new stimulus.

Postulate 3: The stronger the drive, the stronger the response.

Postulate 4: The components of a given stimulus complex may in isolation elicit different responses. When the components are combined in the stimulus complex, the greater the dominance of a given component and the greater the strength of a given response tendency associated with it, the more likely the stimulus complex is to elicit this response.

Deductions

Deduction 3a: The more drive present, the less similar the external stimulus need be to the stimulus which in the past has regularly elicited a response, for it to be elicited with the same strength.

Deduction 4a: If a response has been regularly elicited under a low drive and is now elicited with a high drive of the same kind present, we will observe an increase in "errors," providing the strongest response tendencies to the motor set and the drive are different and that to the motor set is dominant.

Deduction 4b: If a response has been regularly elicited under one drive, and the drive is changed to another without altering the other stimulus components (especially motor set), there will be more errors, providing the appropriate dominant response to the drive-stimulus component from the original drive was the same as that to the motor set, but that to the new drive stimulus is different from that to the motor set, the motor set staying the same.

Deduction 4c: To the extent that a single stimulus component dominates the total stimulus complex, the successive responses given by an individual will be more similar to each other.

Strong emotion leads to stereotypy of responses, as does instruction-induced "motor set," and the "same" physical stimulation. In free association, problem areas will be talked about more frequently than other areas. In the case of errors, we find that certain kinds are quite frequent, i.e. certain types of slips of the tongue and certain kinds of accidents in the accident-prone person. These errors should indicate the life areas in which the person has problems and thus be of diagnostic value to the clinician.

Deduction 4d: Other stimulus conditions being approximately equal, if one arouses feeling about an error he should get real-life responses associated with a similar set, emotion, or drive more quickly than if no feeling is aroused.

BIBLIOGRAPHY

Adler, Mortimer, J. "Liberalism and Liberal Education," *The Educational Record*, XX (1939), 422–24.

Alexander, Carter, and Arvid J. Burke. *How to Locate Educational Information and Data,* Fourth Edition. New York: Bureau of Publications, Teachers College, Columbia University, 1958.

Allport, Gordon W. *Pattern and Growth in Personality.* New York: Holt, Rinehart & Winston, Inc., 1961.

———. *Personality.* New York: Holt, Rinehart & Winston, Inc., 1937.

———. *The Use of Personal Documents in Psychological Science.* New York: Social Science Research Council, Bulletin No. 49, 1942.

American Psychological Association. *Technical Recommendations for Psychological Tests and Diagnostic Techniques.* Washington, D.C.: American Psychological Association, 1954.

Ammons, Helen, and Arthur L. Irion. "A Note on the Ballard Reminiscence Phenomenon," *Journal of Experimental Psychology*, XLVIII (1954), 184–86.

Ballard, P.B. "Obliviscence and Reminiscence," *British Journal of Psychology, Monographs Supplement*, I, No. 2 (1913).

Barzun, J., and H.F. Graff. *The Modern Researcher.* New York: Harcourt, Brace & World, Inc., 1957.

———. "The Nature and History of Experimental Control," *American Journal of Psychology*, LXVII (1954), 573–89.

Berelson, Bernard. *Content Analysis*. New York: The Free Press of Glencoe, Inc., 1952.

Bergmann, Gustav. *Philosophy of Science*. Madison, Wis.: University of Wisconsin Press, 1957.

Bloom, Benjamin S. (ed.) *A Taxonomy of Educational Objectives*. New York: Longmans, Green & Co., Inc., 1956.

Boring, Edwin G. "Intelligence as the Tests Test It," *New Republic*, XXXV, No. 444 (1923), 35–37.

Bowers, R.V. "Discussion and Analysis of the Problem of Validity," *American Sociological Review*, I (1936), 69–74.

Broadbent, D.E. "A Mechanical Model for Human Attention and Immediate Memory," *Psychological Review*, 64 (1957), 205–15.

Bruner, Jerome S., Jacqueline J. Goodnow, and George A. Austin. *A Study of Thinking*. New York: John Wiley & Sons, Inc., 1956.

Brunswick, Egon. "Representative Design and Probabilistic Theory in a Functional Psychology," *Psychological Review*, LXII (1955), 193–217.

———. *Systematic and Representative Design of Psychological Experiments*. Berkeley: University of California Syllabus Series, No. 304, 1947.

Bush, Robert R., and Frederick Mosteller. *Stochastic Models for Learning*. New York: John Wiley & Sons, Inc., 1955.

Campbell, Norman. *What Is Science?* New York: Dover Publications, Inc., 1952.

Cantril, Hadley. *Gauging Public Opinion*. Princeton, N.J.: Princeton University Press, 1947.

Chapanis, A. "Men, Machines, and Models," *American Psychologist*, 16 (1961), 113–31.

Cochran, W.G., and Gertrude M. Cox. *Experimental Designs*. New York: John Wiley & Sons, Inc., 1950.

Cogan, M.L. "The Behavior of Teachers and the Productive Behavior of Their Pupils," *Journal of Experimental Education*, 27 (1958), 89–124.

———. *Pupil Survey*. Copyright ©, 1953, by the President and Fellows of Harvard College.

Coladarci, Arthur P. "Are Educational Researchers Prepared to Do Meaningful Research?" *California Journal of Educational Research*, V (1954), 3–6.

Conant, James B. *On Understanding Science*. New Haven, Conn.: Yale University Press, 1946.

Coombs, C.H. "Theory and Methods of Social Measurement," in D. Katz and L. Festinger (eds.), *Research Methods in the Behavioral Sciences*. New York: The Dryden Press, Inc., 1953.

Cornell, Francis G., Carl M. Lindvall, and Joe L. Saupe. *An Explora-*

tory Measurement of Individualities of Schools and Classrooms. Urbana, Ill.: University of Illinois Bureau of Educational Research, L (1953), Bulletin 75.

Cronbach, Lee J. "Coefficient Alpha and the Internal Structure of Tests," *Psychometrika,* XVI (1951), 297–334.

Dale, Edgar, and Jeanne Chall. "A Formula for Predicting Readability," *Educational Research Bulletin,* XXVII (1948), 11–20 and 37–54.

Davidson, H.P. "An Experimental Study of Bright, Average and Dull Children at the Four-Year Mental Level," *Genetic Psychology Monographs,* 9 (1931), 119–289.

Davis, F.B. *Item Analysis Data: Their Interpretation, Computation, and Use in Test Construction.* Cambridge, Mass.: Graduate School of Education, Harvard University, 1946.

Dewey, John. *How We Think.* Boston: D. C. Heath & Company, 1910.

Dollard, John, and Neal E. Miller. *Personality and Psychotherapy.* New York: McGraw-Hill Book Company, Inc., 1950.

Estes, W.K., S. Koch, K. MacCorquodale, P.E. Meehl, C.G. Mueller, W.N. Schoenfeld, and W.S. Verplanck. *Modern Learning Theory.* New York: Appleton-Century-Crofts, Inc., 1954.

Evaluative Criteria. Washington, D.C.: Cooperative Study of Secondary School Standards, 1950, 1960.

Festinger, Leon, and Daniel Katz (eds.). *Research Methods in the Behavioral Sciences.* New York: The Dryden Press, Inc., 1953.

Flanders, N. "Analyzing Teacher Behavior as a Part of the Teaching Learning Process," *Educational Leadership,* 19 (1961–62), 173–80.

———. *Teacher Influence, Pupil Attitudes, and Achievement.* Prepublication manuscript of a proposed research monograph for the U.S. Office of Education, Ann Arbor, Mich., 1962.

Flesch, Rudolf. *How To Test Readability.* New York: Harper & Row, Publishers, 1951.

Fowler, W. "Cognitive Learning in Infancy and Early Childhood," *Psychological Bulletin,* 59 (1962), 116–52.

Freeman, Frank N. "Tests," *Psychological Bulletin,* XI (1914), 253–56.

French, Elizabeth. *Development of a Measure of Complex Motivation.* Research Report AFPTRC-TN-56-48. Air Force Personnel and Training Research Center, Lackland Air Force Base, Texas, 1956. (Available from Armed Services Technical Information Agency Document Service Center, Dayton 2, Ohio.)

———. "Motivation as a Variable in Work-Partner Selection," *Journal of Abnormal and Social Psychology,* LIII (1956), 96–99.

Fries, C.C. *The Structure of English.* New York: Harcourt, Brace & World, Inc., 1952.

Gardner, D.H. *Student Personnel Service.* Chicago: University of Chicago Press, 1936.

Getzels, J.W. "The Question-Answer Process: A Conceptualization and Some Derived Hypotheses for Empirical Examination," *Public Opinion Quarterly*, VIII (1954), 79–91.

Ghiselin, Brewster. *The Creative Process.* Berkeley: University of California Press, 1954.

Good, Carter V. *Dictionary of Education.* New York: McGraw-Hill Book Company, Inc., 1945.

Gottschalk, L. *Understanding History.* New York: Alfred A. Knopf, Inc., 1951.

————, C. Kluckhohn, and R. Angell. *The Use of Personal Documents in History, Anthropology, and Sociology.* New York: Social Science Research Council, Bulletin 53, 1945.

Gray, W.S., and B.E. Leary. *What Makes a Book Readable?* Chicago: University of Chicago Press, 1935.

Gringes, W.W. *Laboratory Instrumentation in Psychology.* Palo Alto, Calif.: The National Press, 1954.

Guilford, J.P. *Psychometric Methods,* Second Edition. New York: McGraw-Hill Book Company, Inc., 1954.

Gulliksen, H. "Intrinsic Validity," *American Psychologist,* V (1950), 511–17.

Halpin, A.W. (ed.) *Administrative Theory in Education.* Chicago: Midwest Administrative Center, 1958.

Hebb, D.O. "On the Nature of Fear," *Psychological Review,* 53 (1946), 259–76.

————. *A Textbook of Psychology.* Philadelphia: W.B. Saunders Co., 1958.

————. *The Organization of Behavior.* New York: John Wiley & Sons, Inc., 1949.

Heil, L.M., and C. Washburne. "Brooklyn College Research in Teacher Effectiveness," *Journal of Educational Research,* 55 (1962), 347–51.

Hemphill, J.K., D.E. Griffiths, and N. Frederiksen. *Administrative Performance and Personality.* New York: Teachers College, Bureau of Publications, Columbia University, 1962.

Heyns, Roger W., and Ronald Lippitt. "Systematic Observational Techniques," in Gardner Lindzey (ed.), *Handbook of Social Psychology.* Cambridge, Mass.: Addison-Wesley Publishing Company, Inc., 1954.

Hughes, M.M., and associates. *Development of the Means for Assessment of the Quality of Teaching in Elementary Schools.* Salt Lake City: University of Utah Press, 1959.

Hull, C.L. *Principles of Behavior.* New York: Appleton-Century-Crofts, Inc., 1943.

Humphreys, Lloyd G. "Clinical Versus Actuarial Prediction," *Proceedings of the 1955 Invitational Conference on Testing Problems.* Princeton, N.J.: Educational Testing Service, 1956, 129–35.

Jensen, Alfred C. "Determining Critical Requirements of Teachers," *Journal of Experimental Education,* XX (1951–52), 79–85.

Katz, D., and E. Stotland. "A Preliminary Statement to a Theory of Attitude Structure and Change," in Koch, S. (ed.), *Psychology: A Study of a Science.* New York: McGraw-Hill Book Company, Inc., 1959.

Kenny, Douglas T., and Sidney W. Bijou. "Ambiguity of Pictures and Extent of Personality Factors in Fantasy Responses," *Journal of Consulting Psychology,* XVII (1953), 283–88.

Kentucky Symposium. *Learning Theory, Personality Theory, and Clinical Research.* New York: John Wiley & Sons, Inc., 1954.

Lewin, K., R. Lippitt, and R.K. White. "Patterns of Aggressive Behavior in Experimentally Created Social Climates," *Journal of Social Psychology,* 10 (1939), 271–99.

Lindquist, E.F. *Design and Analysis of Experiments in Psychology and Education.* Boston: Houghton Mifflin Company, 1953.

Loevinger, Jane. "Objective Tests as Instruments of Psychological Theory," *Psychological Reports,* Monograph Supplement 9, 3 (1957), 635–94.

———, Goldine Gleser, and P.H. DuBois. "Maximizing the Discriminating Power of a Multiple Score Test," *Psychometrika,* XVIII (1953), 309–17.

Lorge, Irving. "Predicting Readability," *Teachers College Record,* XLV (1944), 404–19.

Lubin, Ardie, and Hobart G. Osborn. "A Theory of Pattern Analysis for the Prediction of a Quantitative Criterion," *Psychometrika,* XXII (1957), 63–73.

Manual of Accrediting Procedures. North Central Association of Colleges and Secondary Schools Commission on Institutions of Higher Education, 1934.

Marquis, Donald G. "Research Planning at the Frontiers of Science," *American Psychologist,* III (1948), 430–38.

McCall, W.A., and J.P. Herring. *Comprehensive Curriculum Test.* New York: Teachers College, Bureau of Publications, Columbia University, 1941.

———, J.P. Herring, and J.J. Loftus. *School Practices Questionnaire.* New York: Laidlaw Brothers, 1937.

McClelland, D.C. *The Achieving Society.* Princeton, N.J.: D. Van Nostrand Co., Inc., 1961.

———, J.W. Atkinson, R.A. Clark, and E.L. Lowell. *The Achievement Motive.* New York: Appleton-Century-Crofts, Inc., 1953.

McGraw, M.G. *Growth, a Study of Johnny and Jimmy.* New York: Appleton-Century-Crofts, Inc., 1935.

————. *The Neuromuscular Maturation of the Human Infant.* New York: Columbia University Press, 1943.

MacKinnon, D.W., in H.A. Murray (ed.), *Explorations in Personality.* New York: Oxford University Press, 1938.

McPherson, Joseph H. *Predicting the Accuracy of Oral Reporting in Group Situations.* Air Force Personnel and Training Research Center, Lackland Air Force Base, Texas, Research Bulletin 54-13, 1954.

McVey, William E. *Standards for the Accreditation of Secondary Schools.* Chicago: University of Chicago Press, 1942.

Medley, Donald M., Harold E. Mitzel, and Arthur N. Doi. *Analysis of Variance Models and Their Use in a Three-Way Design Without Replication.* New York: N.Y. City Division of Teacher Education, Board of Higher Education, Research Report, No. 29, 1955.

————, and H.E. Mitzel. "A Technique for Measuring Classroom Behavior," *Journal of Educational Psychology,* 49 (1958), 86–92.

Meehl, Paul E. *Clinical Versus Statistical Prediction: A Theoretical Analysis and a Review of the Evidence.* Minneapolis: University of Minnesota Press, 1954.

————. "Configural Scoring," *Journal of Consulting Psychology,* XVI (1950), 165–71.

————, and K. MacCorquodale. "On a Distinction Between Hypothetical Constructs and Intervening Variables," *Psychological Review,* LV (1948), 95–142.

————, and Albert Rosen. "Antecedent Probability and Efficiency of Psychometric Signs, Patterns, or Cutting Scores," *Psychological Bulletin,* LII (1955), 194–216.

Mill, J.S. *A System of Logic, Ratiocinative and Deductive.* New York: Longmans, Green & Co., Inc., 1930.

Miller, D.R., and G.E. Swanson. *The Changing American Parent.* New York: John Wiley & Sons, Inc., 1958.

Miller, James G. "Toward a General Theory for the Behavior Sciences," *American Psychologist,* X (1955), 513–31.

Mitzel, Harold E., and William Rabinowitz. *Assessing Social-Emotional Climate in the Classroom By Withall's Technique. Psychological Monographs,* No. 368. Washington, D.C.: American Psychological Association, 1953.

Morsh, Joseph E. *Systematic Observation of Instructor Behavior.* Air Force Personnel and Training Research Center, Lackland Air Force Base, Texas, 1955.

————, George Burgess, and Paul N. Smith. *Student Achievement as a Measure of Instructor Effectiveness.* Bulletin No. TN 55-12. Air

Force Personnel and Training Research Center, Lackland Air Force Base, Texas, 1955.

Mort, Paul R., Walter C. Reusser, and J.W. Polley. *Public School Finance.* New York: McGraw-Hill Book Company, Inc., 3rd Edition, 1960.

Mosier, C.I. "A Critical Examination of the Concepts of Face Validity," *Educational and Psychological Measurement,* VII (1947), 191–205.

Mussen, P.H. (ed.). *Handbook of Research on Child Development.* New York: John Wiley & Sons, Inc., 1960.

Northrop, F.S.C. *The Logic of the Sciences and the Humanities.* New York: The Macmillan Company, 1948.

Olson, Willard C. *Child Development.* Boston: D. C. Heath & Company, 1949.

Parten, Mildred B. *Surveys, Polls, and Samples: Practical Procedures.* New York: Harper & Row, Publishers, 1950.

Payne, S.L. "Interviewer Memory Faults," *Public Opinion Quarterly,* XIII (1949), 684–85.

Pool, Ithiel de Sola (ed.). *Trends in Content Analysis.* Urbana, Ill.: University of Illinois Press, 1959.

Rabinowitz, W., and R.M.W. Travers. "Problems of Defining and Assessing Teacher Effectiveness," *Educational Theory,* III (1953), 212–19.

"Report of the Committee of the American Psychological Association on the Standardization of Procedure in Experimental Tests," *Psychological Monographs,* XIII (1910), No. 1, 107; No. 2, 53; No. 5, 85.

Revised Manual of Accrediting. Commission on Institutions of Higher Education, North Central Association of Schools and Colleges, 1941.

Ruger, Henry A., and Brencke Stoessinger. "On Growth of Certain Characteristics in Man," *Annals of Eugenics,* II (1927), 76–110.

Russell, J.D., and F.W. Reeves. *Administration.* Chicago: University of Chicago Press, 1936.

————, and F.W. Reeves. *Finance.* Chicago: University of Chicago Press, 1935.

Ryans, D.G. *Characteristics of Teachers.* Washington, D.C.: American Council on Education, 1960.

Sears, R.R., E.E. Maccoby, and H. Levin. *Patterns of Child Rearing.* Evanston, Ill.: Row, Peterson, and Company, 1957.

Seeman, Julius, and Nathaniel J. Raskin. "Research Perspectives in Client Centered Therapy," in O.H. Mowrer (ed.), *Theory and Research in Psychotherapy.* New York: The Ronald Press Company, 1951.

Skinner, B.F. *Behavior of Organisms*. New York: Appleton-Century-Crofts, Inc., 1938.

————, "A Case History in Scientific Method," *American Psychologist*, XI (1956), 221–33.

Smith, B.O. "A Concept of Teaching," *Teachers College Record*, 61 (1960), 229–41.

Solley, C.M., and G. Murphy. *Development of the Perceptual World*. New York: Basic Books, Inc., 1960.

Soloman, R.L. "An Extension of Control Group Design," *Psychological Bulletin*, XLVI (1949), 137–50.

Spence, Kenneth W. *Behavior Theory and Conditioning*. New Haven, Conn.: Yale University Press, 1956.

————. "Current Interpretations of Learning Data and Some Recent Developments in Stimulus-Response Theory," in Kentucky Symposium, *Learning Theory, Personality Theory, and Clinical Research*. New York: John Wiley & Sons, Inc., 1953.

Stephenson, William. *The Study of Behavior: A Technique and Its Methodology*. Chicago: University of Chicago Press, 1953.

Stevens, S.S. "On the Theory of Scales of Measurement," *Science*, CLL (1946), 677–80.

Thielen, H. *Dynamics of Groups at Work*. Chicago: University of Chicago Press, 1954.

Thomas, Frank, Elizabeth French, and R.M.W. Travers. "Variables Related to Problem-Solving Effectiveness in Two Different Types of Problem Situation," *Proceedings of the 1955 National Research Council Symposium on Aviation Psychology*. Washington, D.C.: National Research Council, 1956.

Thorndike, E.L. *Adult Learning*. New York: The Macmillan Company, 1928.

————. *Educational Psychology*. New York: Teachers College, Columbia University, 1913.

————. *Measurement of Intelligence*. New York: Teachers College, Columbia University, 1927.

————. *Theory of Mental and Social Measurement*. New York: Teachers College, Columbia University, 1913.

Tiedeman, David V., Joseph G. Bryan, and Philip J. Rulon. *The Utility of the Airman Classification Battery for Assignment of Airmen to Eight Air Force Specialties*. Cambridge, Mass.: Educational Research Corporation, 1953.

Tomkins, S.S. *The Thematic Apperception Test: Theory and Techniques of Interpretations*. New York: Grune and Stratton, Inc., 1947.

Travers, R.M.W. *Educational Measurement*. New York: The Macmillan Company, 1955.

————. "An Enquiry into the Problem of Predicting Achievement,"

Air Force Personnel and Training Research Center Research Bulletin, 54–93. Lackland Air Force Base, Texas, 1954.

————. *Essentials of Learning.* New York: The Macmillan Company, 1963.

————. "The Evaluation of the Outcomes of Guidance," *Educational and Psychological Measurement,* XVIII (1948), 325–33.

Tuddenham, Read D., and Margaret M. Snyder. *Physical Growth of California Boys and Girls from Birth to Eighteen Years. Publications in Child Development,* I, No. 2. Berkeley: University of California Press, 1954.

Underwood, B.J., and R.W. Schulz. *Meaningfulness and Verbal Learning.* Philadelphia: J. B. Lippincott Co., 1960.

Wallace, David. "A Case For and Against Mail Questionnaires," *Public Opinion Quarterly,* XVIII (1954), 40–52.

Wallen, N., and R.M.W. Travers. *Measured Needs of Teachers and Their Behavior in the Classroom.* Final Report, U.S. Office of Education Contract No. 444 (8029), 196.

Waples, Douglas. *The Library.* Chicago: University of Chicago Press, 1936.

Wheeler, R.H. *The Science of Psychology.* New York: Thomas Y. Crowell Company, 1940.

White, R.K., and R. Lippitt. *Autocracy and Democracy.* New York: Harper & Row, Publishers, 1960.

Withall, John. "The Development of a Technique for the Measurement of Social Emotional Climate in the Classroom," *Journal of Experimental Education,* XVII (1949), 347–61.

Wylie, R.C. *The Self-Concept.* Lincoln, Neb.: University of Nebraska Press, 1961.

Zimmer, Herbert. "Validity of Extrapolating Nonresponse Bias from Mail Questionnaire Follow-ups," *Journal of Applied Psychology,* XL (1956), 117–21.

Zook, George F., and M.E. Haggerty. *The Evaluation of Higher Institutions.* Chicago: University of Chicago Press, 1936.

————, and M.E. Haggerty. *Principles of Accrediting Higher Institutions.* Chicago: University of Chicago Press, 1935.

INDEX OF NAMES

INDEX OF SUBJECTS